And Upon This Rock

"Accessible scholarship with pastoral applications! I love this book and will be reaching for it every time I read one of the four gospels, any pericope about Peter, and any of his epistles."

—**Kat Armstrong**, Podcast Host, *Holy Curiosity*

"Peter is the disciple we all recognize in the mirror—bold one moment, broken the next. One day, he's proclaiming Jesus as the Messiah; the next, he's rebuking Him for speaking of the cross. He vows unwavering loyalty, only to deny his Lord when the pressure mounts. He swings a sword in impulse, then preaches a sermon that births a movement. Peter is raw, real, and redeemed—a portrait of grace in motion. This book invites us to walk in his footsteps, to witness his stumbles and triumphs, and to be freshly reminded why Jesus chose him to help build his church."

—**Derwin L. Gray**, Co-Founder, Transformation Church

"*And Upon This Rock* could be titled *The Peter I Never Knew*. Before I read McKnight and Spaulding's compilation, I would have described the fisherman-turned-disciple simply as the impulsive one. But this book led me through a course correction—taking me from Peter's early days as a Christ-follower through his denial and restoration. From there it led me from Peter's time as a Jew/gentile mediator to his latter days as a shepherd. Now I know Peter as a sheep-feeder—exactly who our Lord called him to be."

—**Sandra Glahn**, Professor, Dallas Theological Seminary

"Careful biblical-contextual scholarship that's integrated with the research of real life is rare, but this one hits the mark and delivers hard-won wisdom. It feels like a lucid, insightful adventure with Simon Peter in his world and our world at the same time. Light bulbs in every chapter."

—**Ben Tertin**, Editing Scholar, BibleProject

"'You are Peter, and on this rock I will build my church.' It is an unfortunate idiom of our contemporary biblical imagination that our attention has neglected the leader of the earliest apostolic community, Peter. Or rather, whenever we have engaged with Peter, we have read him as naïve, impulsive, immature disciple; a cipher for our own shortcomings. The Peter whom we meet in the Bible was none of that. This exceptional collection of essays—at the same time academic and deeply personal—reflects on the actual person, ministry, and writings and reveals Peter to be as he truly was: a faithful, mature disciple, who loved his Lord and yearned for the good of the communities of Jesus. At the end, Peter, the rock, is revealed to be a model from whom we can learn about life and ministry, faithfulness, failure, repentance, reconciliation, and the deep joy of being the followers of Jesus. For Peter had the tensile strength needed to be a true friend of Jesus."

—**George Kalantzis**, Professor of Theology, Wheaton College

And Upon This Rock

Peter's Transformative Journey from Fisherman
to Follower to Foundational Leader

EDITED BY

Scot McKnight AND
Nika Spaulding

FOREWORD BY
Lynn H. Cohick

CASCADE *Books* · Eugene, Oregon

AND UPON THIS ROCK
Peter's Transformative Journey from Fisherman to Follower
to Foundational Leader

vCopyright © 2025 Wipf and Stock Publishers. All rights reserved. Except for brief quotations in critical publications or reviews, no part of this book may be reproduced in any manner without prior written permission from the publisher. Write: Permissions, Wipf and Stock Publishers, 199 W. 8th Ave., Suite 3, Eugene, OR 97401.

Cascade Books
An Imprint of Wipf and Stock Publishers
199 W. 8th Ave., Suite 3
Eugene, OR 97401

www.wipfandstock.com

PAPERBACK ISBN: 979-8-3852-3546-9
HARDCOVER ISBN: 979-8-3852-3547-6
EBOOK ISBN: 979-8-3852-3548-3

Cataloguing-in-Publication data:

Names: McKnight, Scot, editor. | Spaulding, Nika, editor.

Title: And upon this rock : Peter's transformative journey from fisherman to follower to foundational leader / edited by Scot McKnight and Nika Spaulding.

Description: Eugene, OR: Cascade Books, 2025. | Includes bibliographical references.

Identifiers: ISBN 979-8-3852-3546-9 (paperback). | ISBN 979-8-3852-3547-6 (hardcover). | ISBN 979-8-3852-3548-3 (ebook).

Subjects: LCSH: Peter, the Apostle, Saint. | Leadership. | Discipleship.

Classification: BS2515 A56 2025 (print). | BS2515 (ebook).

VERSION NUMBER 04/03/25

All contents of the Common English Bible Web Site are: Copyright 2012 by Common English Bible and/or its suppliers. All rights reserved.

The Christian Standard Bible. Copyright © 2017 by Holman Bible Publishers. Used by permission. Christian Standard Bible®, and CSB® are federally registered trademarks of Holman Bible Publishers, all rights reserved.

The ESV® Bible (The Holy Bible, English Standard Version®). ESV® Text Edition: 2016. Copyright © 2001 by Crossway, a publishing ministry of Good News Publishers. The ESV® text has been reproduced in cooperation with and by permission of Good News Publishers. Unauthorized reproduction of this publication is prohibited. All rights reserved.

New American Standard Bible®, Copyright © 1960, 1971, 1977, 1995, 2020 by The Lockman Foundation. All rights reserved. The "NASB," "NAS," "New American Standard Bible," and "New American Standard," are trademarks registered in the United States Patent and Trademark Office by The Lockman Foundation. Use of these trademarks requires the permission of The Lockman Foundation.

NET Bible® copyright ©1996-2017 All rights reserved. Build 30170414 by Biblical Studies Press, L.L.C

THE HOLY BIBLE, NEW INTERNATIONAL VERSION®, NIV® Copyright © 1973, 1978, 1984, 2011 by Biblica, Inc.® Used by permission. All rights reserved worldwide.

Scripture taken from the New King James Version®. Copyright © 1982 by Thomas Nelson. Used by permission. All rights reserved.

Scripture quotations are taken from the New Revised Standard Version Updated Edition. Copyright © 2021 National Council of Churches of Christ in the United States of America. Used by permission. All rights reserved worldwide.

All proceeds from the sale of this book will go to the Center for Women in Leadership (CWL). CWL equips women, in a context that is biblically rooted, theologically robust, and ethnically diverse, to thrive as leaders in the academy and the church. CWL is dedicated to equipping, supporting, and promoting women who are involved in leadership, aspiring to become a leader, or exploring more about leadership.

The Center for Women in Leadership's mission grows from the unapologetic conviction that God has created women to lead in the church and academy for the sake of human flourishing.

Contents

List of Contributors | xi
Foreword | Lynn H. Cohick | xv
List of Abbreviations | xix

1 In the Deep with Peter and Jesus: My Pastoral Life with Peter | NOAH SCHUMACHER | 1

2 Failure to Follow Faithfully: Peter's Denials in Mark | ALICE MCQUITTY | 18

3 Peter: An Apostolic-Pastor in the Making: A Sketch of What Is to Come | SCOT MCKNIGHT | 32

4 A Different Road Traveled: Peter's Conversion | MATTHEW VAN WINKLE | 63

5 Peter's Promenade: An Uncommon Path to Common Discipleship | NIKA SPAULDING | 76

6 Great Confession, Great Correction: How Peter Sees and Mis-Sees Jesus' Messiahship, and What It Means for Christian Discipleship | BRENDEN LANG | 90

7 Death-Defying Hope: The Transfiguration from Peter's Perspective | ELIJAH VAN HOECKE | 105

8 Peter the Pentecostal Pastor: Woulda-Coulda-Shoulda-Boughta-Honda | BRENTON S. FESSLER | 120

CONTENTS

9 Transformative Events in the Early Church
   | Kelly Dippolito | 137

10 The End of Us Versus Them: Peter's Vision and the Expansive, Impartial Love of God | Renjy Abraham | 155

11 Peter the Intercessor (Acts 15): Peter and the Apostolic Council | Robert D. Anderson | 172

12 I Believe in Miracles? The Miraculous Formation of Peter
   | James R. North | 191

13 Tracing the Steps of the Suffering Servant: Peter's Theology for Christians in Pain | Matthew McBirth | 205

14 Reimagining Politics: First Peter's Vision for Public Witness | Taylor Terzek | 221

15 Peter's Shift in Christology: It's Not a Mission, It's a Way of Life
   | J. Leland Stephens | 240

16 Feed My Sheep: Failing Forward in Ministry—A Pastoral Reflection | Matthew Trexler | 257

17 Pastor Peter's Paradigm: Laura Tarro Celebration
   | Scot McKnight | 269

Contributors

Scot McKnight has been teaching the New Testament for more than four decades and is now a Visiting Professor of New Testament at Houston Theological Seminary and at Westminster Theological Centre in the UK. He is the author or editor of more than ninety books, including *The King Jesus Gospel, Kingdom Conspiracy, Pastor Paul, Revelation for the Rest of Us*, as well as commentaries on Galatians, Colossians, Philemon, and James.

Nika Spaulding (ThM in New Testament, DMin New Testament Context) was the Resident Theologian at St Jude Oak Cliff and now serves as a copyeditor for a nonprofit specializing in making biblical knowledge accessible for all. She adores the people of St Jude Oak Cliff and treasures her roommates, Robin and Alex, both women of valor. But, if you listen closely to her heart, it beats loudest for her nieces and nephew. Jayden, Nixon, and AJ bring her the most joy and receive her biggest love.

Renjy Abraham and his wife, Katy, live in the Pacific Northwest with their two children, Ari and Juniper. He continually learns from and with them, for which he is grateful. As the Dean of Scholarship at BibleProject and a principal consultant at Leadership Training Initiative, Renjy is committed to empowering leaders, fostering healthy culture, and helping make biblical literature more accessible. He holds a BS in electrical engineering and an MA in biblical and theological studies and is completing his doctoral research in first-century Judaism and early Christianity. As an Indian American leading in multicultural church and university settings,

Renjy continues to explore the intersection of inclusive leadership development, biblical scholarship, and spiritual formation.

Robert D. Anderson is an adjunct faculty member at Denver Seminary at the Washington, DC, campus. He has a BS in philosophy (Towson University), an MBA (Loyola University of Baltimore), a MA in biblical studies and a CAS in advanced biblical studies (St. Mary's Seminary and University), a PhD in biblical studies (Graduate Theological Foundation) and a DMin (pending from Northern Seminary). He is an author (*Mercy for All*) and contributes to Amplify Christ (LifeStone Ministries). He is the husband of Barbara, father of Rob and Tim, and grandfather of Olivia, Abigail, Lily Mae, and Valerie.

Kelly Dippolito serves as Executive Director of the Center for Women in Leadership. She is passionate about supporting women and freeing them from biblical interpretations that undermine their capacity to lead and thrive. Kelly teaches the Bible with an aim to move believers from biblical familiarity to biblical literacy. She has an MA in Christian studies from Dallas Theological Seminary and a DMin in New Testament Context from Northern Seminary. Kelly and Rich have been married for twenty-nine-plus years and have two adult daughters, one son-in-law, one dog, and two granddogs. Enthusiasm is her superpower.

Brenton S. Fessler has been in local church ministry since 2001 and is the founding and lead pastor of Refuge OC in sunny Orange, California. He is husband to Rachel, and dad to Aubrey, Micah, and Hannah. Brenton's academic journey includes stops at Vanguard University (BA, 2002), Fuller Theological Seminary (MA, 2010), and Northern Seminary (DTM, 2025). When he's not leading, teaching, or studying, you'll probably find him on the golf course, reading a good book, on a date with his wife, or planning the next family vacation.

Brenden Lang is the residency and formation minister at Third City Christian Church in Grand Island, Nebraska. He has a DMin in New Testament Context from Northern Seminary, an MA in Old Testament and Semitic languages from Trinity Evangelical Divinity School, and a BA in biblical interpretation from Nebraska Christian College. His wife, Rachel, pastors alongside him, and they have two children: Hayden and Scottie.

CONTRIBUTORS   xiii

Matthew McBirth serves as a full professor of biblical studies at Ozark Christian College in Joplin, MO, where he strives to raise up servant leaders who love God, love neighbor, and embrace Jesus' beautifully diverse kingdom. He is the husband of Allison, father and Asa and Naomi, and a child of God.

Alice McQuitty serves as the curriculum coordinator and member of the teaching team for Women's Ministry at Irving Bible Church in Irving, Texas, where her husband Andy served as senior pastor for thirty-two years. She is a graduate of Dallas Theological Seminary (ThM) and Northern Seminary (DMin). She has authored and coauthored numerous in-depth Bible studies and delights to see lives transformed through a growing understanding of God's word. Alice and Andy have five adult children and five grandchildren.

James R. North served in pastoral ministry for twenty-two years and is currently enjoying serving as a high school Bible teacher. He holds degrees from North Central University (BS), Fuller Theological Seminary (MDiv), and Northern Seminary (DTM). Married to Kelly, they have three children: Isabelle, Elias, and Olivia. In his free time, James enjoys woodworking, reading, and planning family adventures.

Noah Schumacher serves as the Lead Pastor of Compassion Church in Canton, OH. He also serves as Director for Dream Center Global: a nonprofit committed to transforming local and global communities through sustainable initiatives. Noah has been accompanied in ministry by his wife Michelle of nineteen years. Together, they have three beloved children: Caleb, Kennedy, and Camden. Noah is a graduate of Ashland Theological Seminary with an MDiv as well as graduate of Northern Seminary with a DTM in New Testament Context.

J. Leland Stephens has been blessed to share his journey with his wife, Jenniffer, to whom he has been married for twenty-three years. Together, they have four wonderful daughters. Since retiring from the United States Marine Corps, Leland and his family have dedicated their lives to church planting in military communities outside the continental United States and teaching people how to live the way of Jesus. Leland is a graduate of Denver Seminary with a MA in Christian Studies and Northern Seminary with a DTM in New Testament Context.

Taylor Terzek is a husband to Stephanie and a father to Hudson, Emmy, and Eden. He is a lover of great books, strong coffee, and compelling music. Taylor currently lives in North Carolina, where he has been serving in pastoral ministry for the past decade. You can also find him cohosting the podcast *The Learning Laborers*, which he cocreated to help ministry laborers better incorporate learning into their areas of service.

Matthew Trexler has served for nearly a decade as a Campus Minister with Reformed University Fellowship (RUF) at the University of California, Los Angeles. He is a minister in the Presbyterian Church of America.

Elijah Van Hoecke is the Education Coordinator at Whole Heart International in northern Iraq, where he and his wife Brittany live with their two children. Elijah is pursuing his DTM in New Testament Context at Northern Seminary.

Matthew Van Winkle is an adjunct professor and corporate professional who enjoys hunting for semi-rare books in his free time. When he's not at work, he's spending time with his family or adding to his growing collection. He's a proud husband and father who balances career and hobbies with family life.

Foreword

Lynn H. Cohick
Distinguished Professor of New Testament at Houston Christian University

TRUE CONFESSION: I'M MORE of a "Paul" fan than a "Peter" enthusiast. I've written commentaries on Ephesians and Philippians, and numerous chapters on Paul's teachings, including his views on women's participation in leadership. I've been exploring the Jewish world of Jesus and the interactions of Jews and Christians from the days of my PhD studies in the 1980s. I find the social and cultural contexts of imperial Rome fascinating, especially as the empire's habits and decisions impact the daily life of men, women, and children across its vast lands.

But not so much Peter. I appreciated his testimony about Jesus—"You are the Christ" (Matt 16:16)—but felt annoyed at his need to be noticed ("tell me to come to you, Lord," Matt 14:28) and his cocky, overconfident swagger heading with Jesus into Jerusalem that fateful Passover week (Matt 26:35). So, when my Doctor of Ministry students, who are brilliant and fun, invited me to read their essays from another class on the apostle Peter, I figured that at least their writings would be interesting. After all, I saw their intelligence and good humor during our weeklong course on hermeneutics (yes, hermeneutics can be very fun). I settled into a comfy chair on my back patio, ready for a quiet evening of pleasant reading.

I was completely unprepared for my experience. First, I was unprepared to like Peter as much as I did. In these excellent essays, Peter is brought to life; his story gains texture, depth, nuance. Second, I was unprepared to be spiritually moved, inspired, confronted. The authors' wisdom, their honest, open stories of struggle, disappointment, and hope, drew me into a theological space of reflection and worship. As they shared their stories, my own understanding of discipleship, of Christian community, of failure and forgiveness, became all the richer. Time and again, I would pause at a point in a chapter, reflecting on a pastoral insight, or an all-too-human foible reflected in one of Peter's stories.

What did *not* surprise me was the depth of analysis and theological reasoning that seasons each chapter. I had seen the students' trust of each other, their willingness to go deep on tough questions. Their trust and curiosity make each essay stronger and bolder. Most importantly, they all desire a more passionate, authentic walk with Jesus.

This passion carries over into their academic studies. They ground their essays on the latest and best research, drawing on the most up-to-date thinkers in the fields of biblical studies, spiritual formation, and cultural critique. The chapters share a unified focus, but each has gems of wisdom mined from the author's experience and background. Each chapter focuses on a single episode of Peter's life, creating a comprehensive account of his whole ministry. Because these authors shared a doctoral course together on the apostle, the essays reflect a unity of purpose while still maintaining each author's individual voice and personality. Telling Peter's story within God's story provides an example for believers today who desire to live into God's grand narrative.

I will focus on three areas that characterize this volume: background context; exegetical analysis; and pastoral reflection.

First, the background context creates a solid foundation to explore the life of Peter. These essays present a clear rendering of a complex historical reality that spans from the city of Jerusalem to the Roman province of Asia Minor. Knowledge of Jewish religious customs, leadership structures, and key theological topics place Peter in his world. His words and actions become more understandable seen in the light of first-century habits and assumptions. Institutions like slavery and the imperial cult are explained to better understand the burdens which Peter's communities faced.

Second, the close, careful, imaginative reading of the biblical text draws out the major points of the passages. Some essays consider individual Gospels' portraits of Peter, his calling, journey with Jesus, successes and failures. Others examine the Peter of Acts, focusing on Pentecost, on his healing ministry, his imprisonments, his miraculous escape, his visions, his preaching, and his leadership within the growing church. Still other essays explore his two letters, with their focus on pastoring, on suffering, on engagement with the wider cultural and political world. The whole Bible is used, and so the books of Jonah and Daniel serve as important markers when studying Peter's meeting with Cornelius the Godfearer (Acts 10). Again, in the story about Peter walking on water, we are reminded that Ps 18 describes God reaching down and pulling David out of deep waters (Matt 14:28–31; Ps 18:16, see also Ps 69). As a final example, Isa 53, the suffering servant passage, is studied in light of Peter's congregations' struggles in Asia Minor. Plus, I found so many biblical gems. For example, I had never thought of Elijah and Moses at the Mount of Transfiguration as figures of resurrection hope, a hope that at that point Peter did not fully grasp, but which in his second letter he makes clear that this moment was foundational to his understanding of his own death.

Third, each essay displays great maturity and pastoral wisdom, demonstrated in the fearless approach to difficult subjects, and the honesty in sharing ministry disappointments. One essay walks us through a pastor's severe depression brought on by shrinking congregation numbers (a worldly sign of "failure"), to the assurance that Jesus reaches out his hand to us, even as he did to Peter when he stepped out of the boat into the stormy waves (Matt 14:31). At this moment, Peter "was discovering where trust began and where pride ended." Another essay takes us through the highs and lows of discipleship, from the high of Peter's Confession, to the low of Jesus's Correction, namely that he is the *crucified* Messiah (Matt 16:16–23). About Peter's denials at Jesus's passion, a wise pastor reflects that his pastoral heart was refined and softened, as reflected in the compassion and tenderness with which he writes to believers in 1 Peter (see especially 5:1–11). On resurrection day, Peter shows some hope that what Jesus said, including his transfiguration, might add up to resurrection (Luke 24:12). And just before his ascension, Jesus shares a meal with Peter, who hears Jesus's full acceptance of his declaration of love for his Savior (John 21:15–17). The lesson drawn is that God accepts our love, even in our failures.

My new true confession: I like Peter. Or better said, I like the complicated and challenging Peter that I meet in these pages. And I know myself better by learning about Peter's experiences. Most of all, I understand more deeply the incredible love, compassion, constancy of Peter's Savior and Lord.

Abbreviations

BDAG   Walter Bauer et al. *Greek-English Lexicon of the New Testament and Other Early Christian Literature.* 3rd ed. Chicago: University of Chicago Press, 2000

CGL   *The Cambridge Greek Lexicon.* 2 vols. Edited by J. Diggle et al. New York: Cambridge University Press, 2021

DJG2   *Dictionary of Jesus and the Gospels: A Compendium of Contemporary Biblical Scholarship.* 2nd ed. Edited by Joel B. Green, Jeannine K. Brown, and Nicholas Perrin. The IVP Bible Dictionary Series. Downers Grove, IL: InterVarsity, 2013

DNTB   *Dictionary of New Testament Background.* Edited by Craig A. Evans and Stanley E. Porter. Downers Grove, IL: InterVarsity Press, 2000

DOTP   *Dictionary of the Old Testament Prophets.* Edited by Mark J. Boda and J. G. McConville. Nottingham: InterVarsity Press, 2012

LBD   *The Lexham Bible Dictionary.* Edited by J. D. Barry and L. Wentz. Bellingham WA: Lexham, 2012

NIDOTTE	*New International Dictionary of Old Testament Theology & Exegesis.* 5 vols. Edited by Willem A. VanGemeren. Grand Rapids: Zondervan, 1997
LXX	Septuagint
WUNT	Wissenschaftliche Untersuchungen zum Neuen Testament

1

In the Deep with Peter and Jesus
My Pastoral Life with Peter

Noah Schumacher

The silence was deafening. Terrifying yet calm. I sat by the water's edge of the lake. Not a sound was heard except the small but proud waves rolling over the rocks. I was stuck between a tension of external peace and inner upheaval. Weeks before this moment and up to it were filled with meetings, calls, and endless text messages. Each day there was a new individual or family leaving the church. Though I thought this may happen, it didn't make it any easier to accept. With a firm commitment to leave toxicity behind regarding the ministry, our elder team and I began to make leadership changes. As in most unhealthy environments where tribalism runs rampant, the atmosphere was ripe for taking up offense and causing disunity. I was prepared for fallout. What I was never prepared for was the internal chaos. It all came to a head that quiet day in 2018.

I recall finding a smooth stone and, with unmitigated aggression, skipping it as far as I could on the water. Feeling the release of something deep inside as the stone made its final skip, I let out a shrieking prayer that was more accusatory than lament. With reckless abandon, not caring what lightning may come, I yelled to my Father, "I never signed up for this! Why did you lead me here?" I collapsed back onto the ground weeping before the Lord. Amidst the tears and heaviness,

I realized two things that day: I didn't know who I was, and I didn't understand the ministry I was invited into.[1]

Eugene Peterson hits on what I (and I assume many of us) had envisioned before beginning ministry. Many are drawn into leadership because of the powerful images and stories we discover in Scripture at one time or another. Peterson writes,

> The images forming our pastoral expectations had a good deal more fierceness to them: Moses' bearding the Pharaoh; Jeremiah with fire in his mouth; Peter swashbucklingly reckless as the lead apostle; Paul's careering through prison and ecstasy, shipwreck and kerygma. The Kingdom of God in which we had apprenticed ourselves was presented to us as revolutionary, a dangerously unwelcome intruder in the Old Boy Club of thrones, dominions, principalities, and powers.[2]

Is this not what each of us dreamed of? Sought after? Or were influenced by? We wanted to watch God work miraculously through our efforts. We wanted to encounter the ecstatic milestone prayer gatherings which led us into the third heaven. Many of us romanticized suffering for Jesus while reading Paul's jailhouse and shipwreck stories. I am not too proud to say that I did. And yet, there I was. Not in jail nor on the guillotine block for Jesus. I was by the water with a tattered ego, severe depression, and questioning absolutely everything. People I loved and tirelessly served for years were departing the ministry quicker than I could prevent. Mistakenly at the time, I viewed this as personal rejection and vocational failure. To make matters worse, the church had numbered around 400 members and, when this season of decision making concluded, we were whittled down to 130. It wasn't jail or a shipwreck. It wasn't persecution or even pressure. It was par for the course of being a leader in ministry, and I was not handling it well.

All these years later, it is embarrassing to look back and see myself that unstable and seeking to please anyone and everyone. I was starving for validation but refusing to find it as a child of God. I was hungering for a place of belonging among those I already belonged to in covenant-relationship. My vision and perception of reality was severely immature. Psychologist James W. Fowler explains that faith development involves

---

1. In using the term "ministry" throughout this chapter the focal point will be ecclesiastical ministry. All followers of Jesus are called into full-time ministry with the way they speak, love, serve, and more.

2. Peterson, *Contemplative Pastor*, 29.

six stages of growth. Judging by how he explains each stage it would be accurate to say that many who enter the ministry begin with stage one, called "intuitive faith," and end up crying, screaming, and lamenting their way to further stages of growth, which we as Christians would call discipleship. Looking back on that day by the water, I had a stunted understanding of what God was up to. I was like the one Fowler describes in "stage one" kind of faith, who is "unable to coordinate and compare two different perspectives on the same object."[3] I had my perspective. God had his. Fowler believes these are the kind of individuals who "assume without question that the experiences and perceptions they have of a phenomenon represent the only available perspective."[4] This was me. In fact, this may be many of us.

Before leaving that day, I was praying for the Lord to show me a connection with any other leader from Scripture. I prayerfully and desperately scoured my Bible. Was it Nehemiah or Nathan? Was it Moses or Aaron? Maybe it was Mary or Abraham. Surely it was one of these, but none resonated. Ready to give up and drive home I decided to sit on the Adirondack chair for just a little longer as the sun set. Getting ready to pack up my books and put my chair back I noticed a small skiff making its way to the docks off to my right. The man sat on the middle bench patiently watching and waiting for something to bite the lure he had just gently flung in the water. Right then, the heavens (seemingly) parted, and the Lord guided me to the individual I needed most. How could I have been so foolish? Who in Scripture began their journey with wonderful and (at times) naïve faith? What leader went through a time of testing in leadership? Who plumbed the depths of failure and sorrow in their attempts to follow Jesus and feed his flock? I found the leader. It was Peter. Someone I had just read about a week before! A simple fisherman turned disciple turned pastor turned apostle who, like me that day, encountered Jesus by a lake's edge in a way that transformed his entire life. He went from fisherman Peter to pastor Peter all because of his deep and abiding relationship with Jesus.

In this short chapter we will explore the relationship of Jesus and Peter focusing on three seminal events involving Jesus in the life of Peter. First, we will dive into his calling by Jesus as Peter was washing his nets by the water, focusing on Luke 5:1–10. We will then shift to the time of

---

3. Fowler, *Stages of Faith*, 123.
4. Fowler, *Stages of Faith*, 123.

Peter's testing in the water by Jesus in Matt 14:22–36. In conclusion we will briefly engage Peter's restoration along the water's edge in John 21. These moments illustrate the discipleship journey of every leader who has already, or one day will, experience the growing pains in their attempts to "feed the flock" and rediscover who they are as a Jesus follower.

Jesus Calls Fisherman Peter, Luke 5:1–10

Peter's beginning as a disciple is recalled in Luke 5:1–10, Matt 4:18–22, and Mark 1:16–20.[5] While each presents a glimpse of what took place that day, the Lukan account stands out more so than the rest due to its length and unique description.[6] When Jesus found Peter, he was busy doing his job as a fisherman. It's what he did. It's what he knew. After all he came from Bethsaida (John 1:44) which was called the "fisherman's city." He was a man of the people. He was rough skinned and perhaps also well cultured given the influx of both Jews and Greeks in the region.[7] Peter, like many of us before we began following Jesus, was busy doing what he *thought* was his life's purpose. This all changed the moment Peter got a glimpse of exactly who Jesus was.

According to Luke's account, at first glance Peter didn't even budge. If anything, he was inconvenienced. So, what did Jesus do? Jesus took the teaching right to Peter.[8] It's clear the focal point of this interaction is not the crowd nor the teaching of Jesus. But rather one individual and the rest who were observing. Jesus freely gives Peter his own opinion on what he thinks they ought to do with their fishing net. Again, imagining the annoyance of Peter, he reluctantly obliges. It is what Peter says that is important for us to pay attention to. He says in v. 5, "Master, we have worked

---

5. Unless otherwise noted, all biblical citations will come from the NRSV.

6. Larry Helyer states that what makes Luke's version stand out the way it does is because of the miracle component tied to it. He also further adds that Luke is careful to use this miracle to highlight the shift of allegiance for Peter in how he views Jesus. Helyer, *Life and Witness*, 32–33. Another viewpoint is that Luke may have a fuller form of the story of the first disciples than the one Mark and Matthew have. Or is it that Luke is merging another story of Peter and a miraculous catch of fish? "In a certain way the Lucan story is more logical: the miracle offers a reason why the fishermen would leave everything and follow Jesus. But this logic could well be a Lucan 'improvement' of the Marcan storyline, and we must recognize that there are real inconsistencies in the present Lucan narrative." For more on the form of Luke's version in comparison with the others see Brown et al., *Peter in the New Testament*, 114–19.

7. Cullmann, *Peter*, 22.

8. Gray, *Peter*, 16.

all night long but have caught nothing. Yet if you say so, I will let down the nets." Joel Green, sympathizing with this statement from Peter and connecting the encounter to Mary even, writes that "Jesus's instructions to Peter seem absurd. Not only has a night's work by people who fish by profession produced nothing, but the nets used are for night fishing only. Peter's response, then, echoes that of Mary in 1:34, 38—incredulity leading to service."[9] Thus, on this seemingly normal and mundane day Peter encountered a rabbi-like teacher who brought about a miracle that changed everything. Upon following what Jesus says the catch of fish was simply beyond belief. This simple request from Jesus to use his boat turned into a catalyst for Peter to shift his entire life and profession. Fishing was still the craft he knew well, but now that craft would be assisting the Messiah in bringing in a new kind of harvest.

The clear connection between "catching fish" and "proclaiming the word" is evident in Peter's call story. It is a commission by Jesus that extends to the other would-be disciples observing. Green adds that the relative success in fishing, under Jesus' authority and call, is a prophetic symbol for the overall mission Peter and the disciples (and we) are invited into.[10] Another scholar goes as far as saying that this call story triggers a prophetic "call back" to Jer 16:15–16 with eschatological implications.[11] Speaking on Peter's craft of fishing and his life playing out in the book of Acts this scholar writes,

> Such fishing images turn out to be not just incidental but integral to the very fabric of Peter's apostolic role. The book of Acts offers tantalizing hints of the extent to which these metaphors continue to evoke Peter's past as a fisherman in understanding the future missionary.... He understands God's gospel as reaching out to all nations; and thus he is encouraged to set out into the deep unknown and put down his net for a catch.[12]

---

9. Green, *Gospel of Luke*, 232.

10. Green, *Gospel of Luke*, 231–32.

11. Jeremiah 16:15–16 reads, "'As the Lord lives who brought the people of Israel up out of the land of the north and out of all the lands where he had driven them.' For I will bring them back to their own land that I gave to their ancestors. I am now sending for many fishermen, says the Lord, and they shall catch them; and afterward I will send for many hunters, and they shall hunt them from every mountain and every hill, and out of the clefts of the rocks."

12. Bockmuehl, "Transformation of Simon Peter," 17.

When Jesus found Peter, he did not put to waste who Peter had become and what he had learned. Instead, he took Peter's craft, demeanor, and even talents and led them into a fuller purpose. Peter's beginning, especially as Luke describes it, shows us that Jesus sees past what we were (or are) to enable us to walk a new path of meaning and divine purpose. Often in the grind of ministry we will need to recall our origin stories of when and where it all began. When Jesus found us and the way he found us. In remembering those thin spaces of our past, the Holy Spirit helps us to uncover the pure and unalloyed joy and mystery of our call. Akin to what Peter experienced that day on the boat.

While this may not be a news flash for anyone reading this, it is important to nonetheless remember that ministry expectations we set out with from our beginning are rarely (if ever) in proportion to the lived reality which ensues. This is true for both our internal spiritual expectations as well as our external leadership expectations. Surely Peter had envisioned his future as one marked by continual learning and successes with this new Master who miraculously provided the fish. However, as the Gospels and Acts play out, we can observe a version of Peter that may seem familiar. Michael J. Wilkins explains that

> Jesus' disciples were not that much different than us. These men and women were attracted by Jesus' life and by his teachings, yet they knew that their own lives were nothing by comparison. In one of the early encounters, after Peter witnessed Jesus' miraculous work, "He fell down at Jesus' feet, saying, 'Depart from me, for I am a sinful man, O Lord!'" In the light of Jesus' life, the disciples were only too well aware of their shortcomings.[13]

In every one of our collective call stories, while differences will abound, all can identify with what is said above. We were humbled like Peter and, as Wilkins says, we experienced the light of Christ in which we saw ourselves for who we really were: "I am a sinful man [or woman], O Lord!" What does this recollection of our call do for our longevity in ministry? Simple. It sustains us. Jesus called each of us. He knew where we were then. He knows where we are now. He was patient with Peter on that day as well as many days following. The sustaining presence of Jesus in our lives from the beginning should be cherished and held on to. They are the anchor in which we remember that we were and continue to be worthy. None of us are slaves seeking to earn our place.

---

13. Wilkins, *Following the Master*, 141.

Jesus called us. None of us are orphans wandering to find our place. Jesus already made room at the table for us. With confidence and boldness all of us can declare with absolute conviction we were invited and called into a life of following, serving, and loving. Jesus was with Peter that day and continued. From your beginning to the present, is Jesus not also patiently and loving still with you?

Jesus Invites Pastor Peter into the Deep, Matthew 14:22–36

"Faith in Jesus lets him walk but taking his eyes off his Master makes him sink."[14] This is how one scholar explains the core sentiment found within Matthew's "homiletical vignette"[15] in Matt 14:22–36. The miracle of Jesus walking on water in this pericope and the testing of Peter may be one of the more popular stories in Scripture. As it pertains to the growth of Peter, what ought to stand out most in this story is the faith (foolishness?) of Peter. What ran through his mind when he saw Jesus on the water? What motivated him to think he could in fact do what he saw his own Master doing and step out into the deep? Part foolish. Part admirable. Part familiar. For we too in many regards have stepped out into the deep, locking eyes on Jesus, only to find ourselves sinking in what we thought was stable ground. If this isn't a summary of what life is like in following Jesus and serving his church, I am not sure what is.

Matthew's addition to this story adapted from Mark is full of liturgical flavor. Matthew's intent on elaborating this story to include Peter's leap of faith furthers its applicability to readers in their own journey of following Jesus. As Wilkins referred to above, "Jesus' disciples were not that much different than us."[16] Minus the whole "walking on water" part, of course. But even still, Peter wanted a share in this miraculous event that he saw from Jesus. Who could blame him? One scholar, in highlighting this desire of Peter and the more direct manner in which Peter is desiring to join Jesus on the water writes that

> Peter is not simply challenging Jesus to prove that he can communicate power. He is also challenging his own perseverance and faith. Our English versions of his first sentence might lead us to presume that Peter wants corroborative evidence: "Lord, if

---

14. Bockmuehl, "Transformation of Simon Peter," 72.
15. Bockmuehl, "Transformation of Simon Peter," 72.
16. Wilkins, *Following the Master*, 141.

it is you . . ." This is not quite what the Greek text implies. Peter knows that it is Jesus. He does not know for sure, yet that Jesus is the Messiah—the address, *kyrie*, is, at this stage, nothing but a conventional courtesy, "Sir"—rather than "Lord" . . . a form of address given to anyone in authority. But the *ei* in the Greek, conventionally rendered "if," comes closer to "since": "Sir since it is you, tell me to come to you over the water." In other words, Peter accepts the privileged position of Jesus and, with characteristic eagerness, wants a share in it.[17]

The familiarity found in Matthew's account should be obvious to the seasoned ministry leader. Each of us have, are currently, and/or most likely will sense Jesus leading us into new directions in the future. Directions which lack clarity, purpose, and even common sense. We ourselves will at one time or another eagerly desire a new and refreshing share in the ministry of Jesus wherever that may be. It could be setting out for a new pastoral post. Perhaps it is the Lord calling us to plant a new house church in an unreached community. It could even be leaving traditional ministry for a more marketplace ministry role. No matter the context, just like Peter, we will be invited into waters that will surely test our faith and obedience to his call. What will we do? How steadfast will our gaze be? These questions and more like them keep us moving forward in our development and growth. If our calling anchors us in our understanding why we have been called, our steps outside "our boats" remind us of the "why." Highlighting the deeper part of the story, Ulrich Luz explains that "Peter leaves his boat in a concrete venture of obedience alone and unsupported in the water and grows beyond himself and thus experiences both his own failure and the Lord's support. It [the story] deals with the possibility of exceeding one's own human limitations in faith in the midst of deep despair, fear, misfortune, suffering, and guilt."[18] Peter leaves the boat because Jesus isn't in it. He wants to be where his Master is. With confidence and gusto, he steps out only to be thwarted not by a wave of mighty water but rather a trivial wave of doubt. "One of the loveliest legends . . . that I love better than all others. . . . It expresses the noble doctrine that the human person will be victorious in the most difficult enterprise with faith and hearty courage, while he will be lost by the least touch of doubt."[19] While we wish

17. Thiede, *Simon Peter*, 29.
18. Luz, *Matthew*, 322.
19. Luz, *Matthew*, 322.

it weren't true, it definitely is. This small bit of doubt was accompanied by a supreme rush of fear. A fear that paralyzed him right where he was. "His fear functions as a self-fulfilling prophecy, and he begins to sink."[20] Who among us has not encountered similar emotions accompanied by treacherous feelings of sinking in our ministry? When our funding dries up? When we discern a split upon the horizon? When we discover our identity was not built upon who Jesus says we are but who the people we serve say we are. These situations and more surrounded leaders in ministry who give their all to lead people to deeper faith foundations. But amid all of it, grace abounds for us as it did for Peter.

Present in Matt 14:22–36 is the ever-present love and grace of Jesus. Just as Peter discovered, we find the assurance of Christ's helping hand when we need it most. If we were to boil down this entire scene, it would be a supreme picture of "trust." Peter possessed radical faith and left what was safe and comfortable only to find himself more terrified than he was before. Like the other disciples, Peter is panicked by what he sees. What he thought at first was a ghost turned out to be the same one approaching him who approached him on the beach so long ago. But it was Peter who rightly discerned the moment before him. No one else did. He saw that this test was an opportunity. A chance to challenge his Master ("Lord, if it is you, command me . . .") as well as receive a challenge himself ("Come!").[21] As Peter stepped out of the boat in faith and in faithfulness, he was doing more than meeting Jesus in a storm. He was discovering where trust began and where pride ended. A dreadful and beautiful lesson all of us need to learn at one time or another.

The week before I was aggressively skipping stones, I was huddled on the floor in front of a large wooden altar at the front of a quaint Lutheran sanctuary. I drove to this church and parked my car. I found the secretary and asked if I could simply enter and pray. With eyes bloodshot from tears and a demeanor sure to scare anyone, I was surprised when she escorted me herself to the sanctuary. I sat down and took an agitated deep breath. I was angry with God and those he asked me to lead. During those two hours of prayer, I stepped out into the deep waters where Jesus was. At this point in the ministry, I was sinking rapidly. While metaphorically sinking into deep despair I ran to get a pew Bible nearby. For at that moment I was reminded of Peter drowning in the

---

20. Nolland, *Matthew*, 602.
21. Kirkpatrick, "Pastoral Perspective on Matthew 14:22–33," 334.

dark waters. I wish I could say that I was immediately transformed upon reading Matthew's account. I wasn't. I sat and stared at the large wooden cross before me with the thoughts of suicide and reality of depression slowly losing their grip. I continued to ask the Lord, "Why invite me to make these decisions if it led to failure? Why invite me to come to you in the deep like Peter did if it resulted in my own demise?" These questions and more spewed out from the deepest places of me. I was angry. My eyes were not on Jesus as they should have been. He was the last one I desired to look upon. I wanted to look anywhere else but to him. But it was one simple question he asked in response that led me to seeing this story in an entirely different light. "Since when is obedience toward me failure to you?" I sat there pondering this searing question. Still to this day it haunts me in the best way possible.

In reading this story, who wouldn't assume Peter is failing since he took his eyes off Jesus? But what does this say of the other disciples who never left the boat? Did they succeed? Was their faith with Jesus bolstered that day? Did they disobey? Or was it only one who "failed"? Here is the truth: Peter didn't fail. Did he lack trust for a moment? Yes. If anything, he learned dependency. He learned intimacy. He learned the radical life of trust. A holy sinking a time or two is healthy for all of us, if we embrace it. When you do sense that sinking due to obeying him, remember that you didn't "fail." There are many examples of "ministry failure."[22] These result from being led by the flesh and not the Spirit (Rom 6–8). This is a failure of morality and ethics. But again, it is worth repeating, in ministry, when setting out to obey Jesus and go where he leads, there is no failure. Only learning. Peter learned this deep lesson there on the water with Jesus. That there is no failure in following the call of Jesus. Mistakes? Sure. Hiccups? You bet. Dark nights of the soul? Most definitely. Are we really following him if these are *not* occurring? Unfortunately for Peter, he would soon come to learn what true failure entailed. The kind of failure that, if left unhealed, can destroy the soul and break a person's will completely. Thankfully, Pastor Peter has walked with Jesus. From the calling to the sinking, Jesus was with him, preparing for the time when Peter would need him the most, ironically, near the waters of Galilee.

---

22. For a wide-ranging study on cultivating healthy ministry cultures where moral failures can be dealt with and addressed in healthy ways, see McKnight and Barringer, *Church Called Tov* and *Pivot*.

Jesus Restores Broken Peter, John 21:15–25

In John 21 we have not the climax of Peter's story but perhaps the most pivotal moment in his growth and overall discipleship. There is not ample space to give this moment (and many others from Peter's life) the proper attention they deserve. To best understand the restoration of Peter next to the water that day, we must first look at what precedes this encounter with the resurrected Jesus. Not once or twice, but three times Peter denied being a follower of him, much less knowing him.[23]

Jesus knew what Peter didn't. In his own account, John perfectly captures the passion and pride of Peter in declaring his intent to follow Jesus wherever he calls him to go as well as wherever Jesus himself goes. I imagine all of us at one time or another could relate to this same pride and ego propelling us forward. John records that

> [36] Simon Peter said to him, "Lord, where are you going?" Jesus answered, "Where I am going, you cannot follow me now; but you will follow afterward." [37] Peter said to him, "Lord, why can I not follow you now? I will lay down my life for you." [38] Jesus answered, "Will you lay down your life for me? Very truly, I tell you, before the cock crows, you will have denied me three times. (John 13:36–38)

As any reader will observe, Peter's passion in discipleship has been forged by key moments with Jesus. Moments that challenged him as well as pushed the limits of what he thought was possible. Some of those key moments are when he joyfully stood up for Jesus as the crowds deserted him in John 6, declaring in 6:68, "Lord, to whom can we go? You have the words of eternal life." Peter was also able to witness his own mother-in-law being healed in Matt 8:14–15. There's also that moment when the realization set in that Jesus is the Good Shepherd from John 10:1–21, surely connecting the dots internally to the prophet Jeremiah.[24] Or how about that moment when the subversive nature of leadership was forged upon his conscience as his own feet were washed by Jesus himself in John 13:1–20? These examples and more illustrate the depth of relationship built over time. Thus, to be told that where his master is going, he himself cannot go would be hurtful beyond belief to the heart

---

23. These denials of Jesus from Peter can be found in the following Gospels: Matt 26:58, 69–75; Mark 14:54, 66–72; Luke 22:54–62; and John 18:15–18, 25–26.

24. Jer 10:21; 12:10; 23:1–3; and the whole of Jer 25.

of Peter. Luke, providing another angle of Jesus communicating what was to come regarding Peter's denial says,

> [31] "Simon, Simon, listen! Satan has demanded to sift all of you like wheat, [32] but I have prayed for you that your own faith may not fail; and you, when once you have turned back, strengthen your brothers." [33] And he said to him, "Lord, I am ready to go with you to prison and to death!" [34] Jesus said, "I tell you, Peter, the cock will not crow this day, until you have denied three times that you know me." (Luke 22:31–34)

Jesus' repetition of Peter' name, "*Simon, Simon,*" gives the address a solemn emphasis. While the plural "you" is present, the focus is toward Peter directly. Jesus goes on to assure Peter that he has prayed for him but this time the "you" is being singularly focused. "Notice that the Master did not ask that his servant might be freed from trouble."[25] This is important for us to pay attention to. Jesus knew this testing was coming but did not seek for its absence. The trial and testing had its place in the growth and development of Peter's life. We are no different.

This "sifting" Jesus refers to in v. 32 has multiple meanings, both of which are important for our focus on the restorative actions of Jesus in John 21. "The grain is able to pass through the sieve,[26] which catches the largest waste, or it can retain the grain and let the straw and other impurities pass through."[27] This sifting in the "experiential sieve" of what Peter is walking through from denial to restoration is a test that will provide a shaking and holy disturbance to his own faith and character.[28]

The character of Peter, one scholar states, can be overall summed up as "well intentioned . . . with the desire to do good, yet when the moment called for it, he wavered and became impulsive and unreliable."[29] This summary of his character is clearly on display in each denial pericope. This is why it's so easy to identify with Peter for many of us as leaders. We too have found ourselves impulsive and unreliable. Our actions and disobedience at various seasons have been tantamount to a certain "denial" of the call of Jesus upon our lives. Going further, we

---

25. Morris, *Luke*, 327.

26. A sieve is a utensil consisting of a mesh wire held intact by a frame. It is used to strain liquids as well as solids focusing on the sifting of finer particles.

27. Bovon, *Luke*, 176.

28. Bovon, *Luke*, 176. This is how early Christians understood this concept of testing and the sieve.

29. Vaquilar, "Peter's Journey," 79.

identify with his call from the beginning when we too were enamored with the power of Christ. We drew closer to him as we too stepped out at various times into the deep waters of our calling. All of this is what makes John 21 so pivotal for Peter as well as any of us as leaders in the Church who are in need of deep healing and restoration.

The restoring of Peter in John 21 takes place with all the similarities Peter's own story is accustomed to. The disciples find themselves by the sea of Galilee once more.[30] Jesus has resurrected, and we can assume the disciples, minus one, are still wondering what is next. Peter already knew where he was headed. John 21:3 reads, "Simon Peter said to them, 'I am going fishing.' They said to him, 'We will go with you.' They went out and got into the boat, but that night they caught nothing." Peter was done. He sought to return to what he knew pre-encounter with Jesus. Even after finding out Jesus was raised and seeing him firsthand, Peter still is not able to move forward. The denials usher him into a place of wasted and tattered goods no longer worthy of use. He was destroyed and destitute. Trying to move forward (backward?) led to catching nothing in the nets. Surely as Peter and the rest pulled the nets up, they remembered what happened when they fished *with* Jesus the first time.

There in the distance as John 21:4–11 reveals, they see a man with a small charcoal fire and smoke rising ever so slowly. The man gently calls out to them asking whether they caught anything. Telling them to cast on the right side of the boat, they obeyed. For some of the disciples, and especially Peter, we can imagine this brought back a certain memory. Sure enough, it was the Lord on the shoreline. Peter, putting it all together, leaped into the water leaving the others to bring in the haul of fish that was miraculously caught again. As the others returned to the shoreline, perhaps frustrated that Peter had bailed on them, Peter goes to help them bring the fish to shore. Jesus then invites them to have breakfast with the fish that were caught. He broke bread and passed roasted fish to each.

When they had finished eating Jesus pulled Peter to the side by the shore away from the others. The time for restoration had come. Space does not allow a full unpacking of this exchange.[31] However, we

30. Also called the "Sea of Tiberias" in John 21. Toward the end of the first century this became the more dominant name given to the sea of Galilee. It was named thus in honor of the second Roman emperor, Tiberius.

31. Nick A. Vaquilar explains that John 21:15–19 can be seen as Peter's "rehabilitation." He writes, "In fact, with John 1–20 as a background, one can describe this experience as Peter's rehabilitation, his restoration, and reinstatement into service, his re-commissioning, reaffirmation of his leadership position, establishment of a new

must pay attention to something important that came from Jesus. John 21:18–19 states,

> [18] "Very truly, I tell you, when you were younger, you used to fasten your own belt and to go wherever you wished. But when you grow old, you will stretch out your hands, and someone else will fasten a belt around you and take you where you do not wish to go." [19] (He said this to indicate the kind of death by which he would glorify God.) After this he said to him, "Follow me." (John 21:18–19)

Despite all that had transpired Jesus restored Peter. Following the question of "Do you love me?" being asked three separate times to absolve three separate denials, Jesus casts vision once again for Peter's life and ministry.[32] It wasn't over. Failure was forgiven. There was much more to do, and it did not involve a return to casting nets for fish in the sea. Upon highlighting Peter's pioneering spirit in his younger days, Jesus declares a future that is not easy and will require a new transformation and maturity. A future marked by difficulty, challenge, and even death. But it's the final two words above that restored Peter: "Follow me." Even in the midst of failing Jesus, his grace overcame the pain and agony within his "failed" disciple and he cast vision once again for the life of Peter. Lest we forget, this is Peter the "rock"! The rock symbolizing the revelation that Jesus is the Messiah upon which the church would be built.[33] Where Peter thought he was unworthy, Jesus brought worthiness. Where Peter thought he was forgotten, Jesus remembered him. What was broken and

---

relationship, or transformation of his role." He further writes that, in this exchange, "true denial must be overcome, the bond must be restored, the estrangement must be repaired, the trust must be brought back, and the call and commission renewed." Vaquilar, "Peter's Journey," 88.

32. Ilaria Ramelli is quick to point out that the phrase in 21:15 is best worded as "Do you love me more than you love these things?" In the article the conclusion is that "these things" focuses primarily on the fish and the action of fishing. In essence, "Do you love me more than what you are about to return to? Do you love me more than these 'tools' of your past?" This insight is helpful, for in understanding the question Jesus may pose to us. Do we love him more than what we were about to turn away from him for? Do we truly love this distraction over here or over there more so than he himself? For more on the grammatical construction of 21:15 as well as more pertinent information from the exchange as a whole, see Ramelli, "Simon Son of John," 332–50.

33. For more on Peter's revelation in Matt 16:18 and Jesus communicating that Peter represented the "rock" upon which his church would be built, see Hengel, *Saint Peter*, 16.

in pieces had been pieced back together with two simple words: "Follow me." Can he not also do this with us in our ministries?

Jesus with Peter ... Jesus with Us

Peter's overall transformation from backwoods fisherman to fisher of people extraordinaire makes for one of the most engaging stories in Scripture. Primarily because of the human element. Here we have a man who walked closely with Jesus who at each turn of his life exercised qualities and character that enabled him to find himself and his place as a disciple. As one scholar writes, "It is the profoundly transformative sense of a fallible and imperfect character given grace to make good on his failings: the work of Christ in his life is seen to empower this well-intentioned but rough-hewn and flawed disciple to do the right thing."[34] Where does this then leave us? In every leader (as well as Jesus follower) there is a trajectory and pace. Peter's trajectory was often pointing in various directions at any time. But it was always Jesus who brought the needed recalibration. It was Jesus who patiently and lovingly guided Peter's vision away from self and toward the directives of the kingdom. As leaders we too are in desperate need of this. Jesus, by his Spirit (John 14–16), longs to spend deep and intimate time with us to cast new vision and restore what may be dead or dying. In doing so, he puts us back on a solid trajectory just as he does with Peter in John 21.

The pacing of Peter was also kept in check by Jesus. He knew how to bring Peter to places of prayer and reflection. He also knew when it was time to pull him away from the others on a shoreline and bring restoration into his life. There are seasons of every leader's life where our pace needs to be brought before the Lord to ensure we are tracking with him. With the many demands upon leaders today, it is vital that adopting a Sabbath life is kept as a priority so that ample margin is always present for our pace to be molded into his. How else will we be able to recollect our call stories with joy? How else will we be able to step carefully on the water's surface as the winds blow? How else will we be able to lift our heads up to look Jesus in the eyes as he asks us, "Do you love me?" not once or twice, but perhaps three times?

The grind of serving and loving people can bring weariness and fatigue at any point in the ministry journey. The joy and passion can

---

34. Bockmuehl, "Transformation of Simon Peter," 19.

dissipate at a moment's notice. The seminal moments of our lives and ministry with Jesus can become distant nostalgia. Over time, like any good vehicle, the wear and tear will be just too much, and we will break down. The enemy, if he has his way, will lead us to distractions and a possible denial of our very identity in Christ.

But perhaps like Peter, if we are looking closely, we will discover fresh vision from Jesus. It doesn't matter where our decisions have taken us. No matter the perceived failures or weaknesses. That walk on the shoreline in John 21 shows each of us that our calling still holds true to the very end. It may shift, pause, and need time away for healing. That season of my life when skipping rocks was more therapy than hobby, I found myself taking a pause for healing. In that pause I rediscovered the person of Jesus in fresh and new ways that revitalized and restored my ministry heart. Through that season and the study of Peter's life off and on since then, I learned that each of us can be restored to the proper place Jesus has for us. For his grace never runs dry and our place at his table is always ready. The discovery of ourselves then, as we began with, is tied not to who *we* find ourselves to be, but rather whom *Jesus* has called us to be from the beginning: recipients of grace and passionate followers of himself to the very end.

Bibliography

Bockmuehl, Markus N. A. "The Transformation of Simon Peter." *Crux* 48.3 (2012) 13–22.

Bovon, François. *Luke 3: A Commentary on the Gospel of Luke 19:28—24:53*. Translated by James Crouch. Hermeneia. Minneapolis: Fortress, 2012.

Brown, Raymond, et al., eds. *Peter in the New Testament: A Collaborative Assessment by Protestant and Roman Catholic Scholars*. 1973. Reprint, Eugene, OR: Wipf & Stock, 2002.

Cullmann, Oscar. *Peter: Disciple, Apostle, Martyr*. 2nd rev. ed. Reprint, Waco, TX: Baylor University Press, 2011.

Fowler, James W. *Stages of Faith: The Psychology of Human Development and the Quest for Meaning*. New York: HarperOne, 1995.

Gray, Tim. *Peter: Keys to Following Jesus*. San Francisco: Ignatius, 2016.

Green, Joel B. *The Gospel of Luke*. New International Commentary on the New Testament. Grand Rapids: Eerdmans, 1997.

Helyer, Larry R. *The Life and Witness of Peter*. Downers Grove, IL: IVP Academic, 2012.

Hengel, Martin. *Saint Peter: The Underestimated Apostle*. Translated by Thomas H. Trapp. Grand Rapids: Eerdmans, 2010.

Kirkpatrick, Clifton. "Pastoral Perspective on Matthew 14:22–33." In *Feasting on the Word: Preaching the Revised Common Lectionary: Year A*, edited by David L. Bartlett and Barbara Brown Taylor, 3:332–37. Louisville: Westminster John Knox, 2011.

Luz, Ulrich. *Matthew 1–7: A Commentary*. Rev. ed. Hermeneia. Minneapolis: Fortress, 2007.

McKnight, Scot, and Laura Barringer. *A Church Called Tov: Forming a Goodness Culture That Resists Abuses of Power and Promotes Healing*. Carol Stream, IL: Tyndale, 2020.

———. *Pivot: The Priorities, Practices, and Powers That Can Transform Your Church into a Tov Culture*. Carol Stream, IL: Tyndale, 2023

Morris, Leon. *Luke: An Introduction and Commentary*. Tyndale New Testament Commentaries 3. Downers Grove, IL: InterVarsity, 1988.

Nolland, John. *The Gospel of Matthew: A Commentary on the Greek Text*. New International Greek Testament Commentary. Grand Rapids: Eerdmans, 2005.

Peterson, Eugene H. *The Contemplative Pastor: Returning to the Art of Spiritual Direction*. Grand Rapids: Eerdmans, 1996.

Ramelli, Ilaria. "'Simon Son of John, Do You Love Me?': Some Reflections on John 21:15." *Novum Testamentum* 50 (2008) 332–50. https://doi.org/10.1163/156853608X303525.

Thiede, Carsten Peter. *Simon Peter: From Galilee to Rome*. Grand Rapids: Academie, 1988.

Vaquilar, Nick A. "Peter's Journey as Disciple: An Exegetical-Theological Study of John 21:15–19." *Landas* 26.2 (2012) 79–102.

Wilkins, Michael J. *Following the Master: Biblical Theology of Discipleship*. Grand Rapids: Zondervan, 1992.

2

Failure to Follow Faithfully
Peter's Denials in Mark

Alice McQuitty

Failure. The word itself makes us weak in the knees. Disturbing images come to mind when we hear that word, including perhaps our earliest memories of school days and the menacing red-inked "F" suspended at the top of a paper that would turn a child's cheeks red with shame—and fear. What will happen to me if I fail—this test, this class, this grade, this career, this relationship, this life? Fear of failure can start early in life, and the rest is often spent driven and desperate to avoid it. Thankfully, Jesus offered up his own, red-stained F word to counter our fear: follow. "Follow me," he implored as he began his earthly ministry and beckoned others to join him (Mark 2:14, 8:34).[1]

Any seasoned follower of Jesus knows that the road of spiritual formation is fraught with obstacles, temptations, fears, doubts, and sometimes failure, despite good hearts, good intentions, and even strong convictions about who Jesus is and determined commitments to follow faithfully. Jesus' first disciples experienced this firsthand. There is an enemy afoot determined to derail us, as Peter and Judas discovered, but most times we are our own worst enemy as we wander off the road into the weeds and ditches of trying to experience life on our terms. The comforting element in all of this is that Jesus knows it, predicts it, warns of it,

---

1. All Scripture quotations, unless otherwise noted, are taken from the NET Bible.

and ultimately redeems our failures to fruitfulness through repentance and grace. This is the gospel story.

All four Gospels record the account of Peter's denials, but this essay will anchor in Mark with the assumption of Markan priority as well as with the early tradition that Peter himself is behind the writing of this Gospel. In the words of Eusebius:

> This also the presbyter said: "Mark, having become the interpreter of Peter, wrote down accurately, though not indeed in order, whatsoever he remembered of the things said or done by Christ.... For he was careful of one thing, not to omit any of the things which he had heard, and not to state any of them falsely." These things are related by Papias concerning Mark.[2]

Many modern scholars concur that Mark's Gospel is a faithful representation of Peter's perspective on Jesus' life and teachings as well as on his own discipleship, including the historicity of his denials.[3]

Notable in Mark is the theme of discipleship in which Peter is prominently featured.[4] A brief portrait of Peter and the disciples in Mark will be discussed, followed by an examination of the immediate contexts leading up to Peter's denials. In the pericope of the denials, the significance of Mark's literary structure for his theological agenda will be examined. The final section will include pastoral reflections about dealing with failure and how to stay faithful.

Portrait of Peter and the Disciples

It is widely recognized that Peter occupied a unique and preeminent position within the novice band of disciples.[5] He often functioned as their leader, representative, and spokesman. Peter was first (along with Andrew) commissioned to follow Jesus and become a fisher of people (1:16–17). He is named first in the list of disciples called and appointed to apostleship (3:13–18), after which Jesus renamed Simon as Peter, meaning "rock" (v. 16). Significantly, Jesus gathered and designated the Twelve as apostles, "*so that* they would *be with him* and he could *send them* to preach and to have authority to cast out demons" (3:15–16, emphasis added). In other

2. Eusebius, "Church History," 172–73.
3. Green, *Vox Petri*, 44–45.
4. Hooker, *Saint Mark*, 59.
5. Cullmann, *Peter*, 25–33.

words, their calling was a summons to apprenticeship under him. They were to *be with* him, to learn from him, to become like him in thought and character, and to participate with him in his work.[6] Indeed, they did. They witnessed all his teachings and miracles and even began their own two-by-two ministries in Jesus' name and authority: preaching repentance, casting out demons, and healing the sick (6:7–12). Afterwards, Peter was the first to confess that Jesus is the Christ (8:29).

Peter's confession was a significant turning point in Mark's Gospel because Jesus' response was to begin a whole new teaching about the Son of Man, his favorite self-reference.[7] The term comes from Dan 7:13–14, and Jesus chose it because "this term ties together both suffering and vindication to his vocation to rule."[8] Mark records that Jesus "spoke plainly" of his suffering, rejection, execution, and resurrection—likely to dispel any notion of Peter's that he was a religious-national king.[9] Appalled, Peter took Jesus aside and rebuked him, receiving a harsh rebuke in return. "Get behind me, Satan! You are not setting your mind on God's interests, but on man's" (8:33). Jesus then called the crowd along with his disciples to understand that following him meant self-denial and self-sacrifice. This was the way to true life he told them. Self-preservation was the way of death (8:35). Then the chilling words, "For if anyone is ashamed of me and my words in this adulterous and sinful generation, the Son of Man will also be ashamed of him when he comes in the glory of his Father with the holy angels" (8:38). Would Peter's denials fit into this category?

It has long been a recognized feature of Mark's Gospel that Peter and the other disciples consistently failed to understand the meaning behind the things they saw and heard: the parables (4:13; 7:14–19), the calming of the sea and the storm (4:41; 6:51), the two feedings of the multitudes (6:35–37; 8:21), and now the concept of a suffering Messiah and his cross-bearing followers (8:31–3; 9:9–10, 30–37; 10:32–45).[10] Their failure to comprehend inevitably resulted in a failure of faith that ended disastrously in betrayal, desertion, and denial.

The disciples' incomprehension of Jesus and his mission has garnered much debate about Mark's intent. It has been asserted that this was a polemic against the Twelve who represented a group in Mark's

---

6. Green, *Vox Petri*, 213.
7. Lane, *Gospel of Mark*, 292.
8. McKnight, *Kingdom Conspiracy*, 131.
9. Achtemeier, "Peter," 68.
10. Hooker, *Saint Mark*, 21.

community holding to a false Christology—that Jesus was a *theios aner*, a category in Hellenistic thought of a "divine man" connected to the gods and capable of performing miracles. In this scenario, Mark has Jesus correct this heresy with a theology of suffering and the cross.[11] More likely, Mark is recording accurately Peter's recollection that the disciples simply could not wrap their heads around the theology that Jesus was both the royal Messiah in the line of David and at the same time a Messiah who must be crucified (and his true followers after him).[12] The two theologies could not coexist in their minds. One might wonder if perhaps their failure to understand was a stubborn unwillingness to open their minds to a new way of understanding the Messiah—one that didn't fit their categories or benefit them in a special way.[13] How often do Christians ignore the hard sayings of Jesus because of our own self-interests? However, against a completely negative view of Peter's incomprehension is understanding it as representative of an apocalyptic motif of *human incomprehension in the face of divinely revealed mysteries*.[14] Of course he could not understand! No one could have before the cross and resurrection.

Mark 10:32–45 recounts Jesus' third teaching concerning the fate that awaited him in Jerusalem. James and John ignored it altogether and instead requested to sit on either side of Jesus in his glory. Jesus responded by instructing them yet again that the way to glory is the way of the cross. Would they follow his way to glory?

The Denials in the Immediate Contexts

"Surely, not I?" was the distressed response of each of the Twelve to Jesus' announcement that one of them would betray him (14:19). The setting was a table around which Jesus and the disciples were gathered and partaking of the Passover meal. Although Jesus didn't answer their question, the Greek construction implies they expected a negative answer. It isn't clear however if the question reflects self-confidence or self-doubt on the part of the disciples as to their inclination or ability to commit such treachery. Given Peter's response in the next pericope, one might surmise that his question reflected confidence in his fidelity. It has been suggested that

11. Achtemeier, "Peter," 145–58.
12. Green, *Vox Petri*, 218.
13. Green, *Vox Petri*, 218.
14. Markley, "Reassessing Peter's Imperception," 108.

Mark wanted his readers/hearers to ask themselves whether they would betray Jesus as they were facing persecution or other trials.[15] Jesus affirmed that the betrayer was one of the Twelve, "one who dips his hand with me into the bowl." It calls to mind Ps 41:9, a passage quoted in John's Gospel to explain Judas's defection:[16] "Even my close friend whom I trusted, he who shared meals with me, has turned against me." Jesus indicated that these events were unfolding as part of the divine plan (Mark 14:20–21) and then proceeded to transform their Passover meal into a ceremonial meal of remembrance: breaking the bread ("my body") and sharing the cup ("my blood of the covenant that is poured out for many").

After the Supper, on the way to the Mount of Olives, Jesus predicted the disciples' flight and Peter's denial. The mood must have been quite somber indeed.

> [27] Then Jesus said to them, "You will all fall away, for it is written,
>
> > 'I will strike the shepherd,
> > and the sheep will be scattered.'
>
> [28] But after I am raised, I will go ahead of you into Galilee." [29] Peter said to him, "Even if they all fall away, I will not!" [30] Jesus said to him, "I tell you the truth, today—this very night—before a rooster crows twice, you will deny me three times." [31] But Peter insisted emphatically, "Even if I must die with you, I will never deny you." And all of them said the same thing. (Mark 14: 27–31)

Peter spoke for the whole group in insisting on his loyalty. Unlike the active betrayal by Judas (*paradidōmi*, meaning "to hand over"),[17] the disciples' "falling away" (*skandalisthēsesthe*, future passive indicative)[18] indicates a stumbling along the road because of failing to stay spiritually alert, rather than a complete failure of faith. Although scandalous, their failure wouldn't be final. Jesus will rise and meet them in Galilee.[19] Luke inserts some unique material here to include Satan's involvement in their trial: "Simon, Simon, pay attention! Satan has demanded to have you all, to sift you like wheat, but I have prayed for you, Simon, that your faith may not fail. *When you have turned back, strengthen your brothers*" (Luke 22:31–32, emphasis added). In other words, Simon's

---

15. Brooks, *Mark*, 227–28.
16. Hooker, *Saint Mark*, 336.
17. BDAG, s.v. "παραδίδωμι."
18. BDAG, s.v. "σκανδαλίζω."
19. France, *Gospel of Mark*, 575.

failure would not be the end of his story or his effectiveness as a disciple. Peter, the rock, will turn around and be able to encourage others who also failed to follow faithfully.

But Peter was having none of it. This was the third time in Mark that Peter had the cheek to contradict Jesus. To deny the truth of what Jesus said was to call him a liar, which brushes up against blasphemy. Not only did Peter fail to understand Jesus and his mission, but he also failed to understand himself. For all his bravado, the "rock" had feet of clay. Though everyone else might be weak, he would be strong. His trust was in himself and his own ability to stay faithful. It would be a very short path to denying Jesus, not once, but three times that very night. He would fulfill Jesus' prophecy.

As the disciples arrived at Gethsemane, Jesus singled out Peter, James, and John to "remain here and stay alert" (14:34). These three had witnessed the raising of Jairus's daughter and the transfiguration. Now they would witness Jesus's agony and his struggle to accept the Father's will.[20] This was the crucial test of Jesus' own faithfulness which must become the model for his followers. Although all three of them failed to stay awake, Jesus focused his rebuke on Peter, likely because he had been so adamant about his loyalty. "Simon, are you sleeping? Couldn't you stay awake for one hour? Stay awake and pray that you will not fall into temptation. The spirit is willing, but the flesh is weak" (Mark 14:37–38). The use of Simon's given name, rather than his apostolic name Peter, seems to indicate his failure as a disciple in this moment. The command to stay awake and pray was an admonition to remain spiritually vigilant so that they could face the "severe testing of loyalties" that would shortly come.[21] If Peter the rock cannot stay strong enough in one hour, how will he remain steadfast in the coming test?[22] He won't. None of them will. Jesus withdrew again to pray twice more and twice more found them asleep. This sequence of threes anticipates Peter's threefold denial.[23]

When Judas "the betrayer" showed up with an armed crowd to arrest Jesus, Jesus did not resist. Instead, he insisted once again that "the Scriptures must be fulfilled" (14:49 NIV). When the disciples realized that Jesus would not resist, they did exactly as he predicted. They all deserted him and fled, including perhaps the author of Mark's Gospel,

---

20. Garland, *Mark*, 539.
21. Lane, *Gospel of Mark*, 520.
22. Hooker, *Saint Mark*, 349.
23. Helyer, *Life and Witness*, 60.

mentioned only as a "young man" with good intentions to follow Jesus, who instead fled naked into the night rather than stand loyally beside him (14:50–51).

Peter's Denials

Continuing Mark's theme of discipleship, Peter's denials are juxtaposed with the Jewish trial of Jesus.[24] The scenes shift back and forth between Jesus' interrogation inside the court of the high priest and Peter's interrogation outside in the courtyard. This type of literary device is called "framing"[25] or "sandwiching,"[26] and allows two stories to be compared or contrasted. In this case, the structure of the narration contrasts the faithfulness of one with the unfaithfulness of the other.[27]

> The effect of this way of telling the story (in contrast with Luke, who records Peter's denial before Jesus' hearing) is to throw Jesus and Peter into sharp contrast. Each will be under pressure, but whereas Jesus both in his silence and in his final dramatic utterance will stand firm, Peter will crumble. Jesus will go to his death, but with his witness to his mission undimmed; Peter will escape, but at the cost of his integrity as a disciple of Jesus.[28]

With that in mind, try to imagine the scenes as you read Mark 14:53–72.

> [53] Then they led Jesus to the high priest, and all the chief priests and elders and experts in the law came together. [54] And Peter had followed him from a distance, up to the high priest's courtyard. He was sitting with the guards and warming himself by the fire. [55] The chief priests and the whole Sanhedrin were looking for evidence against Jesus so that they could put him to death, but they did not find anything. [56] Many gave false testimony against him, but their testimony did not agree. [57] Some stood up and gave this false testimony against him: [58] "We heard him say, 'I will destroy this temple made with hands and in three days build another not made with hands.'" [59] Yet even on this point their testimony did not agree. [60] Then the high priest stood up before them and asked Jesus, "Have you no answer? What is this that they are

---

24. Kuruvilla, *Mark*, 320.
25. Rhoads and Michie, *Mark as Story*, 51, cited in Herron, "Mark's Account," 177.
26. Kuruvilla, *Mark*, 321, citing Tom Shepherd, *Markan Sandwich Stories*, 267–310.
27. Kuruvilla, *Mark*, 321, citing Tom Shepherd, *Markan Sandwich Stories*, 267–310.
28. France, *Gospel of Mark*, 598.

testifying against you?" ⁶¹ But he was silent and did not answer. Again the high priest questioned him, "Are you the Christ, the Son of the Blessed One?" ⁶² "I am," said Jesus, "and you will see *the Son of Man sitting at the right hand* of the Power and *coming with the clouds of heaven.*" ⁶³ Then the high priest tore his clothes and said, "Why do we still need witnesses? ⁶⁴ You have heard the blasphemy! What is your verdict?" They all condemned him as deserving death. ⁶⁵ Then some began to spit on him, and to blindfold him, and to strike him with their fists, saying, "Prophesy!" The guards also took him and beat him.

⁶⁶ Now while Peter was below in the courtyard, one of the high priest's slave girls came by. ⁶⁷ When she saw Peter warming himself, she looked directly at him and said, "You also were with that Nazarene, Jesus." ⁶⁸ But he denied it: "I don't even understand what you're talking about!" Then he went out to the gateway, and a rooster crowed. ⁶⁹ When the slave girl saw him, she began again to say to the bystanders, "This man is one of them." ⁷⁰ But he denied it again. A short time later the bystanders again said to Peter, "You must be one of them, because you are also a Galilean." ⁷¹ Then he began to curse, and he swore with an oath, "I do not know this man you are talking about!" ⁷² Immediately a rooster crowed a second time. Then Peter remembered what Jesus had said to him: "Before a rooster crows twice, you will deny me three times." And he broke down and wept.

Mark's structure parallels Jesus and Peter in two separate but simultaneous trial scenes,²⁹ albeit Jesus' trial was a quasi-legal one while Peter's was a test of his faith and loyalty. Peter had initially fled with the other disciples at Jesus' arrest but to his credit had apparently recovered his composure sufficiently to follow Jesus again "to be with him" but "at a distance." Jesus was led inside a lion's den of Jewish leaders looking for a way to put him to death (v. 53) while Peter warmed himself by a fire among the guards in the courtyard (v. 54). While the "chief priests and the whole Sanhedrin" were probing for incriminating testimony against Jesus and many falsely accused him, Jesus twice remained silent. When finally asked point blank if he was "the Christ, the Son of the Blessed One," Jesus boldly confessed his identity as the Son of God (*egō eimi*, "I am") and went even further to claim his identity as the Son of Man, whose victory would be at the right hand of God (v. 62).³⁰ Jesus' faithfulness to his identity and

---

29. Kuruvilla, *Mark*, 327.
30. Kuruvilla, *Mark*, 321, 326.

calling resulted in condemnation "worthy of death." At that point he was physically abused and ironically commanded to prophesy—ironic because at that very moment, Peter was in the courtyard fulfilling Jesus' prophecy about himself. Accused by a lone servant girl of being associated with "that Nazarene Jesus," Peter flatly denied understanding anything about Jesus.[31] This was a lie with a smack of the truth. Truly he had failed many times to understand Jesus throughout his discipleship journey—this was a culmination of that process.[32] At this point, Peter removed himself to the entryway, and a rooster crowed. That should have served as a warning to Peter, but it didn't seem to register with him.[33]

The servant girl found Peter again, and this time pointed him out to those standing nearby as "one of them." Again, Peter denied it, only this time the verb tense changed to an imperfect, indicating that he kept on denying, and in the process of talking too much revealed his Galilean accent.[34] Peter's third denial was accompanied by curses and swearing, "I do not know this man you are talking about." The object of Peter's curse is not specified in the text. The early NIV translates this as Peter calling down curses on himself if he is lying. However, there is a distinct possibility Peter is anathematizing (*anathematizein*) Jesus![35] The persecuted Christians who would have heard/read Mark would have been struck with the threefold interrogation of Peter as like what happened in Pliny the Younger's court (61–112 CE).[36] Pliny was a Roman lawyer in the late first century. He would ask the accused whether they were Christians, and if they confessed, he would ask them a second and third time, threatening them with punishment. He would later conclude that cursing Christ was something which "those who are really Christians cannot be made to do" (*Epistula* 10.96.5).[37] If Peter carried his denial to the point of blasphemy or apostasy as Mark seems to imply, then it

---

31. The word deny (*arneomai*) has several nuances: to deny something is true, to disdain association with, to repudiate, or disown. BDAG, s.v. "ἀρνέομαι."

32. Garland, *Mark*, 566.

33. Some of the most important manuscripts do not include the first crowing. That the rooster crowed "the second time" after the third denial is also unique to Mark. The other three Gospels record a single crowing. Most of the textual variants in vv. 68 and 72 of Mark likely represent attempts to harmonize Mark to the more traditional single crowing. See Williams, *Mark*, 252 and France, *Gospel of Mark*, 618.

34. Garland, *Mark*, 566–67.

35. Lampe, "St. Peter's Denial," 348, 354.

36. Lampe, "St. Peter's Denial," 348.

37. Cited in Lampe, "St. Peter's Denial," 354.

makes his failure even more breathtaking and his restoration later even more remarkable.[38] In the narrative structure of this whole pericope, the greatest irony is that "the charge of blasphemy is laid on Jesus, not on Peter, who actually deserves it."[39]

The contrast between Jesus' powerful affirmation and Peter's shameful denial could not be more poignant or tragic. The rooster crowed "the second time," and Peter broke down and wept as he remembered what Jesus had said, not only the denial prediction, but perhaps too his words in 8:38, "If anyone is ashamed of me and my words . . . the Son of Man will be ashamed of him when he comes in his Father's glory."[40] The intensity of Peter's sorrow is indicated by the verb phrase *epiballō* ("to throw oneself")[41] *eklaien*, "to weep."[42] The phrase is difficult to translate but indicates a deep gut-wrenching sorrow, likely mixed with shame and regret. "The rock" had cracked and crumbled into a pile of sand.[43]

Peter is not mentioned again until the resurrection in Mark 16 when the women came to the tomb to anoint Jesus' body. When they entered the tomb "a young man dressed in a white robe" announced that Jesus had risen, and he gave them a specific message, "But go, tell his disciples, even Peter,[44] that he is going ahead of you into Galilee. You will see him there, just as he told you." Jesus singled out Peter for special attention. Every awful thing that had happened to Jesus, to Peter, and to all the disciples, Jesus had told them about in advance. Now he was reminding them of something else he had previously told them. He would go ahead of them to Galilee, the place where they all started following him. It hints of a new start after failure. The narrative of Mark ends abruptly with the women fleeing from the tomb in terror and bewilderment, saying nothing to anyone because they were afraid. Certainly, the reader/hearers of Mark would know that the women did tell, that Peter was indeed forgiven

38. Garland, *Mark*, 567.
39. Kuruvilla, *Mark*, 330.
40. Herron, "Mark's Account," 273.
41. BDAG, s.v. "ἐπιβάλλω."
42. BDAG, s.v. "ἔκλαιεν."
43. Garland, *Mark*, 573.
44. Most versions translate the *kai* as *and*. "Go tell his disciples and Peter. . ." but Hengel sees an *inclusio* with 1:16 in this "unnecessary" phrase to indicate that for Mark, Peter was the most important guarantor of the tradition and was also the most authoritative disciple of Jesus—this against an anti-Petrine view of this Gospel. See Hengel, *Saint Peter*, 42.

and restored, and that he became a foundational pillar in the first church at Jerusalem, but that story is for other chapters.

Pastoral Reflections on Peter's Denials

For all his positive, even endearing qualities, Peter was deeply flawed and often fallible, as are all disciples of Jesus at times—made especially painful when those flaws are revealed, typically in times of trial or temptation. And yet, it is in the fire of our trials and failures that our character is not only revealed but refined. While failure can feel like the end of the world, Peter would tell us that it is not. It can be an important part of our formation and transformation if we respond with humility and repentance. Peter became an embodied example of forgiveness and a fresh start. There is an almost palpable tenderness and compassion in his first epistle toward wavering believers in Asia Minor that likely sprung out of his own deeply disappointing failure (1 Pet 5:1–11).[45]

But no one wants to fail. How would Pastor Peter advise us to remain faithful in times of trial? Drawing from his writings, Peter would advise us to develop humility and a firm reliance on God.

> [5] And all of you, clothe yourselves with humility toward one another, because God *opposes the proud but gives grace to the humble*. [6] And God will exalt you in due time, if you humble yourselves under his mighty hand [7] by casting all your cares on him because he cares for you. (1 Pet 5:5–7)

Peter thought he had what it took to stay strong. He was the self-confident leader of the Twelve and thought he was above the others. "Even if all fall away, I will not." His self-reliance, his failure to heed to Jesus' warnings, and his refusal to accept Jesus' teachings about the way of faithful discipleship led to his downfall. Jesus doesn't need or want our bravado.[46] He knows our flesh is still weak, no matter how willing the spirit is. He calls us to trust him especially when following him is costly.

Secondly, Peter would exhort us to stay alert. Busy schedules and constant distractions make us susceptible to the insidious temptations of our enemy.

---

45. Helyer, *Life and Witness*, 61.
46. Lane, *Gospel of Mark*, 555.

> [8] Be sober and alert. Your enemy the devil, *like a roaring lion*, is on the prowl looking for someone to devour. [9] Resist him, strong in your faith, because you know that your brothers and sisters throughout the world are enduring the same kinds of suffering. (1 Pet 5:8–9)

Three times Jesus had warned Peter and the others to stay awake, to watch and pray. Three times they failed. Three times Peter denied Jesus. There is a connection. Spiritual watchfulness is imperative because the flesh is weak and because there is an enemy determined to devour us. The primary way we stay spiritually alert is through prayer. Peter again: "For the culmination of all things is near. So be self-controlled and sober-minded for the sake of prayer" (1 Pet 4:7). All too often in the hustle and bustle of life and the constant demands of ministry, a consistent prayer life is the first thing to go, but prayer is the essential priority for us, as it was for Jesus.

Finally, our own denials take much more subtle forms than Peter's. Most of us do not face prison or death for our faith. We do however live in a highly contentious culture, so we might be overly reluctant to share our faith. We might not even want others to know we are Christians for fear of being mocked or rejected. We conform to the world's standards and self-centered approach to life rather than following the way of the cross. Peter's words once more:

> [16] But if you suffer as a Christian, do not be ashamed, but glorify God that you bear such a name. [17] For it is time for judgment to begin, starting with the house of God. And if it starts with us, what will be the fate of those who are disobedient to the gospel of God? [18] And *if the righteous are barely saved, what will become of the ungodly and sinners?* [19] So then let those who suffer according to the will of God entrust their souls to a faithful Creator as they do good. (1 Pet 4:16–19)

For any number of reasons, we all fail to follow Jesus faithfully at times. If you or someone you know has experienced a failure recently, Pastor Peter would tell you to humbly and truly repent and then get up and keep following Jesus. He is way ahead of you. Your stumbling and failings do not surprise him. He has already arranged for your forgiveness, and he plans to use your failures to conform you to Christ. Though you might fail him time and again, he will never fail you. Keep following the one who was faithful unto death, and failure will not get the final word.

Bibliography

Achtemeier, Paul J. "Peter in the Gospel of Mark." In *Peter in the New Testament: A Collaborative Assessment by Protestant and Roman Catholic Scholars*, edited by Raymond E. Brown et al., 57–73. 1973. Reprint, Eugene, OR: Wipf & Stock, 2002.

Bockmuehl, Markus N. A. *Simon Peter in Scripture and Memory: The New Testament Apostle in the Early Church*. Grand Rapids: Baker Academic, 2012.

Bond, Helen K., and Larry W. Hurtado, eds. *Peter in Early Christianity*. Grand Rapids: Eerdmans, 2015.

Brooks, James A. *Mark*. The New American Commentary 23. Nashville: B&H, 1992.

Brown, Raymond E., et al., eds. *Peter in the New Testament: A Collaborative Assessment by Protestant and Roman Catholic Scholars*. 1973. Reprint, Eugene, OR: Wipf & Stock, 2002.

Calvin, John. *Commentary on a Harmony of the Evangelists Matthew, Mark, and Luke*. Logos. 3 vols. Grand Rapids: Eerdmans, 1949.

Cullmann, Oscar. *Peter: Disciple, Apostle, Martyr*. Waco, TX: Baylor University Press, 2011.

Eusebius of Caesarea. "The Church History of Eusebius." In *Eusebius: Church History, Life of Constantine the Great, and Oration in Praise of Constantine*, edited by Philip Schaff and Henry Wace. Nicene and Post-Nicene Fathers, series 2, vol. 1. New York: Christian Literature, 1890.

France, R. T. *The Gospel of Mark: A Commentary on the Greek Text*. Grand Rapids: Eerdmans, 2002.

Garland, David E. *Mark*. NIV Application Commentary. Grand Rapids: Zondervan, 1998.

Green, Gene L. *Vox Petri: A Theology of Peter*. Eugene, OR: Cascade Books, 2020.

Helyer, Larry R. *The Life and Witness of Peter*. Downers Grove, IL: IVP Academic, 2012.

Hengel, Martin. *Saint Peter: The Underestimated Apostle*. Grand Rapids: Eerdmans, 2010.

Herron, Robert Wilburn Jr. "Mark's Account of Peter's Denial of Jesus: A Representative History of Interpretation of Mark 14:54, 66–72." PhD. diss., Rice University, 1990.

Hooker, Morna D. *The Gospel According to Saint Mark*. Black's New Testament Commentary. London: Continuum, 2006.

Kuruvilla, Abraham. *Mark: A Theological Commentary for Preachers*. Eugene, OR: Cascade Books, 2012.

Lampe, G. W. H. "St. Peter's Denial." *Bulletin of the John Rylands Library* 55 (1973) 346–68.

Lane, William L. *The Gospel of Mark*. New International Commentary on the New Testament. Grand Rapids: Eerdmans, 1974.

Markley, John R. "Reassessing Peter's Imperception in Synoptic Tradition." In *Peter in Early Christianity*, edited by Helen K. Bond and Larry W. Hurtado, 99–108. Grand Rapids: Eerdmans, 2015.

McKnight, Scot. *Kingdom Conspiracy: Returning to the Radical Mission of the Local Church*. Grand Rapids: Brazos, 2014.

Rhoads, David, and Donald Michie. *Mark as Story: An Introduction to the Narrative of the Gospel*. Philadelphia: Fortress, 1982.

Thiede, Carsten P. *Simon Peter: From Galilee to Rome*. Grand Rapids: Academic Books, 1988.

Wessel, Walter W., and Mark L. Strauss. *Mark*. Rev. ed. Expositor's Bible Commentary 9. Grand Rapids: Zondervan, 2010.

Williams, Joel F. *Mark*. Exegetical Guide to the Greek New Testament. Nashville: B&H Academic, 2022.

3

Peter: An Apostolic-Pastor in the Making
A Sketch of What Is to Come

Scot McKnight

THE MOST INTERESTING PUZZLE pieces in the formation of earliest Christianity can be found in the pages of the New Testament. A few of these pieces are connected to rock, to stone, to foundation, and to cornerstone/coping stone. One of the major colors in these pieces, which compel us to gather the pieces together, is a color called "Simon Peter." One Peter piece of the puzzle appears in Matt 16:17–19, where Simon, nicknamed "Rock" (*Petros*), forms the Rock (*petra*) upon whom or which, Jesus, the just-confessed Messiah, will build nothing less than his church, or "assembly."[1] Next to this puzzle piece we would need to slide into our immediate working space 1 Cor 3:10–15, and it can be observed that it is a similar and stronger, but not identical, color as the Matt 16 piece of the puzzle. In 1 Cor 3 we learn, not that Peter is the foundation, but that Paul laid down Christ, whom he calls the only foundation. A tandem piece of the puzzle is noticeable in Peter himself, that is if we assign authorship to him, because his puzzle piece has the identical color as Paul's, with the foundational role given to Christ (1 Pet 2:4–8). Two puzzle pieces, which came out of the box still connected, can be found in Eph 2:20–21, one piece is the color of Paul and another that of Peter. These two pieces they

---

1. Parallels found at Mark 8:27–33 and Luke 9:12–22, with a connected tradition at John 1:35–42.

are ready to connect, not only other to other apostles but also to prophets, here assigned a foundational role in the formation of the church. The Ephesians piece of this puzzle fits snugly with Rev 21:14, where we read the "city's wall" has "twelve foundations and on them the Lamb's twelve Commissioners' twelve names."[2]

These rocky, stony pieces of the New Testament don't fit together as snuggly as we might expect, which is how puzzling works. It is hard to disagree with Christ being the foundation, and for most of us that puzzle piece can be put where it belongs, with the assumption that all the others will interlock. But how is Christ the foundation piece if the apostles and prophets are too? In which case, one has to ask how in the world anyone would have colored either the apostles and prophets, and especially one man, Peter, with a color similar to that flat foundational piece of Christ. Is he, or for that matter the other apostles, merely foundation-like pieces on the foundation of Christ?

To back up, Matt 16:17–19 is hardly ambiguous in its affirmation of Cephas or Peter as the Rock, and as the Rock, the foundation for the church. If the Rock is Peter, another puzzling challenge puzzles us: when did the Rock get his nickname? And, when he got that nickname, was it in Aramaic (*Cephas*) or Greek (*Petros*)? Was it as a young man in multilingual Bethsaida, his hometown, or was it in those earliest meetings with Jesus fleshed out in John 1:42–43, or was it when Jesus called the Twelve in Mark 3:16 (cf. Luke 6:14), or was it when Simon confessed Jesus as Messiah, at which moment Jesus names him the Rock? And did Jesus merely convert Peter's Greek name gained in Bethsaida into an Aramaic name? Regardless of timing, the name Rock has a similar color to those other foundation pieces. Some in the early church had the temerity to label Simon as the foundation of the church. If that was a clear foundation in earliest churches, I want us to be willing to ask, Why did Paul become the Lead Apostle, with someone seemingly assigning Peter the role as the Former Lead Apostle? Was that reassignment made by Luke in ordering the Acts of the Apostles as he did, first emphasizing Peter but with Peter giving way to Paul? We have but at most two letters from Peter and we've got a shelf full of letters from Paul. Even the staunchest of Roman Catholics admit Paul's got the bigger role in the New Testament. More important for you and for me in this book is that Paul's status and letters

---

2. All translations in this chapter are from McKnight, *Second Testament*.

have pushed Peter off the stage, at least for Protestants, for providing a paradigm for pastoring.

In this study I want to offer a sketch of Peter as a pastor, knowing of course he never calls himself a pastor.[3] He does, as if he is speaking from experience, urge his co-elders to "pastor God's flock" (1 Pet 5:2). One could buttress such an inference by asserting that Peter ought not to be telling others to do what he does not also himself do. Peter's role as an apostle meant he pastored people, but as an apostle he also pastored other pastors. But before we get to Peter as pastor, I want to put in place three other terms: convert, apostle, and witness. Peter's pastoral ministry was because he was converted, because he was summoned by Christ to be a commissioner or apostle, and because he was a witness of the sufferings (and more) of Christ.

Peter as Convert

The Synoptic Gospels present Peter as a fisherman from Capernaum (Mark 1:16–20; Matt 4:18–22; Luke 5:1–11). Yet the Gospel of John, never afraid to present details Synoptic specialists often ignore, informs us that Peter and his brother, Andrew, along with Philip and Nathanael, were from a fishing village called Bethsaida or, as some suggest, the

---

3. I will not enter here into a discussion about method in studying the historical Peter, apart from saying there are three basic approaches: to take the New Testament texts as reliable for information about Peter, to subject them to critical scrutiny with some, or more than some, bits surviving historical scrutiny (Hengel; Dunn is more open to Peter being behind 1 Peter), and a recent fresh approach in pondering memories about Peter from later texts (Bockmuehl). This book enters the discussion through the first approach. Bockmuehl's memory approach nonetheless permits him to write up a helpful sketch of what the New Testament texts present: Bockmuehl, *Simon Peter*, 19–33. For wider sketches, Perkins, *Peter*; Dunn, *Beginning from Jerusalem*, 189–96, 212–29, 378–415; Dunn, *Neither Jew nor Greek*, 724–54. For a narrative approach to Peter in the Gospels, with an exploration of the pattern about Peter, see Wiarda, *Peter in the Gospels*. The pattern is one of reversed expectations that respond to Peter's positive intentions. The most comprehensive study I have seen is Lieu, *Peter in the Early Church*.

I want to offer a word about the history of scholarship. It is hard today for many to recognize, though some remember, the impact of Martin Hengel's massive study, *Judaism and Hellenism*, with its follow-ups in both smaller volumes and a multitude of essays. He proved that Hellenism had penetrated Judaism. The bright light of Hengel, however, was eclipsed by E. P. Sanders's even more impactful *Paul and Palestinian Judaism*, who corrected Hengel's German Lutheran distortions of Judaism, but his studies remain of significance for the careful reader. See Hengel, *Judaism and Hellenism*; Hengel, *Jews, Greeks, and Barbarians*; Sanders, *Paul and Palestinian Judaism*; Sanders, *Judaism*; Sanders, "Common Judaism Explored."

location of their fishing businesses,[4] technically on the east side of the Jordan where it flowed into the Sea of Galilee (John 1:35–42, 44). As such, Bethsaida has at times been seen as the hometown of the apostles. Archaeologists get under one another's skin over Bethsaida's precise location, whether it is Tell Bethsaida (Et-Tell), called Julias for just a few years by Herod Philip,[5] or el-Araj, on the West side of the Jordan and in Galilee, and much closer to the shoreline of the lake. Or, as Markus Bockmuehl, perhaps the world's most significant Peter scholar today, wonders: Was Tell Bethsaida the city with el-Araj as the fishing site for the more official Tell Bethsaida?[6] What matters more than the precise location is that Peter's hometown was multilingual with very little evidence for a Jewish presence. That Acts 4:13 calls Peter an *agrammatos* and *idiotēs* ("uneducated and novice") both fits Bethsaida's multilinguality and Peter's lack of a rhetorical education.[7] That his parents named him Simon connected him with perhaps a patriarch, Simeon, or more likely with Simon Maccabeus. The name Simon jumped in numbers following the Maccabean and Hasmonean period.[8] One could speculate that his parents were Jewish resisters. That he was observant speaks of his parents' piety as well as his, and complicating that piety would have been his life experience outside the social norm (Acts 10:14, 11:8).[9] Peter's portrait in the Gospels, thus, reveals a courageous and even resistant

---

4. On Bethsaida as it pertains to Peter, Freyne, "Fisherman from Bethsaida"; also Appold, "Peter in Profile." For a more extensive set of studies, Arav and Freund, *Bethsaida*, vols. 1–4.

5. E.g., Josephus, *Antiquities* 18.27–28; cf. *War* 2.168. The oddity of naming Bethsaida after "Julia" is that she became a disgrace to her emperor-father, Augustus, so others contend Julia refers to Augustus's wife, Livia Julia, who was given different descriptions according to the situation and date. Or, perhaps Philip renamed Bethsaida prior to disgraces of Julia. For discussion, see Strickert, "Renaming of Bethsaida."

6. Bockmuehl, *Remembered Peter*; Bockmuehl, *Simon Peter*, 171–74. See also Evans, *Jesus and the Remains*, 5–17.

7. Sean Adams discusses the power of Peter's speaking in how some connect supernatural empowerment (e.g., Luke 21:12–15) to Peter's lack of training. See Adams, "Tradition of Peter's Literacy." In the church tradition, then, Peter becomes a "textbroker" (143).

8. See Williams, "From Shimon to Petros." She disputes the view that Simon was called Petros in his pre-Jesus days, and that the singular shift occurred when Jesus changed it from Simon *Peter* to *Kēphas*. She thinks the name change to *Kēphas* was indicative of his conversion, or his new life, and the intimacy Jesus had with him and the Zebedee sons, who also had nicknames. The Greek name played better in the diaspora.

9. Paul's harsh criticism of Peter's lack of observance, then, cannot be blamed on his growing up in Bethsaida.

Jewish man of Torah observance (cf. Mark 8:32; 14:29, 31), but nothing reveals such a character more than his sword slashing in Gethsemane (John 18:10). He was at least enthused by a Jewish eschatology shaped by a national restoration (Acts 2:26, 39; 3:19, 22–25; 5:31). Bockmuehl wisely observes that "life in a minority context frequently dilutes or heightens religious zeal."[10] Peter's was the latter.

In such a context Simon, soon to be called Cephas or Petros/Peter, encounters Jesus.[11] The story is told, as mentioned, in two or three ways (Mark 1:16–20; Matt 4:18–22; Luke 5:1–11; John 1:35–42). The Markan-Matthean narrative shows signs of a story reduced to its basics in order to provide for churches a synopsis of a conversion or call story. The Lukan story stands on its own and can be supplemented with the Markan-Matthean and Johannine accounts. Pressed by the crowd at the shoreline, Jesus spots two boats "standing along the lake" (Luke 5:1–2). The fishermen were "rinsing their nets." Jesus boards into Simon's boat, which could indicate a flourishing fishing business on his part. Jesus asks Simon to launch the boat out into the lake, from which location Jesus, sitting, teaches the crowd. In a down moment, Jesus asks Simon to return to deeper waters and let down his anchored nets. Simon, calling Jesus "Superintendent" (*epistatēs*),[12] however deferential he was, resists Jesus's request and then does what Jesus asks. An overwhelming catch ensues, so much the nets "were ripping," requiring help from other boats, and so overwhelming the boat was sinking. Fishermen gonna fishermen.

The impact on Peter was a confession of sin, which is a non sequitur for anyone other than those who know stories of Christian conversion. Everyone else was shocked by the fishing story, including those other fishermen who were "in common," or partnership, with Peter, Zebedee's sons (5:10). Their fishing business partnership also indicates a flourishing business. Perhaps it was Zebedee's business. At this point Jesus calms the fears of Simon and reveals to him that "from now on you will be catching [*zōgreō*] humans" (5:10). The Greek term means to catch alive, or in the military, to take alive.[13] Using the image fishing for what the apostles were

10. Bockmuehl, *Simon Peter*, 176.

11. For more on Peter and conversion, see Matthew Van Winkle, "Different Road Traveled," 63–75 below.

12. Used but six times, each in Luke, in the New Testament (5:5; 8:24, 45; 9:33, 49; 17:13). Peter uses the term of Jesus at 5:5, probably 8:24, 45, and 9:33; John at 9:49; and the scaly-skinned at 17:13.

13. More than three decades ago a student of mine, Greg Vadala, wrote an extensive paper on this passage and was the first to make me aware of the significance of the verb

to do connects with Jer 16:15–16.[14] Once on shore the men all choose to leave the fishing business to others to follow Jesus (5:11).

A gurgle in current scholarship bubbles up with Markus Bockmuehl, who discounts Luke 5:1–11 as a conversion story.[15] In brief, his theory is that a much later text in Luke 22:31–32 indicates both that Peter had not been converted and that his conversion was in the future. The text reads:

> Simōn Simōn, Look! Satanas called out for [all of] you to sift [you] as wheat. I have pleaded for you that your allegiance doesn't eclipse and you, *when turning back*, strengthen your siblings. [The Greek term behind the italics is *epistrephō*, a term that translates at times the Hebrew *shuv* (to turn, to convert).]

For sure, *epistrephō* is a conversion term even in Luke (Luke 1:16–17). Which leads to Bockmuehl's question: "When, or where, or how does Peter's turning occur?" Even more, he writes, "even on this last night of his ministry, Luke's Jesus evidently still anticipates Peter's conversion as in the *future*." He offers, however indirectly, a definition of (his lack of) conversion by pointing to the lack of "turning, conversion, or even repentance" on the part of Peter in Luke up to this point. Luke 5:1–11 is a "call," which it is, but we ought to be wary about reifying an experience like Peter's into a singular call vs. conversion. He adds to his point by contending Peter's baptism goes unrecorded, and neither did his confession of Jesus as Messiah lead to repentance—leading to doubts about any conversion prior to Luke 22. He thinks Luke left the moment of conversion open for readers to fill in the gaps.[16] Bockmuehl, though he suggests a conversion post-trial of Jesus and pre-Pentecost, that is, at Easter, even without the terms he so wants to appear, makes three fundamental mistakes in proposing the absence of Peter's conversion prior to his proposed date. First, he fails to define conversion adequately. Second, because of an inadequate definition of conversion, which I will discuss shortly, to see the elements of conversion already present in Luke 5, including repentance, which begins with a genuine confession of sin.[17]

---

used by Luke.

14. Still unsurpassed is Wuellner, *"Fishers of Men."*

15. Bockmuehl, *Simon Peter*, 153–63. Dunn makes much of the Acts 10–11 narrative as Peter's conversion (to a gentile mission); see Dunn, *Beginning from Jerusalem*, 389–96. Peter's radical shift of mind from observance of food laws to the greater freedom away from such (Acts 10:1–16, 28) is what Dunn has in mind.

16. Bockmuehl, *Simon Peter*, 156–57.

17. David Horrell disputes Bockmuehl's use of 1 Pet 1:3 as an indicator of a later

Third, he reifies the term *epistrephō* in Luke 22 to mean religious conversion, when it more likely refers to a returning to his former condition (Gen 8:12; 21:32; 44:13; Exod 4:20; 34:31; Num 16:50; Deut 1:7, 40; 4:30; 10:5; et al., not all of which translate *shuv*).

Measuring conversion solely by specific terms present in a narrative can lead one astray.[18] Conversion expresses a person's self-reflective, dialectical interaction with a group's expectations for inclusion. Thus, it is both individual and corporate. For Peter at this time in his life a conversion to Jesus would involve a self-understanding in interaction with Jesus's kingdom-coalition-understanding. I make use of two definitions of conversion, one from the major scholar of conversion theory, Lewis R. Rambo, and one from a faith and human development scholar, James Fowler. These two scholars provide eyes to see conversion already in Luke 5:1–11 as well as in Luke 18:28–30, both of which precede Bockmuehl's lock on Luke 22:31–32. Rambo defines conversion in these terms: "Conversion is what a group or person *says* it is. The process of conversion is a product of the interactions among the convert's aspirations, needs, and orientations, the nature of the group into which she or he is being converted, and the particular social matrix in which these processes are taking place."[19] When the orientation shifts from the interaction of individual and group to the individual herself, Fowler defines conversion in these terms: "Conversion is a significant recentering of one's previous conscious or unconscious images of value and power, and the conscious adoption of a new set of master stories in the commitment to reshape one's life in a new community of interpretation and action."[20] Put succinctly, a primary indicator of conversion is a revised autobiography or a significant shift in a person's self-perception or life, which is exactly what we see in Luke 5:1–11, as we find both a clear self-reflection and we know from the pages of the Gospels the course of Peter's life shifts following that moment. Confession of sin as seen in Luke 5's story cannot be snipped off from repentance. And even more important, we see the same shift *in Peter's own terms*, as expressed in the Synoptic Gospels. Here is Luke's version of Peter's own autobiographical reflection, one that sums up his life with Jesus thus far:

---

conversion; see his "Peter Remembered," 199–200.

18. In what follows I make use of McKnight, *Turning to Jesus*, 50–52.
19. Rambo, *Understanding Religious Conversion*, 7 (italics original).
20. Fowler, *Stages of Faith*, 282 (italics original).

Petros said, "Look! We, releasing our stuff, followed you." (Luke 18:28)

The Markan and Matthean forms, instead of using an aorist participle ("releasing") as in Luke, used an aorist indicative ("we released all things"; Mark 10:28). Peter looks back at some moment in the past when something happened that changed his life dramatically. A self-reflected change in one's autobiography is the telltale sign of conversion. Conversion has a beginning, conscious or not, but does not finish until one's life is over, which means Christian conversion is a process of making Jesus's story into one's story, of one's story fitting into Jesus's story. Peter's incorporating himself into the kingdom story began on the northern shore of the Sea of Galilee.

Peter's conversion begins with a theophanic/christophanic revelation that produces insight into who Jesus is and that leads to a confession of sin, which is the A-side of which repentance is the B-side. Peter's confession leads to a decision to abandon the fishing business and to daily embodied acts of being with Jesus, listening to him, learning from him, following him, and imitating him. John Carroll, then, is closer to the mark in writing that "the language of repentance and forgiveness does not appear, but Simon is the first of many sinners whose lives will be transformed through encounter with Jesus."[21] Peter's confession flows directly from a profound encounter with Jesus himself, from "proximity to supercharged, sacred presence."[22] Peter's conversion then is a Jesus-event, not a philosophical event. Yet, failure bubbles up in Peter's storied conversion often, sometimes as representative of others and sometimes on his own. He was formed as a disciple through the experiences of failure, one term for which (especially in Matthew) is *oligopist-*, or "little faith" (Matt 14:31; cf. 6:30, 8:26, 16:8).

From this moment on in the narratives we find about Peter, the man's entire life was recentered around Jesus and his kingdom vision. At the foundation, if I may now reuse that term, of Peter's pastoral experience was personal conversion from one way of life—Jewish, observant, and probably on the radical spectrum socially—to another way of life—observant in a Jesus way, and probably still radical. It is reasonable to think Peter, if his Bethsaida and parental context above are absorbed, joined the kingdom coalition of Jesus because he saw potential for a

21. Carroll, *Luke*, 124.
22. Spencer, *Luke*, 133.

revolution, a reformation, or for a revival for Galileans and perhaps Judeans. That opening sermon in Nazareth (Luke 4:16–30), whether Peter was there or heard about it, stoked Peter's fires. He was proud of his newfound friend and Superintendent, and was proud to be part of this budding kingdom coalition.

Peter as Apostle

Peter's pastoral ministry and his apostolic ministry overlapped so much one can't spot the pastoral in the apostolic. He was an apostle-pastor, an evangelist-pastor, a church-planting-pastor, and a fishing-pastor. According to the book of Acts, an apostle *must be* someone who followed Jesus from the beginning and who was "a witness of his resurrection" (Acts 1:21–22). Jesus himself turned some disciples into apostles, naming them such and commissioning them to extend and expand the kingdom vision. The earliest textual evidence for this in the Gospel traditions can be found in Mark 3. Following the sketch of Jesus's early Galilean mission (1:14—3:6), and realizing the intensity of suspicions, reactions, and rejections of Jesus—plotting his death (3:6)—Jesus "slipped away" with this "Apprentices" only to be followed by a "great mass" from the surrounding regions (3:7–8). The crowds adored Jesus, many were healed, and he was "rebuking them often not to make him apparent" (3:12). Withdrawing was the aim. So he "ascends to the mountain" with those he wanted with him (3:13). Mark's wording now provides the critical detail:

> He made twelve, whom he named "Commissioners," that they would be with him, and that he would commission them to announce and to have authority to toss out demons. (3:14–15)

Mark names them at this point. His list is followed with adjustments in Matthew (10:2–4), Luke (6:13–16), and Acts (1:13). Three general observations for Peter learning a pastoral way of life in his apostolic commission can be brought to the surface.

First, there are twelve Commissioners, and one cannot dispute the inevitable connection the choice of that number makes with the twelve tribes of Israel, though ten were dispersed at the time of Jesus.[23] The number twelve, while it has the suggestion of the reunification of the twelve tribes in the glorious future for Israel, echoes the leadership of

---

23. McKnight, "Jesus and the Twelve," 181–214.

twelve at Qumran (1QS 8:1; 1QSa 17–22; 4Q159, frgs. 2–4:3–4; 1QM 2:1–3; 11Q19 57:11–14) and perhaps the Testament of Judah and the Testament of Benjamin, which I cite here:

> And after this Abraham, Isaac, and Jacob will be resurrected to life and I and my brothers will be chiefs (wielding) our scepter in Israel. (T. Jud. 25:1)

> Then shall we also be raised, each of us over our tribe, and we shall prostrate ourselves before the heavenly king. (T. Ben. 10:7)

Joshua 4 lurks behind the choice of this number twelve, too. There the covenant was renewed with the children of Israel. Notice these lines, and I cite from John Goldingay's *The First Testament*:

> When the entire nation had come to an end of crossing the Yarden, Yahweh said to Yehoshua: "Get yourselves twelve stones from here, from the middle of the Yarden, from the place where the priests' feet stood steady. Take them across with you and set them down at the place where you stay the night to night." (Josh 4:1–3)

The connection of the Jordan, the twelve, the baptism in the Jordan River, and entry into the land, each with loud echoes in the ministry of Jesus, suggests Jesus acquired his vision for twelve apostles from the renewal of the covenant in Joshua. Jesus will himself appoint these same twelve to rule over Israel, like judges not kings, in the "Restoration" (Matt 19:28; cf. 8:11–12).

Second, they are called "apostles" or, as I have it, "Commissioners" because they are officially commissioned by Jesus for a task, namely, both to be "with Jesus" (Mark 3:14) and to expand the work Jesus himself had been doing (Mark 6:6–13; Matt 9:35—11:1, 28:16–20; Luke 9:1–6, cf. 10:1–12). Mission as commission is imitation if being with Jesus forms the foundation. To carry out this commission the twelve needed empowerment and authority (Mark 3:15; Matt 10:1, 28:18; Luke 9:1) to exercise the powers of healing, exorcism, and teaching (esp. Matt 10:5–42). A noticeable correlation jumps up for attention, in the narrative of Matthew, between the ministry of Jesus (8:1—9:34; 15:24) and the Commissioners (10:5–10). What he had done in chapters 8 and 9 they were commissioned do in chapter 10.

Jesus's summons to Peter to follow him leads to the understated, even unrecognized, but profound feature of *being with Jesus*. Our cohort led several insightful discussions about Peter and Jesus as presented in the Gospels. Presence with Jesus forms the foundation on which Peter was to expand the mission of Jesus, *and so learn both discipleship formation and, as an extension, pastoral ministry*.[24] Peter learned the cruciform life from a confession followed up by a denial of Jesus's own words that chased away the very foundation on which Peter built both his confession and denial. Peter's mind went through a whiplash shift when it came to Jesus's suffering.[25] Peter becomes a wannabe water walker with the Water Walker, but sinks and is rescued.[26] The same must be said of the impact of the transfiguration on Peter, even if many in the Western church ignore the transfiguration.[27] This had to have impacted his discipleship and pastoral care. As is visible to all readers, he was in the inner circle of Jesus's followers (e.g., Mark 9:2), accompanied Jesus from the earliest days to the crucifixion, to Galilean appearances, and then Peter continues his leadership on the day of Pentecost (Acts 2).[28] As an apostle, however, Paul informs the Galatians that he worked out a semi-official agreement with Peter for Paul to be an apostle to the gentiles ("the foreskin [people]") and Peter to the Jews ["circumcised"] (Gal 2:7–9). The book of Acts presents Peter as one who went toe-to-toe with Jerusalem's leaders (Acts 3–5)[29] as he ministered to Judeans and was the leading apostolic figure, both theologically and administratively, in the earliest church.[30] The encounter and evangelism of Cornelius of Joppa stands out in the Lukan portrait of post-Pentecost Peter, which flips the script about Jonah.[31] Luke sounds like Paul. Those twelve chapters of Petrine ministry almost end when Peter "journeyed to another place" (Acts 1–12; 12:17),[32] but Peter appears

---

24. In this volume, see James North, "I Believe in Miracles?" 192–205 below; and Brenden Lang, "Great Confession, Great Correction," 90–104 below.

25. See Leland Stephens, "Peter's Shift in Christology," 241–57 below.

26. On this episode, see Nika Spaulding, "Peter's Promenade," 76–89 below.

27. On the transfiguration, see Elijah Van Hoecke, "Death-Defying Hope," 105–20 below.

28. For Pentecostal Peter, see Brenton Fessler, "Peter the Pentecostal Pastor," 121–37 below.

29. On the encounters of Peter with the authorities, see Kelly Dippolito, "Transformative Events," 138–55 below.

30. Hengel, *Saint Peter*. Dunn's suggestion that the earliest preaching had something to do with Peter, too, carries weight. His sketch includes the resurrection, redefining messiahship, the appointment of the Son of God in power, Jesus's exaltation as Lord, the bestower of the Spirit, and the soon coming Son of Man—all shaped by a Christ devotion. See Dunn, *Beginning from Jerusalem*, 212–29.

31. See Renjy Abraham, "End of Us Versus Them," 156–72 below.

32. For discussion, Dunn, *Beginning from Jerusalem*, 378–415.

prominently in the famous Jerusalem Council.³³ Wherever he went, and scholarship disputes where he went, not much later he was nonetheless back in Jerusalem and present as a slightly demoted apostle for the Jerusalem Council when James, the brother of Jesus, led the discussion (Acts 15). Peter disappears from Acts at that point, but he appears (1) in Galatians as one who in Jerusalem showed hospitality to Paul (Gal 1:18) and as one of the "Reputables" (2:2, 6), and then in Antioch as one who had fallen out of favor with Paul's gospel (2:11–14),³⁴ (2) in Corinth as "Kephas [*Kēpha*]," a rival apostle (1 Cor 1:12, 3:22, 9:5, 15:5), and then (3) in Peter's delineation of his mission churches in eastern, central, and northern Asia Minor (Pontus, Galatia, Cappadocia, Asia, and Bithynia; 1 Pet 1:1). If we back up to the claimed agreement of Paul with Peter in front of the Reputables in Jerusalem, that is, to Gal 2:7–9, and if we read 1 Peter as many scholars do, that is, a letter written to at least some gentile converts, then we must conclude that Peter's gospel mission expanded from Paul's and Luke's framing of it. Peter's churches had plenty of gentiles. The standard texts to support at least a partial, if not more, gentile makeup of 1 Peter's churches, include the following:

> As heeding children, not being remodeled by the desires of your former ignorance . . . (1:14)
>
> Knowing that you were liberated not by perishable things—silver and gold—from your useless behavior passed on from your fathers . . . (1:18)³⁵
>
> The ones once: *not people* but now: God's people, the ones *not shown compassion* now have been shown compassion. (2:10; from Hos 1:6, 9)
>
> For the time that has passed is adequate to effect the ethnic groups' will, having journeyed and flaunting sensuality's, desires, wine-soaking, parties, symposia bashes, and nonobservant

---

33. On which, see the essay in his volume by Robert Anderson, "Peter the Intercessor," 173–91 below.

34. For a thesis challenging scholarship on the social context for Peter's withdrawal in Antioch, see Gibson, *Peter Between Jerusalem and Antioch*. A sudden rise of resistance in the rise of Agrippa gave rise to James's and Peter's concern with Pauline open-table fellowship. Peter did not believe in gentile Judaizing and wanted to eliminate cause for persecuting the Jewish believers in Jerusalem. Hence, Peter again shows to be a mediator.

35. Elliott, *1 Peter*, 370.

idolatries, in which they consider it foreign you aren't running with them into the same dissolution flood, insulting ... (4:3-4)

It is very difficult for me to think Peter would describe a life of former observance of the Torah with such terms.[36] One might enter into pages of insoluble consternation seeking to prove that "the elect temporary residents of the Diaspora" (1:1) were actually Jewish believers in the diaspora, that it is like Jas 1:1 in other words, but the evidence above has convinced much of scholarship that 1 Peter's audience was primarily gentile, if also mixed. Of course, Peter would have had a natural connection with diaspora Jews.[37] All to say that *as an apostle Peter's ministry did not follow Paul's script strictly.*[38] The tension between Peter and Paul, which may be present in at Corinth among the congregants, though clearly calmer in 1 Cor 9, could have been connected to rival missionary work.[39] Peter's apostolic ministry then had to learn mission and pastoral work in the context of tension with other leaders. That mission, too, included ministering to both Jews and gentiles as Paul's own apostolic mission did. Peter's pastoral ministry, which began in Galilee and expanded into Judea and beyond into the diaspora, was a multiethnic apostolate.

Some highlights of his Judean mission deserve brief mention. Peter was the day of Pentecost's preacher extraordinaire in that he interpreted its spontaneous tongue speaking as the days of Joel (Acts 2:1—41; Joel 2:28–32). Peter becomes an irritant to Jerusalem's temple authorities because of his preaching about Jesus (Acts 3:1—4:31) and healing (e.g., 5:12–16). He supervises the followers of Jesus following the sudden deaths of Ananias and Sapphira (4:36—5:11). Opposition to Peter led to inquiries and more, leading to arrests and imprisonments and physical abuse (4:18–22, 5:18–42). It was Peter and John who were commissioned by other Commissioners to Samaria to evaluate and affirm the expansion of the gospel through deacon Philip, if also to denounce the foolishness of another man named Simon (8:18–24). Peter's role was to pray for the endowment of the Spirit upon the new believers in Samaria (8:14–25).

Next, we see Peter traveling to Lydda where he healed a man (9:32–35); then Joppa, where Peter raised Tabitha, a woman Apprentice

---

36. For one good example, see van Unnik, "Critique of Paganism."

37. Elliott, *1 Peter*, 94–97.

38. So also Omerzu, "Petrus und Paulus." Christina Eschner finds Peter closer to Paul than to James in early Christian tensions; see "Petrus in der Mitte."

39. Developed in the important study on Peter by Hengel, *Saint Peter*.

(9:36–43). A major event occurs in Acts in the crossing of boundaries to the gentiles with Peter and Cornelius. Bolstered (if not more) by a vision, Peter preaches the gospel about Jesus to Cornelius and then observes the work of God in his life—so much, Peter and fellow Jewish believers "were beside themselves because the Holy Spirit gift had also been poured out on the ethnic groups" (10:44–46). These gentiles spoke in tongues, convincing Peter of the work of God among them, and he urged them to be baptized (10:47–48). So important is this expansion to gentiles that Peter has to give an account to the "Commissioners and siblings" in Jerusalem when he returns (11:1), though he was now under a watchful eye of Jewish believers for his behaviors among the gentiles. That is, "You entered into [fellowship] with the foreskin [people] and you ate with them" (11:3). So Peter told them the whole story, which is how he compellingly convinces others that God's work has stretched out beyond Judea (11:4–18). The growth of the kingdom mission of Jesus through these early Judean and gentile believers provoked king Herod Agrippa I to kill James, son of Zebedee, and to plot the death of the now imprisoned Peter (12:1–5). The story goes that Peter was visited by an angel who miraculously liberated Peter from jail and led him to Mary's house, which was filled with praying believers (12:6–17). As mentioned, Peter figures as a major, though not final, voice in the Jerusalem Council.

Any breezing through these stories reveals an apostle whose ministries were uber-charismatic and powerful. Peter witnessed miracle after miracle, conversion after conversion, prayer time after prayer time, and excitement on top of expectation, if not mixed with some fear, of imprisonment and even death. Suffering and the gospel mission accompanied Peter's apostolic mission, that was through and through pastoral.

Third, and briefly, Peter is first among equals. In the list of the apostles, which reflects both the evangelists' own dates and locations of writing but also the days when the apostles were present with Jesus in Galilee and Judea, Peter is always first. It begins with Mark's bare listing of Peter first: Jesus "made the Twelve, and he placed the name 'Petros' on Simōn" (Mark 3:14), which becomes in Matthew "first, Simōn—who is called Petros" (10:2). Luke mostly repeats Mark at both Luke 6:14 and Acts 1:15. That he was first is not just evidenced in Matthew. Peter famously first proclaimed Jesus as the Messiah (Mark 8:29 and parr.). The innermost circle of Commissioners not only has Peter but his house seems to be the headquarters for the kingdom coalition (Matt 8:14) and he becomes the first one to speak on numerous occasions. So much so that Peter can be seen as the spokesperson for the Commissioners (e.g., 14:28; 15:15; 16:16, 18, 22–23; 17:4, 24; 18:21; 19:27; 26:33, 35, 40, 69, 73, 75). He not only leads the church in the first twelve chapters of Acts but offers decisive evidence for gentile conversion and Spirit-baptism without having observed the law (Acts 10–11, 15).

Peter, as Martin Hengel reminds us, has become the "underestimated apostle" because Paul has become the esteemed apostle for the Protestant church. Markus Bockmuehl, who calls Peter "the neglected stepchild" in scholarship,[40] has shown that (what he frames as) the memory of Peter was strong beyond the first century as the church grew and expanded. His background in Bethsaida outfitted him for a mediating role between Paul and Jerusalem. The Pauline version of the church gets so much press in the New Testament that it established the underestimation of Peter in the Protestant church. Underestimated he was but influential he was as well. Each of the evangelists make Peter the most significant apostle:

> Mark sees and hears Jesus through Peter's eyes and ears; for Matthew, Peter is the messianic congregation's bedrock and gatekeeper; for Luke, the pioneering convert, evangelist, and strengthener of believers; for John, the spokesman and shepherd of Jesus's flock.[41]

He was at least a rival to Paul and for many he was the apostle of apostles, the first among equals. I'm persuaded he was behind the Gospel of Mark and Matthew's Gospel can hardly contain Peter's importance (16:13–20). Inasmuch as Mark's Peter forms the view of Peter in both Matthew and Luke, and inasmuch as John, too, makes him the most prominent apostle, we are driven to admit the singular influence of Peter on the entire Gospel tradition. As an apostle, however, his pastoral life has also been underestimated, and it is the purpose of this volume to give the man some time on the platform.

Peter as Witness

In 1 Pet 5:1 Peter claims he is a "witness," which translates the Greek term *martus*. At the time of Jesus and Peter this term had not yet acquired the definition of a "martyr," even though today some popular writers and preachers like to provoke by saying a *martus* in the days

---

40. Bockmuehl, *Simon Peter*, xiii.
41. Bockmuehl, *Simon Peter*, 5.

of Jesus and the early church was *not about verbal witness* (read: evangelism) but instead was about *embodied life*. The reverse is the case.[42] Preparatory to Peter's pastoral work was a life of witnessing what he had heard from Jesus and what he saw about Jesus.

What Peter witnessed, which means saw and then spoke about, was "Christos's sufferings" (5:1). Pick your Gospel and read the second half and you will know what Peter witnessed—what Christians have customarily called the passion narrative (e.g., Mark 10–15).[43] Having heard Jesus numerous times indicate that the long shadow of John the Baptist's gruesome murder loomed over himself (Mark 6:14–30), Peter walked with Jesus into Jerusalem with dark clouds brooding. Peter witnessed Jesus's entry, his tipping over tables in the temple, his disputes with the authorities and the parables he told to interpret what was happening and why, Jesus's predicting the temple's demise, his peculiar identification of himself with the wine and bread at the quasi-Passover meal, Jesus's lamenting terms about Peter's denials, his tortured prayers in Gethsemane, his arrest and bouncing from one place to another as Jesus was tried and judged worthy of crucifixion, his visibly abused body, his march to Golgotha, his crucifixion, his abuse, his half-truth *titulus*, his mocking, his exhaustion, his asphyxiation, and his death. That's what Peter means when he says he was a witness of "Christos's sufferings." These are the events that seared Peter's memory with unforgettable graphic images, with sounds and colors and voices and smells, with events that cry out for meaning and interpretation, with regrets upon regrets, with times with Jesus following the passion that somehow brought enough grace for Peter to be restored, and then empowered, and then driven into an apostolic ministry that added up to an unimpeachable conclusion: "Christos's sufferings" were both an injustice and a template to be followed over and over by those who followed Jesus. Peter's witness of "Christos's sufferings" then was a witness of Jesus and those who denied themselves and who died in a Calvary that sucked the death of many others into the vortex of a resurrection that overwhelmed without denying that suffering.

Put directly, the many suffering passages in 1 Peter extend and expand the sufferings of Christ (1:6–8; 2:18–25; 3:13–17; 4:1–6, 12–19; 5:8–9, 10).[44] One has to wonder if Peter's own painful memories of his

---

42. See Elliott, *1 Peter*, 819–20, followed by Bockmuehl, *Simon Peter*, 129–30.

43. In this volume, see the (cohort favorite) study of Alice McQuitty, "Failure to Follow," 18–31 below.

44. For a study of Peter and suffering see Matthew McBirth, "Tracing the Steps of

own failure factor into his theology of suffering. The suffering of Peter's churches, which is clearly about social status as well as verbal and physical abuse (1:1; 2:11–12, 18–25; 3:16; 4:3–5), deserved interpretation. Peter sees these extensions of Christ's sufferings as a "testing" (1:6–8), as an opportunity to follow in the sufferings of Christ (2:21–23) and to witness for Christ, both verbally and by doing good (3:13–17), and as an opportunity for becoming holy (4:1–2)—all fully immersed in a cosmology that (1) recognizes the reality of Satan's participation in their suffering and its desire for death (5:8–9), (2) knows God is on their side (5:10–11), and (3) hopes in an eschatology of a future judgment that will disestablish injustice and establish justice, which Peter refers to often as a salvation that, while present (e.g., 1:9, 10; 3:21), thematizes itself as the future (1:5, 9; 2:2; 4:18). Christos's sufferings extend for Peter into the life of those whom he calls "the elect temporary residents" and "exiles" (1:1; 2:11).[45]

As a witness to "Christos's suffering" Peter is also one who has a "common life," or share "in the splendor about to be apocalypse" (5:1). Peter's theme of cruciformity then is wider than the cross; his cruciformity is a Christoformity in that the believer is conformed by the power of the Spirit over time to the life, death, resurrection, and ascension of Christ.[46] Peter does not stop in his Christoformity at the suffering of Christ; he takes us into the throne room of God where the glory of God floods all creation with the splendor and majesty of God enthroned over all (cf. 1:5, 7, 12, 13; 4:13; 5:1 with Rev 21–22). Each of these themes could be developed at length, but space prohibits development.

Peter's witness must be expanded, however, beyond his participating and observing and reporting about the sufferings of Christ. An early Christian tradition, affirmed by several, was that Peter was the voice behind the Gospel of Mark. Eusebius provides the critical information in the living memory of the early church:

> We direct lovers of learning to them, but at present we must include along with the words of his [Papias's] that we have already been set down a tradition that he has recorded about Mark the evangelist, in these words:

---

the Suffering Servant," 206–21 below.

45. For the social status understanding of these terms, see Elliott, *1 Peter*, 84–103, rooted in his important monograph, Elliott, *Home for the Homeless*. I follow his interpretation in McKnight, *1 Peter*, 23–26, 47–52.

46. McKnight, *Pastor Paul*, 4–6.

> And the presbyter used to say this: Mark was Peter's translator, and he wrote down accurately, though not in order, what he remembered [hearing] about what the Lord had said and done. For he had not heard the Lord or been his follower, but later, as I said, was Peter's. Peter used to teach using short examples, but he did not compose an ordered account of the Lord's sayings, with the result that Mark did not err in writing the particulars he remembered. For he took forethought for one thing, not to falsify or omit anything of what he had heard in the accounts he wrote.

This is what is said by Papias about Mark.[47]

Clement of Alexandria, again as quoted by Eusebius from the former's *Hypotyposes*, adds,

> . . . while that according to Mark came about by this [divine] plan. When Peter had publicly preached the Logos in Rome and spoken the Gospel by means of the Spirit, those who were present, being many, asked Mark to record what Peter had said in writing, since Mark had accompanied him for a long way and had remembered his sayings. He did so, and gave the Gospel to those who requested it. When Peter learned of this, he neither prevented it nor encouraged it.[48]

New Testament scholars tend not to trust Eusebius or the traditions he claims to pass on, and the above are from Papias and from John the Elder. Yet, there are signs today of scholars affirming the general impression that Peter was behind Mark. The evidence is clear in what it affirms while the historicity of the tradition has been disputed. I suspect Papias heard a solid memory about the origins of Mark's Gospel. If so, I contend Peter's witness in the early church involved *teaching others what Jesus said and did*. That is, Peter's witness became the Gospel of Mark.[49] Peter's teaching was about the

---

47. Eusebius, *History of the Church* 3.39.14–16. The tradition is found in Irenaeus, *Against Heresies* 3.1.1, cited by Eusebius, *History of the Church* 5.8.2–4. The word "translator" (*hermēneutēs*) does not mean "translator" in that he moved Peter's (supposed) Aramaic into Greek, but that Mark was Peter's mediator from an oral teaching setting to a written text. Thus, Elder, *Gospel Media*, 238–44; Hengel, *Saint Peter*, 36–48. Many dispute the connection of Peter to Mark. For discussion, see Bond, "Was Peter."

48. Eusebius, *History of the Church* 6.14.6–7.

49. From a different angle, and mostly confirming, see Bockmuehl, *Simon Peter*, 13–16, 131–41.

public kingdom mission of Jesus and his tragic death in Jerusalem. If Mark lacks literary artistry it could be because Mark was committed to passing on to others only what he remembered Peter teaching. Both Matthew and Luke would clean up Mark, but *their witness is so deeply dependent on Mark, and Mark on Peter, that the Synoptic Gospels are the deposit of the apostle Peter's witness.* Underestimated, indeed.

I continue now with Peter as a witness beyond the sufferings of Jesus. If Peter is behind Mark, and that means if Peter's public teaching in Rome was about Jesus, then we should be scouting for evidence of echoes of Peter's time with Jesus in 1 Peter.[50] Scholars have performed this task with intricacy. Here are some possible echoes:

1. In 1 Pet 1:3 the use of "who gave us life again" (*anagennaō*) could reflect the new birth account in John 3, or it could (also) reflect, along with 1 Pet 3:21, Peter's experience of the new life given him as a result of his restoration (John 21).
2. In 1 Pet 1:8 it is said the original readers of the letter had never seen Jesus, with the possible implication that the author had: "Whom, not seeing, you love, in whom now not seeing, but trusting you are overjoyed with inexpressible and splendored joy."
3. In 1 Pet 5:1 the author says he was a "witness" of "Christos's suffering," and what he witnessed of that suffering is more than visible in 2:22–25.
4. In 1 Pet 5:5 the term behind "fasten" is *engkomboomai*, which may echo Jesus wrapping himself with a towel in John 13:4's famous towel and basin scene.

Does 1 Peter echo any sayings of Jesus? The answer is yes, and the problem is that these echoes could be dependence on a Gospel or actual echoes by Peter of what Jesus said. The connection of Peter to Mark supports at least consideration of the second option.[51] The following are the most likely echoes that Peter's witness included telling others what Jesus had said.

1. 1 Pet 1:4 could echo Matt 25:34.
2. 1 Pet 1:11 could echo Luke 24:26–27.
3. 1 Pet 3:14; 4:14 could echo Matt 5:10.

---

50. I am dependent here upon Achtemeier, *1 Peter*, 9–12.
51. A listing of all suggested possibilities can be found in Achtemeier, *1 Peter*, 10n97.

4. 1 Pet 2:12 could echo Matt 5:11–12.
5. 1 Pet 1:6, if one is persuaded of #3 and #4, could echo Matt 5:12.
6. 1 Pet 4:7 could echo Luke 21:31, 34, 36.
7. 1 Pet 4:8 could echo Matt 18:21–22.
8. 1 Pet 5:8 could echo Mark 13:35.

Paul Achtemeier rightly warns that echoes like these are rooted in Peter's Greek and the Gospels' Greek. That would more support 1 Peter's dependence on the Gospels than Peter's recollections of Jesus's Aramaic sayings that would have been translated into Greek by Peter himself. Complicating this set of texts is the previous point in this section in witness: if Peter is behind Mark, one might expect more echoes of Markan sayings than Matthean or Lukan sayings. The data above are a bit of a wash, but with one proviso: If Peter is behind 1 Peter and the Gospel of Mark, it is likely that at times Peter echoes Jesus's sayings and deeds.

Peter's pastoral ministry, to which we will now turn, was founded on his conversion, his apostolic ministry, and his witness to the fullness of Jesus and his life. Pastoral ministry to this day requires rooting in the same elements. The ideal of pastoring is a convert confident of being called who pastors people on the basis of a personal witness.

Peter as Pastor

When I use the term "pastor" for Peter I evoke the term he used of his co-elders and (as least for himself) witnesses who are charged to "pastor God's flock among you, mentoring" (1 Pet 5:1–2). The early Christians did not provide a dictionary for others to know the meanings of their terms, and neither do our wonderful lexica do much more than provide glosses. Terms take on hues and glows in specific contexts even if a general direction of a term sings its distinct song with clarity. Pastor, I infer, points at a person who cares for another person and a fellowship in a multitude of directions, including in the spiritual, relational, emotional, physical, and social themes of life. Pastors pastor people, which intends to push back against thinking pastors (simply) preach to people.

When I read 1 Pet 5's words to the elder-pastors my mind cannot bracket John 21, that famous passage in which Jesus asks Peter three times if he loves him.⁵² Peter responds three times with "I do." John has played mind games with a seven thousand times seven thousand pastors, professors, and (tongue-in-cheek) Dallas Theological Seminary students who are word study specialists by shifting vocabulary from *agapaō* to *phileō*. (Some of whom are students in this cohort.) The conclusion is that these terms are synonyms and ought not to be distinguished between self-sacrificing and friendship love. John himself uses both for God's love of humans, for God's love for the Son, Jesus's love for humans, and human love for Jesus (3:16, 35; 5:20; 8:42; 11:5, 36; 13:34; 15:19; 16:27).⁵³ What matters for us is that the question-and-answer leads each time to the same charge: "Feed/pastor my lambs/sheep" (21:15, 16, 17). Jesus assigned the pastoral function to Peter. Peter was a pastor because he pastored people. Noticeably, sheep are not Peter's; they are Jesus's ("my"; 21:15, 16, 17). The pastoral/shepherd function finds expression metaphorically in feeding and pastoring/tending. Thus, the pastor provides nurturance for the people assigned to her by God.

Back to 1 Pet 5. As a "co-elder" Peter can urge the "elders among you" to engage themselves as pastors. An elder in the early church evoked age (older rather than younger), veneration, respect in the community, as well as wisdom offered to others.⁵⁴ The term almost certainly suggested a team or council of sages for the churches. It is beyond a temptation for many to think they know the early churches had a plurality of elders and pastors and mentors. Perhaps and probably, but hardly certain. Complicating the issues is that the congregations were house churches with household members, not least with the (household's) elders (male and female) leading. So age, wisdom, leadership, and household overlap one another. The term will have at times meant age and at other times a more official leadership role (cf. 1 Tim 5:1–2 with 5:17, 19; Titus 1:5). Its relationship to mentor ("bishop" or "overseer"; 1 Tim 3:2; Titus 1:7; Phil 1:1) is underdetermined in the New Testament texts and one is wise to appreciate overlaps in sense, as in Acts 20:17, 28. It is as elders and probably witnesses that the elders are instructed to pastor the people by mentoring them into Christoformity.

---

52. On the restoration of Peter in John 21, see Matthew Trexler, "Feed My Sheep," 258–69 below.

53. Thompson, *John*, 442.

54. Elliott, *1 Peter*, 813–16. For more, see Campbell, *Elders*; Stewart, *Original Bishops*.

The term Peter uses in 1 Pet 5:1, *poimainō*, roots itself in the world of shepherding and herding domestic animals. In its transferred-to-humans sense it connotes caring for, looking after, cherishing, nurturing, managing, and controlling.[55] Peter more or less defines the term "pastor" with the term "mentoring" (NIV: "watching over them"; 5:2; cf. CD 13:9–10).[56] To repeat, Peter would not have been ordering his co-elders what to do if he had not done or was not doing the same. As pastor, Peter mentored, cared for, protected, supervised, administered, fed, and nurtured the among-you-flock of God, and in v. 3 he reframes the flock as "the part [assigned to you]." David Horrell, in his study of the memory of Peter at work in 1 Peter, concludes that "since Peter gives his instruction to the elders here precisely as co-elder, it seems that the letter at least implicitly 'constructs the *image of Peter as shepherd,'* evoking a role more fully depicted in John 21."[57] As pastor, he has a responsibility to a select group of people; as an apostle his group of people is all the churches he has formed and over which he probably appointed elders, mentors, and deacons who would have pastored those people. His people were spread over all of Asia Minor, he had some apostolic-pastoral responsibilities in Corinth, and then certainly in Rome.[58] Spread out they may have been but his view of pastoring was local. As he puts it, "among you" and "the part [assigned to you]" (5:2, 3).

Peter's concerns for these elder-pastors boils down to one major term ("mentoring") and four specifics, with the added bonus of an eschatological reward for the faithful (5:2–4). First, they are to mentor people not because they have to, not because it is a duty, and not because it is required, but "willingly" (*hekousiōs*). Pastoring lacks heart when it is done as a duty or by compulsion. Second, the elders are to mentor people "consistent with God," which can be taken as a modifier of the previous

---

55. *CGL*, 1151. For a more extensive bibliography, with emphasis on Paul as pastor, see McKnight, *Pastor Paul*, 198n26.

56. The NA28 recognizes the reading of this term can be challenged, inasmuch as a *presbyter* is (supposedly) being instructed to perform the role of an *episkopos*. That alone, along with the evidence of it being found in major early and extensive manuscripts, provides the ground for including *episkopountes*. It has been observed by some that the term merely repeats *poimanate*. First Peter is pre-monarchical bishop, as many have observed (e.g., Elliott, *1 Peter*, 827).

57. See Horrell, "Peter Remembered," 193. He discusses 5:1–4 on pp. 188–93.

58. Bockmuehl, *Simon Peter*, 99–150. For a hard-hitting discussion, see Barnes, "'Another Shall Gird Thee.'" Barnes argues Peter was burned alive in Rome in AD 64. For the archaeological evidence, see Lampe, "Traces of Peter Veneration."

point or, as I take it, as a separate point. Peter wants pastors to operate in ways consistent with God and God's will. Elliott gets it just right in writing, "It indicates that to which Christian volition is fundamentally oriented; namely, the will of God."[59] In his third point we come to the problem of simony (Acts 8:9–24). The elders are to mentor God's flock "not for shameful gain but emotionally" (1 Pet 5:2). The negative has been a concern forever but my translation of the positive veers away from the NIV ("eager to serve") and the CEB/NRSVue ("eagerly"). The Greek term is *prothumōs*, which is glossed with enthusiastically, desiringly, keenly, and eagerly. The term is used in the New Testament only here,[60] and it poses itself against working for the money. The term is made of the term *thumos*, which suggests passionate commitment. Emotionally, then, is my gloss, with the sense of having one's heart and passion and work ethic aligned with the pastoral work. I think "emotionally" strikes the right balance. This term describes the pastor who doesn't watch the clock but who spots the work to be done and, because she is committed to pastoring the people, attends to the people under her care. This term comes with an important warning: the term also points us to the kind of effort that is prone to burnout.

Fourth, Peter urges the elders to mentor God's flock "not as ruling over" but instead "becoming models for the flock" (5:3). Here Peter echoes Jesus's famous words to Zebedee's sons in Mark 10:35–45, when Jesus got after their desire for glory and connected such a desire for power to the ways of Rome. Every pastor faces the seduction of power and the abuse of authority. Power easily shifts into willpower, and willpower into domineering and abuse. Peter warns the elders that when mentoring becomes domineering, pastoral care becomes abuse.[61] The alternative transcends non-abuse because it becomes exemplary living. In early August 1944 Dietrich Bonhoeffer wrote to his friend and future biographer, Eberhard Bethge, and sketched an outline for a book. Which doesn't matter here. What does is his sketch of the proposed chapter three: "The church is church only when it is there for others. . . . The church must participate in the worldly tasks of life in the community—not dominating but helping and serving. . . . In particular, *our* church will have to confront the vices of hubris, the worship of power, envy, and illusionism as the roots of all

---

59. Elliott, *1 Peter*, 828.

60. But see *prothumia* in Acts 17:11; 2 Cor 8:11, 12, 19; 9:2; *prothumos* in Mark 14:38; Rom 1:15.

61. McKnight and Barringer, *A Church Called Tov* and *Pivot*.

evil.... It will have to see that it does not underestimate the significance of the human 'example' (which has its origin in the humanity of Jesus and is so important in Paul's writings!); the church's word gains weight and power not through concepts but by example."[62] Bonhoeffer promised he would write more about this in the future, which he did not survive to accomplish. Charles Marsh refers to Bonhoeffer's piece in a recent collection of essays called *People Get Ready: Twelve Jesus-Haunted Misfits, Malcontents, and Dreamers in Pursuit of Justice*. About 150 pages later in that same volume, in an essay by Jacqueline Bussie about Flannery O'Connor, the author says of moral exemplars, "Aren't moral exemplars precisely the ones who reverse the cliché—those who don't merely *reflect* their cultural moment, but who instead *refashion* it into a product of their liberating vision? True followers of the gospel don't merely *portray* their era, but instead in a very real sense *produce* it."[63]

Example, exemplification, imitation, and modeling form the center of all genuine mentoring.[64] Not all are made to mentor. Pastors cannot not be. Their mottos need to buckle up with *Follow me* and *Do as I do* and *Watch me*. Jesus shaped the path for Peter, both as seen in the Gospel of Mark's central sections as well as in 1 Pet 2:21's famous "leaving behind an outline, so you could follow in his steps." The elders who mentor by providing an example are being called to re-embody the life Peter learned from Jesus. The reward for these elder-mentors will be "an unfadeable, splendorous crown" (5:4).

Peter has but a short word for the "younger men," and it is not clear nor is it compelling whether or not these are future elders, younger converts, or just younger males in the assembly.[65] Wherever one stands on the options, these younger men are instructed to pursue wisdom, to find a sage or mentor, and to "order" themselves "under" such a sage.

---

62. Bonhoeffer, *Letters and Papers*, 503–4. Charles Marsh, who put me on to this piece by Bonhoeffer, made reference to it in his foreword to Slade, *People Get Ready*.

63. Bussie, "Race, Grace, and God's Typewriter," 148.

64. For imitation in Paul, see esp. Copan, *Saint Paul*, 45–69; Hood, *Imitating God in Christ*.

65. See the admirable sketch in Elliott, *1 Peter*, 836–40. He contends these are recent converts.

Lived Theology

Before shutting off the lights on this conversation about Peter as a pastor, I want to mention the major themes in Peter's vision for the people in his churches. One can get lost in a discussion of the relationship of 1 Peter to Pauline theology, and there are similarities. Yet, the theology of 1 Peter has its distinctive in its lack of distinctiveness. He sounds like Paul at times (3:16; 4:10–11, 13; 5:10, 14); at other times he doesn't; but 1 Peter also does not have a glaringly distinct theological view—as we find in Paul, in Hebrews, in James, and in 1 John. First Peter, in fact, mediates between the theology of Paul and Jewish-Christians.[66] Following a brief overview of some themes, I want to turn to how Peter pastored people to a lived theology. Peter's ultimate concern is *salvation*, which has begun in the present but is not complete until the final day. Suffering features in Peter's understanding of a life leading to salvation. Salvation for Peter operates through "blood-sprinkling" (1:2) and being "liberated" by "Christos's priceless blood" (1:18–19) and being "devoted [to God, purified, made holy] by heeding the truth" (1:22). Believers have "tasted" the Lord himself (2:3) and been "cured" (2:24) so they can be led to God (3:18). His terms for salvation include being given a new life (1:3, 23; 2:2, 24; 3:7, 18), inheritance (1:4–5), and ultimately God's blessing (3:9). Notice the number of times salvation-as-deliverance appears (1:5, 9, 10; 2:2; 3:20–21; 4:18) and, as well, a similar interest in the topic of grace (1:10, 13; 3:7; 5:5, 10, 12). Though 2 Pet 1:4 ushers readers into participation in Christ more explicitly than is found in 1 Peter, the "in Christ" as well as suffering and glory with Christ themes of 1 Peter are noticeable. Deliverance for Peter happens by and with participation (cf. 1 Pet 4:13, 16; 5:1).[67] What is noticeable is that for Peter the time of salvation remains in the future (1:5, 9; 2:2; 4:18). People are not so much already saved as they are being saved. Pastoring people for Peter means pastoring people into and toward deliverance from sin in its systemic wholeness, which will not be complete until the apocalypse.

---

66. Dunn, *Neither Jew nor Greek*, 727–29. Bockmuehl sees the memories of Peter to be of a mediating nature. See Bockmuehl, *Remembered Peter*. On p. 176, he writes that Peter's "upbringing would have left him culturally and perhaps linguistically better equipped than James to envisage the gospel's outreach from Jerusalem to Antioch and Rome." On p. 180, he speaks of Peter as "centrist, bridge-building." So also Pheme Perkins, who writes, "Peter represents a policy of accommodation and adaptation to the changing circumstances of the community." See Perkins, *Peter*, 185.

67. For an essay length exploration, see Edwards, "Participation in Christ."

The location of deliverance in the world is the *church* (2:1–10) as the family and household of God (4:17).[68] The believers in Peter's churches are called to hope (1:13), holiness (1:14–16), awe before God (1:17–21), and love (1:22–24), all of which is enveloped in a theory of both personal and communal growth (2:1–8). In particular, the people of the church are to pursue holiness, or devotion to the God who alone is holy (1:14–16, 18, 22; 2:1–2, 5, 9, 11–12, 15, 20; 2:24; 3:6, 13, 15, 17; 4:1–6, 18). Those who live out this life, which is a following of Christ (2:18–25), will exemplify a compelling witness to the liberation that can be found in Christ—and this exemplary life is a public life (2:12, 15; 3:1–6, 16) that will come to expression in verbal witness (1:12, 25; 2:9; 3:15; 4:6).

Themes and theology have never been enough. Theology unlived is not theology. Theology that is lived is what theology is designed to be.[69] The life lived by the believer, in fact, is the only theology that matters finally. It is a public life with a public witness that can be distinguished from political activism.[70] Which leads me to look at a very important, and sometimes ignored, term in 1 Peter. That word group is *agathopoieō/agathopoiia/agathopoios*, and the idea is all about publicly "doing good." In a Jewish context the term evokes the term *tov* (good), which is a master moral category of the Hebrew Bible.[71] In a Greco-Roman context the term suggested not just doing good but doing public benevolence, like building bridges or providing food during a famine *for the common good*.[72] Notice these verses in 1 Peter:

> . . . if to Governors, as one sent by him for making it right for bad-doers but public praise for good-doers. (2:14)

> Because so is God's will: in doing good to silence the ignorance of imprudent humans. (2:15)

> But if, doing good and suffering, you are resilient, this is grace with God. (2:20)

> . . . as Sarra heeded Abra'am, calling him "lord"—of whom you have become children, doing good and not being in awe of any dread. (3:6)

---

68. Developed extensively by Smith, *Strangers to Family*.
69. Marsh et al., *Lived Theology*.
70. See in this book Taylor Terzek, "Reimagining Politics," 222–40 below.
71. Stoebe, "*Tov*."
72. Winter, *Seek the Welfare*, 12–23.

> For its better to suffer for doing good—if this be God's will—than for doing bad. (3:17)
>
> So, let the one suffering consistent with God's will present themselves with good deeds to the allegiant Creator. (4:19)

Lived theology, a theology generated by salvation and lived in the context of the church family, is a visible life of doing good for the common good. Jesus said much the same, and this is an echo that almost no one suggests, in Matt 5:16, saying, "So shine your light before humans so they may see your beautiful works and splendor your Father in the heavens." The Greek terms behind "beautiful works" are *ta kala erga*, which is a Greek version of the Hebrew sense of doing good and the alternative Greek expression, *agathopoi-*, which appears to be mostly a Christian neologism.

I finish with this. When Peter was preaching to Cornelius, he summed up the public ministry of Jesus in these words:

> The word that he commissioned to Yisraēl's descendants, gospelling peace through Yēsous Christos—this one is Lord over all—you know the utterance that happened through the whole of Youdaia (beginning from the Galilaia after the dipping that Yōannēs announced), [the utterance about] Yēsous the one from Nazara, as God christened him with Holy Spirit and power, who crossed through [the land] doing good works and curing all those over-ruled by the Accuser because God was with him. (Acts 10:36–38)

Peter's summary of Jesus was that he was one traversing the paths of Galilee *doing good*, and he did so in the power of the Spirit because God was with him. Peter could not have not had Jesus on his mind when he pastored the people in his churches with instructions to be people of public good works. Lived theology, in other words, reveals a theology words can never quite get right. Peter's words about pastoral care are not instructions of a philosopher exploring subjects. Peter's words flow from a convert who was an apostolic witness whose churches prompted him to pastoral care. His important words for pastors in 1 Pet 5:1–5, then, are words of one who, like a pastor after three decades of caring for people, has words of wisdom for those who have the ears to hear and the heart to absorb the wisdom of a sage.

So much can be learned from Peter as a pastor, which is why the first essay in this volume is the story of what Noah Schumacher learned from Peter as he went through difficult times personally and pastorally.[73]

Bibliography

Achtemeier, Paul J. *1 Peter: A Commentary on First Peter*. Hermeneia. Minneapolis: Fortress, 1996.
Adams, Sean A. "The Tradition of Peter's Literacy: Acts, 1 Peter, and Petrine Literature." In *Peter in Early Christianity*, edited by Helen K. Bond and Larry W. Hurtado, 130-45. Grand Rapids: Eerdmans, 2015.
Aland, Barbara, et al., eds. *Novum Testamentum Graece*. 28th ed. (NA28). Stuttgart: Deutsche Bibelgesellschaft, 2012.
Appold, Mark. "Peter in Profile: From Bethsaida to Rome." In *Bethsaida: A City by the North Shore of the Sea of Galilee*, edited by Rami Arav and Richard A. Freund, 3:133–48. Kirksville, MO: Truman State University Press, 2004.
Arav, Rami, and Richard A. Freund, eds. *Bethsaida: A City by the North Shore of the Sea of Galilee*. 4 vols. Bethsaida Excavations Project. Kirksville, MO: Truman State University Press, 2009.
Barnes, Timothy D. "'Another Shall Gird Thee': Probative Evidence for the Death of Peter." In *Peter in Early Christianity*, edited by Helen K. Bond and Larry Hurtado, 76–95. Grand Rapids: Eerdmans, 2015.
Bock, Darrell L., and Robert L. Webb, eds. *Key Events in the Life of the Historical Jesus: A Collaborative Exploration of Context and Coherence*. WUNT 247. Tübingen: Mohr Siebeck, 2009.
Bockmuehl, Markus N. A. *The Remembered Peter: In Ancient Reception and Modern Debate*. WUNT 262. Tübingen: Mohr Siebeck, 2010.
———. *Simon Peter in Scripture and Memory: The New Testament Apostle in the Early Church*. Grand Rapids: Baker Academic, 2012.
Bond, Helen K. "Was Peter Behind Mark's Gospel?" In *Peter in Early Christianity*, edited by Helen K. Bond and Larry Hurtado, 46–61. Grand Rapids: Eerdmans, 2015.
Bond, Helen K., and Larry Hurtado, eds. *Peter in Early Christianity*. Grand Rapids: Eerdmans, 2015.
Bonhoeffer, Dietrich. *Letters and Papers from Prison*. Edited by John W. de Gruchy. Dietrich Bonhoeffer Works 8. Minneapolis: Fortress, 2010.
Bussie, Jacqueline A. "Race, Grace, and God's Typewriter: Loving the Canceled Flannery O'Connor." In *People Get Ready: Twelve Jesus-Haunted Misfits, Malcontents, and Dreamers in Pursuit of Justice*, edited by Peter Slade et al., 141–66. Grand Rapids: Eerdmans, 2023.
Campbell, Robert A. *The Elders: Seniority Within Earliest Christianity*. Studies of the New Testament and Its World. Edinburgh: T. & T. Clark, 1994.
Carroll, John T. *Luke: A Commentary*. New Testament Library. Louisville: Westminster John Knox, 2012.

---

73. See Noah Schumacher, "In the Deep with Peter and Jesus," 1–17 above.

Copan, Victor A. *Saint Paul as Spiritual Director: An Analysis of the Concept of Imitation of Paul with Implications and Applications to the Practice of Spiritual Direction.* Paternoster Biblical Monographs. 2007. Reprint, Eugene, OR: Wipf & Stock, 2008.

Dunn, James D. G. *Beginning From Jerusalem.* Christianity in the Making 2. Grand Rapids: Eerdmans, 2008.

———. *Neither Jew nor Greek: A Contested Identity.* Christianity in the Making 3. Grand Rapids: Eerdmans, 2021.

Edwards, Dennis R. "Participation in Christ in 1 Peter." In *Cruciform Scripture: Cross, Participation, and Mission,* edited by Christopher W. Skinner et al., 144–59. Grand Rapids: Eerdmans, 2021.

Elder, Nicholas A. *Gospel Media: Reading, Writing, and Circulating Jesus Traditions.* Grand Rapids: Eerdmans, 2024.

Elliott, John H. *1 Peter: A New Translation with Introduction and Commentary.* Anchor Bible 37B. New York: Doubleday, 2000.

———. *A Home for the Homeless: A Social-Scientific Criticism of 1 Peter, Its Situation and Strategy.* 2nd ed. 1990. Reprint, Eugene, OR: Wipf & Stock, 2005.

Ellis, E. E., and Max Wilcox. *Neotestamentica et Semitica: Studies in Honour of Matthew Black.* Edinburgh: T. & T. Clark, 1969.

Eschner, Christina. "Petrus in der Mitte zwischen Paulus und Jakobus? Zum Verhältnis dieser drei Apostel des Urchristentums." In *Peter in the Early Church: Apostle—Missionary—Church Leader,* edited by Judith Lieu, 511–35. Bibliotheca Ephemeridum Theologicarum Lovaniensium 325. Leuven: Peeters, 2021.

Eusebius of Caesarea. *The History of the Church: A New Translation.* Translated by Jeremy M. Schott. Berkeley: University of California Press, 2019.

Evans, Craig A. *Jesus and the Remains of His Day: Studies in Jesus and the Evidence of Material Culture.* Peabody, MA: Hendrickson Academic, 2015.

Fowler, James W. *Stages of Faith: The Psychology of Human Development and the Quest for Meaning.* San Francisco: HarperSanFrancisco, 1981.

Freyne, Sean. "The Fisherman from Bethsaida." In *Peter in Early Christianity,* edited by Helen K. Bond and Larry W. Hurtado, 19–29. Grand Rapids: Eerdmans, 2015.

Gibson, Jack J. *Peter Between Jerusalem and Antioch: Peter, James and the Gentiles.* Vol. 2. WUNT 345. Tübingen: Mohr Siebeck, 2013.

Goldingay, John. *The First Testament: A New Translation.* Downers Grove, IL: IVP Academic, 2018.

Gupta, Nijay K., et al., eds. *Cruciform Scripture: Cross, Participation, and Mission.* Grand Rapids: Eerdmans, 2021.

Hengel, Martin. *Jews, Greeks, and Barbarians: Aspects of the Hellenization of Judaism in the Pre-Christian Period.* Translated by John Bowden. Philadelphia: Fortress, 1980.

———. *Judaism and Hellenism: Studies in Their Encounter in Palestine During the Early Hellenistic Period.* Translated by John Bowden. 2nd ed. Philadelphia: Fortress, 1974.

———. *Saint Peter: The Underestimated Apostle.* Translated by Thomas H. Trapp. Grand Rapids: Eerdmans, 2010.

Hood, Jason B. *Imitating God in Christ: Recapturing a Biblical Pattern.* Downer's Grove, IL: IVP Academic, 2013.

Horrell, David. "Peter Remembered in 1 Peter? Representations, Images, Traditions." In *Peter in the Early Church: Apostle—Missionary—Church Leader,* edited by Judith Lieu, 179–208. Bibliotheca Ephemeridum Theologicarum Lovaniensium 325. Leuven: Peeters, 2021.

Jenni, Ernst. *Theological Lexicon of the Old Testament.* 3 vols. Translated by Mark E. Biddle. Peabody, MA: Hendrickson, 1997.

Josephus, Flavius. *The Works of Josephus: Complete and Unabridged.* Translated by William Whiston. Peabody, MA: Hendrickson, 2003.

Lampe, Peter. "Traces of Peter Veneration in Roman Archaeology." In *Peter in Early Christianity*, edited by Helen K. Bond and Larry Hurtado, 273–317. Grand Rapids: Eerdmans, 2015.

Lieu, Judith, ed. *Peter in the Early Church: Apostle—Missionary—Church Leader.* Bibliotheca Ephemeridum Theologicarum Lovaniensium 325. Leuven: Peeters, 2021.

Marsh, Charles, et al., eds. *Lived Theology: New Perspectives on Method, Style, and Pedagogy.* New York: Oxford University Press, 2016.

McCready, Wayne O., and Adele Reinhartz, eds. *Common Judaism: Explorations in Second-Temple Judaism.* Minneapolis: Fortress, 2008.

McKnight, Scot. *1 Peter.* NIV Application Commentary. Grand Rapids: Zondervan, 1996.

———. "Jesus and the Twelve." *Bulletin for Biblical Research* 11:2 (2001) 203–31.

———. *Pastor Paul: Nurturing a Culture of Christoformity in the Church.* Theological Explorations for the Church Catholic. Grand Rapids: Brazos, 2019.

———, ed. *The Second Testament: A New Translation.* Downers Grove, IL: IVP Academic, 2023.

———. *Turning to Jesus: The Sociology of Conversion in the Gospels.* Louisville: Westminster John Knox, 2002.

McKnight, Scot, and Laura Barringer. *A Church Called Tov: Forming a Goodness Culture That Resists Abuses of Power and Promotes Healing.* Carol Stream, IL: Tyndale Momentum, 2020.

———. *Pivot: The Priorities, Practices, and Powers That Can Transform Your Church into a Tov Culture.* Carol Stream, IL: Tyndale Elevate, 2023.

Omerzu, Heiki. "Petrus und Paulus im Lichte des Galaterbriefes: Zwei Apostel im Spannungsfeld zwischen Jerusalem und Antiochia." In *Peter in the Early Church: Apostle—Missionary—Church Leader*, edited by Judith Lieu, 283–309. Bibliotheca Ephemeridum Theologicarum Lovaniensium 325. Leuven: Peeters, 2021.

Perkins, Pheme. *Peter: Apostle for the Whole Church.* Studies on Personalities of the New Testament. Columbia: University of South Carolina Press, 1994.

Rambo, Lewis. *Understanding Religious Conversion.* New Haven: Yale University Press, 1993.

Sanders, E. P. "Common Judaism Explored." In *Common Judaism: Explorations in Second-Temple Judaism*, edited Wayne O. McCready and Adele Reinhartz, 11–23. Minneapolis: Fortress, 2008.

———. *Judaism: Practice and Belief, 63 BCE–66 CE.* 4th ed. London: SCM, 1992.

———. *Paul and Palestinian Judaism: A Comparison of Patterns of Religion.* Minneapolis: Fortress, 1989.

Slade, Peter, et al., eds. *People Get Ready: Twelve Jesus-Haunted Misfits, Malcontents, and Dreamers in Pursuit of Justice.* Grand Rapids: Eerdmans, 2023.

Smith, Shively T. J. *Strangers to Family: Diaspora and 1 Peter's Invention of God's Household.* Waco, TX: Baylor University Press, 2016.

Spencer, F. Scott. *Luke.* Two Horizons New Testament Commentary. Grand Rapids: Eerdmans, 2019.

Stewart, Alistair. *The Original Bishops: Office and Order in the First Christian Communities*. Grand Rapids: Baker Academic, 2014.

Stoebe, H. J. "*Tov*." In *Theological Lexicon of the Old Testament*, edited by Ernst Jenni and Claus Westermann, 2:486-495. Translated by Mark E. Biddle. Peabody, MA: Hendrickson, 1997.

Strickert, Frederick. "The Renaming of Bethsaida in Honor of Livia, a.k.a. Julia, the Daughter of Caesar, in Josephus, *Jewish Antiquities* 18.27–28." In *Bethsaida: A City by the North Shore of the Sea of Galilee*, edited by Ravi Arav and Richard Freund, 3:93–113. Bethsaida Excavations Project. Kirksville, MO: Truman State University Press, 2009.

Thompson, Marianne Meye. *John: A Commentary*. New Testament Library. Louisville: Westminster John Knox, 2015.

van Unnik, W. C. "The Critique of Paganism in 1 Peter 1:18." In *Neotestamentica et Semitica: Studies in Honour of Matthew Black*, edited by E. E. Ellis and M. Wilcox, 129-42. Edinburgh: T. & T. Clark, 1969.

Wiarda, Timothy. *Peter in the Gospels: Pattern, Personality, and Relationship*. WUNT 127. Tübingen: Mohr Siebeck, 2000.

Williams, Margaret H. "From Shimon to Petros: Petrine Nomenclature in the Light of Contemporary Onomastic Practices." In *Peter in Early Christianity*, edited by Helen K. Bond and Larry W. Hurtado, 30–45. Grand Rapids: Eerdmans, 2015.

Winter, Bruce W. *Seek the Welfare of the City: Christians as Benefactors and Citizens*. First-Century Christians in the Graeco-Roman World. Grand Rapids: Eerdmans, 1994.

Wuellner, Wilhelm H. *The Meaning of "Fishers of Men."* New Testament Library. Philadelphia: Westminster, 1967.

4

A Different Road Traveled

Peter's Conversion

Matthew Van Winkle

In the summer of 2017, I found myself in a profound theological crisis. It wasn't a crisis of unbelief, but rather a crisis of belief, particularly in understanding how salvation is depicted in the New Testament. This crisis was especially relevant to my mission of planting a church in Minneapolis, a mission driven by the desire to witness new people embracing Christianity. It is in this context that I began to question the very nature of conversion, a fundamental aspect of evangelicalism.[1] As the story goes, I'm in Minneapolis to start this church so that we can see converts, and I'm trying to figure out what conversion even means. Not a great start at this point. And because conversion is such a deep part of evangelicalism, it means that in my crisis and as a good evangelical, I go to Paul to figure out what is going on with conversion, with a slight dose of James, to ensure we have a healthy amount of responsibility. Never once did I consider looking at the apostle Peter and the Gospels.

But here we will do just that. In a book about Peter, we will look at his conversion; however, as good evangelicals, we will also talk about Paul. I want to start the conversion conversation with Paul because his conversion is often seen as paradigmatic among Christians and move to

---

1. Tang, "Church Plants."

Peter's conversion once we have defined some terms.² I hope that we will see similarities in these two events. Further, I want to focus the conversation about Peter on the Gospel of Mark. Luke certainly has a turning back (*epistrephō*) that he uses to speak of Peter in Luke 22, and John has Peter and Jesus make amends over the charcoal fire (*anthrakia*).³ Mark appears to be an apocalypse that may or may not be a collection of stories from Peter himself, where Peter is an essential figure in the apocalyptic drama. We will begin and end with Mark's story. First, we will discuss how Mark works, then Peter's involvement in its writing. Then, we will briefly discuss Paul's conversion on the road to Damascus and return to discuss Peter's conversion in Mark. To wrap it up, we'll examine how this revelation will help us in our ministries.

Finally, before we leave the introduction, I want to talk about the word "conversion." Generally, this word is used when someone is changing from one ideology to another. One might convert from the Democratic Party to the GOP, or from being a Cubs fan to a Guardians fan. A distinct change is in view here. I think we must accept that Peter and Paul did not change from one religion to another. They simply followed the God of Israel as they always had. Of course, the revelation (apocalypse, if you will) that the story of Israel had found its completion in the person of Jesus and that he was indeed Israel's God incarnate was undoubtedly a new step for them. However, it was simply a step that completed the story as they knew it. Is conversion, as we understand it, the best word to describe this phenomenon? I am not convinced it is. If not conversion, what will be the best way to describe this event? Let us step forward and see.

Mark—Genre and Authorship

Mark's Gospel gives us a possible direct link to Peter's thoughts on Jesus's ministry, but Mark is not simply regurgitating random moments. Mark is an expert storyteller sandwiching narratives to drive a point home.⁴ As we'll see, Mark is acquainted with Jewish apocalyptic writing. However, I keep mentioning "Mark," so to be clear, I will assume that John Mark of the Acts narrative is in mind here. While there are arguments to be had on all sides, 1) the identity of "Mark" is not paramount to any argument I'm about

---

2. See Peace, *Conversion in the New Testament*.
3. Bockmuehl, *Simon Peter*, 163.
4. Lane, *Mark*, 11–12; Witherington, *Mark*, 36–37.

to make, and 2) the evidence of John Mark being the "interpreter" of Peter is well enough attested to move forward with that assumption.[5]

Genre

Mark has been described as a passion narrative with a long introduction. But why is this the case? Sure, all of the Gospels focus on the passion, but Mark devotes 19 percent of his narrative to the passion, while 15 percent of Matthew and Luke are dedicated to the last week.[6] Mark is also known for the "Messianic Secret" in which Jesus is keeping secret his mission as Messiah. Ben Witherington does not think that there is a Messianic Secret motif in Mark, and I think I am inclined to agree with Witherington's argument. However, I believe the true nature of Mark as apocalyptic has led to this understanding.[7] For example, if I want to have a surprise birthday party for my wife (which I would never do because she hates those) I do in fact have a secret, but the secret is kept so that the reveal is better. Mark's Jesus does not keep the secret; he points to what is consistently "unveiled" about Jesus. "Mark is a book of secrets, of veils, of mysteries."[8]

We must define apocalyptic properly: in apocalyptic, God reveals to the seer a fuller understanding of what is happening and, at times, what will happen in the world. We should think of Elisha's servant in 2 Kgs 6:17, who had his eyes opened to see the truth of heaven's armies around the Syrian army. Or of Daniel, who is shown a vision of four beasts and has the vision explained to him. As N. T. Wright explains, "As a literary genre, 'apocalyptic' is a way of investing space-time events with their theological significance."[9] In the first case, Elisha prays that the servant's eyes are opened, which causes him to see the truth: God is the revealer, the servant is the seer, and the armies are the revealed. In the case of Daniel, what is assumed to be an angelic being reveals the truth of the vision to Daniel, making Daniel the seer, the angel the revealer, and the true meaning of the vision the revealed.

---

5. For more on the John Mark arguments, see Witherington, *Mark*, 21–26; Lane, *Mark*, 7–12, 21–23; Edwards, *Mark*, 3–6; that being said, this paper will look at the evidence that Peter was behind Mark's material.

6. Witherington, *Mark*, 5.

7. Witherington, *Mark*, 40–41; Witherington, *Christology of Jesus*, 263–67.

8. Wright, *New Testament*, 390.

9. Wright, *New Testament*, 392.

In Mark, Jesus is the one being revealed, and on one occasion God fills the role of revealer. To investigate this more, let's look at Mark 8:11—9:8, which will allow us to demonstrate two things. First, it will provide a basis for the idea set forth that Mark is writing in an apocalyptic genre. Second, this section will be even more important once we begin looking at Peter's conversion. For now, let's look at the genre. This section begins with the Pharisees asking for a "sign from heaven" (8:11 NRSV), and Jesus responds that they will not be given one. On the boat on the way to "the other side" (8:13), Jesus tells the disciples to beware of the yeast of the Pharisees and Herod. Of course, this confuses the disciples because they don't even have any bread. Jesus picks up on their ignorance and tries to get them to understand what he means, finally asking, "Do you not yet understand?" (8:21).

Now, the crew is in Bethsaida, and Jesus has a blind man brought to him. Here we have Jesus's two-stage healing miracle, first with the blind man being able to see a little and then the blind man being able to see entirely. Jesus sends him away, saying, "Do not even go into the village" (8:26). Mark's following location is Caesarea Philippi, where Jesus asks dual questions, "Who do people say that I am?" and "Who do you say that I am?" (8:27, 29). Peter here has the correct answer. He seems like he finally understands something! Jesus, having garnered what can only be described as a discipleship victory, begins the next part of the discipleship training, telling his disciples "that the Son of Man must undergo great suffering, and be rejected by the elders, the chief priests, and the scribes, and be killed, and after three days rise again" (8:31). Peter then pulls Jesus aside and rebukes him, because Jesus's words are not fit for a Messiah as Peter understands it. This is the completion of the story above with the blind man. The throughline is understanding/seeing with the disciples not understanding, and Jesus then trying to get them to understand on the boat, which corresponds to the blind man. Then Peter confesses who Jesus is! But does he see clearly as the blind man does at the end of the story? No, Peter only "sees" a little. He knows that the trees are people/Jesus is the Messiah, but something is still missing. Jesus then tells the crowd and the disciples what this following will cost them. Here, we notice that Jesus continues the discipleship training even though Peter clearly misses the forest for the trees.

Mark then skips six days[10] and tells the story of the transfiguration. Peter gets antsy and decides the three disciples on the mountains should make three dwellings for Jesus, Elijah, and Moses. "Then a cloud overshadowed them, and from the cloud there came a voice, 'This is my Son, the Beloved; listen to him!'" (9:7). Peter does not know what is happening until the voice from heaven, and as John Markley notes, "Peter's imperception and fear during this revelatory moment are the natural responses of a human seer witnessing the mysteries of the divine realm."[11] Who is Revealed? Jesus. Who is the Revealer? God himself. Who is the representative Seer? Peter. Just as Peter didn't understand earlier because not everything had been revealed to him, he begins to see clearly as God has revealed who Jesus is. The whole section leads to this point, where the seeing/understanding comes to a crescendo. The Messianic Secret exists only because there is a consistent revealing/apocalypse of who Jesus is in the book of Mark.

Authorship and Peter

Mark also seems to get information from Peter. This connection is well attested in the early literature from Papias to Justin Martyr, Clement to Irenaeus, leading James Edwards to say, "The tradition that Peter was a key source for Mark's Gospel—indeed, that the Second Gospel was in many respects 'Peter's memoirs'—found, as far as we know, unanimous agreement in the early church."[12] Lane even sees a similarity between Paul's sermon in Acts 10 and Mark's general outline.[13] Helen Bond discusses some of the objections to a Petrine connection, and I think she makes two points that highlight why Peter's story can speak to people even today. First, Bond points out that while Peter is not given a glowing portrait in the Gospel, Mark's Peter can provide hope to those struggling to follow Jesus in their current situation.[14] Second, Bond points out that stories of Peter's seeming ignorance were told in light of his work postresurrection.

---

10. I think it's important to note that this is the first time Mark has told us a specific number of days between two events.

11. Markley, "Reassessing Peter's Imperception," 106.

12. Edwards, *Mark*, 5n9, the best of the footnote, in my opinion, being Papias in Eusebius, *Ecclesiastical History* 3.39.15; Justin Martyr, *Dialogue with Trypho* 106; Clement in Eusebius, *Ecclesiastical History* 6.14.6–7; and Irenaeus, *Against Heresies* 3.1.1.

13. Lane, *Mark*, 10–11.

14. Bond, "Was Peter," 57.

There seems to be not just the apocalyptic seer motif around Peter but also a bit of dramatic irony at the same time.[15]

What can that tell us about Peter and his conversion? At its core, we can begin to talk about the conversion of Peter as ongoing discipleship instead of a one-time event, and we'll look more at this after we've taken a look at Paul and his conversion. Looking at the stories above in Mark 8:11—9:8, Jesus engages with those following him, both the disciples and the crowd, to move them toward a fuller understanding of who he is and what the kingdom is. We even see this in Mark's language in the narrative, with seeing/understanding being synonymous. Further, this discipleship was a continual apocalypse of Jesus as the Messiah and his kingdom. It stands to reason that Peter would even describe the events as such.

But you say we already have a conversion story in Acts! Paul's conversion should inform us about Peter's conversion, how it works, and what we can glean. First, I want to say that we do not need Paul's conversion story to make sense of Peter's conversion story. With our information, we could make a good argument, and I hope that after you have read this the first time, you come back and evaluate this statement. However, because Paul's conversion is so paradigmatic in Christianity, and more data is never bad, we will turn to Paul's conversion in Acts and Galatians.

Paul's Conversion in Acts and Galatians

Paul's conversion is reported three times in Acts (9:1–19, 22:4–16, 26:9–19), and we'll look at each individually. However, I would like to tip my hand early. As stated above, conversion is discipleship, not simply a one-time event. McKnight points out, "Prayer for forgiveness, with its claims of repentance, will be acceptable to God only if the supplicant turns from sin."[16] Discipleship is leaning into this and following God instead of the sinful desires we have followed before. However, at the same time there does seem to be an entry into discipleship, that being the call. As we look at how Paul's conversion is communicated and how Paul communicates his conversion in the next section, we'll notice that Paul refers to the event on the Damascus Road (Damascus Experience going forward) as a call. And this is how we should see conversion: continued discipleship.

---

15. Bond, "Was Peter," 59.

16. McKnight, *Turning to Jesus*, 33; McKnight separates call, repentance, and discipleship (p. 47), which may be appropriate, but I also think that we can feasibly combine repentance and discipleship as the turning involves the following as well.

Conversion is transformation of some kind, a change in identity to identifying with Jesus.[17] For that transformation to take place, a call is made. For some, this is the call of/from an advocate, but for Paul and Peter that call was from Jesus himself.[18] Hopefully, we'll see this soon with Paul and then continue to see the same with Peter.

Before we move to that, I want to make a note about the language of call here. While call and calling in the evangelical milieu usually has overtones of vocational ministry, here the call is simply the call to follow. For Paul specifically, the call will be to more than simply following, but it does not need to be that way. Jesus called those around him to a deeper level of discipleship, and there is no evidence all of them went into some sort of vocational ministry like the apostles.[19] Here in this chapter, we are talking more about the call to come and follow Jesus than anything else.

Acts 9 is Luke's narrative telling of Paul's Damascus Experience.[20] Paul is headed up to Damascus to imprison some he considers heretics, and on the way, he has an experience. He hears a voice asking why Paul is persecuting him.[21] Paul replies by asking who is speaking, and the voice says it is Jesus. Paul then follows the instructions to go into the city. Meanwhile, a certain Ananias is told that Paul is there and that he is ready for a man named Ananias to go see him. Ananias knows of this individual and is rightfully afraid.[22] But Jesus says to Ananias, "Go, for he is an instrument whom I have chosen to bring my name before Gentiles and kings and before the people of Israel; I myself will show him how much he must suffer for the sake of my name" (9:15–16). Ananias goes and prays for Paul, and Paul is baptized. "For several days he was with the disciples in Damascus, and *immediately* he began to proclaim Jesus in the synagogues, saying, 'He is the Son of God'" (9:19b–20; emphasis mine). Naturally, his former allies are now opponents, and they are seeking to kill him, so Paul escapes to Jerusalem. In Jerusalem, he speaks "boldly in the name of the Lord" (9:28). Once again, his former allies are opponents, and they are seeking to kill him, so Paul escapes. He goes home to Tarsus this time, and we do not hear from him for a bit.

17. McKnight, *Turning to Jesus*, 4.
18. For more on the advocate, see McKnight, *Turning to Jesus*, 84–90, 145–51.
19. McKnight, *Turning to Jesus*, 47.
20. For authorship of Luke see Keener, *Acts*, 1:402–14.
21. The identification of the church with Christ himself is beautiful here, but once again we'll move on because that's not why we're here!
22. One might say there's a bit of Jonah energy here.

The second account of Paul's Damascus Experience is in Acts 22. This time Paul speaks in Jerusalem to his "brothers and fathers" (22:1). Much of the narrative remains the same, but we get an addition to Ananias's speech to Paul adding in part, "The God of our ancestors has chosen you to know his will, to see the Righteous One and to hear his own voice; for you will be his witness to all the world of what you have seen and heard" (22:14–15). Paul's Damascus Experience, as seen in Acts 22, is not simply a point of change from one religion to another but a call by God himself to new work. Paul relates that it was not just Ananias who was aware of this call, as in Acts 9, but Ananias told Paul that at the time.

The final account of Paul's Damascus Experience is in Acts 26 when Paul gives the account to King Agrippa. Once again, a new addition to the call is made, but this time, it is from Jesus himself: "I have appeared to you for this purpose, to appoint you to serve and testify to the things in which you have seen and to those in which I will appear to you" (26:16–18).[23] Craig Keener notes that this is the most thorough accounting of what Jesus said to Paul, and it happens to be where Jesus's words in Acts 9 to Ananias are finally fulfilled: "before Gentiles and kings" (9:15).[24]

Paul also talks about his Damascus Experience in Gal 1:15–16.[25] It's a brief couple of lines, but they reinforce what we have said above. "But when the one who set me apart from birth and called me by his grace was pleased to reveal his Son in me so that I could preach him among the Gentiles" (Gal 1:15–16a). Paul uses the calling language here to describe what happened because he did not stop believing in the God of Abraham, Isaac, and Jacob. He now understood by grace that Jesus was the faithful Messiah of Israel. Is there a conversion? Absolutely, but it was in how Paul thought of who Jesus and his followers were, not in a move like we might see today.[26]

An additional note pertains to this Galatian retelling. We should note that Paul was called, and the Son was apocalypsed.[27] We should hear echoes of Mark screaming back: the unveiling/revealing of the Son strikes again, this time in a completely different arena. Ultimately, I

---

23. I have chosen to go with "things in which you have seen" and not "things in which you have seen me."

24. Keener, *Acts*, 4:3516.

25. "Apart from some fairly idiosyncratic voices in recent centuries, nearly all scholars have affirmed that Paul wrote Galatians." Keener, *Galatians*, 6.

26. DeSilva, *Galatians*, 146.

27. Wright, *Galatians*, 76.

believe that Krister Stendahl wins the day when he says, "The emphasis in the accounts is always on this assignment, not on the conversion. Rather than being 'converted,' Paul was called to the specific task of apostleship to the Gentiles."[28] The crescendo of the Damascus Event stories in Acts shows more of what Paul heard than any other retelling. And now, finally, we return to the call and discipleship of Peter.

Peter's Call and Discipleship

Looking at Mark 1 as a unit, we start with the announcement of gospel. Mark, famously, doesn't start with a genealogy or prologue but dives straight into John the Dipper.[29] Mark has three uses of the word "gospel" (*euangelion*) in Mark 1 (the emphasized areas show Mark's use of this word, translated here with "good news"):

- The beginning of the *good news* of Jesus Christ, the Son of God. (1:1)
- Now after John was arrested, Jesus came to Galilee, proclaiming the *good news* of God, and saying, "The time is fulfilled, and the kingdom of God has come near; repent, and believe in the *good news*." (1:14–15)

And, you're not going to believe this, but Mark does not use the word again until 8:35, right in the middle of the passage we looked at earlier.[30] However, in Mark 1 gospel comes up right before Peter's call, which is why it is so important in context. Peter's call, as well as his brother Andrew's call, is reported like this in Mark:

> As Jesus passed along the Sea of Galilee, he saw Simon and his brother Andrew casting a net into the sea—for they were fishermen. And Jesus said to them, "Follow me and I will make you fish for people." And immediately they left their nets and followed him. (1:16–18)

"Fish for people" certainly feels a bit odd, so we will say "Fishers of People"! Sunday School memories aside, Mark shows here what we have been building to: the first thing he mentions about Peter is a call to follow. And what Peter does is respond to the call. Notice the similarities

---

28. Stendahl, *Paul Among Jews and Gentiles*, ch. 2.

29. Minor homage here to Scot McKnight's New Testament translation, *The Second Testament*.

30. Keener, "Mark 1.1," 00:50.

between what we said about Paul and Peter's reaction here. Paul immediately starts proclaiming Jesus exactly what he was told to do, and Peter immediately follows Jesus precisely what he was told to do. We should also note, "We are on safer ground if we learn to admit that the texts tell us only part of the story."[31] And this is all the more important, because of how Mark has shaped the telling of this story right next to Jesus's final use of gospel in the opening.

The next time we see gospel used is in Mark 8:35. Mark's use of gospel in chapter 8 coincides with Jesus's teaching on the cost of discipleship. Mark has blended call and discipleship with gospel here, and once we realize that chapter 9 starts with "Truly I tell you, there are some standing here who will not taste death until they see that the kingdom of God has come with power" (9:1) we see that Mark is foreshadowing the apocalypse to come in the next chapter. It seems Mark sees the transfiguration as the culmination of the apocalypse of the gospel.[32]

We now have a fairly complete picture of Peter's call, and initial phases of discipleship. There was a call to follow Jesus, followed by discipleship that included: Peter's mother-in-law being healed (1:29–31), going to search for Jesus after he left early to pray (1:35–39), being listed first among the twelve (3:16), multiple parables, the calming of two storms (4:38–41; 6:49–51), and thousands eating miraculously provided food (6:44; 8:9). This is discipleship on a grand scale, all setting Peter up for walking in the miraculous, while also explaining who this God is.[33]

And yet, Peter still fails. Moving to John's Gospel, we see an intimate portrait of denial and restoration. Peter's trio of denials around a charcoal fire are juxtaposed to Jesus's threefold question about Peter's love for him, once again around a charcoal fire. In Acts Peter gives multiple speeches to his brothers and sisters but when it is time for the mission to go outside the walls of the traditions, he must be told three times, "What God has made clean, you must not call profane" (Acts 10:15). And then after the vision, Peter finally says that now he "truly understands that God shows no partiality" (Acts 10:34). The same man who quoted Joel noting the Spirit would be poured out on all flesh is just now realizing that God doesn't show partiality. This is the man who saw Jesus do miracles in gentile areas (Mark 5:1–20). Yet it isn't until just now in Acts that Peter truly understands. Was Peter's conversion a conversion as we would imagine it?

31. McKnight, *Turning to Jesus*, 42.
32. Lane, *Mark*, 313–314.
33. For more on the miraculous see ch. 12 by James North in this work.

I believe the answer is no. Peter heard a call, just as Paul did, to discipleship under the Messiah and to spread the good news of the kingdom, but Peter did not have the persecution narrative that Paul did.

In the stories we have, Peter's movement shows him continually learning and growing, simply being a disciple as he goes. The growing isn't complete until deep into the second story of Acts. While there might be some dramatic narrative movement in Acts, I think that it's clear that we are moving forward in time the whole time. Peter's call is simple: just come and follow. Peter's discipleship is much more developed and lengthier, but I don't think that we can divorce the discipleship from the call in the entirety of conversion. In fact, Peter's discipleship is a larger piece of the puzzle than the call.

For Us Today

I hope that we have moved to look at Peter's conversion more holistically and that conversion as a whole in the New Testament is shown to be more complex and should be described as the call and discipleship overall. That should help us look at how we interact with the New Testament. I'd like to tell a few stories that hopefully will illustrate some of how we need to rethink what it means to become a Christian.

Recently, there was an uproar about a church that did some borderline things. A huge outcry came from multiple sides against multiple individuals who were in the controversy. Here's the thing: both sides claimed they were right, and part of their defense was how many people had come to Christ recently through the various warring ministry factions. And to show how nebulous this is, you probably have an idea of what uproar I am talking about, but we could be thinking of different ones! This conflict just happens over and over, and the defense is only that there are people coming to Christ. Given the above, why are we counting those who are converted? If the point is for call and discipleship, as we have seen above, why are we counting those who have simply raised their hands? Don't show me how many people have said yes, show me how many people are being discipled.

For example, I have had multiple call and response times. My dad kept a calendar that marked the first time that I responded for salvation. But that was not the only time that I responded to a call for repentance. Furthermore, it wasn't even the time that I would count as my conversion if we were keeping track. But for my dad, it mattered, and it mattered enough for it to be memorialized on a keepsake calendar. So, if we're counting conversions, do we count every time I went "down to the altar" or responded in some other way?

And what about those who were socialized into the faith?[34] These individuals who were nurtured into the church and never knew a time without faith in Christ, when was their conversion? Did they receive a call and discipleship just like those who hold to a more personal decision approach to faith? Further, how do we respond to those who have gone through the liturgical process to come into the faith? Are they even less saved because the church was a part of the process, or do they end up in a super-saved bucket?!

While all this may seem reductive, I think these are important questions for us today, and the answers must lie in the stories the texts tell us. This is why we spent so much time looking at Peter's conversion and the elements we can see in them, the call and the discipleship. And while I certainly do not want to overgeneralize any thoughts on conversion as it's clear, "Conversion can't be reduced to a formula any more than love can be set out as an equation."[35] The truth is Jesus meets us all where he needs to meet us, and the call on the shores of the Sea of Galilee is just as important as the call on the road to Damascus. However, I do not want to leave you without hope.

Just as Jesus was revealed to Peter on the mountain, conversion will take place by the revealing of Jesus to those who need to see him. And the most beautiful part of this is we have partnered with him to reveal him to others. We are the ones who have been set forth as Christ's Ambassadors, to be his advocates on earth and to reveal who he is to those who don't know him. While I do believe that the call ultimately comes from God, we need to remember that Andrew wasn't on the mountain for the transfiguration. Andrew got that revelation from Peter.[36]

And further, Jesus isn't here in person to disciple those around us. Matthew 28:20 gives us the imperative to make those disciples. The continual desire for the Godhead to partner with humanity to bring about his purposes for the earth hasn't changed since the garden, and we are the ones who get to work with God in this endeavor.

---

34. This paragraph is deeply indebted to McKnight's work: *Turning to Jesus*, 1–25.

35. McKnight, *Turning to Jesus*, 77.

36. Or James and John I guess, but wouldn't you be upset if your sibling saw that and you heard it from a friend instead?

Let's take these ideas, call and discipleship through the revelation of Jesus Christ, and go forward with them.

Bibliography

Bockmuehl, Markus N. A. *Simon Peter in Scripture and Memory: The New Testament Apostle in the Early Church*. Grand Rapids: Baker Academic, 2012.
Bond, Helen K. "Was Peter Behind Mark's Gospel?" In *Peter in Early Christianity*, edited by Helen K. Bond and Larry W. Hurtado, 46–61. Grand Rapids: Eerdmans, 2015.
DeSilva, David A. *The Letter to the Galatians*. New International Commentary on the New Testament. Grand Rapids: Eerdmans, 2018.
Edwards, James R. *The Gospel According to Mark*. Pillar New Testament Commentary. Grand Rapids: Eerdmans, 2002.
Keener, Craig S. *Acts: An Exegetical Commentary*. 4 vols. Grand Rapids: Baker Academic, 2012.
———. *Galatians: A Commentary*. Grand Rapids: Baker Academic, 2019.
———. "Mark 1.1: Forty Minutes on Mark's First Verse." Sept. 11, 2020. https://www.youtube.com/watch?v=-Rj5AO_WrlY.
Lane, William L. *The Gospel According to Mark*. New International Commentary on the New Testament. Grand Rapids: Eerdmans, 1974.
Markley, John R. "Reassessing Peter's Imperception in Synoptic Tradition." In *Peter in Early Christianity*, edited by Helen K. Bond and Larry W. Hurtado, 99–108. Grand Rapids: Eerdmans, 2015.
McKnight, Scot. *Turning to Jesus: The Sociology of Conversion in the Gospels*. Louisville: Westminster John Knox, 2002.
Peace, Richard. *Conversion in the New Testament: Paul and the Twelve*. Grand Rapids: Eerdmans, 1999.
Stendahl, Krister. *Paul Among Jews and Gentiles, and Other Essays*. Philadelphia: Fortress, 1976.
Tang, Len. "Church Plants as Evangelism Laboratories." *Fuller Studio*, Nov. 29, 2023. https://fullerstudio.fuller.edu/theology/church-plants-as-evangelism-laboratories/.
Witherington, Ben. *The Christology of Jesus*. Minneapolis: Fortress, 1997.
———. *The Gospel of Mark: A Socio-Rhetorical Commentary*. Grand Rapids: Eerdmans, 2001.
Wright, N. T. *Christian Origins and the Question of God*. Vol. 1: *The New Testament and the People of God*. Minneapolis: Fortress, 1992.
———. *Galatians*. Commentaries for Christian Formation. Grand Rapids: Eerdmans, 2021.

5

Peter's Promenade
An Uncommon Path to Common Discipleship

Nika Spaulding

> *"Look! Look! Look!" cried Lucy. "Where? What?" asked everyone. "The Lion," said Lucy. "Aslan himself. Didn't you see?" Her face had changed completely and her eyes shone.*[1]

> Immediately he made the disciples get into the boat and go ahead of him to the other side, while he dismissed the crowds. After dismissing the crowds, he went up on the mountain by himself to pray. Well into the night, he was there alone. Meanwhile, the boat was already some distance from land, battered by the waves, because the wind was against them. Jesus came toward them walking on the sea very early in the morning. When the disciples saw him walking on the sea, they were terrified. "It's a ghost!" they said, and they cried out in fear. Immediately Jesus spoke to them. "Have courage! It is I. Don't be afraid." "Lord, if it's you," Peter answered him, "command me to come to you on the water." He said, "Come." And climbing out of the boat, Peter started walking on the water and came toward Jesus. But when he saw the strength of the wind, he was afraid, and beginning to sink he cried out, "Lord, save me!" Immediately Jesus reached out his hand, caught hold of him, and said to him, "You of little faith, why did you doubt?" When they got into the boat, the

---

1. Lewis, *Prince Caspian*, 131.

wind ceased. Then those in the boat worshiped him and said, "Truly you are the Son of God." (Matt 14:22–33 CSB)[2]

WHEN THE FOUR PEVENSIE siblings found themselves back in Narnia to help Prince Caspian reclaim his rightful place upon the throne, the youngest, Lucy, sees Aslan and knows he is beckoning them all to take a different path than the one they were attempting. After a feeble attempt at persuading them to take the less sensical path, Lucy bitterly follows her older siblings instead of heeding Aslan's summons. Later Lucy learns that even though her older siblings outvoted her, Aslan still expected her to follow him. When Lucy receives her gentle rebuke from the loving lion, she no longer represents the youngest of the Pevensie siblings but instead represents every person who has been called by God but wavers. Lucy will learn from this encounter what it means to follow Aslan even when it makes no sense. While C. S. Lewis might have had any number of situations in mind when he penned this story, he easily could have been pondering the moment Peter jumps out of the boat in Matt 14:22–33. Like Lucy, Peter, too, will learn what it means to follow God without wavering.

Except for Luke, the Gospel writers all deem Jesus' shuffling across the Sea of Galilee worthy of mention. The clear Christological implications of this incident jump off the pages. For starters, Jesus' declaration of "It is I" (*ego eimi*) is "not bad grammar but a conscious echo of the divine name of Yahweh, as in Exod 3:14."[3] Secondly, walking on water represents solely divine activity.[4] Finally, in Mark's account—likely Matthew's source—he has Jesus "passing by," alluding to Exod 33:22 and clearly paralleling Job 9, where God alone walks on water and passes by Job.[5] For Mark, Matthew, and John this pericope strengthens the case for Jesus' deity and claim as the Son of God.[6] But Matthew does a little more. Where Mark and John focus the spotlight on Christ alone doing things reserved only for God, Matthew widens his lens to include unique material of Peter attempting his own sea strut. What exactly is Matthew

2. All Scripture will be CSB unless otherwise noted.
3. Blomberg, *Matthew*, 235.
4. Luz, *Matthew*, 319.
5. Keener, *Gospel of Matthew*, 406.
6. Keith Warrington concludes about all three sections, "For the writers, Jesus demonstrates similar divine authority which begs the questions, 'Who is he?' and 'Should we worship him?'" Warrington, *Miracles in the Gospels*, 206.

doing when he alone inserts the short scene of Peter getting out of the boat, walking, doubting, sinking, yelling, being rescued, and returning to the boat? Is this a true story or a story that tells the truth? Is Peter foolhardy or full-heartedly trying to follow Christ? To Pete or not to Pete, that seems to be the question. We will step out of the boat together and show that Peter, much like Lucy, must follow the command of Christ and, though faith is often mixed with doubt, even little faith saves and brings you closer to seeing Jesus (or Aslan) more clearly.

Why does Matthew alone include this story about Peter? Assuming Mark and John had knowledge of this Petrine event, their omission stems from redactional decisions to focus entirely on Christology. For Matthew, this intrusion of Peter into Jesus' big Christological moment fits with his double emphasis on the person of Jesus and the suitable response of the church. From the Sermon on the Mount through the postresurrection appearances, "Matthew served then, as it can still serve, as a great instruction manual on the person of Jesus and the nature of discipleship."[7] Rather than bifurcating sections on Jesus' true nature and how disciples should respond, Matthew—writing to a church under duress—often is "addressing Christological issues with his right hand . . . at the same time delivering teaching on discipleship with his left."[8] For Matthew, his sea-crossing pericope does highlight the uniqueness of Jesus as the Son of Man, but by telling Peter's part he simultaneously speaks about discipleship.

At this point, one could fairly ask, "Does Peter *really* represent discipleship for every person given his preeminent position among the disciples?"[9] Is this a picture of discipleship or a picture of Peter's discipleship? Was Lewis writing about Lucy or all of us? Where Mark gives Peter a prominent position, Matthew "has taken over this feature and expanded it noticeably."[10] Moving forward, Peter will be the main spokesperson for the group and will alone be told he received special revelation from God the Father about the true identity of Jesus (Matt 16). Furthermore, regardless of how you interpret Jesus' words—either upon Peter or upon Peter's confession—the church will be built with Peter somewhere near the foundation. Yet, preeminence does not equate to par excellence. Later Peter will tell Jesus he will not die in Jerusalem; he tries to build homes

---

7. Wright and Bird, *New Testament in Its World*, 578.

8. Davies and Allison, *Saint Matthew*, 513.

9. For a discussion of Peter as the leader of the disciples see Helyer, *Life and Witness*, 36–40.

10. Brown et al., *Peter in the New Testament*, 105.

at the Mount of Transfiguration and must be told to listen; and he wants to limit the number of times forgiveness should be offered.[11] Perhaps the feats and foibles of Peter make him even more exemplary of a typical disciple. Rather than most important, he "appears only as the most representative of the disciples. What all of them represent, do, and think comes to particularly strong expression in his person."[12] Peter speaks for the whole group, but he does so as one among them. When Matthew writes about Peter, he writes about typical discipleship.

Rather than seeing Peter as exceptional, then this sea-walking scene makes better sense when we see Peter as archetypal.[13] Matthew—writing to a young church facing duress—knows that "similar calls will be made to many of Jesus' followers in the days to come and they can draw comfort from Peter's experience in that when their faith wavers, Jesus' arm will not."[14] Great writers will tell you that if you wish to capture your reader by placing them in your character's shoes, specificity not generality creates this effect. Matthew does this with Peter. Although Peter participates in an exceptionally specific moment, Matthew expects this story and others like it to paint broad strokes about discipleship. In the same way Jesus calls the disciples to become fishers of men (Matt 4:19) and calls them to go out, giving them power over unclean spirits and diseases (Matt 10:1), Jesus also calls Peter to walk on water.[15] Calling and doing the seemingly impossible comes part and parcel for discipleship in Matthew. Specific yet universal. Peter as the archetype means "on this occasion, Peter was the miracle; this was a miracle just for him, *and for any other follower who is prepared to respond positively to Jesus' commission, 'Come'*" (emphasis mine).[16] Peter represents discipleship not just for the hyper-devoted Christian, but for all who hear the beckoning call of Christ.

But what exactly is the call? If it is a metaphor for following Christ into the storms of life, did Matthew fabricate this story for pedagogical flair? If he did, where did he get the idea? All these questions deserve

11. Reeves, *Matthew*, 327–30.

12. Cullmann, *Peter*, 31.

13. Discussing the redactional differences between Mark and Matthew's accounts, Carlisle states "Matthew, editing his narrative to speak to the whole question of the true meaning of Christian discipleship, uses Peter as an archetype of this view." In other words, Matthew explicitly uses Peter here as a fill-in for all disciples. Carlisle, "Jesus' Walking on the Water," 151–55.

14. Warrington, *Miracles*, 207.

15. Brown, et al., *Peter in the New Testament*, 82.

16. Warrington, *Miracles*, 208.

consideration as they will fill out the finer brush strokes of what Matthew hopes to teach about discipleship through Peter. We will start by discussing the background texts that might have informed Matthew and then move into what Peter's stroll might mean for us.

Matthew most likely used Mark as one of his main sources for his Gospel.[17] We also know that Mark depended on Peter for much of his eyewitness testimony in his Gospel.[18] Which begs the question, why does this material show up in Matthew and not in Mark?[19] Did Peter forget to mention to Mark that he once walked on water—a feat I doubt many people would keep to themselves? Or, did Matthew invent this material for redactional purposes? Some see this epiphany as "central to the story line and not merely part of the story."[20] Others take issue with that position and claim, "Such understandings are not exegesis; they proceed from the presuppositions of the expositor."[21] Gundry—wishing to correct those who wrongfully claim that he considers Matthew *entirely* midrash—writes in his second edition, "I am not backing down from my thesis that at numerous points these features exhibit such a high degree of editorial liberty that the adjectives 'midrashic' and 'haggadic' become appropriate."[22] With Matthew's literary flourishes and Mark's omission, debating the historicity of this event might prove as futile as the disciples attempting to row across the lake that night. Perhaps the "best approach is to set aside the question of the historicity of the event and to focus instead on what the narrative meant to Matthew."[23] After all, regardless of

---

17. There are a few minority scholars that hold to a Matthean priority, but for this paper I am assuming that Matthew used Mark in his writings. For a brief discussion, see Wright and Bird, *New Testament in Its World*, 581–83.

18. As early as the first two centuries, writers like Papias claim Mark was Peter's "interpreter." Kuruvilla, *Mark*, 2.

19. We also recognize that Peter might have told Mark about this incident, but "the story would not have served a constructive purpose in Mark's Gospel which attempts rather to play down his exploits in strength or weakness of faith, preferring instead a sober account based on a balanced amount of information." Thiede, *Simon Peter*, 29.

20. Keener briefly states that the historicity of this story cannot be decided easily and sets it aside after offering this position represented by Meier. Keener, *Matthew*, 406.

21. Morris, *Matthew*, 380.

22. Gundry, *Matthew*, xxiii. Gundry famously proposed a stronger element of midrashic, or creative, redaction, in the first edition of his Matthew commentary. That edition led to his dismissal from the Evangelical Theological Society on the grounds that he violated the principles of inerrancy. In this second addition he softens the language some, but his argument deserves thoughtful consideration.

23. Hare, *Matthew*, 168.

whether this event happened, Matthew has his reasons for including it, and those reasons can at least partially be derived from the sources that inform our understanding of this miracle.

Even if Matthew watched his buddy Peter hop out of the boat, by choosing to tell this story he would evoke in his readers' minds similar sea walking and rescue stories. Yet, the question remains, which stories would they remember? From the non-Jewish sources, they might remember the *Epic of Gilgamesh* when the tavern keeper reminds Gilgamesh, who wishes to cross the ocean, "Only Shamash the hero crosses the ocean: apart from the Sun God, who crosses the ocean?"[24] Gilgamesh agrees with Job: only a God can traverse *upon* the water. Or, they might think of Josephus's scathing critique of Caligula when he wrote, "And other pranks he did like a madman as when he laid a bridge . . . so he enclosed the whole bay within his bridge, and drove his chariot over it; and thought, that as he was a god, it was fit for him to travel over such roads as this was."[25] Caligula, too, agrees with Job, but seriously overestimates his god-like power. Real gods need no bridges.

In addition to gods, Hellenistic literature also included heroes or divine men who had the ability to stride on the sea if they "are in a special way sons of God or achieve divine powers by magic—or unless in their audacity they invade dimensions that are reserved for the divine."[26] For example, Orion—a demigod born from a father who is a god and human mother—was given the "power to stride across the sea" from his dad, Poseidon.[27] Orion must borrow his father's divinity; perhaps Matthew's readers imagined in the same way Peter borrows Jesus'. In Iamblichus's *Life of Pythagoras*, he "receives a magical arrow that can carry him over bodies of water, mountains and other obstacles that hinder ordinary travelers."[28] Because of an intrusion from the magical world, a human receives the ability to walk upon water. With these non-Jewish sources swirling in one's mind, "the miracle would thus strike a gentile audience as particularly

---

24. *Epic of Gilgamesh*, tablet 10, lines 71–77.
25. Josephus, *Antiquities*, 71–77.
26. Luz, *Matthew*, 320.
27. Apollodorus, *Library* 1.4.
28. It should be noted, McPhee sketches out several Greco-Roman mythological accounts that some argue parallel sea-crossing miracle, but he ultimately argues that they do not bear enough resemblance to Jesus' story. McPhee, "Walk, Don't Run," 763–77, 769.

marvelous and incomprehensible."[29] As we have already discussed, however, Matthew hopes to do more with this text than just shock and awe at Jesus' abilities. If he hopes to say something more about discipleship, then these texts have little to offer. Furthermore, Matthew's primary audience would not have been gentiles, but Jewish Christians who would be more likely to have Solomon rather than Sophocles floating in their heads. The Greco-Roman sources make much of the divinity of Jesus, but looking at the Jewish sources helps us to more fully understand what Matthew hoped to communicate by including Peter's participation.

Much like the Greco-Roman sources, the Jewish sources unequivocally declare that only God can walk on water. They also go a step further and claim water is the special domain of Yahweh.[30] In both the creation account and exodus tradition God masters and tames the chaotic waters. Job 9 in the Masoretic text picks up this idea of God at creation "trampling upon" and "treading upon" the sea. Those metaphors "suggest God's dominance and power over the sea, which in ancient Near Eastern mythology was often depicted as the monster of chaos, the principle of evil, disorder, and death that opposed the creator god(s)."[31] This imagery of God conquering the waters appears throughout the Old Testament (Hab 3:15; Ps 77:20; Isa 51:9–10) and other Jewish literature (Wis 14:3 and Sir 24:5–6).[32] As Jesus makes the sea his promenade, Matthew intends for his Jewish readers to make the connection between Yahweh treading upon the waters and now Christ treading upon the same sea that gave his experienced fishing buddies fits. But Jesus does more than walk, he also saves and for that Matthew probably had other Old Testament sources in mind.

When Matthew wrote about Jesus extending his hand to save Peter, a few places in the Old Testament might have caused his Jewish readers some déjà vu. After reading Peter's rescue, a reader versed in the Jewish Scriptures might start humming the tune of Ps 18. David writes that after taming the sea, God "reached down from on high and took hold of me; he drew me out of deep waters" (v. 16).[33] Or, perhaps they might hear David's other melody as he compares the threat of enemies to a sea rescue. In Ps 144:7 David asks God to "reach down from on high; rescue

29. McPhee, "Walk, Don't Run," 777.

30. Heil, *Jesus Walking*, 34.

31. Meier, *Marginal Jew*, 914.

32. For a thorough discussion of Jewish background literature see Meier, *Marginal Jew*, 914–19, and Heil, *Jesus Walking*, 37–56.

33. Davies and Allison, *Matthew*, 508.

me from deep water and set me free from the grasp of foreigners."[34] Or, might the reader—like Peter—look away from Jesus and notice the sea and boat and think of Ps 107 and Jonah 1? Both passages include a ship being battered by the waves, sailors crying for rescue, and the sea stilling, thus rescuing those upon it.[35] Matthew intends for his readers to think of the many times God rescues from the sea—the domain of chaos, darkness, and travail—when Jesus rescues Peter.

Those parallels deserve consideration, but Matthew probably gave a smirk and a wink when he heard his readers hum a different tune. Again, for Matthew Christology matters in this passage and he knows that by writing Jesus walks on the sea, rescues with his outstretched hand upon the sea, and calms the sea he is giving readers a nudge in the side. Wink, wink, Jesus is Yahweh. As we have already mentioned, however, Matthew wants to say something more than Mark and John do with this story. Matthew also parallels Ps 69, and by doing so he can add to "Jesus is Yahweh" with "And discipleship looks like this, and always has."[36] When Matthew as the narrator uses his omniscient voice to tell us Peter's perspective, he evokes the same point of view as the individual in Ps 69.[37] In the LXX the corresponding vocabulary to Matthew's Greek reveals the close relationship between the two passages.

Term or Phrase	Psalm 69	Matthew 14
"save me" (*sōzō egō*)	v. 1	v. 30
"waters" (*houdatas*)	vv. 1 and 14	vv. 28 and 29
"deep waters" (*thalassa*)	v. 2	v. 26
"sweeps over" (*katapontizō*)	vv. 2 and 15	v. 30

34. Harrington, *Matthew*, 227.

35. Harrington, *Matthew*, 226.

36. Here are some of the lines from Ps 69 that parallel Peter's experience: v. 1 Save me, God, for the water has risen to my neck. v. 2 I have come into the deep water, and a flood sweeps over me. v. 14 Rescue me from the miry mud; don't let me sink. Let me be rescued from those who hate me and from the deep water. v. 15 Don't let the floodwaters sweep over me or the deep swallow me up. v. 17 Don't hide your face from your servant, for I am in distress. Answer me quickly! v. 18 Come near to me and redeem me.

37. Heil notes the parallels when he states, "OT background for the extreme distress of Peter is provided by Ps 69. The situation of the psalmist in this lament of an individual is the same as that of Peter: distress from overwhelming waters from which only God can save." Heil, *Jesus Walking*, 61.

Term or Phrase	Psalm 69	Matthew 14
"crying" (*krazō*)	v. 3	v. 30
"O Lord" (*kurios*)	v. 13	v. 30

By connecting Peter to Ps 69, Matthew reminds his readers that discipleship includes lament, crying out to God, facing hardship, and trusting in God alone to rescue. Peter represents an archetype, and his words harken back to this archetypal prayer where "the troubles are not specific, which is in keeping with the purpose of the Psalms to provide templates of prayers for later worshippers who have similar, though not identical, issues."[38] By putting the words of Ps 69 in the mouth of Peter, Matthew very cleverly teaches his readers that just like in the days of old, followers of Yahweh—and in this case, specifically Jesus who is Yahweh—should expect trouble and tribulation. And just as in the days of old, the strong hand of God still reaches down into the miry depths to set disciples onto solid ground—or solid boats.

You might be wondering, if we were always going to arrive at Ps 69 as the proposed background literature that most informed Matthew's writing of this passage, why did you have me row so hard through the other literature first? I wanted to show how universal facing danger, chaos, and even death is to the human condition. Regardless of whether Matthew's readers hailed from Jewish or Greco-Roman backgrounds, the sea represented a chaotic and dangerous realm that posed a real threat to any would-be traversers.[39] This background explains the plethora of writ-

---

38. Longman, *Psalms*, 346.

39. In addition to Greco-Roman and Jewish sources, the Buddhist Jataka—stories from the previous lives of Buddha—also has a parallel worth mentioning in the footnotes. It is not included in the text above because the collection of Jataka come from the fifth century CE—much later than our biblical sources. However, these Buddhist stories sometimes include materials that are found in sculptures from much earlier pre-Christian times. Since the dating remains difficult, we put this material in the footnotes to not potentially weaken the argument above. However, since the argument states that this story of a rescue upon the sea represents a universal experience, this story deserves some consideration. Jataka 190 tells of a man wishing to visit his master but when he arrives at the river the ferry is no longer available. So, the man thinks joyful thoughts about Buddha and that empowers him to walk on the river. When the man reaches the middle, he sees the waves and he began to sink. So, he thinks stronger thoughts about Buddha and then continues on the surface. This represents a close parallel to Matt 14, but the striking dissimilarity teaches us something about the Christian experience vs the Buddhist. For the Buddhist, he experiences rescue not from another but through

ers in Matthew's day and earlier who use the sea imagery and humanity's attempt to tame it or need of rescue from it. The world is chaotic and life is hard—either bend the world toward your will (Caligula) or cry out to the one who lovingly saves (David, Peter, and the rest of us disciples). Peter—as our representative—teaches all disciples to cry out to God for rescue, but he also teaches us a bit more.

A quick peek at more recent reception history, and you might also conclude that Peter teaches us to think before we leap. One scathing critique asserts, "It goes too far to cast Peter's request as an admirable example of discipular desire to obey Jesus' commands. The content of the request bespeaks doubt more than desire, because the desire arises out of the doubt."[40] This critique finds friends as others have concluded "by [Peter's] example believers are taught to beware of over-much rashness" and Peter "confuses enthusiasm . . . with faith."[41] If scholars make negative interpretations, then pastors are sure to follow. Which might explain why George Morrison to his large congregation in Glasgow preached, "Peter's temperament which put him in this danger. . . . The other disciples were all safe and sound. It never occurred to them to leave the vessel. They were men of sagacity and common sense, and knew the difference between land and water."[42] Tough crowd for Peter. While we might grant that in most cases common sense calls for staying in the boat, there is nothing common about following Jesus, and most of the time he was hardly sensical to his closest followers. And, by coloring Peter's decision in such a negative light, we miss out on what this event continues to teach us about discipleship.

For starters, disciples should want to be near Jesus. Chrysostom interprets Peter's decision as an act of love and not pride when he notes Peter does not ask for Christ to command him to simply to walk but instead to command him to come *to Jesus*.[43] Augustine gives a favorable interpretation because in his estimation Peter has genuine trust in Christ's power,

---

his own ability to conjure thoughts of the other. For Peter, he is saved by the other. The Buddhist saves himself. Christ saves Peter. The Jataka story is cited by Luz, *Matthew*, 321.

40. Gundry, *Peter*, 11.

41. For a helpful survey of favorable and unfavorable interpretations of Peter's decision see Bruner, *Matthew*, 77.

42. Wiersbe, *Classic Sermons*, 47.

43. Bruner, *Matthew*, 77.

not his own.[44] Furthermore, if Peter should have stayed in the boat, Christ could have easily rebuked his request—a song and dance they rehearse often. Instead, "Jesus has acknowledged the propriety of the disciple's desire to act as his Lord acts (*imitatio Christi*)."[45] After all, didn't Jesus tell Peter to follow him? If we allow for Peter to have favorably stepped out of the boat then Matthew is teaching us "disciples were expected to imitate their masters, and Jesus is training disciples who will not simply regurgitate his oral teachings but who will have the faith to demonstrate God's authority in practice as well."[46] If we bear in mind that it "took courage for the apostle to venture on the water at all" then suddenly Matthew says even more about discipleship.[47] Trusting God for salvation is one big part, but discipleship also includes love of Christ, imitation of Christ, and courage to do the loving and imitating thing.

Admittedly, the Peter detractors have one glaring indictment to make against our sea-walking disciple: he takes his eyes off Christ, sees the storm, doubts, and sinks. But doesn't this too teach us about the nature of discipleship? That Peter presented here as "paradoxically a model both of faith and of lack of faith" is a lesson for disciples who also find themselves wavering in storms.[48] If we are honest with ourselves, does not most of discipleship involve a dance oscillating between confidence and frailty, faith and doubt, water walking and drowning rescue? Do we not often say, "I believe, help my unbelief"?[49] Certainly, most of us would not want to be called "little faith one" by our Savior, but Matthew reserves this word for believers only—never non-believers.[50] Little faith does not mean no faith. And, "Peter's actions through which he displays his little faith, teach us that what counts is Jesus' saving presence, not the Christian's strength of will or courage."[51] Disciples need to hear "fear not, take courage, be bold" but what a relief that when they fail they also

---

44. Bruner, *Matthew*, 77.

45. Davies and Allison, *Saint Matthew*, 507.

46. Keener, *Matthew*, 407.

47. Morris, *Matthew*, 383.

48. Hagner, *Matthew*, 423.

49. The more gracious of commentators recognize doubt as the normative discipleship experience. See, e.g., Blomberg, *Matthew*, 236; Helyer, *Life and Witness*, 39; Brown, et al., *Peter in the New Testament*, 83.

50. Hare, *Matthew*, 170.

51. Davies and Allison, *Matthew*, 513.

can hear from Peter's example, "I got you, I'm right here, little faith is sufficient because I'm a big savior."

Doubt happens. Lucy doubted. Peter doubted. By including this story, Matthew allows us to learn a vital lesson about doubt in the life of the Christian. Rather than viewing faith and doubt as mutually exclusive convictions, disciples do better to realize "doubt is not opposed to faith; in the typical case it is part of faith."[52] And, rather than seeing faith as mental assent, we should learn to see it as trust in God. Trust can happen amidst doubt. Peter doubts, but he still cries out to Jesus to save him. He shows us that "doubt and pain do not prove the absence of faith. Instead, the Christian may have the dispositional faith combined with concurrent doubt."[53] In other words, in the swirling doubt, in the chaotic wind and waves, in the crashing fears, we can still say "help me," and that is enough.

Back in Narnia, Aslan again asks Lucy to persuade her siblings to follow a difficult path. Afraid, she puts her face into his mane, and "there must have been magic in his mane. She could feel lion-strength going into her. Quite suddenly she sat up. 'I'm sorry, Aslan,' she said. 'I'm ready now.'"[54] Back in Galilee, Jesus asks the disciples who they think he is. Peter must have received his lion-strength from the boat incident because he answers that Jesus is the Messiah, the Son of the Living God. Jesus replies, "Blessed are you, Simon son of Jonah, because flesh and blood did not reveal this to you, but my Father in heaven."[55] Perhaps doubt paves a path for conviction. By including this Petrine account, Matthew continues to teach us about the nature of discipleship, and those who teach this passage have the same invitation. Of course, we should beckon disciples to follow Christ with great faith often requiring courage. Peter reminds us, though, that the good news about following Jesus is that even when we doubt, fail, and falter, the strong hand of God will still be stretching toward us. And we may just find that in that faltering, we gain a renewed sense of strength and commitment.

---

52. Smith, *Why Faith Is a Virtue*, 159.
53. Smith, *Why Faith Is a Virtue*, 162.
54. Lewis, *Prince Caspian*, 150.
55. Matt 16:17.

Bibliography

Apollodorus. *The Library*. Translated by J. G. Frazer. Loeb Classical Library 121. London: Heinemann, 2001.

Blomberg, Craig L. *Matthew*. New American Commentary 22. Nashville: Broadman, 1992.

Brown, Raymond E., et al., eds. *Peter in the New Testament: A Collaborative Assessment by Protestant and Roman Catholic Scholars*. 1973. Reprint, Eugene, OR: Wipf & Stock, 2002.

Bruner, Frederick Dale. *Matthew 13–28: A Commentary; The Churchbook*. Rev. ed. Grand Rapids: Eerdmans, 2007.

Carlisle, Charles Richard. "Jesus' Walking on the Water: A Note on Matthew 14:22–33." *New Testament Studies* 31 (1985) 151–55.

Cullmann, O. *Peter: Disciple, Apostle, Martyr*. Translated by Floyd V. Filson. Philadelphia: Westminster John Knox, 2011.

Davies, W. D., and Dale C. Allison. *A Critical and Exegetical Commentary on the Gospel According to Saint Matthew*. International Critical Commentary. Edinburgh: T. & T. Clark, 2004.

The Epic of Gilgamesh: The Babylonian Epic Poem and Other Texts in Akkadian and Sumerian. Edited by A. R. George. New York: Penguin, 2000.

Gundry, Robert Horton. *Matthew: A Commentary on His Handbook for a Mixed Church Under Persecution*. 2nd ed. Grand Rapids: Eerdmans, 1994.

———. *Peter: False Disciple and Apostate According to Saint Matthew*. Grand Rapids: Eerdmans, 2015.

Hagner, Donald A. *Matthew 14–28*. Word Biblical Commentary 33B. Nashville: Nelson, 2008.

Hare, Douglas R. A. *Matthew*. Interpretation. Louisville: John Knox, 1993.

Harrington, Daniel J. *The Gospel of Matthew*. Sacra Pagina. Collegeville, MN: Liturgical, 1991.

Heil, John Paul. *Jesus Walking on the Sea: Meaning and Gospel Functions of Matt 14:22–33, Mark 6:45–52, and John 6:15b–21*. Rome: Biblical Institute, 1981.

Helyer, Larry R. *The Life and Witness of Peter*. Downers Grove, IL: IVP Academic, 2012.

Josephus, Flavius. *The Works of Josephus: Complete and Unabridged*. Translated by William Whiston. Peabody, MA: Hendrickson, 2003.

Keener, Craig S. *A Commentary on the Gospel of Matthew*. Grand Rapids: Eerdmans, 1999.

Kuruvilla, Abraham. *Mark: A Theological Commentary for Preachers*. Eugene, OR: Cascade Books, 2012.

Lewis, C. S. *Prince Caspian*. The Chronicles of Narnia 4. New York: HarperTrophy, 2002.

Longman, Tremper. *Psalms: An Introduction and Commentary*. Tyndale Old Testament Commentaries. Downers Grove, IL: IVP Academic, 2014.

Luz, Ulrich. *Matthew 8–20*. Hermeneia. Minneapolis: Fortress, 1989.

McPhee, Brian D. "Walk, Don't Run: Jesus's Water Walking Is Unparalleled in Greco-Roman Mythology." *Journal of Biblical Literature* 135 (2016) 763–77. https://doi.org/10.15699/jbl.1354.2016.3084.

Meier, John P. *A Marginal Jew: Rethinking the Historical Jesus*. Vol. 2: *Mentor, Message, and Miracles*. New York: Doubleday, 1994.

Morris, Leon. *The Gospel According to Matthew*. Grand Rapids: Eerdmans, 1992.

Reeves, Rodney. *Matthew*. Story of God Bible Commentary. Grand Rapids: Zondervan, 2017.

Smith, Philip D. *Why Faith Is a Virtue*. Eugene, OR: Cascade Books, 2014.

Thiede, Carsten P. *Simon Peter: From Galilee to Rome*. Exeter: Paternoster, 1986.

Warrington, Keith. *The Miracles in the Gospels: What Do They Teach Us About Jesus?* Peabody, MA: Hendrickson, 2016.

Wiersbe, Warren W., ed. *Classic Sermons on the Apostle Peter*. Kregel Classic Sermon Series. Grand Rapids: Kregel, 1995.

Wright, N. T., and Michael F. Bird. *The New Testament in Its World: An Introduction to the History, Literature, and Theology of the First Christians*. Grand Rapids: Zondervan Academic, 2019.

6

Great Confession, Great Correction
How Peter Sees and Mis-Sees Jesus' Messiahship, and What It Means for Christian Discipleship

BRENDEN LANG

THE LAST SEVERAL YEARS have witnessed a surge in discussion about the meaning and need for discipleship. Many books, blogs, and even organizations have been developed to address just this issue. Of course, not everyone agrees about what discipleship is or how we should go about it. For some, discipleship looks like Bible education—helping people grow in their understanding of God and Scripture. For others, it looks like growing in the context of a community—getting people in small groups where they can learn to live in right-relationships. Still others see discipleship ultimately as an exercise in multiplication—we are to make disciples, who make disciples, who make disciples, who make disciples . . . These ideas are not mutually exclusive, and there's value in all of them. We should be studying the Scriptures, we ought to be growing in community, and we must be sharing Jesus with others! But in our drive to get discipleship right, have we somehow missed what it is fundamentally about? What is discipleship as it was imagined by Jesus? Or perhaps a better question: who is a disciple according to Jesus?

Typically, theologies of discipleship begin with, or are at least centered around Jesus' Great Commission to "make disciples."[1] But here, I want to

---

1. Matt 28:19 (NRSV).

suggest a better place to start, namely with Peter's Great Confession. For one, the Great Confession provides the very words many believers use when they begin their journeys as disciples. In my own church, we ask everyone to recite these words when they are baptized and/or become members of the church. Second, and more to the point, the Great Confession provides the immediate context for Jesus' clearest statement about what it means to be a disciple, albeit in a part of the story that is more frequently neglected—what I like to call the "Great Correction." What follows then is a study of the Great Confession and Great Correction, especially as this story is recorded in the Gospel of Mark.[2]

Literary Context

To appreciate the significance of this story according to Mark, we first need to see how it fits within the literary context of the Gospel. Scholars have made a variety of proposals about the structure of Mark, but many see a threefold division within the book.[3] In part one (Mark 1:1—8:21), Jesus ministers in and around Galilee where he is designated and acts as the Messiah. In part two (Mark 8:22—10:52), Jesus travels on the way to Jerusalem as he teaches how to follow in the way of the Messiah (i.e., how to

---

2. The Great Confession and Great Correction can be found in Mark 8:27—9:1 and Matt 16:13-28. Luke omits Jesus' rebuke of Peter, but the remaining parts of the story can be found in 9:18-27. John also refers to the Great Confession in 1:41-42, though the details and chronology differ from the Synoptics. Matthew's version of the story has held primacy of place in the history of Christian discussion, largely because of the additional comments Jesus makes about Peter and the church. This essay will comment from time to time on Matthew's idiosyncrasies but will focus primarily on Mark's version of the story, and for a few different reasons. First, whereas Mark ties the Great Confession and Great Correction together as one story, Matthew breaks them up through the transitional vocabulary, "From that time on . . ." (Matt 16:21). Moreover, early church tradition identifies Peter as the source of this Gospel. Though modern critical scholarship holds an appropriately skeptical view of traditions such as these, this tradition does fit with some of the modern scholarly assumptions about the location and date for the book of Mark. Though a Petrine origin for the Gospel material cannot be verified, the possibility still opens fascinating interpretive questions. What would it imply if Peter was the source of a Gospel that takes a particularly low view of the disciple? And what would stories like the one in view communicate to Roman Christians, who were facing persecution themselves, in light of traditions about the manner of Peter's death? See discussion in Perrin, "Mark," 554-56.

3. See discussion in Perrin, "Mark," 555-56.

be a disciple). Then in part three (Mark 11:1—16:8), Jesus spends his final week in Jerusalem where, on the cross, he is crowned as Messiah.[4]

The second part—Mark's roadmap for discipleship where the Great Confession occurs—is framed by stories of Jesus healing people of blindness—the only two such stories in Mark.[5] Providing sight was evidently a regular feature of Jesus' ministry given that we read many similar stories in the other Gospels. But since these are the only two sight-restoring stories in Mark, and given their locations in the book, namely at major turning points, many scholars have seen a greater significance to these accounts than mere historical reporting: the stories symbolize the spiritual condition of Peter and the rest of the disciples who "have eyes, and fail to see."[6]

The first healing story which immediately precedes the Great Confession is especially significant in this regard. Mark records how a person who had been blind is healed in two stages. At first, the man comes to see, but not completely: "I can see people, but they look like trees, walking."[7] After this, Jesus fully restores his sight so that he comes to see "everything clearly."[8] Why did it take Jesus two tries to fully restore the man's vision? Was the one who stilled the storm and multiplied the loaves not powerful enough to give full sight in one attempt? When we view the story from a purely historical perspective, we're left wondering. But when we consider the literary context, we too gain clarity: the two-stage process by which the man came to see physically is symbolic of the process by which Peter would come to see spiritually.

The Great Confession

Here now we can focus in on the first part of the story. The episode begins with Jesus traveling with Peter and the disciples to the villages of Caesarea Philippi.[9] For the casual reader, this may seem like a small

---

4. On the process of Jesus moving from Messiah-designate to Messiah-enthroned, see Bates, *Salvation by Allegiance Alone*, 50. As for discussion about the cross as the locus of Jesus' coronation in Mark, see Wright and Bird, *New Testament in Its World*, 572–74.

5. Mark 8:22–26; 10:46–52.

6. Mark 8:18. On this, see Garland, *Mark*, 312–13; France, *Gospel of Mark*, 322–23.

7. Mark 8:24.

8. Mark 8:25.

9. For a robust discussion of the history and geography of Caesarea Philippi as it

detail, but for Peter, this was an electric setting—a place that would have ignited his inner passions and was ripe for bold claims. Caesarea Philippi was located at the base of Mount Hermon about twenty-five miles north of the Sea of Galilee. The city had previously been called Panias due to a shrine there dedicated to the Greek god Pan, the god of flocks and fertility. This shrine was set near a watery cave, which in that cultural context was thought of as a portal to the underworld.[10] In this light, we can better appreciate Jesus' reference to the "gates of Hades" in Matthew's version of the story: "And I tell you, you are Peter, and on this rock I will build my church, and the gates of Hades will not prevail against it."[11] While the gates of Hades may have seemed to overtake Pan's shrine, they would prove no match for Jesus' temple (i.e., the church).

The physical terrain also helps us better appreciate Jesus' references to rocks in Matthew's version. First, he calls Simon as Peter (Greek: *Petros*), which sounds like the Greek word for rock (*petra*).[12] Then Jesus adds that he would build his church "on this rock" (Greek: *epi tautē tē petra*). Whether Jesus had Peter in mind with this latter reference has been a matter of contentious debate. Protestants have often been eager to read other options here lest Roman Catholic claims about papal primacy prove true. I, for one, cannot see how identifying Peter as this rock necessarily legitimates such claims.[13] Nevertheless, whether Jesus meant to refer to Peter, himself, or something altogether different, the cliff face against which Caesarea Philippi's religious complex was built would have provided a "vivid" backdrop for Peter and all who were present.[14] The pagan temples built along these rocks would eventually crumble, but the Church founded on Jesus' rock would endure forever.

Mark, of course, makes no mention of rocks in his telling of this story. But the city's political associations loom large in the background. Around 20 BCE, Caesar Augustus gave the area to Herod the Great who

---

pertains to the Great Confession, see Phillips, "Peter's Declaration."

10. Phillips, "Peter's Declaration," 290.

11. Matt 16:18.

12. The same is true of Simon's other surname wherein Aramaic *Cephas* sounds like *ceph*, "rock."

13. D. A. Carson bemoans, "If it were not for Protestant reactions against extremes of Roman Catholic interpretation, it is doubtful whether many would have taken 'rock' to be anything or anyone other than Peter." See Carson, "Matthew," 368.

14. Phillips, "Peter's Declaration," 293.

then built a temple there in honor of the emperor.[15] Later in 2 BCE, Herod's son, Philip the tetrarch, further developed the city and named it Caesarea Philippi to further glorify the emperor, and it seems himself.[16] Thus it was no small step along the discipleship pathway for Peter to confess here, "You are the Messiah." Here at a site where people worshiped the emperor, and which was named after the emperor and his client ruler, Peter boldly declared that Jesus was God's anointed ruler, king of heaven and earth.

This royal claim is, in fact, part of the significance of the title messiah, though this gets lost on many modern readers. The significance gets lost even more so when versions translate the title as "Christ."[17] For many readers, Christ is thought to be little more than Jesus' last name. As a result, our confessions easily devolve into shallow affirmations of a guy who happens to be related to God. But in calling Jesus the "Christ," or as the NRSV translates it, "Messiah," Peter meant so much more.

At its most basic level, the Hebrew term messiah (*māšîaḥ*) means "anointed one" (i.e., one who has oil smeared on them).[18] In the Hebrew Bible, this title is given to a variety of priestly and royal figures who were appointed for special tasks. This list includes figures like Aaron, Saul, David, members of the Davidic dynasty, and even the Persian emperor Cyrus. Broadly and theologically speaking, the task these messiah figures had in common was to link heaven and earth.[19] This may not be immediately apparent, but it becomes clearer when we survey usage of the verbal form *māšaḥ*, "to anoint." For example, the first time we see this verb is in Gen 31:13 where it refers to an event when Jacob had poured oil on a stone. Jacob had had a dream while sleeping on the stone of angels climbing up and down a ladder which connected heaven and earth.[20] So

15. Phillips, "Peter's Declaration," 290.

16. Josephus only indicates that Philip named it after the emperor: "When Philip, also, had built Paneas, a city, at the fountains of Jordan, he named it Cesarea" (Josephus, *Antiquities* 18.28). However, coins issued later by Philip show the full name, Caesarea Philippi. The addendum "Philippi" no doubt served to distinguish this city from the Caesarea by the sea (i.e., Caesarea Maritima). But we shouldn't think Philip was motivated purely by concern for clarity. He had no small honor to gain by linking his name with Caesar's at this city. For numismatic evidence, see Ma'oz, "Banias," 138.

17. See ESV, NASB, NKJV, and NET to name a few.

18. Oswalt, "מָשַׁח."

19. I am indebted here to the work of Tim Mackie, Jon Collins, and the Bible Project in their podcast series *The Anointed*. Check out Mackie and Collins, "'Christ' Is Not a Name."

20. Gen 28:10–22.

to commemorate the moment and mark the place as a "gate of heaven," Jacob sets up the rock and anoints it.[21] Similarly, the verb is used several times later in reference to the tabernacle and its holy objects.[22] The tabernacle was the place where God's presence was manifest with the Israelites. So having been anointed, the tabernacle and its objects were established as holy places where heaven met earth.

Once again, understanding this background can help us better appreciate some of the unique statements in Matthew's version of the story. If the cave at Caesarea Philippi was like the "gates of Hades," so as the Messiah, Jesus was like the gate of heaven.[23]

Mark, no doubt, had a similar conception of Jesus. This is why, for example, when Jesus is designated as the Son of God (i.e., the Messiah) at his baptism, and when he is declared the Son of God at his crucifixion, barriers that divided heavenly spaces from earthly spaces are "torn" (Greek: *schizō*) apart.[24] In other words, in and through Messiah Jesus, God was now "in our midst and on the loose."[25] But there's more we can say about the title messiah that is helpful for understanding Peter's confession in Mark.

Though nonroyal, religious figures could be called a messiah in the Hebrew Bible, the term increasingly came to have royal connotations. In the books of Samuel and the Psalter in particular, we see the term frequently applied to David and his dynasty. Of special importance are uses like that found in Ps 2, where God promises that his anointed Son would rule, not just over Israel, but over all the nations. Also significant are uses such as those found in Ps 89 where an exilic poet recalls God's promises to the anointed David. In this poem, he remembers that David and his line were to rule "forever" as the "highest of the kings of the earth."[26] Promises such as these were formative for Jews in the centuries leading up to the time of Jesus when they were without a Davidic king and living under foreign domination. The promises fostered hope that a

---

21. Gen 28:17–18. Note that the verbal form used here is the synonym *yāṣaq* "to pour out" (an obvious play on the name, Isaac [Hebrew: *yiṣḥāq*]).

22. Exod 29:36; 30:26; 40:9–11; Lev 8:10–11; Num 7:1, 10, 84, 88; Dan 9:24.

23. Cf. John 1:35–51 where the themes of Jesus' messiahship and Jacob's dream are brought together in the context of Peter's (brother's) Great Confession.

24. Mark 1:10, 15:38.

25. Garland, *Mark*, 48.

26. Ps 89:27–29.

new king would one day rise to set the world to right for God's people.[27] This is what Peter correctly saw about Jesus in the politically charged setting of Caesarea Philippi. And it's consistent with one of Mark's main purposes for writing the Gospel—to establish in ink the good news that Jesus is the Messiah, king of heaven and earth.[28]

The Great Correction

Now if a primary purpose for Mark was to make the explosive claim that Jesus is the Messiah, then a complimentary purpose must have been to explain why he is a *crucified* Messiah.[29] After all, virtually no one saw this coming—certainly not Peter. Mark makes this point by connecting Peter's Great Confession with Jesus' Great Correction.[30] The second half of the story begins this way: "Then he began to teach them that the Son of Man must undergo great suffering, and be rejected by the elders, the chief priests, and the scribes, and be killed, and after three days rise again. He said all this quite openly. And Peter took him aside and began to rebuke him."[31]

Here, Jesus gives the first of three predictions in Mark about what would happen to him.[32] Jesus was to suffer, be killed, and only then be raised to reign. And this evokes a surprisingly bold reaction, even for the deep-feeling Peter: he rebukes Jesus.

27. See the discussion on the origins of messianism in Evans, "Messianism," 699–700.

28. See discussion in Wright and Bird, *New Testament in Its World*, 560–61. See also Craig Evans who carefully makes the case that Mark's claim about Jesus' messiahship constitutes a counterclaim against Roman pretensions: "The Markan evangelist presents Jesus as the true son of God and in doing so deliberately presents Jesus in opposition to Rome's candidates for a suitable emperor, savior, and lord." Evans, *Mark*, lxxxix.

29. Wright and Bird, *New Testament in Its World*, 560–61.

30. In contradistinction, Luke does not include the Great Correction and Matthew more clearly separates out this episode through the transitional vocabulary, "From that time on . . ." (Matt 16:21). Of course, this phrase is more than a simple transition for Matthew. Jack Kingsbury has argued influentially that this phrase is rather a structural formula which marks dramatic new phases in the story of Jesus both here and at Matt 4:17. See Kingsbury, *Matthew*, 7–25. With this in mind, one could well argue that even though the book shifts dramatically in 16:21, Matthew may yet have viewed the two episodes as unfolding in the same setting. Nevertheless, in Matthew, Jesus' passion prediction "is no longer Jesus' direct response to Peter's confession as it was in Mark; instead, Jesus begins a new instruction." See Luz, *Matthew*, 381.

31. Mark 8:31–32.

32. See also Mark 9:31; 10:32–34.

Rebuke isn't exactly a word we use in everyday English, but it doesn't sound good. And in the original Greek (*epitimaō*), it wouldn't have sounded any better. More than a simple correction, the term connotes ideas of censure and even dishonor. Elsewhere in Mark, this same word is used to describe what Jesus shouted toward a demon in Mark 1:25, as well as to the chaotic, almost devilish storm in Mark 4:39. So it's shocking to find Peter doing the same thing to the one he just called the Messiah. But it's there. And it's because a crucified Messiah didn't fit Peter's theology. Like the blind man who could see, but not clearly, Peter saw Jesus for who he was, but not fully. He saw Jesus as king, but not as a crucified king.

Now at this point, Jesus has not yet named that he would be crucified, only "killed." But this would have been problematic enough for Peter. A common perception at that time was that the messiah would be like a victorious war hero. Of course, not all Jews thought about the messiah the same way. Some even anticipated two messiahs.[33] But based on the available literature, we may presume that many, including Peter, would have resonated with prayers like this from the first-century BCE Psalms of Solomon:

> See, O Lord, and raise up their king for them, a son of David, for the proper time that you see, God, to rule over Israel your servant. And undergird him with strength to shatter unrighteous rulers. Cleanse Jerusalem from the nations that trample it in destruction, to expel sinners from the inheritance in wisdom, in righteousness, to rub out the arrogance of the sinner like a potter's vessel, to crush all their support with an iron rod; to destroy lawless nations by the word of his mouth, for gentiles to flee from his face at his threat, and to reprove sinners by the word of their heart.[34]

Now it should be said that the view expounded in this prayer was not a complete innovation at the time of Jesus. The seedbed for texts like this may be found in some of the very texts cited earlier from the Hebrew Bible. But it must also be said that the seedbed for Jesus' prediction about his fate was there in the Hebrew Bible as well. For example, Jesus mentions the "Son of Man."[35] Throughout the Gospel, he often uses this title

---

33. See the discussion on the Messiah in Second Temple Judaism in Strauss, "Messiah."

34. Pss. Sol. 17:23–27 (Lexham English Septuagint).

35. Mark 8:31.

to refer to himself.³⁶ But Son of Man is more than a self-referential phrase for Jesus.³⁷ Verses like Mark 13:26 and 14:26, which describe the Son of Man as "coming" on the "clouds" of heaven, suggest that Jesus saw himself as the "Son of Man" of Dan 7:13. So too, verses like Mark 8:38, which envision the Son of Man in a heavenly courtroom, suggest that Jesus was thinking about Daniel's judicial figure. Of course, the allusion can easily be missed because of translation inconsistencies. The NRSV translates the Aramaic *bar ' ĕnāš* as "one like a human being" in Dan 7:13. This translation is perfectly legitimate, but it masks the fact that this is the equivalent of the Greek *ton huion tou anthrōpou* which the NRSV translates as "Son of Man" in Mark 8:31 and elsewhere. The allusion would be more obvious if the translations were the same. Nevertheless, the link is there. And it matters for this discussion because Daniel's Son of Man is a representative of humans who is raised to reign over all the kingdoms of the earth, but only *after* a season of suffering. That is, the Son of Man (like the messiah) is presented as king of heaven and earth, but his rule comes only *after* many great trials.

Jesus also explains that he would "suffer," "be rejected," and "killed." In these statements, one can hear echoes of Isa 53 which describes yet another representative, a servant (as Jesus also likes to call himself) who is described with similar terms.³⁸ The vision begins by stating that this servant would "prosper" (Hebrew: *yaśkîl*), "be exalted" (Hebrew: *yārûm*), "lifted up" (Hebrew: *niśśā'*), and "very high" (Hebrew: *gābah mə' ōd*).³⁹ These terms are not exclusive to royalty, but the biblical writers did find them appropriate at times to describe God's anointed, and even God himself.⁴⁰ And yet, as the passage goes on, it becomes clear that the servant's path to exaltation was not so simple. Though he gained a "portion with the great" he was first a "man of suffering."⁴¹ Though he would "prolong his days," he first "poured out himself to death."⁴²

Scholars today disagree about the interpretation of this vision, whether it was fulfilled at some level in its original Babylonian context

---

36. Mark 2:10, 28; 8:38; 9:9, 12, 31; 10:33, 45; 13:26; 14:21, 41, 62.
37. For discussion of Jesus' use of the phrase "Son of Man," see Wright, *Jesus*, 510–19.
38. See discussion in Watts, "Mark," 175–82.
39. Isa 52:13.
40. See for example Jer 23:5–6; Ps 89:19; 2 Sam 5:12; Ezek 19:11; Isa 6:1.
41. Isa 53:3, 12.
42. Isa 53:10, 12.

and/or whether the prophet did have or could have had Jesus in mind.[43] The point here is not to make the case that Isaiah (or Deutero-Isaiah, if you will) was clearly, consciously describing the crucified Jesus. Actually, quite the opposite. Though our questions may have changed, the confusion about the vision's meaning has been around since its conception.[44] As Isa 53:1 itself states, "Who has believed what we have heard?"[45] Paraphrase: "This is anything but straightforward!" If it were, Jesus' words wouldn't have been so shocking to Peter. But they were. Rather, the point is that the seedbed, or perhaps better, the trajectory for how Jesus would one day understand his vocation as the Messiah could be found here, and in Dan 7, and elsewhere in the Hebrew Scriptures. You just had to have eyes to see it.[46]

So just as Peter rebuked Jesus, Jesus now rebukes Peter that he might come to see more clearly: "Get behind me, Satan! For you are setting your mind not on divine things but on human things."[47] Then calling the crowd who was right there with them, Jesus adds, "If any want to become my followers, let them deny themselves and take up their cross and follow me. For those who want to save their life will lose it, and those who lose their life for my sake, and for the sake of the gospel, will save it."[48]

---

43. For a summary of the interpretive options and issues, see Goldingay, "Servant of Yahweh," 700–707.

44. John Goldingay argues that the vision was intentionally ambiguous so that readers might discover themselves in the drama: "The openness of the pronouns in the vision left it open for audiences to find their place in it. When subsequent generations of Jews looked at this scene, they found themselves in it, though they left the portrayal of exaltation for the Messiah. When the first Christians looked at this scene with the risen Christ, they knew that Christ had been the realization of this vision, and the vision then helped them to understand who he was. They also knew that it was God's vision for them. As is often the case with a vision or a poem, there is no need to limit it to only one such referent." See Goldingay, *Isaiah*, 303.

45. Isa 53:1.

46. This, in fact, seems to be what the writer had in mind in Isa 53:1. The speakers ("we") come across as those who have been healed through the servant's vicarious death, such that they now understand what the unhealed will struggle to hear and see. So Watts: "In taking the literary perspective of looking back on the event, [Isa 53:1] affirms the efficacy of God's action in his servant. Whereas the problem all along has been that God's people were blind and deaf to his purposes (e.g., Isa 42:18–25; 48:8), because of this extraordinary act they finally see, hear, and understand the new thing that God was doing." See Watts, "Mark," 178.

47. Mark 8:33.

48. Mark 8:34–35.

Here now we find Jesus' clearest statement about what it means to be a disciple. In Mark, to be a disciple means following Jesus, and following Jesus means doing as he did (or at least as he would).[49] This is the significance of the part of the book that this story begins. As we have outlined above, Jesus here begins to journey "on the way" to Jerusalem—that is, to the cross. And as he goes, he teaches about the *way* of the Messiah, which is the *way* of the cross. For Peter and the disciples who followed Jesus quite literally, the road provided the classroom where they were taught how to follow him conceptually. They were to deny themselves and take up their crosses—perhaps literally, but certainly metaphorically. Metaphorically speaking, this meant they were to be the sort of people who would sell all they have and give it to the poor.[50] It meant they were to welcome and show hospitality to the marginalized and the lowest classes of society.[51] It even meant assuming the position of those who belonged to the lowest classes of society.[52] The cross, in fact, implied as much. In the first century Roman world, crucifixion was reserved for rebels and slaves.[53] So to willingly take up one's cross, as Jesus did and calls all followers to do, was to humble oneself as though one was a slave.

Of course, Peter never seems to get the point, at least as far as Mark records his part in the story. The three passion predictions Jesus makes in this part of the book find their match in Peter's three denials in the next. And Peter's not alone. None of the Twelve ever seem to get it. When we get to the abrupt and open ending of the book, we are left wondering if anyone is still following Jesus.[54] He is "going ahead," but no one is said to be following.[55] And so as readers, we are drawn into the story. Will we follow him? Are we up for the task?

---

49. Gombis, *Mark*, 14–15.
50. Mark 10:17–31.
51. Mark 10:13–16.
52. Mark 9:33–37; 10:35–45.
53. Fiensy, "Crucifixion."
54. For discussion about the unusual ending to Mark, see Perrin, "Mark," 558.

55. Mark 16:7. At the very least, none of the Twelve are present. Mark does highlight several women disciples who stayed with Jesus through the crucifixion and were there for his burial and at the empty tomb. From the other Gospels, we know that these women were also the first to preach the good news of the resurrected Jesus. Yet, in Mark's Gospel, even they say nothing, presumably for rhetorical effect: If they don't proclaim the good news, will the reader step in?

Pastoral Takeaways

I fear that in the modern American church, we've lost sight of the task: the call to discipleship, which is the call to follow Jesus in the way of the cross. Like Peter, we might confess Jesus as the Messiah. But we haven't worked out the implications of what it means to say he is the Messiah, that is, the crucified Messiah. We've embraced the Jesus of the confession without the Jesus of the correction. This is not to say that we don't welcome the Jesus who died on the cross for our sins. But aside from what the cross means for our eternal destiny, we have little more use for the cross. It's a nice token, a sign of God's love for you and me, even the sacrifice that saves us. But it has next to no bearing on our lives beyond that. And this couldn't be further from the task of discipleship. If being the Messiah meant carrying a cross, if this was the way of King Jesus, then this is also the nature of his kingdom, and it's the call on our lives as kingdom-citizens as well.

So how can we do better? If our goal is to get discipleship right, then what needs to change? First, in imitation of Jesus (which as we've been discussing is the nature of discipleship), we as disciple-makers must make sure people understand what they are confessing when they confess Jesus as the Christ. Sometimes we are so eager to draw people to first-time decisions that we understate the costs involved with such decisions. Yes, grace costs us nothing (at first, at least). But following Jesus costs us everything. We don't do anyone any favors by rushing them to decide things they don't realize they are deciding. We let them down and set them up for defeat. To be clear, I'm not suggesting that individuals must become Bible scholars before they can become Christians. The issue here isn't about Bible knowledge so much as it is about the scale of one's commitment. Becoming a disciple of Jesus means giving him allegiance above all else, and allegiance is expressed not just with our words, but also with our lives.[56] So just as Jesus informed the crowds who were there with him and Peter, we would do well to inform would-be followers of the true costs involved. In the words of Dietrich Bonhoeffer: "Whenever Christ calls us, his call leads us to death."[57]

Second, we must remind our people again and again of the true nature of discipleship. Part of our task as pastors is to help people see more clearly with each new day how to follow Jesus wherever they go, whether

---

56. Bates, *Salvation by Allegiance Alone*.
57. Bonhoeffer, *Discipleship*, 81.

it be at home, the workplace, on social media, or in the public sphere. This is an ongoing, never-really-ending process of pastoral encouragement and prophetic rebuke. Clearly, it was an ongoing process for Peter and the other disciples. As far as the Gospel of Mark is concerned, they never quite got there. But that too might be part of the point. A disciple by nature is always in process. The word "disciple" itself implies as much. At its most basic level, the term disciple means "apprentice," or "learner."[58] So while a disciple may become a teacher, by the very nature of the role, a disciple remains a student. Though they may become a leader, a disciple remains forever a follower. This is the irony of Christian discipleship. Jesus calls us to full allegiance, and we may confess full allegiance. But I suppose unless our journey leads quite literally to a death on a cross, we'll never fully get there. So we must keep on learning just as we keep on leading. And this leads to the third and final point.

As pastors, we must strive to model cruciform living ourselves. Unfortunately, church leaders (myself included) sometimes struggle with this the most. We ought to know as well as anyone that the nature of the kingdom, and thus the nature of the church is self-denying, sacrificial, and upside-down. And yet, the churches we build and the ministries we lead too often look (or strive to look) more like the self-concerned, self-promoting organizations of American capitalism. This is not to say that we have nothing to learn from the business world. Having humility entails a willingness to learn from others. But what if church leaders began to lead in such a way that business leaders couldn't help but look to us? What if, like Jesus, our lives and leadership were so radically different from anything our culture has to offer that the crowds couldn't help but pay attention? What if through the faithful witness of our lives, we could show that despite the cost of following Jesus—and it is a high cost—God's faithfulness is higher? What could happen then?

With Peter, you might say that we have such a faithful witness. Mark may paint Peter in a less than favorable light, but if tradition is correct that Peter is the source for Mark's Gospel, then we might see Christlike humility in how Peter helped shape Mark's Gospel. And though Mark ends with Peter denying Jesus at the cross, if tradition is correct about the manner of his death, then Peter finally, fully got what it means to be a disciple: He denied himself, took up his cross, and followed Jesus right up to his own crucifixion in Rome around 64 CE.

---

58. BDAG, s.v. "μαθητής."

We are only left to imagine the impact Peter's witness might have had on Mark's Roman audience when they received the gospel just a few years later during their own season of suffering. Quite a lot, I suspect. But we don't need to imagine the impact his life and legacy left beyond the pages of Scripture. This essay, this book, two thousand years of church history, and two billion present-day Christians, all result, at least in part, from Peter's own development and decision to carry the cross when given a second chance. As successors of the ministry that was first passed along to Peter, we too have a chance to get discipleship right. Jesus is going ahead. May we take up our cross and follow.

Bibliography

Bates, Matthew W. *Salvation by Allegiance Alone*. Grand Rapids: Baker Academic, 2017.

Bonhoeffer, Dietrich. *Dietrich Bonhoeffer Works*. Vol. 4: *Discipleship*. Edited by Geffrey B. Kelly and John D. Godsey. Translated by Barbara Green and Reinhard Krauss. Minneapolis: Fortress, 2001.

Carson, D. A. "Matthew." In *The Expositor's Bible Commentary: Matthew, Mark, Luke*, edited by Frank E. Gaebelein, 8:1–599. Grand Rapids: Zondervan, 1984.

Evans, Craig A. *Mark 8:27—16:20*. Word Biblical Commentary 34B. Nashville: Nelson, 2001.

———. "Messianism." In *DNTB*, 698–707.

Fiensy, David A. "Crucifixion." In *LBD*, s.v.

France, R. T. *The Gospel of Mark*. Grand Rapids: Eerdmans, 2002.

Garland, David E. *Mark*. The NIV Application Commentary. Grand Rapids: Zondervan, 1996.

Goldingay, John. *Isaiah*. Edited by W. Ward Gasque, Jr., et al. Understanding the Bible Commentary Series. Grand Rapids: Baker, 2001.

———. "Servant of Yahweh." In *DOTP*, 700–707.

Gombis, Timothy G. *Mark*. Edited by Tremper Longman and Scot McKnight. Story of God Bible Commentary. Grand Rapids: Zondervan Academic, 2021.

Josephus. *The Works of Josephus: Complete and Unabridged*. Translated by William Whiston. New updated ed. Peabody, MA: Hendrickson, 1987.

Kingsbury, Jack Dean. *Matthew: Structure, Christology, Kingdom*. Philadelphia: Fortress, 1975.

The Lexham English Septuagint. Edited by Ken Penner. 2nd ed. Bellingham, WA: Lexham, 2019.

Luz, Ulrich. *Matthew 8–20: A Commentary on Matthew 8–20*. Translated by James E. Crouch. Hermeneia. Minneapolis: Fortress, 1989.

Mackie, Tim, and Jon Collins. "'Christ' Is Not a Name." *The Anointed* (Podcast). Mar. 13, 2023. https://bibleproject.com/podcast/christ-not-name/.

Ma'oz, Zvi Uri. "Banias." In *New Encyclopedia of Archaelogical Excavations in the Holy Land*, edited by Ephraim Stern, 1:136–43. Jerusalem: Israel Exploration Society, 2008.

Oswalt, John. "מָשַׁח." In *NIDOTTE* 2:1123–27.

Perrin, Nicholas. "Mark, Gospel of." In *DJG2*, 553–66.
Phillips, Elaine A. "Peter's Declaration at Caesarea Philippi." In *Lexham Geographic Commentary on the Gospels*, edited by Barry J. Beitzel and Kristopher A. Lyle, 286–97. Bellingham, WA: Lexham, 2016.
Strauss, Mark. "Messiah." In *LBD*, s.v.
Watts, Rikk E. "Mark." In *Commentary on the New Testament Use of the Old Testament*, edited by G. K. Beale and D. A. Carson, 111–251. Grand Rapids: Baker Academic, 2007.
Wright, N. T. *Jesus and the Victory of God*. Minneapolis: Fortress, 1996.
Wright, N. T., and Michael F. Bird. *The New Testament in Its World: An Introduction to the History, Literature, and Theology of the First Christians*. Grand Rapids: Zondervan Academic, 2019.

7

Death-Defying Hope

The Transfiguration from Peter's Perspective

Elijah Van Hoecke

Introduction: Viewing the Transfiguration
from Peter's Perspective

If you were to ask Peter to identify the most significant moment from his time with Jesus, what would his answer be? The great catch(es) of fish? The healing of his mother-in-law? The Last Supper? The resurrection appearances? A case could be made for any one of these important events. However, in the letter of 2 Peter—when Peter is close to death and intent on reassuring his readers of his apostolic authority—it is to none of these experiences that Peter points. Instead, he reminds his fellow Christians that he was one of the privileged few who experienced the glorification of Jesus "when [they] were with him on the sacred mountain."[1] This experience—what we often call "the transfiguration"—impacted Peter to the extent that he was still thinking about it at the very end of his life.[2]

---

1. 2 Pet 1:18. All Scripture quotations throughout this chapter are taken from the NIV.

2. Even if one holds to pseudonymous authorship of this letter, it remains significant that one of Peter's disciples would point to the transfiguration as the defining marker of Peter's authority and apostleship.

Many scholars and theologians have undertaken the task of analyzing the transfiguration from exegetical and theological perspectives.[3] It is a fascinating story which houses a whole host of deep Christological truths. Christ's glorious nature is revealed not just to the three disciples who accompany Jesus up the mountain, but also to the generations of believers who have read or heard the story since that day. The transfiguration presents a "gospel in microcosm," pointing both backwards (to the prophets of old) and forward (to the resurrection).[4] However, the present chapter—in keeping step with the broader project of this book—will be focused on the transfiguration experience from the perspective of Peter. As we will see, the Synoptic accounts carefully present this story in a manner which invites us to consider the perspective of Peter and his companions. The transfiguration as an event centers on Jesus, but its impact is felt most keenly by his disciples. In fact, one could argue that the most significant "metamorphosis" which occurred on the mountain was the change inside of Peter's heart—where Christ confronted his despair with death-defying hope.[5] However, in order to fully appreciate the hope which was presented to Peter at the transfiguration, we must first understand why his experience of the previous week would have caused him to feel so disillusioned.

The Context of Peter's Experience: Confusion and Doubt

Peter's discipleship journey was filled with ups and downs (one could say he hit some *rocky* patches). He was the only disciple to walk on the water with Jesus, but it didn't take long for him to begin sinking under the waves. Peter pulled a sword on one of the guards sent to arrest Jesus, but then repeatedly denied knowing him. Fast forward fifty days, however, and Peter is boldly preaching the message of Jesus in the streets of Jerusalem! The most dramatic of these high-to-low experiences occurred just a week before the transfiguration.

---

3. The transfiguration has loomed much larger in the theological tradition of the Eastern church than it has in the West. For an Eastern perspective, see Andreopoulos, *This Is My Beloved Son*. For a Western perspective, see Schreiner, *Transfiguration of Christ*.

4. Trites, "Transfiguration of Jesus," 78.

5. Andreopoulos, *This Is My Beloved Son*, 90.

Peter Identifies the Messiah[6]

By the time Peter arrived in the region of Caesarea Philippi (Mark 8:27), he had seen Jesus do all kinds of amazing things—everything from healing blind men to feeding multitudes to walking on water. There was little doubt left in Peter's mind that Jesus was the Messiah, the anointed one who would bring God's salvation to Israel. Knowing this, Jesus created a perfect opportunity for Peter to declare his faith in front of his fellow disciples, for whom he often acted as the designated spokesman and representative.[7] When prompted, the disciples of Jesus had no problem explaining the theories of the crowds regarding Jesus' identity: "Some say John the Baptist; others say Elijah; and still others, one of the prophets" (Mark 8:28). It was Peter, however, who answered Jesus' next question—"Who do you say I am?"—with boldness and certainty: "You are the Messiah" (8:29). Although they are warned to keep this declaration to themselves (8:30), it is clear that Peter had captured in his statement at least part of the truth about Jesus' identity. However, it didn't take long for Peter's own ideas about messiahship to cause him to step way out of line.

Peter Rebukes the Messiah

Once his identity as the Messiah was firmly established in the minds of the disciples, Jesus began to describe the fate that awaited him in Jerusalem—suffering, rejection, death, and resurrection. Ostensibly, this was the first time that Jesus had "spoke[n] plainly about this," and it marks an important shift in the ministry and teaching of Jesus (Mark 8:32).[8] As usual, Peter felt the need to share his thoughts on the matter; he tactfully pulled Jesus aside and rebuked him for describing his messianic mission in such bleak terms. Jesus, however, responds with a startling rebuke of his own, and ensures that the other disciples hear it as well: "Get behind me Satan! You do not have in mind the concerns of God, but merely human concerns" (8:33). It is probably impossible for modern Westerners to fully appreciate the shame and embarrassment which would have overwhelmed Peter in such a moment. Any honor he may have been feeling from his bold confession would have dissolved in an instant.

6. For an in-depth discussion of these events in Mark 8, refer to the chapter by Brenden Lang, "Great Confession, Great Correction," 90–104 above.

7. Marcus, *Mark*, 633.

8. Evans, *Mark*, 35.

Like salt in a wound, Jesus' speech to the crowd in 8:34–38 would have pained Peter even more. Not only was Jesus going to suffer, but those who wished to follow him would suffer as well. What's more, when Jesus called out "anyone [who] is ashamed of me and my words," it is hard to imagine that Peter would not have felt singled out. Peter's categories for what the reign of the Messiah would be like were all being turned upside down. Jesus had resigned to give himself over to death, and he expected his followers to be willing to do the same. Peter spent the week leading up to the transfiguration listening to teachings which were "rife with affliction and death."[9] He had been rebuked in front of his friends and fellow disciples, and this would have likely shaken his confidence both in his rabbi and in himself. Suffice it to say, Peter's heart was in dire need of a fresh infusion of hope at this point of the journey, and Mark 9:1 provides a hint that such an experience was on the horizon.

The Kingdom Promise—A Glimmer of Hope

Virtually every biblical commentator points out that it is impossible to understand the prediction of Mark 9:1 (that "some who are standing here will not taste death before they see that the kingdom of God has come with power") without considering the transfiguration account which follows in 9:2–13.[10] It seems safe to assume, then, that the disciples would not have been sure what to make of Jesus' strange saying in the moment. However, it does function as a hint to the reader that Peter may not have fallen so far as to be unredeemable. Right in the midst of the "prophecies of Jesus' impending death," Jesus offers a glimmer of hope. Yes, the Messiah was going to die, but that didn't mean that the Kingdom of God could be stopped—and some of his foolish disciples were going to get to see proof of exactly that. Six days later, Peter found himself climbing a mountain with James, John, and Jesus.

Peter's Transfiguration Experience: Death-Defying Hope

Although it may seem strange to focus our study of the transfiguration on the perspective of the disciples, it should be pointed out that the text

---

9. Schreiner, *Transfiguration of Christ*, 9.

10. See, for example, Stein, *Mark*, 417. See also Knights, "Metamorphosis and Obedience," 219.

leads us to do exactly that. Strangely enough for a scene centered around the glory of Jesus, Jesus himself behaves rather passively.[11] Jesus does not participate in the dialogue of the scene. Instead, we are presented with two viewpoints: (1) that of the disciples, and (2) that of God the Father.[12] Rather than give us a description of the physical or metaphysical details of the actual transfiguration, the entire narrative focuses on what the disciples *saw* and *heard*. Most importantly, the voice from heaven is directed *at the disciples*, not Jesus.[13] The whole experience is designed for the benefit of these three disciples, especially Peter. Furthermore, the literary design of the passage encourages its readers/listeners to experience this divine moment alongside the three terrified apostles. At this point, I would encourage you to immerse yourself in Peter's experience by reading Mark 9:1–13 for yourself.

"Up a High Mountain"—Peter Enters Sinai

It is impossible to know what was going through Peter's mind as he climbed the "high mountain" with Jesus. The mere fact that Jesus has allowed Peter to join him on the hike (despite the "Satan" ordeal) probably helped to assure Peter that he still had a place in Jesus' inner circle. In any case, the Synoptic authors make it very clear that Peter is entering a holy space—a space almost identical to that of Sinai. Several clues point in this direction—the mountain setting (v. 2), the weeklong time interval (v. 2), the change in Jesus' appearance (vv. 2–3), the cloud (v. 7), and the voice of God (v. 7).[14] In case there is any doubt left in the reader's mind about the Sinaitic setting of this experience, Mark tells us that the two prophets who actually spoke to God on Sinai (Elijah and Moses) have appeared next to Jesus on the mountain! Mark could not have made this more obvious for us—Peter is about to have a Sinai experience where he will come face to face with the God of Israel.

---

11. To be clear, Jesus is the *theological* center of this passage. *He* is the "beloved son." What I argue here, however, is that the disciples are the *dramatic* center of the passage. The people and events in Mark 9:2–8 orbit around Jesus, but the camera (to use a cinematic analogy) foregrounds the reaction of the disciples.

12. Green, "Transfiguration," 970. Using Luke's narrative, Green distinguishes between the viewpoint of the disciples (9:32–33) and the viewpoint of God (9:34–35).

13. Stein, *Mark*, 416.

14. Hooker, "What Dost Thou Here," 60. See also Marcus, *Mark*, 631.

Although the ultimate effect of Peter's mountaintop experience will be hope and confidence, it should be noted that in the moment he was absolutely terrified (v. 6), just like the Israelites at Mt. Sinai.[15] Peter had arrived in what Robert Gundry calls a "suburb of heaven,"[16] and it is in this divine space that Peter sees Jesus undergo a miraculous transformation—his itinerant rabbi from Nazareth was being glorified right before his very eyes! Mark tells us that Jesus' clothes became dazzling white (like the Ancient of Days in Dan 7), and Luke adds that the face of Jesus changed in appearance (Luke 9:29).[17]

This new vision of Jesus strikes terror into Peter's heart. Peter encounters the glory of YHWH—the God whom he had worshiped since childhood and the God whom his ancestors had worshiped for centuries—in the person of Jesus. If this story is indeed being framed as a Sinai experience, Jesus has been placed in the slot that YHWH would normally fill.[18] This is, of course, the central Christological claim of the passage—that Jesus shares in God's divine glory. He does not reflect glory (like the face of Moses); he himself possesses a glory which is normally hidden to the world but which Peter sees in a moment of spectacular revelation—even before the glory cloud appears.[19] This apocalyptic view of Jesus alone would have made a lasting impact on Peter's psyche. However, more actors enter the stage at this point.

Two More Prophets—A Sign That Death Does Not Win

Bible commentators have debated the significance of Elijah and Moses's presence on the mountain of transfiguration since the time of the early church fathers.[20] However, rather than rehash all of these views, we want to focus our discussion on a more specific question: what would the presence of Elijah and Moses communicate to Peter in light of his consternation caused by the death predictions of Jesus?

Peter had been distressed by Jesus' most recent teachings, which emphasized the role of suffering and death. To be fair, Jesus also predicted his

15. Cf. Exod 19:16; Heb 12:18–21.
16. Gundry, *Mark*, 457.
17. Evans, *Mark*, 36.
18. Friedeman, "Jesus' Divine Glory," 70.
19. Friedeman, "Jesus' Divine Glory," 69.
20. For a thorough discussion of the interpretive options, see Schreiner, *Transfiguration of Christ*, 78–88.

own resurrection, but Peter and the other disciples didn't seem to know what Jesus could mean by that—probably because it was so far outside of the scope of what their daily experience told them was possible.[21] Could anyone—even the Messiah—really escape death? *Enter Elijah and Moses.* These are two prophets of God who seem to have cheated death in one sense or another. According to Deut 34:7, Moses lived well beyond the average life expectancy—120 years in all! Of course, Moses is still reported to have died and there is no indication in the text that he was resurrected. However, the mysterious nature of his burial (by the hand of God and in an undisclosed location—cf. Deut 34:6) led many Jewish interpreters to speculate about whether Moses had really died after all.[22]

Elijah, on the other hand, is taken to the skies in a heavenly chariot and thereby escapes death altogether.[23] Whereas Moses's relationship with death is ambiguous, Elijah's is explicitly victorious.[24] The death-defying stories of these two prophets—coupled with the fact that they were in some sense alive enough to have a conversation with Jesus—are evidence that death does not have the final word over God's servants. Elijah and Moses would have been refreshing signs of resurrection hope in the midst of a gloomy week of death predictions. Maybe God could vindicate Jesus' death after all? Of course, for Peter all of these thoughts would have hit home much later, when he reflected on the experience. In the actual moment he was simply terrified!

"Let Us Put Up Three Shelters"—Peter's Blunder

We have all experienced a time in our lives when we were so flustered or shocked that we found ourselves speaking without thinking. This is exactly what Mark tells us happens to Peter when he finds himself standing face-to-face with two national heroes and a transfigured Jesus (9:6). However, the fact that Mark still includes Peter's offhand remark indicates that it plays into the significance of the transfiguration—and more specifically, Peter's personal experience of this divine moment.[25]

---

21. Kazmierski, *Jesus, the Son of God*, 116.
22. Marcus, *Mark*, 637.
23. Cf. 2 Kgs 2.
24. This could account for why Elijah is named before Moses in Mark's narrative (an unnatural order "corrected" by Matthew and Luke).
25. Derrett, "Peter and the Tabernacles," 16. Derrett argues that Peter's remark is crucial because it sits at the center of the transfiguration narrative, and the narrative

Peter begins with a true observation paired with an inadequate address: "Rabbi, it is good for us to be here" (9:5a). Mark has likely included Peter's use of the title "rabbi" to contrast it with the divine title God will use for Jesus in v. 7: "my Son."[26] This is a strike against Peter. However, his basic assertion that it is "good" for the disciples to experience this moment is undeniably correct, and it further buttresses the argument that this whole experience has been provided for the benefit of Peter and his companions. Peter then goes on to suggest that he, James, and John should build shelters (or tents) for Jesus and the other two prophets (9:5b). This seems to be the part of Peter's speech for which Mark feels compelled to make excuses, and scholars have debated why this seemingly innocuous offer of hospitality is problematic. We will look at the two most compelling arguments which have been made.

One explanation for why Peter's suggestion is misguided is that he still has not fully come to terms with who Jesus really is. In the previous chapter he declared Jesus to be the Messiah, but he seems to think that this puts Jesus on the same level as Moses and Elijah, rather than above them.[27] Peter offers to build each of them a tent (perhaps to function as "Tents of Meeting"), and therefore has not comprehended that Jesus is playing the part of YHWH—rather than a prophet—in this Sinaitic scene.[28] The other problem with Peter's suggestion is that it assumes this moment of glory can be prolonged indefinitely.[29] Peter would prefer to set up camp in this heavenly space rather than return back down the mountain, where death and demons await. However, Jesus has already made it clear that he is headed to Jerusalem to face rejection and death (8:31). Suggesting an extended stay on the holy mountain is another way for Peter to attempt to put off (or even avoid) this gloomy outcome. It is no surprise, then, that when the glory cloud appears, the voice of God offers an indirect rebuke of Peter's suggestion.[30]

---

itself sits at the center of Mark's Gospel.

26. Stein, *Mark*, 417–18.
27. Schreiner, *Transfiguration of Christ*, 100–101.
28. Friedeman, "Jesus' Divine Glory," 70.
29. Carlston, "Transfiguration and Resurrection," 239. See also Evans, *Mark*, 37.
30. Stein, *Mark*, 418. See also Trites, "Transfiguration of Jesus," 76.

"This Is My Son"—Jesus' Identity and Authority Confirmed

None of the figures on the mountain have time to respond to Peter's blundering suggestion before the glory cloud makes its appearance. However, both of Peter's misguided assumptions (that Jesus is on the same level as the other prophets and that the death of Jesus can be avoided) are addressed by the voice of God coming from the cloud: "This is my Son, whom I love. Listen to him!" (9:7). Keen readers of Mark's Gospel will recognize this sonship language from the story of Jesus' baptism. However, there is an important grammatical difference: whereas the baptism declaration was addressed *to Jesus* ("you are . . ."), the transfiguration declaration is addressed *to the disciples* ("this is . . .").[31] Again, we see that this moment is primarily directed toward the disciples, not Jesus.

Any confusion about Jesus' status is immediately dispelled by the Father's clear statement. Jesus is not just a prophet—like Elijah or Moses—he is the Son of God. Jesus has not come up the mountain to pay homage to these ancient heroes; rather, Elijah and Moses have appeared to pay homage to Jesus![32] Jesus is superior to all other mediators of YHWH's presence, for he himself embodies the glory and presence of God.[33] This is accentuated by the disappearance of Elijah and Moses in the very next verse. By revealing the identity of Jesus to Peter, God has affirmed the confession that Peter made in 8:29 (that Jesus is the Messiah), but he has also gone far beyond that: Jesus is God's own Son.[34] The phrase "whom I love" (or "beloved" in the NASB) is a callback to Gen 22:2, where God told Abraham to sacrifice the "son whom you love." The implication is that God himself endorses Jesus' march toward death. Jesus' path of suffering does not compromise his divine sonship, nor does his sonship prevent him from suffering. This reference to Abraham and Isaac also offers hope to Peter in the midst of his own doubts—just as Isaac was vindicated through obedience, so too would Jesus be vindicated.

---

31. Evans, *Mark*, 38. The same grammatical shift is preserved in Luke's Gospel, but Matthew synchronizes the two statements, putting them both in the third person.

32. Hall, "Synoptic Transfigurations," 44.

33. Marcus, *Mark*, 640. See also Schreiner, *Transfiguration of Christ*, 101.

34. One could argue that this sonship language is simply another way of describing Jesus' messianic status, since David was also referred to as God's son (e.g., Ps 2). However, the narrative context of this declaration—where Jesus is embodying the Sinaitic glory of YHWH—indicates that the divine sonship of Jesus is something altogether more significant than that of David. Jesus' sonship is not just relational; it is also ontological.

"Listen to Him!"—A Hope-Inspiring Rebuke

The second half of the Father's speech is a simple command: "listen to him!" The voice is instructing these disciples to listen to the voice of Jesus, his beloved Son. It also represents an indirect rebuke of Peter's foolish decision in the previous chapter to chastise Jesus for talking about his impending death (cf. 8:32). Peter's role is not to instruct Jesus, but to *be instructed* by him. Even though there has been a shift in Jesus' teaching over the previous week—toward the subjects of death, suffering, and cruciform discipleship—Peter is still required to heed his words.[35] If not, he will be unprepared for the suffering which awaits him.[36]

It may be hard at first glance to see how this rebuke could be a source of hopefulness. However, one must remember who is speaking: YHWH, the very source of life. If God is affirming Jesus' death prediction, he is also affirming his resurrection prediction. Any doubt that Jesus would be vindicated by God the Father is extinguished by this forceful command. The death of Jesus "is by no means a tragedy or mistake, or a withdrawal of God's favor."[37] Furthermore, the phrase "listen to him" hearkens back to the prediction in Deut 18:15–19 which states that a prophet like Moses will be raised up and the Israelites "must listen to him."[38] This further endorses the teachings of Jesus, since this prophet is said to speak with the words of YHWH (18:17), and anyone who does not listen to him will be "call[ed] to account" (18:19). No wiggle room is left for Peter in his response to Jesus. Peter can rest assured that all of Jesus' words are coming straight from YHWH—the words of death and the words of life. If he can bring himself to walk through the valley of the shadow of death with Jesus, he will find the life, glory, and vindication of God on the other side.

Was Peter's Transfiguration Experience Effective?

We have examined the role that the transfiguration was designed to play in Peter's discipleship experience. After a difficult week of gloom and dread, the transfiguration was meant to bolster Peter's inner hope—to assure him that this Messiah he claimed to follow was truly the Son of God

---

35. Evans, *Mark*, 38.
36. Edwards, *Gospel According to Mark*, 268.
37. Stein, *Mark*, 420.
38. Marcus, *Mark*, 634.

and would be vindicated on the other side of death. Jesus felt it necessary to inspire Peter and his companions with a vision of his eternal glory, that they might face the dark road ahead.[39] It was a sign that Peter would not be allowed to "return to the happiness of his discipleship before the Passion was announced" nor would he be allowed to set up an eternal camp on the heavenly mountain.[40] Peter was being called to come to terms with all of Jesus' mission—his eternal sonship, his difficult teachings, his brutal death, and his glorious resurrection. However, the passage leaves us wondering about whether the transfiguration was actually effective. Did any of this hope and assurance sink into Peter's soul?

Evidence That Peter's Confusion and Doubt Still Lingered

If Peter was transformed by the transfiguration experience, it is safe to say that it was not instantaneous.[41] Even after Peter's mountaintop experience, he still—along with the other disciples—fails to grasp the significance of Jesus' death and resurrection (Mark 9:10, 32). Rather than ask Jesus about the meaning of his resurrection, the disciples use their hike down the mountain to ask Jesus about the role of Elijah. It's as if they had already forgotten what the voice in the cloud made very clear: *pay attention to Jesus, not the prophets of old who have disappeared before your very eyes!*

Later, in the garden of Gethsemane, Peter chooses to draw blood in an attempt to save Jesus from death, despite knowing that Jesus had long preached about its inevitability (Mark 14:47; cf. John 18:10). Although he claimed to be ready to die alongside Jesus (Mark 14:31), Peter denies knowing him three times after the arrest (14:66–72). That being said, all of us who are on the path of discipleship with Jesus realize that transformation is a *process*, and there is good evidence to suggest that Peter's experience on the mountain planted seeds of change that slowly (but surely) reformed his imagination over time to see hope in the death and resurrection of Jesus.

---

39. Andreopoulos, *This Is My Beloved Son*, 86. See also Schreiner, *Transfiguration of Christ*, 10.
40. Ramsey, *Glory of God*, 146.
41. Schreiner, *Transfiguration of Christ*, 10–11.

Evidence That the Hope of the Transfiguration Took Root

Although Peter continued to stumble and blunder his way to Resurrection Sunday, a careful reading shows signs of increased awareness and acceptance of Jesus' fate. Despite his lack of comprehension discussed above, Peter never again rebukes Jesus for talking about death. In fact, Peter never rebukes Jesus about anything ever again. This alone is evidence that Peter learned something on the mountain (i.e., "listen to him!"). Furthermore, although Peter's claim to be willing to die alongside Jesus turns out to be false, the statement itself implies that he has accepted the fate of Jesus. His swordplay in the garden ought to therefore be seen as the impulsive reaction of a loyal friend taken by surprise, rather than a seriously thought out response to the crisis at hand. Because Mark's Gospel ends so abruptly, we must rely on Luke to see the full extent of Peter's transformation.

We don't get a lot of details about the internal reaction of Peter to the resurrection. We do know, however, that as soon as he heard the report of the women, he ran to the tomb to see for himself (Luke 24:12a). Such a response is evidence that he thought God had done something miraculous. If Peter was sure about the permanency of Jesus' death, he would not have bolted to see the empty tomb.[42] Peter left the tomb "wondering to himself what had happened" (24:12b). However, it is very possible (and one might argue common) for someone to believe that a wonderful miracle has taken place without being exactly sure of all the details.[43] This interpretation of Peter's reaction is supported by the words of the beloved disciple, who writes that he also ran to the tomb, where he "saw and believed," but still "did not understand from Scripture that Jesus had to rise from the dead" (John 20:8–9). Just like the beloved disciple, the empty tomb caused Peter to experience a mixture of belief and bewilderment. This is a sign that Peter's imagination (and the beloved disciple's imagination) had been prepared for this moment.

Certainly by the time he stood up to preach to the Pentecost crowds gathered in Jerusalem (Acts 2), Peter's belief in the resurrection of Jesus had been solidified. This may seem at first like a weak piece of evidence for the effectiveness of the transfiguration—didn't all of the disciples

---

42. The rest of the disciples serve as an example of those who "did not believe the women" and therefore do not run to the tomb like Peter (Luke 24:11).

43. For more on Peter's experience with miracles, see James North, "I Believe in Miracles?," 192–205 below.

believe in Jesus' resurrection by that point? Well, maybe not. Matthew tells us that some of the apostles were still doubting by the time Jesus ascended into heaven![44] The boldness and eloquence with which Peter preaches the gospel of Jesus Christ to his fellow Jews shows not only that he was empowered by the Holy Spirit, but also that he had been thinking deeply about the resurrection for some time. It is obvious that his faith in Jesus' power over death already had deep roots by the time the Spirit descended, and this may be because he (along with James and John) had been prepared more than others for the in-breaking of God's kingdom. The glory of the resurrection and the glory of the Holy Spirit's arrival had already been previewed by Peter in the face of Jesus when they stood on the heavenly mountain together.

2 Peter 1:12–19—The Lasting Impact of the Transfiguration

The confidence with which Peter put his hope in the glory and the resurrection of Jesus never wore off, and it seems like the transfiguration had a significant part to play in this enduring faith. Second Peter 1:12–19 provides the most conclusive evidence that this is true.[45] Take a moment to read the passage for yourself.

By the end of his life, Peter was still reflecting on his mountaintop experience and sharing it with other disciples to assure them that his gospel was trustworthy: "We were eyewitness of his majesty. . . . We ourselves heard this voice that came from heaven when we were with him on the sacred mountain" (1:16, 18).[46] Out of all of the events to which Peter could have pointed to bolster his message—including the resurrection appearances—he chose to mention the transfiguration. This is as surprising as it is revealing. The transfiguration played a much larger role in Peter's discipleship journey than it tends to play in our own (at least for those of us in the Western tradition). Peter was convinced that he would soon be "putting aside" the "tent of [his] body" (i.e., dying), and he felt it important to "refresh [the] memory" of his disciples concerning the transfiguration so that they "will always remember these things" (1:13, 15).[47] Peter be-

---

44. Cf. Matt 28:16–17.
45. For questions about the authorship of this letter, see n2 above.
46. Beck, "Transfiguration," 686.
47. Interestingly, Peter refers to his death as a "departure" (or exodus), the same word used by Luke to describe the conversation between Moses, Elijah, and Jesus at the transfiguration: "They spoke about his *departure*, which he was about to bring to

lieved that the transfiguration story provided a stamp of approval for his message, proving that it was "completely reliable," unlike the "fabricated stories" of false teachers.[48] The transfiguration experience had grounded Peter's faith in Jesus Christ and had planted within him a death-defying hope; he assumed it could do the same for others.[49]

Conclusion: Adopting Peter's Transfiguration Experience

The transfiguration of Jesus left an indelible mark on Peter's soul. God provided this experience for Peter at just the right time, when he was wrestling through doubt and confusion. This heavenly moment—both intimate and glorious—reassured Peter of his place by Jesus' side and also gave him hope that death would not be the end. The God of Israel had power over death (as evidenced by the arrival of the two prophets) and Jesus, as God's beloved Son, would be vindicated on the other side of an unjust death. Furthermore, Peter was commanded to listen to and obey the Son, which would eventually mean picking up his own cross and trusting that God would vindicate him as well.[50]

This transformative power of the transfiguration is not limited to those who experienced it firsthand. Mark, Matthew, and Luke all chose to include this narrative in their Gospel accounts, and Peter described it in his final letter. This textual evidence suggests that the first generation of apostles believed that each subsequent generation needed to ponder the transfiguration of Jesus for themselves—to experience it alongside Peter, James, and John. We too climb the heavenly mountain, we too worship Jesus as the beloved Son, and we too experience the divine glory—glory which transforms both us and our surroundings.[51] Like Peter, we receive a firm command to listen to and obey Jesus, even when he leads us into dark places. However, we are also given assurance that death does not have the last word—the power of God will ultimately

---

fulfillment at Jerusalem" (Luke 9:31, emphasis added). For a deeper study of this linguistic link, see Trites, "Transfiguration of Jesus," 75.

48. 2 Pet 1:19, 2:3.

49. Andreopoulos, *This Is My Beloved Son*, 7.

50. For more on the martyrdom of Peter see J. Leland Stephens, "Peter's Shift in Christology," 241–57 below.

51. For personal transformation, see Hooker, "What Dost Thou Here," 60; Andreopoulos, *This Is My Beloved Son*, 21. For the transformation of creation see Beck, "Transfiguration," 686; Ramsey, *Glory of God*, 147.

give victory to all of his suffering servants. May this give us the courage to return back down the mountain and engage a world filled with death on behalf of the God of life.

Bibliography

Andreopoulos, Andreas. *This Is My Beloved Son: The Transfiguration of Christ*. Brewster, MA: Paraclete, 2012.

Beck, D. M. "The Transfiguration." In *The Interpreter's Dictionary of the Bible*, edited by George Arthur Buttrick, 4:686–87. New York: Abingdon, 1962.

Carlston, Charles Edwin. "Transfiguration and Resurrection." *Journal of Biblical Literature* 80 (1961) 233–40.

Derrett, J. Duncan M. "Peter and the Tabernacles." In *Studies in the New Testament*. Vol. 6: *Jesus Among Biblical Exegetes*, 16–27. New York: Brill, 1995.

Edwards, James R. *The Gospel According to Mark*. The Pillar New Testament Commentary. Grand Rapids: Eerdmans, 2001.

Evans, Craig A. *Mark 8:27—16:20*. Rev. ed. Word Biblical Commentary 34B. Grand Rapids: Zondervan Academic, 2015.

Friedeman, Caleb T. "Moses, Elijah, and Jesus' Divine Glory (Mark 9.2–8)." *New Testament Studies* 70 (2024) 61–71.

Green, Joel B. "Transfiguration." In *Dictionary of Jesus and the Gospels*, edited by Joel B. Green et al., 966–72. 2nd ed. Downers Grove, IL: IVP Academic, 2013.

Gundry, Robert H. *Mark: A Commentary on His Apology for the Cross*. Grand Rapids: Eerdmans, 1993.

Hall, Stuart. "Synoptic Transfigurations: Mark 9, 2–10 and Partners." *King's Theological Review* 10.2 (1987) 41–44.

Hooker, Morna. "'What Dost Thou Here, Elijah?' A Look at St. Mark's Account of the Transfiguration." In *The Glory of Christ in the New Testament: Studies in Christology*, edited by L. D. Hurst and N. T. Wright, 59–70. Oxford: Clarendon, 1987.

Kazmierski, Carl R. *Jesus, the Son of God: A Study of the Markan Tradition and Its Redaction by the Evangelist*. Forschung zur Bibel 33. Würzburg: Echter, 1979.

Knights, Chris. "Metamorphosis and Obedience: An Interpretation of Mark's Account of the Transfiguration of Jesus." *Expository Times* 121 (2010) 218–22.

Marcus, Joel. *Mark 8–16*. Anchor Yale Bible 27A. New Haven: Yale University Press, 2009.

Martin, Thomas W. "What Makes Glory Glorious? Reading Luke's Account of the Transfiguration Over Against Triumphalism." *Journal for the Study of the New Testament* 29 (2006) 3–26.

Ramsey, Michael. *The Glory of God and the Transfiguration of Christ*. New York: Longmans, Green, 1949.

Schreiner, Patrick. *Transfiguration of Christ: An Exegetical and Theological Reading*. Grand Rapids: Baker Academic, 2024.

Stein, Robert H. *Mark*. Baker Exegetical Commentary on the New Testament. Grand Rapids: Baker Academic, 2008.

Trites, Allison A. "The Transfiguration of Jesus: The Gospel in Microcosm." *Evangelical Quarterly* 51 (1979) 67–79.

8

Peter the Pentecostal Pastor
Woulda-Coulda-Shoulda-Boughta-Honda

BRENTON S. FESSLER

> The book of Acts is the best source that we have to demonstrate what normal church life is supposed to look like when the Holy Spirit is present and working in the church. Here we find a church that has passion for God, is willing to sacrifice—even to the point of martyrdom—and is a miracle-working church. Why would we think that God wants the church to be something different today? Would anyone seriously rather have the church in Calvin's day or the church in twentieth-century America as the model of normal church life?
>
> —Jack Deere, *Surprised by the Power of the Spirit*[1]

Introduction

HOW OFTEN DO YOU think about the Roman Empire? Much has been made about this question, no doubt helped along by a viral TikTok trend and various memes.[2] Regardless of your gender, or answer to this question, I would like you to imagine you found yourself in Rome.

Your taxi driver drops you at the Colosseum, and you're overwhelmed. All of the photos you have seen up until this point don't do it

1. Deere, *Surprised by the Power*, 114.
2. Dickson, "Obsessed with the Roman Empire."

justice, and for a quick second you imagine yourself as Maximus—Russell Crowe's character from the movie *Gladiator*—squaring up against the emperor. As you make your way around the arena, you even allow your imagination to hear the cries from first-century crowds for more bloodshed—perhaps even from early Christians.

Leaving the Colosseum, you meander through the Titus Arch and grab a gelato to stave off the sweltering summer heat. As you continue walking slightly northwest, you can see the Palatine Hill to your left, where the wealthy elite of imperial Rome used to show off their palatial houses. A few more steps bring you to the Roman Forum, which served as the hub of daily life in ancient Rome. You feel the need to pinch yourself—the buildings and structures are like a visual candy shop, tantalizing your historical imagination to no end.

But if you walk too fast you will miss a hidden gem along the way. Just off the beaten path, a stone's throw from the Forum, you come to a building with large letters above the entrance: *PRIGIONE DEI SS APOSTOLI PIETRO E PAOLO. MAMERTINUM.* A quick glance at the maps app on your phone will help decipher this is the *Mamertine Prison*. Dig a little deeper and you'll read how this is the reported prison where both the apostle Peter and apostle Paul were held (at different times) while under arrest in Rome.

Figure 1. Mamertine Prison, photo by David Vazquez

The reliability of those facts might be suspect, and you're smart enough to realize that somewhere along the way over the last two millennia the details have become stuff of legend. Not to mention some good marketing strategy for tourism. We'll probably never know how things actually happened or ended up for those two pillars of the early Christian church—did Paul ever make it to Spain? And was Peter really crucified upside down, as *tradition* likes to tell us? Even still, their stories and influence cannot be ignored—both then, and now.

Leaving Paul alone for the time being, I can't help but wonder about Peter in prison. In my mind I see him as an old man in this city, weathered by the years and hunched over by time. He might be in chains, or at least confined to a room he cannot escape. *But that doesn't mean he has to stay there.* Because if Peter just closes his eyes for a minute, he is instantly transported back to another time and place—where he can feel the breeze on his face, hear the birds chirping in the air, smell the saltiness of the sea, and almost taste the fresh catch of the day.

In Rome, Peter is as far away from the fishing village of Galilee as you can get.

In Rome, Caesar is in charge of the empire, yet Peter knows a different story.

In Rome, Peter may meet his end, but he will hold the ground.

Unlike his moment of capitulation and denial in Pilate's courtyard just before Jesus' crucifixion, I imagine this time—at the end of his life—Peter will be strengthened by his own experiences since meeting Jesus the Nazarene. He might even harken back to his ancestors and draw strength from the stories of Shadrach, Meshach, and Abednego—who, when faced with another king's fury, exclaimed: *"O King . . . we do not need to defend ourselves . . . the God we serve is able to deliver us . . . and even if he does not, we want you to know, Your Majesty, that we will not serve your gods or worship the image of gold you have set up."*[3]

Our creative imagination is sparked while walking around Rome and at the steps of the entrance to the Mamertine Prison. Yet all of us are left to ponder this question: How did Simon the fisherman become the apostle Peter and find the strength to remain committed to King Jesus? The only answer that seems fitting from the text: the Holy Spirit's empowering presence.[4]

My Pentecostal Journey

I am a fourth-generation Pentecostal pastor, having followed my (maternal) great-grandfather, grandfather, and father into ministry as a card-carrying, ordained minister within the Assemblies of God (AG). Let's be honest: Pentecostals are "still the kids on the other side of the tracks with our Evangelical brothers and sisters"[5] and might even be the

---

3. Dan 3:16–18. Unless otherwise noted, all Scriptures used are taken from NIV.

4. A gentle nod to Gordon Fee's widely influential book of the same name.

5. A Pentecostal friend who teaches at an Evangelical university recently shared this story: "Some days I am so reminded that we as Pentecostals are still the kids on the

laughingstock of Christian denominations. It's true. Pastors and scholars from other traditions don't understand us all that well, and we're often the punchline of more than a few jokes. But it doesn't help to play the victim or exclaim, "Woe is me!" Sometimes we are quite good at inflicting the harm and shame on ourselves in our actions or communication: insert here the many stories of Pentecostal snake handlers, "holy rollers," and Jericho marches in the church fellowship hall.

My experience is somewhat unique. While my great-grandfather and grandfather pastored small AG churches in rural communities of Arkansas, Texas, Alabama, Missouri, Mississippi, and Virginia, my dad felt a call to ministry in the military and served as a Navy chaplain for more than two decades. That adventure took us to military bases all over the world, including Scotland and Japan. These were my formative years, where "church" never looked like the *wild* version of a Pentecostal community that you hear about. The setting of military chapels is rather ecumenical—and so I grew up going to church with Methodists, Baptists, Lutherans, Pentecostals, Presbyterians, Episcopalians, and Anglicans. I'm grateful for the rich depth this afforded me as a child, and it continues to pay wonderful dividends into my life as a pastor.

All that to say, I have still been able to experience some of the *crazy* aspects of Pentecostalism firsthand. In junior high I attended my first youth summer camp, tagging along with the local AG church in the neighboring city of the Marine Corps base. It was at that camp where I first learned that "Holy Spirit Night" was on Thursday nights. In subsequent camps and weekend retreats over the years, the equation held true: On the second-to-last night, you were encouraged (nay, expected?) to have an encounter and experience with the Holy Spirit, which was verified by speaking in tongues. Side note: I was definitely glad to be a teenager in the '90s, because other ministers have since told me how, during the 1970s and 1980s, camp leadership would even "lock the doors" of the sanctuary or meeting hall to prevent any from leaving until everyone had spoken in tongues.

Recovering Pentecostal friends of mine often tell stories like this, of how they were *shamed* or *guilted* into speaking in tongues during

---

other side of the tracks with our Evangelical brothers and sisters. I am on the search committee for a director of an academic center on the Holy Spirit [at the university]. I am the *only* female, and the *only* Pentecostal on the committee. Some of their questions amuse me and others make me so angry. They can be so fearful of the work of the Spirit that they demean our language and our perspective."

adolescence. Some even chose to adopt a *fake version* of this heavenly language, using "*Shoulda-Woulda-Coulda-Boughta-Honda*" or something similar in repetitive fashion, with eyes closed and hands raised to pass the test with their youth leaders or pastors. I cringe each time I hear those kinds of stories. But if I'm being honest, they also help shape and inform my own pastoral leadership as I shepherd a community of people on a journey of discovering and experiencing all three members of the Trinity—Father, Son, and Holy Spirit—in pure and genuine ways.

I would like to contend that our praxis as Pentecostals must be rooted in good and faithful Biblical theology. And for that, we need to rediscover the stories from Scripture, specifically in the life of the apostle Peter, who is the first disciple to preach publicly following the great outpouring of the Holy Spirit on the day of Pentecost as detailed in Acts. This chapter seeks to contribute to the ongoing reassessment and appreciation of Simon Peter's Pentecostal empowerment which led to the birth and expansion of the early Christian church—on the highways and byways, in the nooks and crannies, fishing villages, ports of trade, and all throughout backwater towns of the Roman Empire, of which we still feel the effect today.

Peter as Pentecostal Guide

A study on the apostle Peter offers many valuable insights for pastors and ministry leaders, primarily due to his transformation from a simple fisherman to a foundational leader in the early Christian church. Simon's journey embodies themes of redemption, leadership development, and pastoral care, which are crucial for effective ministry today. Furthermore, Peter's Pentecostal experiences and his subsequent actions as a Spirit-filled leader provide a powerful model for all Christian leaders.

Pentecostal preachers and pastors have historically focused on themes of revival, spiritual renewal, and the active role of the Holy Spirit in the believer's life. Acts 2 is a crucial and bedrock text for Pentecostals, especially since Peter's sermon marks the first significant Christian preaching after the coming of the Holy Spirit at Pentecost. Peter's transformation from a hesitant disciple to a powerful proclaimer of the gospel is often highlighted as an example of how the Holy Spirit can empower believers to help expand God's kingdom. And Peter's surprising *chutzpah* after Pentecost offers the perfect archetype and guide for a normative understanding of the Holy Spirit, especially when we contrast this with some of Peter's previous failures and fearfulness—walking *and* sinking in the water (Matt 14:22–33), being called Satan (Matt 16:23), and the denial of Christ (Luke 22:54–62).

But First, Simon

While Shakespeare reminds us rather poetically how "a rose by any other name would smell as sweet,"[6] there is still something quite powerful about names, especially ancient ones. I'm captivated by the litany of name-change moments in Scripture, because they often speak of something so powerful going on in the life of the person at hand: Abram to Abraham (Gen 17:1–5); Sarai to Sarah (Gen 17:15); Jacob to Israel (Gen 32:28); Hoshea to Joshua (Num 13:16); Solomon to Jedediah (2 Sam 12:24–25); Naomi to Mara (Ruth 1:20); and Saul to Paul (Acts 13:9). When it comes to Simon, Craig Keener aptly points out that this was "perhaps the most popular masculine name of the period."[7] It was such a common name that we see it show up nine times in the New Testament.[8] The frequency of the name Simon required a distinguishing name to accompany it (such as "Peter"). Hengel agrees: the use of nicknames is common, and since "Simon was the most commonly used personal name during the century before and after the turn of the era, it would make sense that a nickname"[9] be used, especially since there was a second Simon among the circle of the twelve disciples.

Keener suggests "nicknames normally signified something about the person."[10] But up until this point, Simon has not been anything special. Yet, despite his countless missteps or failures, Jesus sees something within Simon—his *Pentecostal potential*, no doubt—and forecasts a new reality and role for Simon as Peter (*petros*). Some would contend that

---

6. Shakespeare, *Romeo and Juliet*, act 2, scene 2.

7. Keener, *Acts*, 1:742.

8. Simon Peter (the disciple of our focus), Simon the Zealot (another disciple), Simon the brother of Jesus (the other brothers were James, Joseph, and Judas), Simon the leper (the owner of the home where Jesus' head was anointed), Simon from Cyrene (who helped carry the cross), Simon the Pharisee (the owner of the home where Jesus' feet were washed), Simon Iscariot (father of Judas), Simon the sorcerer (who asked to buy Holy Spirit power), and Simon the tanner (who Peter stayed with in Joppa on the way to Cornelius).

9. Hengel, *Saint Peter*, 55.

10. Keener, *Acts*, 1:742.

at first Simon is a weak reed[11] in the wind, but after being empowered by the Holy Spirit on the day of Pentecost, he comes to embody his new name and identity: *Rocky*.[12]

Robbing Peter to Pay Paul

Peter is often resigned to a sermonic trope in our pulpits or Bible study groups. Because of this, theologian Gene Green uses the backdrop of *Peter Pan* to point out how the apostle Peter "is one of the 'lost boys' of Christian theology. Indeed, he could be regarded as their *captain*."[13] Why? Let's just say Protestants have felt alienated from Peter since the time of the Reformation. That's when the "Roman Catholic Church claimed him and the keys of the Kingdom. Peter was the one who had authority, and his successors continue to maintain it. On the other hand, Luther and all those who followed him and his Reformation compatriots ended up with Paul as their patron."[14] I know this has been true for me, as I know Paul better than Peter.

As I've heard it said, *Peter is for the Jews what Paul is for the gentiles*. And since I would theologically find myself more closely aligned with gentiles, I often choose to go down the road of Paul, rather than Peter. This is certainly the case in Protestant New Testament scholarship. For instance, Todd Still confesses that in his academic writing career, he has "robbed Peter to pay Paul."[15] As a Catholic friend once quipped, he finds it odd when Protestants balk at the idea of venerating Mary, because Protestants are *often guilty of venerating Paul*! Markus Bockmuehl further explains the dilemma: "the primary-source material at our disposal [for the study of Peter as a historical and historic figure] is woefully thin."[16] Bockmuehl even quotes Hengel when he says that Peter "has long been the *underestimated* disciple."[17]

And almost like a prosecuting lawyer attempting to discredit a witness or suspect, Bockmuehl lays out the incriminating evidence:

11. Pawson, *Simon Peter*.
12. Keener, *Acts*, 1:742.
13. Green, *Vox Petri*, 28.
14. Green, *Vox Petri*, 28.
15. Still, "Images of Peter," 161.
16. Bockmuehl, *Remembered Peter*, 3.
17. Bockmuehl, *Remembered Peter*, 7.

"Simon Peter is not self-evidently pivotal from the point of view of theology. He is not a major New Testament author or early Christian thinker, let alone a central subject of Christian faith or doctrine."[18] And in material or literary terms, "Peter himself left us next to nothing. Two short letters of uncertain date and origin are attributed to him in the New Testament. . . . The narrative traditions of Acts, too, offer rather more detail about Paul's travels than about those of Peter . . . in other words: *why bother with Peter at all?*"[19]

Even still, a thorough rebuttal is needed, and Bockmuehl rises to the occasion by switching seats to become the defense attorney. He contends that after Jesus, Peter "is the most frequently mentioned individual not only in the gospels, but in the New Testament as a whole."[20] A quick count will find Peter is mentioned 156 times and Cephas nine times, which outshines Paul's 158 times (though Luther and Pauline scholars might demand a recount!). We must see Peter for who he is and the role he carries for the early church—he is, after all, a "key figure for understanding the earliest Gentile mission and its ability to sustain a continuing relationship, however troubled, with the original Palestinian Jesus movement."[21] And even on more theological and ecclesiological lines, the *remembered* Peter "voices the disciples' faith in Jesus as the Messiah and becomes the church's first and leading witness to his words, his deeds and his resurrection. In other words, Peter speaks to Jesus of the church and to the church of Jesus."[22]

The Purpose of Pentecost

Back to the subject at hand, I am firmly convinced Peter's own pneumatology does not begin on the day of Pentecost, but rather extends from his developing Christology—having watched and known the ministry of Jesus firsthand. After all, as Gordon Fee has noted, the Spirit is "the power for Jesus' life and mission. Not only is Jesus conceived of the Holy Spirit (Luke 1:35), but his entire earthly ministry is lived out by the power of

---

18. Bockmuehl, *Remembered Peter*, 4. He goes on to say how "Romans, the Deutero-Pauline letters and most of the Apostolic Fathers and Apologists are strikingly silent about Peter."

19. Bockmuehl, *Remembered Peter*, 4–5.
20. Bockmuehl, *Remembered Peter*, 7.
21. Bockmuehl, *Remembered Peter*, 7.
22. Bockmuehl, *Remembered Peter*, 7.

the Spirit."²³ Pentecost reminds us of God's presence, that we need his power to go with us, like Moses's demand for God to go "with them" (Exod 33:15). Fellow Pentecostal scholar Robert Menzies even describes how the pneumatology from Peter's speech in Acts 2 "is missiological rather than soteriological in nature. The Spirit of Pentecost is, in reality, the Spirit for others—the Spirit that compels and empowers the church to bring the 'good news' of Jesus to a lost and dying world."²⁴

The ecclesiological challenge in understanding the point and purpose of Pentecost goes back to the old feud between Peter and Paul. Menzies lays out the issue in matter-of-fact terms: "The tendency in Protestant churches has been to read Luke in the light of Paul. Paul addresses pastoral concerns in the church; [but] *Luke writes a missionary manifesto*. Perhaps this explains why Protestant discussions of the Spirit have centered more on his work in the Word and sacraments, the 'inner witness' of the Spirit, and less on his mission to the world."²⁵ This should not surprise us, as God himself acts as a missionary when he *sends* his Son, and then *sends* his Holy Spirit. Amos Yong picks up on this point: "While there are human characters—human missionaries—galore in the Acts account (e.g., Stephen, Peter, Paul, and others), the central missionary is divine. The Spirit is sent out from heaven and sends out Jesus's disciples and followers to bear witness to the Father in the name of his Son."²⁶

Let us now turn to Acts 2:1–4, the primary text regarding the day of Pentecost. The scene is perhaps so familiar, especially for Pentecostals, that it has lost its impact for modern readers. The room where Jesus' followers were gathered almost seems chaotic, but let us quickly break the passage down, one element at a time.

Wind. This is a clear image for God, even going back to the early days of creation. In Hebrew it is the word *ruach*, meaning "wind," "breath,"

---

23. Fee, *Listening to the Spirit*, 175. He elaborates in his own footnote (on p. 207) on this issue: "The Holy Spirit descends on him at his baptism (3:21–22); he is led by the Spirit into the desert for the time of testing (4:1); he returns from the desert into Galilee in the power of the Spirit (4:14); and it was in the 'power of the Lord' that he healed the sick (5:17). . . . 'God anointed Jesus of Nazareth with the Holy Spirit and power, and he went around doing good and healing all who were under the power of the devil, because God was with him' (Acts 10:38)."

24. Menzies, "Spirit in Luke–Acts," 104.

25. Menzies, "Spirit in Luke–Acts," 105.

26. Yong, *Mission after Pentecost*, 13.

or "spirit." The corresponding Greek word is *pneuma*. Both *ruach* and *pneuma* are commonly used in passages referring to the Holy Spirit. The first occurrence of the word in the Bible is in the second verse: "The Spirit of God [*ruach elohim*] was hovering over the waters" (Gen 1:2).[27]

Fire. Like wind, fire is also a strong image for God in Scripture. For instance, fire is a symbol of God's presence when he is making a new covenant with Abram (Gen 15:17). And in one of the most significant stories from the Old Testament, the angel of the Lord "appeared to [Moses] in flames of fire from within a bush. Moses saw that though the bush was on fire it did not burn up" (Exod 3:2).[28] With such strong biblical backdrop from the Old Testament, it should not be surprising to us that Luke describes "tongues of fire that separated and came to rest on each of them" (Acts 2:3), as this speaks of God's presence.

Tongues. When Luke continues to describe the scene in Acts 2, he tells how all of the disciples "were filled with the Holy Spirit and began to speak in other tongues as the Spirit enabled them" (Acts 2:4). For the first time in Scripture, but certainly not the last, believers are seen and heard to be *speaking in tongues*. Beyond just a supernatural event, some scholars have long seen this moment as a reversal of Babel.[29] Yet the subject of speaking in tongues is often the dividing line for most, and questions abound (*Is it normative past the stories from Scripture? Is it required for being filled/baptized with the Spirit? Why tongues?*). We find ourselves in good company, for these questions even challenged early Pentecostal pioneers. In some ways, I would respond: *Why not tongues?* The tongue is the most *powerful* muscle in the human body for speaking good or evil. It makes perfect sense to allow God control of our tongues, for his glory.

---

27. *Ruach* appears nearly four hundred times in the Old Testament. For example: "breath of life" (Gen 6:17); the "wind" that God sent over the earth to cause the flood waters to recede (Gen 8:1).

28. When Moses led the people out of Egypt, Yahweh accompanied them "in a pillar of *fire*" (Exod 13:21). And "the *fire* of the Lord fell and burned up the sacrifice" (1 Kgs 18:38) even after Elijah poured water on the altar.

29. Dunn, *Jesus and the Spirit*, 150. See Keener, *Acts*, 1:842–44, for more on this debate.

Witness (Acts 1:8)

While it is good and well for us to discuss what happened in the room on the day of Pentecost, and to notice the very biblically based imagery, we should turn more of our focus on what happened outside and beyond the room. Jesus sets the tone: "You will receive power when the Holy Spirit comes on you; and you will be my witnesses in Jerusalem, and in all Judea and Samaria, and to the ends of the Earth" (Acts 1:8). Thus, the purpose of the Holy Spirit is empowerment for witness. Simply put, the Holy Spirit "empowers the Church."[30] And since the day of Pentecost was a regular day on the calendar for the Hebrew people, set apart for bringing the firstfruits of the harvest in offering to Yahweh, Henry Swete is quick to draw the connection on how easy it is "to see the appropriations of such a day for the coming of the Divine Gift which is the first-fruits of the spiritual harvest."[31]

For Peter, the gift of the Holy Spirit is for empowerment of witnessing about Jesus. "As soon as they emerged from the upper room, Peter, who had earlier denied that he knew Jesus, stood and preached fearlessly to the multitude. Peter's actions demonstrate that one aspect of the Spirit's empowerment is boldness to preach."[32] We see this happening on the day of Pentecost (Acts 2), when Peter is before the authorities (Acts 4), when the gentile Pentecost happens at Cornelius's house (Acts 10), and when the apostle Paul lays his hands on the believers (Acts 19). "When the Spirit has come upon his people there shall be power; but, according to the text, not power per se or for us, but for a higher task: 'you shall be my witnesses.'"[33] The mission is not Pentecost, but Pentecost empowers the mission. Let us not seek the gift of the Holy Spirit as a spiritual badge of honor to set us apart from those who are not lucky enough to have *a dose of the Holy Ghost*. As my dad always says: May we seek the *Giver* of the gift, not just the gift.

In an earlier meal, Jesus instructs his disciples: "Do not leave Jerusalem, but wait for the gift my Father promised, which you have heard me speak about" (Acts 1:4). From this verse, Keener points out how Luke emphasizes the "disciples cannot succeed in Christ's mission

---

30. Thiselton, *Holy Spirit*, 50.
31. Swete, *Holy Spirit*, 55.
32. Martin, *Toward a Pentecostal Theology*, 21.
33. Bruner, *Theology of the Holy Spirit*, 160.

without Christ's power."[34] Bruner challenges us: "Significantly, the object of the spiritual witness shall not be the gift, power, or baptism of the Holy Spirit. Jesus is the object, but more than object, he is first of all the subject of the witness of the Spirit."[35]

Forgiveness

We now turn our attention to the end of John's Gospel, when Jesus appears to the disciples after the resurrection. They are holed up in another room behind locked doors, hiding for fear that what happened to *him* will happen to *them*. When he (miraculously) appears, "Jesus said, 'Peace be with you! As the Father has sent me, I am sending you.' And with that he breathed on them and said, 'Receive the Holy Spirit. If you forgive anyone's sins, their sins are forgiven; if you do not forgive them, they are not forgiven'" (John 20:21–23). This passage is sometimes referred to as the Johannine Pentecost because of the action of Jesus: *breathing* on his disciples and *sending* the Holy Spirit. And in addition to being sent by Jesus, Peter and the disciples are empowered (compelled?) to forgive the sins of others. F. B. Meyer calls this "a distinct equipment for service."[36]

If you strike up a conversation with a cessationist today, they will try to convince you that the spiritual gifts on display in the New Testament ceased after the time of the disciples. However, I would wager none of them believe forgiveness has ceased. With these simple words by Jesus to his friends (John 20:21–23), he has made forgiveness a spiritual gift. In some ways, perhaps forgiveness should be the calling card of Christians around the world—that we forgive more often than we hold on to unforgiveness. And because of the sins we have committed, along with the sins others have committed against us, we will need the Spirit's power to forgive.

---

34. Keener, *Between History and Spirit*, 531

35. Bruner, *Theology of the Holy Spirit*, 160. He goes on: "The apostles are his (genitive possessive) witnesses, belonging to him and in his possession. The power of the baptism of the Holy Spirit is first and foremost a power which joins to Christ."

36. Meyer, *Peter*, 234.

Justice

As we learn from the second epistle attributed to Peter, we have the opportunity to "participate in the divine nature" (2 Peter 1:4). But what does this look like? I would contend that we participate in the divine nature when we seek justice, for which we need the Spirit's help. Finnish Pentecostal scholar Veli-Matti Kärkkäinen picks up on this theme when he says the "Spirit works for the freedom of those under oppression, whatever form that may take."[37]

Justice for the oppressed is a part of the divine mission, as this is the very story of Exodus—God heard their cries and *sent* someone (Moses) to rescue them. And this is the story of Jesus (John 3:16). God's Spirit is "graciously inviting the followers of Christ to collaborate in the work of liberation and justice."[38] Amos Yong says "post-Pentecost missiology is no respecter of persons. 'God shows no partiality' (Acts 10:34) in catching up all who are available for recruitment by the divine wind. Peter is an evangelist even as the gentile Cornelius is an instrument of divine witness."[39] The gentile Pentecost (Acts 10) should wake us up to Spirit-empowered justice: Free the slaves, care for orphans, and let women preach! As my friend David says, we are called to *Neighborliness*.[40] Yong describes this as Spirit-empowered *neighborly witness*.[41]

Conclusion: Pentecostal Living

Here's what I know about pastors: we strive earnestly to "pastor people by becoming a Spirit-prompted presence . . . [we embed ourselves in our own] community and seek fresh words for that community . . . [and hopefully] are seen as the presence of God in the community."[42] But Pentecostal preaching and living cannot be limited to those of us who

---

37. Kärkkäinen, *Spirit and Salvation*, 427.
38. Kärkkäinen, *Spirit and Salvation*, 427.
39. Yong, *Mission After Pentecost*, 277.
40. Docusen, *Neighborliness*.
41. Yong, *Mission After Pentecost*, 281: "The witness of ancient Israel was to care for the alien and stranger in their midst, even as the witness of the first followers of Jesus as Messiah was to live blameless lives before and around their unbelieving neighbors. As repeatedly observed in the New Testament letters, the call was for gospel truth to be lived out or interpersonally embodied and communally incarnated before a neighboring/watching world."
42. McKnight, *Pastor Paul*, 19.

are card-carrying members of a Pentecostal denomination. The Spirit will not be boxed in like that. I am very encouraged by recent stories of how the Spirit is going wild again (as in the book of Acts), and giving visions and dreams to men and women, young and old, all over the world. Sounds like the prophetic call of Joel, if you ask me. We would be smart to hoist the sails and catch the wind of the Spirit, to be empowered to bring greater witness to the good news of Jesus. After all, "The experience of Pentecost can and must be repeated in the experience of all who would become Christians."[43]

To that end, may this be our guiding (Pentecostal) prayer: *"Living Breath of God, you who brooded over the waters at creation, come now, and fill our spirits. Living [Ruach] of God, you who conceived Jesus by the Virgin Mary, pour out your gifts in abundance. Living Breath of God, you who groan for the redemption of the whole creation, breathe in us."*[44]

Bibliography

Alvarez, Emilio. *Pentecostal Orthodoxy: Toward an Ecumenism of the Spirit*. Downers Grove, IL: InterVarsity, 2022.

Bird, Michael F. *A Bird's-Eye View of Luke and Acts: Context, Story, and Themes*. Downers Grove, IL: IVP Academic, 2023.

Bockmuehl, Markus N. A. *The Remembered Peter: In Ancient Reception and Modern Debate*. WUNT 262. Tübingen: Mohr Siebeck, 2010.

———. *Simon Peter in Scripture and Memory: The New Testament Apostle in the Early Church*. Grand Rapids: Baker Academic, 2012.

Bond, Helen K., and Larry W. Hurtado, eds. *Peter in Early Christianity*. Grand Rapids: Eerdmans, 2015.

Bruner, Frederick Dale. *A Theology of the Holy Spirit: The Pentecostal Experience and the New Testament Witness*. Reprint, Grand Rapids: Eerdmans, 1986.

Charette, Blaine, and Robby Waddell, eds. *Spirit and Story: Pentecostal Readings of Scripture: Essays in Honor of John Christopher Thomas*. New Testament Monographs 41. Sheffield: Sheffield Phoenix, 2020.

Deere, Jack. *Surprised by the Power of the Spirit: Discovering How God Speaks and Heals Today*. Grand Rapids: Zondervan, 1996.

Dickson, E. J. "Why Are So Many Men Obsessed with the Roman Empire?" *Rolling Stone* (blog), Sept. 16, 2023. https://www.rollingstone.com/culture/culture-features/men-obsessed-roman-empire-explained-tiktok-1234826340/.

Docusen, David. *Neighborliness: Love Like Jesus; Cross Dividing Lines; Transform Your Community*. Nashville: W Publishing, 2022.

---

43. Dunn, *Baptism in the Holy Spirit*, 53.
44. Plantinga, *Morning and Evening Prayers*, 120–21.

Dunn, James D. G. *Baptism in the Holy Spirit: A Re-Examination of the New Testament Teaching on the Gift of the Spirit in Relation to Pentecostalism Today.* Philadelphia: Westminster, 1970.

———. *Jesus and the Spirit: A Study of the Religious and Charismatic Experience of Jesus and the First Christians as Reflected in the New Testament.* Grand Rapids: Eerdmans, 1997.

Fee, Gordon D. *God's Empowering Presence: The Holy Spirit in the Letters of Paul.* Peabody, MA: Hendrickson, 1994.

———. *Listening to the Spirit in the Text.* Grand Rapids: Eerdmans, 2000.

Gibson, Jack J. *Peter Between Jerusalem and Antioch: Peter, James, and the Gentiles.* WUNT 2/345. Tübingen: Mohr Siebeck, 2013.

Green, Gene L. *Vox Petri: A Theology of Peter.* Eugene, OR: Cascade Books, 2019.

Helyer, Larry R. *The Life and Witness of Peter.* Downers Grove, IL: IVP Academic, 2012.

Hengel, Martin. *Saint Peter: The Underestimated Apostle.* Grand Rapids: Eerdmans, 2010.

Kärkkäinen, Veli-Matti. *Pneumatology: The Holy Spirit in Ecumenical, International, and Contextual Perspective.* Grand Rapids: Baker Academic, 2002.

———. *Spirit and Salvation.* A Constructive Christian Theology for the Pluralistic World 4. Grand Rapids: Eerdmans, 2016.

———. *Toward a Pneumatological Theology: Pentecostal and Ecumenical Perspectives on Ecclesiology, Soteriology, and Theology of Mission.* Edited by Amos Yong. Lanham, MD: University Press of America, 2002.

Keener, Craig S. *Acts: An Exegetical Commentary.* 4 vols. Grand Rapids: Baker Academic, 2012.

———. *Between History and Spirit: The Apostolic Witness of the Book of Acts.* Eugene, OR: Cascade Books, 2020.

Keener, Craig S., and L. William Oliverio Jr., eds. *The Spirit Throughout the Canon: Pentecostal Pneumatology.* Journal of Pentecostal Theology Supplement Series 48. Boston: Brill, 2022.

Lossky, Vladimir. *The Mystical Theology of the Eastern Church.* Crestwood, NY: St. Vladimir's Seminary Press, 1976.

Macchia, Frank D. *Jesus the Spirit Baptizer: Christology in Light of Pentecost.* Grand Rapids: Eerdmans, 2018.

Martin, Lee Roy, ed. *Toward a Pentecostal Theology of Preaching.* Cleveland: CPT, 2015.

McDonnell, Kilian, and George T. Montague. *Christian Initiation and Baptism in the Holy Spirit: Evidence from the First Eight Centuries.* 2nd ed. A Michael Glazier Book. Collegeville, MN: Liturgical, 1994.

McKnight, Scot. *Pastor Paul: Nurturing a Culture of Christoformity in the Church.* Theological Explorations for the Church Catholic. Grand Rapids: Brazos, 2019.

Menzies, Robert. "The Spirit in Luke–Acts: Empowering Prophetic Witness." In *The Spirit Throughout the Canon: Pentecostal Pneumatology*, edited by Craig S. Keener and L. William Oliverio Jr., 75–105. Journal of Pentecostal Theology Supplement Series 48. Leiden: Brill, 2022.

Meyer, F. B. *Peter: Fisherman, Disciple, Apostle.* Kerry: CrossReach, 2018.

Pawson, David. *Simon Peter: The Reed and the Rock.* Berkshire, UK: Anchor Recordings, 2014.

Plantinga, Cornelius. *Morning and Evening Prayers.* Grand Rapids: Eerdmans, 2021.

Skaggs, Rebecca. *1, 2 Peter and Jude Through the Centuries*. Wiley Blackwell Bible Commentaries. Hoboken, NJ: Wiley, 2020.

———. *1 Peter, 2 Peter, Jude*. Blandford Forum: Deo, 2012.

Skaggs, Rebecca, and Priscilla Benham. *Revelation: Pentecostal Commentary*. Pentecostal Commentary Series. Dorset: Deo, 2009.

Spittler, Russell P., ed. *Perspectives on the New Pentecostalism*. Grand Rapids: Baker Book House, 1976.

Still, Todd. "Images of Peter in the Apostolic Fathers." In *Peter in Early Christianity*, edited by Larry W. Hurtado and Helen K. Bond, 161–67. Grand Rapids: Eerdmans, 2015.

Swete, Henry B. *The Holy Spirit in the New Testament*. London: Macmillan, 1921.

Taylor, Barbara Brown. *The Preaching Life*. A Cowley Publications Book. Lanham, MD: Rowman & Littlefield, 1993.

Thiselton, Anthony C. *The Holy Spirit—In Biblical Teaching, Through the Centuries, and Today*. Grand Rapids: Eerdmans, 2013.

Yong, Amos. *The Hermeneutical Spirit: Theological Interpretation and Scriptural Imagination for the 21st Century*. Eugene, OR: Cascade Books, 2017.

———. *Mission after Pentecost: The Witness of the Spirit from Genesis to Revelation*. Grand Rapids: Baker Academic, 2019.

———. *Revelation*. Belief: A Theological Commentary on the Bible. Louisville: Westminster John Knox, 2021.

9

Transformative Events in the Early Church

Kelly Dippolito

It's amazing how much trouble a miraculous healing can get you into.

One way of discovering this trouble is to map the pattern of the narrative in some early chapters in Acts. In what follows, we sketch that map, which reveals the prominence of Peter as a "pastor" of that Jerusalem assembly. His leadership is revealed in his collaboration with others and courageous example of boldness before the temple establishment. The map also reveals the growth of the early church, both in numbers and resolve.

Cycle of Clashes Between Disciples and Religious Authorities

Acts 3 and 5 record clashes between the religious leadership in Jerusalem and the freshly Spirit-filled apostles. Covering the span of time between Pentecost and the stoning of Stephen, the movement in the narrative describes persecution and the church's response in order to demonstrate the working out of the Spirit in the life of the community. Luke's purpose is not to provide a history of the infant church's difficulties; rather, he offers the reader an account of the circumstances through which the Spirit led the church "to discover and rediscover its mission."[1]

In the aftermath of their clashes with Jewish leaders, the community of disciples learned that the cost of obedience is high, and they rejoiced

1. González, *Acts*, 49.

in that. They discovered that to follow Christ means being receptive to the promptings of the Spirit to confront systems opposed to the gospel, both in the culture and in the church.[2] Their witness was comprised of both "mutual responsibility" to one another and the miracles and teaching they professed in the name of Jesus.[3]

This rhythm of private community and public involvement moves the narrative in Acts from Jerusalem to the surrounding regions. A group of believers gathered in a relatively private setting experienced the filling of the Spirit on the day of Pentecost in Jerusalem. When they spoke in different languages, the disturbance attracted a crowd who accused them of drunkenness and unwittingly became Peter's sermon audience. The new community bonded with a private commitment of generosity to each other; while walking in public to the temple, Peter and John encountered a forty-year-old man with lifelong disabilities and gave him what they had, faith and healing in Jesus's name, which drew them into a clash with the religious leadership in Jerusalem.

A cycle begins: miracle, arrest, leadership reacts, apostles respond, leadership threatens, apostles released.[4]

Peter and John prayed privately with their friends, a community who yearned for boldness and valued sharing and honesty, sensitive to the Spirit; as the apostles went about in public spaces, many signs and wonders occurred.

The cycle accelerates: miracle, arrest, supernatural release from prison, leadership reacts, apostles respond, leadership threatens, apostles punished and released.[5]

The church continued to grow in numbers and needs, requiring the group to privately commission leaders to organize food distribution. Stephen was publicly scorned and stoned, leading to persecution that scattered the community throughout Judea and Samaria.

---

2. González, *Acts*, 8.
3. Gaventa, *Acts of the Apostles*, 41.
4. Garland, *Acts*, 43.
5. Bock, *Acts*, 236.

Event	Private Community	Public Involvement
Pentecost	Spirit falls on believers (2:1–4)	Crowds gather (2:5–13)
		Peter addresses crowd (2:14–41)
Church established First clash with authorities	Community life flourishes (2:42–47)	Peter and John heal man with disabilities (3:1–10)
		Peter addresses the crowd (3:11–26)
		Peter and John under arrest (4:1–4)
		Leadership reacts (4:5–7)
		Peter responds (4:8–12)
		Leadership threatens (4:13–18)
		Peter reiterates that they will continue speaking in Jesus' name (4:19–20)
		Leadership threatens and releases them (4:21–22)
Church grows and encounters internal conflict Second clash with authorities	Church prays, asks for boldness (4:23–31)	Signs and wonders (5:12–16)
	Everything owned in common (4:32–37)	Apostles arrested (5:17–18)
		Angel releases apostles from cell, they continue to teach (5:19–21a)
	Ananias and Sapphira withhold, struck dead (5:1–11)	Leadership reacts (5:21b–28)
		Peter responds (5:29–32)
		Leadership threatens, Gamaliel intervenes (5:33–39)
		Apostles flogged and released (5:40–42)
Church expands leadership, addressing internal tensions and needs Third clash with authorities targets a new leader	Community criticized for neglecting non-Jewish widows, selects leaders for food distribution, including Stephen (6:1–7)	Stephen performs signs and wonders (6:8)
		Opposition spread false accusations (6:9—7:1)
		Stephen responds (7:2–53)
		Stephen stoned (7:54—8:1a)
Church suffers severe persecution and scatters Gospel spreads	All but the apostles scatter; Saul imprisons men and women (8:1b–3)	Scattered church proclaims the Word throughout the region (8:4)

The Community of the Church Formed (Acts 2)

God's pouring out of the Spirit upon the believers at Pentecost set the trajectory for the church community toward opposition from religious authorities. The divine encounter dramatically shaped who they were and who they will become. Jesus promised the gift of the Spirit and his function was to bear witness to Jesus crucified, resurrected, and ascended. "In response to that witness, many join the believers, and the community continues to generate awe. Alongside this reception of the gospel, however, grows a negative reaction that culminates in Stephen's death and the flight of believers in the face of persecution."[6] Joy and sorrow coexisted for the church.

Clash I: Spirit-Led Kerfuffle (Acts 3:1–10)

> Peter and John encounter a man being carried through the Beautiful Gate, a daily ritual for the 40-year-old with disabilities. His circumstances warrant that he provide for himself by asking for alms from those entering the temple. With anticipation in his eyes, he appeals to Peter and John. Fresh from his experience on the day of Pentecost, Peter obeys the prompting from the Spirit and addresses the man. Acknowledging his lack of monetary resources, Peter offers his most valuable possession, Jesus. Peter confidently takes the man's hand and he feels a strengthening in his body. He jumps and walks, praising God! The crowds at the temple witness the miracle, amazed and astonished that the alms-asker has been healed by a supernatural encounter with a Jesus-follower.[7]

Immediately after receiving the Spirit, the disciples' daily lives are punctuated by miracles. In Acts 3, we find the record of the first miraculous event since Jesus's ascension. With this new development of their faith journey, they entered a season that required them to step into the authority they observed Jesus carrying. Hence, believing for a miracle is not only "replicating the kind of work Jesus performed in his ministry" but also an indication of maturing in faith and boldness in action.[8] It is

---

6. Gaventa, *Acts of the Apostles*, 83.

7. *Author's note*: Summaries of the relevant Bible passages are presented as a creative writing exercise.

8. Bock, *Acts*, 162.

apparent that Jesus worked through the apostles and the church as his witnesses to bring flourishing and goodness.[9]

During the church's infancy, routines and norms were established among the community of believers privately while also garnering public attention. As the power of Jesus was displayed, earthly power structures became threatened and uneasy, setting off the aforementioned pattern: miracle, arrest, leadership reacts, apostles respond, leadership threatens, apostles released.

Peter's first clash with religious authorities in Jerusalem was the result of healing a man with disabilities who asked for alms at the temple. Both the man's circumstances and the location are significant to appreciating the tension underneath the text. As a person with disabilities, the man was barred from entering the temple, which prevented him from entering the sanctuary or the presence of God.[10] However, the pedestrian traffic at the temple created a predictable place to ask for alms (donations). The gate specified in Acts 3:2 is identified as "Beautiful," which is likely a descriptor rather than a name. The Nicanor Gate was made of bronze and "heavily adorned," which would fittingly be called beautiful, and "allowed access" to the Court of Women and Gentiles, a popular area to enter the temple.[11] Even Peter and John's movements in that area warrants our attention, as it "reaffirms the involvement of the early community at the temple."[12]

The miracle itself was a holistic saving, with physical and spiritual ramifications. "Although the lame man seeks money, Peter and John gave him far more, full restoration to health and salvation in Jesus' name."[13] Reflective of the early church's commitment to holding all assets in common, Peter lacked money to donate, so his actions sufficed as his offering. As he uttered, "Stand up and walk," Peter reached for the man's hand (Acts 3:6–7 NRSV).[14] While Peter's boldness is strongly associated with his words to the crowd and the authorities, there is a moment of courage that can only be attributed to the Spirit: Peter lifted the disabled man prior to the healing having occurred in the man's body (Acts 3:7). Harkening back to Old Testament prophets who spoke of future events as

9. Bock, *Acts*, 164.
10. Garland, *Acts*, 38.
11. Bock, *Acts*, 160.
12. Bock, *Acts*, 159.
13. Garland, *Acts*, 37.
14. All Scripture will be NRSV unless otherwise noted.

if they had already occurred (the prophetic perfect tense), Peter was so certain of the Spirit moving in him and the power of God to heal that he looked straight at the man and offered his right hand preemptively. This is a post-Pentecost Peter—the disciple who made eye contact with Jesus while denying him in the courtyard (Luke 22:61) has matured into a confident apostle. "The miraculous is not only the one healed but [also] Peter and John, who now live on the other side of the journey of Jesus as his true witnesses."[15]

Clash I: Peter Addresses the Crowd (Acts 3:11—4:2)

> Like on the day of Pentecost, Peter speaks to the gathered crowd. Instantly deflecting the attention away from himself and John, he tells them the gospel story, recounting the events that had taken place not too long before in that very city of Jerusalem. Peter witnessed those events: the arrest of Jesus, his crucifixion, and his resurrection. Peter's powerful sermon to the crowd is interrupted by being arrested by the religious leaders of the temple.

Peter's address to the crowds who gathered in wonder at the healing also reflects his personal development. He has moved from an "incomplete understanding" of Jesus to a robust articulation of the significance of Christ as the fulfilment of the Scriptures.[16] The text reveals that Peter's influence shaped the theological understanding of the early church soon after the resurrection, likely in the first five years of the church, establishing the "Christological-soteriological bases of the Christian kerygma."[17]

Recounting the facts of Jesus's life and ministry, Peter included many of the same themes in Acts 3:12–26 that he said to the Pentecost onlookers in Acts 2:14–40.[18] The content came from eyewitness account; Peter bore witness to his own experience alongside Jesus and reconciled it with his biblical understanding: "Scouring the [Old Testament] Scripture helps the disciples make sense of what they had seen with their eyes. They understand that what happened to Jesus is the pinnacle of the unfolding story of salvation history."[19] The apostles' fresh interpretation of Scripture was key

---

15. Jennings, *Acts*, 42.
16. Brown et al., *Peter in the New Testament*, 160.
17. Hengel, *Saint Peter*, 101. See also Bock, *Acts*, 165.
18. Garland, *Acts*, 38–39.
19. Garland, *Acts*, 41.

to their message. Drawing on the "old promises" gives the church roots, which was "a form of legitimization for the new community."[20]

The thrust of Peter's message to the crowd is summarized by, "Repent therefore, and turn to God" (Acts 3:19). Peter's goal remained clear and consistent. His address issued an appeal to the crowd to consider the claims of Christ. Restraint respected the audience, leaving individuals with the responsibility of their choices: "It is when religion is imposed that it does damage."[21]

Clash I: Arrest and Peter's Response (Acts 4:3–22)

> Peter and John were detained overnight since the healing occurred in the late afternoon and it was now evening. The next morning the temple elites question Peter and John on whose authority they performed this miracle. Peter, again the spokesperson, is empowered by the Spirit to answer. His frank response focuses the discussion on the good deed performed in the name of resurrected Jesus Christ. The religious leaders express astonishment by the boldness coming from men not as educated as themselves and are perplexed as to how to manage these Jesus companions. They are unable to deny the miracle; the healed man is standing in their presence. A command to stop speaking in Jesus's name is imposed on Peter and John in hopes that their message would not spread further among the people. Their response shifts the burden to the religious leaders, pointing out that they could judge whether Peter and John should obey God or men. Peter and John are resolute; they will not be silent. Fearing the crowds who were still praising God for the miraculous healing, the temple elites issue another threat of silence before releasing Peter and John.

"In the name of Jesus Christ of Nazareth, stand up and walk" (Acts 3:6). What began as a walk to the temple evolved into an arrest and altercation with the authorities. Peter's command to the man with disabilities in Acts 3:6 set a chain of events in motion that, while unsurprising, certainly confirm that "speaking holy words has serious consequences."[22] The disturbances in the city attributed to the church created inevitable

---

20. Bock, *Acts*, 181.
21. Bock, *Acts*, 200.
22. Jennings, *Acts*, 45.

conflict with the power structures of the temple.[23] Therefore it follows that the accusation pointed at Peter and John spoke to the issue of authority: "By what power or by what name did you do this?" (Acts 4:7). Asking this question makes it plain that they understood that these events had occurred under another authority, in a location that they had authority over.[24] Their responsibility and leadership of the temple, the center of Judaism, was threatened.

Acts 4:8 specifies that Peter was filled with the Spirit before he uttered a response to the religious authorities. The importance of this phrase cannot be underestimated. It was by the Spirit's power that Peter spoke with boldness and conviction in a demanding situation. Although the leaders' evaluation of Peter and John limited them to "uneducated" and "ordinary" (Acts 4:13), the Spirit alive in them was extraordinary, underscoring the necessity of the Spirit to enable disciples to be effective witnesses.[25] Strategically, Peter opened his response by labeling the healing a "good deed," also translated as an "act of kindness" (NIV), in an effort to establish goodwill, since acts of that sort were regarded highly favorably in the first-century Roman Empire (Acts 4:9).[26] His statements were short and powerful, ending with: "There is salvation in no one else, for there is no other name under heaven given among mortals by which we must be saved" (Acts 4:11). With this conclusion, Peter affirmed Jesus as preeminent, thereby answering their question of authority.

The characteristics of "boldness" merit further consideration (Acts 4:13). Described as a courage combined with a "steely frankness," the boldness associated with Peter and John is confident, assured, not pointed or agenda driven.[27] Crucial to a proper understanding is differentiating boldness from "fawning speech that seeks to flatter and placate"; the apostles did not seek the approval or goodwill of the religious leaders.[28] They only sought the favor of God and the guidance of the Spirit, forcing us to recognize that "boldness is not the result of character refinement or moral formation ... it comes from without, from the Spirit of God."[29]

---

23. González, *Acts*, 9.
24. Bock, *Acts*, 190.
25. Garland, *Acts*, 46.
26. Bock, *Acts*, 190–92.
27. McKnight, *Acts*, 55.
28. Garland, *Acts*, 45; see also Bock, *Acts*, 195.
29. Jennings, *Acts*, 48–49.

The boldness of Peter and John rankled the "politically cautious elite."[30] They are understandably perplexed and frustrated by their loss of control over the temple and the people.[31] Since they cannot deny the healing, the evidence standing in front of them, they must control the flow of information by silencing the church, classic "damage control."[32] Reasserting their power was accomplished by issuing an order for Peter and John to cease speaking or teaching in the name of Jesus. Peter and John refused. The rhetorical strategy of their refusal was to acknowledge their earthly authority and insist that they judge if the apostles should obey God (Acts 4:19). Fearing the people, who were praising God for the miracle, the temple authorities were flummoxed as to how to punish Peter and John, settling on more threats before releasing them. They were released, "not for the sake of justice, but 'because of the people.'"[33]

Peter and John's Accusers

An evaluation of the characters ruffled by Peter and John's teaching and miracles illustrate the first-century dynamic between Judaism and Rome. We observe an idea of the scale of the opposition to the apostles in reviewing the descriptions of people involved and considering their spheres of influence (listed in order of appearance with details supplied by both the NRSV and NIV):

First clash in Acts 4:1–8:

- Priests
- Captain of the temple guard
- Sadducees
- Rulers, elders, and scribes
- Annas, the high priest
- Caiaphas, John, and Alexander
- Others of the high priestly family

---

30. Keener, *Acts*, 196.
31. González, *Acts*, 62.
32. Bock, *Acts*, 198.
33. González, *Acts*, 62.

Second clash in Acts 5:17–22:

- High priest and associates, Sadducees
- Council and whole body of elders of Israel (NRSV)
- Sanhedrin, the full assembly of the elders of Israel (NIV)
- Temple police/officers
- Captain of the temple guard
- Chief priests
- Member of the council, Gamaliel, a Pharisee

The involvement of the Sadducees reflects that they had the most to lose as temple authorities. Not only did they control the Sanhedrin, they also maintained influence and status by positioning themselves in a power-sharing arrangement with Rome.[34] The Sanhedrin's jurisdiction extended beyond the temple into the city, functioning as a "municipal and regional senate, with perhaps an average of seventy members."[35] Although Jesus's most hostile interactions in the Gospels involved the Pharisees, the apostles' clashes in Jerusalem paint the Sadducees as more hostile to the early church.[36] However, in the second clash, Gamaliel, a Pharisee, emerged as a wise, reasoned member of the Sanhedrin. True to core Pharisaic values, Gamaliel persuades the Sanhedrin to pursue tolerance, smoothing the situation with a position of noninterference.[37]

Analyzed in its entirety, the list of characters involved in the clashes between the apostles and the religious authorities confirms that the power structure of Jerusalem utilized law enforcement, spiritual oversight, and formal power structures to oppose the message and power of Jesus.

Clash I: The Church Prays (Acts 4:23–31)

> With their leaders back in the embrace of the believing community, prayers of praise rise to the heavens along with a petition for God to see the threats against them and give them boldness to speak and miracles to perform.

---

34. Bock, *Acts*, 238.
35. Keener, *Acts*, 192.
36. Bock, *Acts*, 237–38.
37. Keener, *Acts*, 214–16.

Upon their return "to their friends," also translated as "to their own people" (NIV), Peter and John gave the church a report (Acts 4:23). The church demonstrated the fruit of being Spirit filled in their response of praise and worship. They quoted Ps 2 and drew from Hezekiah's prayer in Isa 37:16–20, Old Testament truths that expressed their trust in God's sovereignty plus their anguish over the situation without complaint.[38] They concluded by praying a petition for boldness, desiring to spread the gospel while anticipating persecution. They demonstrated an awareness that boldness came through the Spirit rather than being a product of personal courage.

> It is a mark of success for the community that in preaching the word its members have walked the path of Jesus and have suffered rejection. The reliance on God, the resting in God's justice, the willingness to suffer persecution, the desire to preach Jesus, and the call to God to show himself—all are signs of a healthy community. The presence of rejection and opposition is not a surprise, nor is it sought, but suffering is embraced when it comes from God. Turning to God leads to boldness.[39]

Persevering through prayer, relying on the Spirit, cultivating unity, and gathering together defined the community of believers, as does having generosity among themselves to address everyone's needs. "They shared everything they had" (Acts 4:32, NIV).

Clash I: Spirit-Led Sharing and Honesty Upheld as Community Values (Acts 4:32—5:11)

> The community shares generously and with joy. But a married couple sold property and deceitfully withheld their profits. They die at Peter's feet. The fear of the Lord seizes the community.

The opposite of obeying the Spirit is resisting the Spirit. The narrative provides an example of an "instant-judgment miracle" that offers a sharp contrast to the general description of the church.[40] Ananias and his wife Sapphira sold a piece of property and lied to Peter about the price they received, thereby dishonestly withholding from the community. Each fell dead at Peter's feet.

---

38. Bock, *Acts*, 210; see also Garland, *Acts*, 45–46.
39. Bock, *Acts*, 210.
40. Bock, *Acts*, 219.

What appears severe needs context: the community's healthy function is as important as its mission.[41] God saw and corrected the internal workings of the group. Reassuringly, the situation with Ananias and Sapphira is "presented as a unique judgment at a sensitive point in the church's early days."[42] The result was a fear of God within the church, extending to all who learned about the event.

Clash II: Conflict with Religious Authorities Escalates (Acts 5:12–42)

> The apostles continue meeting at Solomon's Portico, healing the sick and ministering to the demon oppressed. Their reputation permeates Jerusalem and its neighboring towns; people came from across the region with the hope of being healed in Peter's shadow. Provoked by jealousy of the healings taking place in Jerusalem, the high priest and Sadducees arrest the apostles and detained them. Yet the Spirit intervenes, releasing the apostles from their cells and sending them into the temple at dawn to preach and teach. Not knowing this, the high priest arrives and calls together the religious leaders, preparing to confront their prisoners only to learn that they had been freed from their cells overnight. The captain braves the crowds to regather the apostles before the religious authorities. Again, the high priest questions them. Peter gives a predictable response—we must obey God—followed by an abbreviated version of their witness.
>
> At this, the religious authorities hit their breaking point and react in rage. A highly respected Pharisee on the council steps in to provide leadership and order by having the apostles removed from the meeting and then addressing his fellow councilmen with reason and logic. He reminds them of other teachers who had come and gone: if this is not of God, it will fade; if it is of God, then we are fighting against God. The group recognizes his wisdom. The apostles are flogged, threatened, and released.
>
> The apostles continue ministering at the temple and from house to house, rejoicing in their suffering and disgrace, with a deep commitment to proclaiming the gospel of Jesus Christ.

---

41. Bock, *Acts*, 212.
42. Bock, *Acts*, 220.

Interestingly, less ink is spilled in Acts on the subsequent clashes with religious authorities in Jerusalem. The brevity of the account in Acts 5 underscores the increasing resistance and quickening tension. The cycle repeated with escalations. The growth in attention and reputation caused by performing "many signs and wonders" resulted in the church growing in number (Acts 5:12–16). Word of healings spread such that people laid the sick in the streets hoping that Peter's shadow would touch them (Acts 5:15). "Many people in antiquity regarded one's shadow as part of one's body, so it is not surprising that some would seek for contact with at least Peter's shadow."[43] The culmination of these events precipitated a response from religious leadership (Acts 5:17–18).[44]

Filled with jealousy, the Sadducees arrested the apostles. So far in the text, two escalations are noteworthy: the second clash is based on many unspecified miracles rather than a single occurrence, and apostles, plural, are arrested instead of a limited subset involved in a particular infraction. This detainment is designed to suppress their rising influence and make a public statement.

But God escalated his response as well. An angel released the apostles from the prison, instructing them to stand in the temple and spread the gospel (Acts 5:19–20). They did as directed. Again, the apostles experienced confirmation that relying on the Spirit for boldness and guidance is key to living a Christian life, publicly and privately.

As in the earlier clash, the religious leaders feared the people and modified their reaction accordingly. Due to their close relationship with Rome, and the Roman expectation of peace, the leaders were mindful of any disturbance that could be construed as subversive or leading to rioting. Even the people chosen to extricate the apostles from the crowd feared being stoned, "a detail that interestingly anticipates the stoning of Stephen."[45] Sternly reminded of the Sanhedrin's command to stop teaching in Jesus's name, Peter replied with the directness and boldness associated with his Spirit-filled demeanor: "We must obey God rather than any human authority" (Acts 5:28).

Hearing his response, the Sanhedrin erupted in rage and wanted to kill the apostles (Acts 5:33). But one man, a Pharisee named Gamaliel, contributed the powerful observation that "if [Christianity] is of God, you will not be able to overthrow them—in that case you may even be found

43. Keener, *Acts*, 208.
44. Bock, *Acts*, 233.
45. Gaventa, *Acts of the Apostles*, 107.

fighting against God!" (Acts 5:38–39). The clashes between the religious authorities and the apostles since Acts 3 crescendo at this moment, "the high point . . . of the entire story of resistance up to this point."[46] Behind Gamaliel's statement is wondering if this is of God. In Luke's account the reader learns that the Spirit guided, empowered, and emboldened the apostles and the church, confirming that this is indeed from God.

While the apostles were spared from death, the Sanhedrin had them flogged, a form of torture that typically involved thirty-nine lashes and was sometimes fatal.[47] When considered in the context of their experiences as Jesus's disciples and as Spirit-filled believers, "these actions of torture are bound to the actions of liberation as the full-orbed reality of following Jesus."[48] The apostles returned home rejoicing that God had considered them worthy of suffering dishonor in his name. The capacity to rejoice is evidence of the Spirit's work among the apostles and the church, just as it "became characteristic of Christian martyrs throughout the early centuries of persecution."[49] And every day they continued to preach and teach in his name, both privately in homes and publicly at the temple (Acts 5:42).

Clash II: The Church Selects Leaders (Acts 6:1–7)

> Division occurs in the church over the distribution of food. To address the need for ministry leadership, Stephen, a man of faith and the Holy Spirit, is selected. The community commissions him and six others with prayer and the laying on of hands. The reputation of the church grows, as does their numbers, including drawing priests into the fold.

Whereas the first clash between Peter and John with the religious authorities was instigated by a specific healing in which individuals were arrested followed by the church immediately praying about the situation, the second clash is described more broadly: "many signs and wonders" led to the arrest of the group of apostles and the church gathered to pray "during those days" (Acts 5:12; 6:1).

---

46. Gaventa, *Acts of the Apostles*, 110.
47. González, *Acts*, 83.
48. Jennings, *Acts*, 61.
49. González, *Acts*, 83.

From the text we learn that the church distributed food daily to widows in the church (Acts 6:1). This comports with the community's generosity and sensitivity to Spirit-led giving noted in earlier passages. Stemming from issues between "the Hellenists" and "the Hebrews," ethnic tension impacted the unity of the group (Acts 6:1).[50] Additional workers were needed to lead and guide food distribution; therefore, the apostles gathered the community and worked toward a consensus. Seven men were appointed by the group.

Stephen, "a man full of faith and the Holy Spirit," was chosen as a leader and commissioned through prayer and the laying on of hands (Acts 6:5–6). With that dispute settled, the church grew, and we read a special notation that "a great many of the priests became obedient to the faith" (Acts 6:7). In light of the increasing persecution of Peter and the apostles by the religious leaders, including chief priests, the transformation of priests into believers is notable and likely provoked the next event recorded in Acts, the stoning of Stephen.[51]

Clash III: The Stoning of Stephen (Acts 6:8—8:4)

> Stephen, leader in the church and of its food distribution ministry, obeys the Holy Spirit by performing many miracles. His activity draws the ire of some synagogue leaders, who conspire against him with rumors of blasphemy. Stephen responds to the leaders with an epic Spirit-led sermon. While Stephen looked into the heavenlies unto the glory of God, the enraged crowd dragged him outside Jerusalem and stoned him. Saul, later to be known as Paul, approves.
>
> That very day persecution broke out against the church in Jerusalem. Everyone except the apostles scatter throughout the region. With focus and determination Saul inspects residences for community members, taking both men and women to prison. But the scattered remember what the Lord had done in Jerusalem in their midst, and they proclaim the word wherever they go.

The cycle of miracles, arrests, and responses erupted into violence when Stephen was targeted for persecution. Many elements of the third and final

---

50. Bock, *Acts*, 255.
51. Gaventa, *Acts of the Apostles*, 116.

clash in Jerusalem are intensifications of the elements in the prior conflicts: the event, the people targeted, the arrest, and the punishment.

	CLASH I Acts 3	CLASH II Acts 5	CLASH III Acts 6
Event	Healing of man with disabilities	Many signs and wonders	Stephen did great wonders and signs among the people
People Targeted	Peter and John	The apostles	Stephen
Detainment	Arrested	Arrested	Seized
Response	Sermon by Peter ("boldness")	Sermon by Peter	Very long sermon by Stephen
Punishment	Do not teach or speak in Jesus' name	Do not teach or speak in Jesus' name Flogged	Stoned
After	Church prays Ananias and Sapphira	Apostles rejoice Church selects and prays over Stephen as leader of food distribution	Severe persecution begins Church scattered

There was no time for the church to gather privately to pray after Stephen was stoned. "That day a severe prosecution began against the church in Jerusalem" (Acts 8:1).

Stephen is the offspring of a Pentecost-shaped community for whom boldness was modeled, expected, and prayed for. "The pattern of prophetic witness is demonstrated fully by Stephen."[52] Importantly, Stephen is the first identified believer to whom a miracle is assigned outside of the twelve apostles. Thus, signs and wonders are not limited to the apostles; rather, they flow from the Spirit without regard for title or status.[53] The Spirit empowered all believers in the church to bear witness to the gospel.

The church was born on Pentecost in Jerusalem. The church was scattered out of Jerusalem on the day Stephen was stoned. The apostles remained, yet the geographical borders of their ministries eventually

---

52. Johnson, *Prophetic Jesus*, 178.
53. Keener, *Acts*, 229.

expanded, evidenced by Peter going to Caesarea in Acts 10. Faith in Jesus and reliance on the Spirit had been cultivated while in Jerusalem, therefore when they were displaced, they retained their "sense of connection as a group of communities bound together by Jesus."[54] They remained faithful and obedient to God's call and leading.

What Does This Mean for Us?

Acts 2–9 record the development of the early church from Pentecost to clashes to persecution. The rhythm of the life of the early church is given by Luke to provide an example for Spirit-led living, both private and public. This theme is repeated throughout the passages surrounding Peter's clashes with the religious authorities. Peter's boldness to the Sanhedrin was evidence of the Spirit working in his life, empowering him to speak frankly at a moment of scrutiny and pressure. His example moved the group to request the same Spirit-empowerment, as they recognized that it had come from God, not Peter, and was for everyone, not just the apostles.

Evaluating our own rhythms of private-public living is a courageous exercise in self-reflection and awareness. We have an opportunity to live out kingdom principles as illustrated by the early church, but it requires an honest assessment of ourselves.

Are we, as individuals and a faith community, open and receptive to the Spirit's empowerment and leading?

Are we, as individuals and a faith community, honest and vulnerable to request prayer, sharing our experiences with others?

Are we, as pastors and leaders, encouraging the whole church to embrace Spirit-led boldness and ministry?

Are we, as volunteers and people in the pews (or chairs), leaving ministry to pastors or are we stepping into our own kingdom assignments?

The Spirit who came upon the church at Pentecost is for you, too. The Spirit-led boldness that Peter experienced in his time of extreme distress and pressure is available for you, too. The Spirit-empowered life is for you, too.

---

54. Bock, *Acts*, 227.

Bibliography

Bock, Darrell L. *Acts*. Baker Exegetical Commentary on the New Testament. Grand Rapids: Baker Academic, 2007.

Brown, Raymond Edward, et al., eds. *Peter in the New Testament: A Collaborative Assessment by Protestant and Roman Catholic Scholars*. 1973. Reprint, Eugene, OR: Wipf & Stock, 2002.

Garland, David E. *Acts*. Teach the Text Commentary Series. Grand Rapids: Baker, 2017.

Gaventa, Beverly Roberts. *The Acts of the Apostles*. Abingdon New Testament Commentaries. Nashville: Abingdon, 2003.

González, Justo L. *Acts: The Gospel of the Spirit*. Maryknoll, NY: Orbis, 2001.

Hengel, Martin. *Saint Peter: The Underestimated Apostle*. Translated by Thomas H. Trapp. Grand Rapids: Eerdmans, 2010.

Jennings, Willie James. *Acts*. Belief: A Theological Commentary on the Bible. Louisville: Westminster John Knox, 2017.

Johnson, Luke Timothy. *Prophetic Jesus, Prophetic Church: The Challenge of Luke–Acts to Contemporary Christians*. Grand Rapids: Eerdmans, 2011.

Keener, Craig S. *Acts*. New Cambridge Bible Commentary. New York: Cambridge University Press, 2020.

McKnight, Scot. *Acts*. New Testament Everyday Bible Study. Grand Rapids: HarperChristian Resources, 2022.

10

The End of Us Versus Them

Peter's Vision and the Expansive, Impartial Love of God

RENJY ABRAHAM

TWO MESSENGERS OF GOD, in the same city, hundreds of years apart, face a similar decision: Will God's extravagant love guide them to uproot the social division of their world and embrace the expansion of God's family?

Acts 10 is the story of two worlds colliding. Peter, a foundational leader of the early church, receives a message from God and visits a Roman centurion, Cornelius, a gentile military officer involved with the oppression of Israel, joining a Jewish leader for peaceful conversations—to a first-century audience, this encounter was scandalous. Luke saturates this story with divine activity to underscore that God initiated and blessed this gathering. It is no accident that God places Peter in this situation because, as one of the early church pastors, he will lead a monumental transformation of Jesus' community into a people who love and include all previously forbidden "others."

Luke, the author of Acts, uses Peter and Cornelius's interaction to forge a mutualistic path for Jewish and gentile relations. He intentionally designs Peter's encounter with Cornelius to shift the first-century emerging church from a Jewish-centered movement to a community defined by its indiscriminate welcome. Luke uses ancient literary design methods to activate stories familiar to his audience and challenge readers to extend

God's expansive love to everyone. He structures the narrative to present Peter as 1) an inverse of the prophet Jonah, 2) a fulfillment of Daniel's dream, and 3) a witness to another Pentecost. Acts 10 urges contemporary Christian communities to reject false ideas about divine partiality and invites them to embrace mutualistic inclusivity anchored in the way of Jesus, one so strong that love extends to all.

A Scandalous Encounter—Acts 10

While in Joppa, God gives Peter a vision of a sheet with various animals, some of which are unclean, according to the Torah. Peter hears a divine voice command him to "rise" and "eat" (v. 13). Yet, as a loyal Jewish person, Peter resists because he never has and never would eat these forbidden animals. The voice said to Peter, "Do not call anything impure what God has made clean" (v. 15). This vision repeats three times. God's Spirit nudges Peter to visit the Roman centurion Cornelius in Caesarea. When they meet, Cornelius falls at Peter's feet in reverence. Peter tells Cornelius to stand and enters his home to find a large gathering. Peter shared with them that "God does not show favoritism" (v. 34), that "Jesus Christ . . . is Lord of all" (v. 35), and that "God anointed Jesus of Nazareth with the Holy Spirit and power" (v. 38). The Holy Spirit interrupts Peter's speech and "fell upon all who heard" (v. 44), and the people begin "speaking in tongues" (v. 46). Peter recognizes that the same Spirit who empowered Jesus and fell upon the Jewish followers of Christ is now dwelling with these gentiles.

Readers unaccustomed to strict dietary laws tied to religious belief and practice have difficulty feeling the weight of this moment. Peter's Jewish family, friends, mentors, and his entire community have operated with a conviction that eating these things would dishonor God. Food laws are fundamental to Peter's identity and social reputation. Loyal Jewish people, including Jesus followers of the time, would not dream of doing something this scandalous.[1]

---

1. Recent scholarship on Acts 10–11 is in dispute about whether or not earliest Jewish believers continued to follows the laws of kashrut (food laws) and to what degree (or not) gentile believers were to observe laws of kashrut. The Paul within Judaism school of thought believes Jewish believers practiced kashrut laws while gentile believers were expected to follow laws for them in the law of Moses. A good example of such a study is Oliver, *Torah Praxis*, 320–64, on Acts 10. *Editor's note*: Note. —Scot McKnight.

Jewish and Gentile Relations in Antiquity

First-century history reveals a particularly sharp social divide between Jews and gentiles. In 167 BCE, Antiochus Epiphanes IV stormed the Jerusalem temple and erected a statue of Zeus.[2] He repurposed the Israelite altar and sacrificed a pig, an unclean animal according to the Torah. This blatant act of disregard for Torah ignited a Jewish rebellion and movement to reclaim their identity and resist the economic and political powers, forcing them to compromise their loyalty to God to survive. Antiochus's desecration of the temple was a foundational event that directly affected Jewish identity well into the new millennia as new, yet familiar, foreign forces continued to occupy Judea and its surrounding region. Rome ruled with similar arrogance by the first century, reminiscent of Antiochus's reign.[3]

Antiquity offers no picture of a unified Judaism, as many groups differed on several important issues, including ideas about God, how to interpret and practice the Torah, and how to respond to these surrounding cultural pressures. Some, like the Herodians, were willing to compromise their ways to enjoy the benefits of positive association with the ruling group.[4] Others wanted to conquer the gentile world to punish these foreign peoples for the pain they were believed to have caused.[5] Christianity began as a sect of Judaism, so these various attitudes toward the gentile world influenced the early followers of Jesus. Even in the early church, a nationalistic interpretive thread through some communities suggested that Jesus would return to conquer the world and establish a new Israel to rule over all the other nations.[6] Gentiles could be a part of this new kingdom, but only if they converted to Judaism, and gentiles

---

2. This was standard Hellenistic strategy when rulers conquered to unite two groups around common deity worship.

3. Wright, *People of God*, 158.

4. Sim and McLaren, *Attitudes to Gentiles*.

5. "See, O Lord, and raise up their king for them, a son of David, for the proper time that you see, God, to rule over Israel your servant. And undergird him with strength to shatter unrighteous rulers. Cleanse Jerusalem from the nations that trample it in destruction, to expel sinners from the inheritance in wisdom, in righteousness, to rub out the arrogance of the sinner like a potter's vessel, to crush all their support with an iron rod; to destroy lawless nations by the word of his mouth, for gentiles to flee from his face at his threat, and to reprove sinners by the word of their heart" (Ps. Sol. 17:23–27); Bird, *Origins of the Gentile Mission*.

6. The Hebrew Bible has passages that represent this perspective (e.g., Zech 14:12–19); Boyarin, *Jewish Gospels*, 4–5.

would not be awarded equal status in the community.[7] How do followers of the way of Christ navigate the cultural pressures and widespread social norms that divide people? Through Peter's dream and subsequent events, it appears that God is helping them find a new way forward. Yet, they will discover that it is not necessarily "new."

Literary Design

Acts 10 redefines who can fully participate in Jesus' church and challenges how they should receive people outside their community. Luke makes his case by designing his literature with echoes from and connections to familiar narratives in the Hebrew Bible. He follows first-century scribal practices and storytelling.[8] Ancient authors consistently use concept and keyword repetition, location, and character references to activate other familiar stories they assume the reader knows to invite consideration of theological and social implications of the narrative.[9] Luke presents his account of the Peter-Cornelius encounter in a way that establishes Peter as an inversion of the prophet Jonah and fulfillment of Daniel's dream, who is also a witness to the second Pentecost described in Acts.

Two Worlds Colliding: Peter and Cornelius

Peter was a fisherman by trade and a part of the Jewish peasant class. He is known as the one who denied Jesus three times (Luke 22:55–65). Even so, after the resurrection, over a meal, Jesus provides a threefold restoration and entrusts Peter to care for his followers (John 21). Peter becomes a prominent leader in the early church and a primary spokesperson starting on the day of Pentecost (Acts 2). By the time he meets Cornelius, Peter is only influential in this small Jewish sect, and the broader Jewish religious rulers comment on Peter's lack of education and ordinariness (Acts 4:13).[10]

As a centurion, Cornelius had the power to arrest people and have them flogged based on whim.[11] Not only is he a gentile, but he represents

---

7. Wall, "Peter, 'Son' of Jonah," 75.
8. Brown et al., *Peter in the New Testament*, 44.
9. Wall, "Peter, 'Son' of Jonah," 83.
10. Wright and Bird, *New Testament in Its World*, 756.
11. Cornelius was a Roman military officer stationed in Caesarea, a strategic

the harsh Roman rule of an occupying empire to the Jewish community. Jewish people despised the imperial leadership both for military might and wealthy nobility because it reminded them of their vulnerability and economic disparities. However, Luke uses two previous stories of centurions to subtly prepare his audience to anticipate that Cornelius might not be exactly what they would expect of a Roman centurion.[12] First, a centurion manifests loyalty to Jesus and rests in Jesus' authority (Luke 7).[13] In turn, Jesus raises this gentile military enemy as an example of extraordinary faith in front of the Jewish community. Then, a centurion appears at Jesus' execution and declares Jesus' innocence (Luke 23:47).[14] In this culminating moment, Luke chooses an authoritarian gentile adversary as the character who perceives this unjust event. The centurion garners the audience's sympathy by simply asserting what happened to Jesus was wrong. Luke expects readers to upload these previous centurion stories to soften their attitudes toward Cornelius.

Luke also presents a mystery to his audience by showing that, somehow, the Spirit of God had already been working in Cornelius's life, softening his heart to the ways of Christ before Peter ever showed up. Luke does this by mentioning Cornelius's generosity to the poor and calling him a "Godfearer," a term reserved for pagan gentiles who were open to Judaism's ideas and practices (Acts 10:2).[15] As a Godfearer, Cornelius's familiarity with Jewish ways had primed him to receive Peter. God was already working to heal and restore Cornelius's humanity long before he knew about Jesus or got baptized. The author prepares the audience

---

imperial port that opened up trade routes in the southeastern part of the empire. Luke mentions that Cornelius has servants and attendants, which speaks to his wealth, prominence, and influence in the city (Acts 10:7); Wright, *Acts for Everyone*, 158; Helyer, *Life and Witness*, 75.

12. Luke refers to a "centurion" only a handful of times throughout Luke–Acts, the two-volume unified work.

13. A centurion's servant is deathly ill and sends for Jesus' help. Luke captures this story with all the ethnic, social, and economic tensions involved. The centurion does not approach Jesus himself, but the request comes through Jewish elders of the city (Luke 7:1–3). The Jewish elders vouch for the centurion, appealing to his love for Israel and his generosity in building the local synagogue (Luke 7:4). Then, as Jesus is on the way to the centurion's home, the centurion again communicates through mediators, who graciously ask Jesus not to come but to merely speak the command, and the servant will be healed. The centurion honors Jesus by navigating the Jewish and gentile divisions (sending mediators) and not placing Jesus in a position to compromise the cultural and religious codes (not inviting Jesus to his home); Green, *Gospel of Luke*, 284.

14. The Greek word can be translated righteousness or innocent. Bock, *Luke*, 377.

15. Brown et al., *Peter in the New Testament*, 153.

for the surprise that God's love is expansive; even an enemy gentile can participate as a full member of Christ's family. Luke sets the stage for a curious encounter that kicks off while Peter is in Joppa.

Peter Inverts Jonah

Luke activates the Jonah story to present Peter as an inversion or antithesis of Jonah. Jonah gets irritated when faced with God's directive to extend God's forgiving love to Assyrian gentiles and ends up alone, hateful toward the people God loves. On the other hand, Peter trusts God's command and willingly extends that love, teaching his community to do the same. Luke cues Jonah's story by placing the events in the same city, Joppa, and referencing it four times in Acts 10 and ten times in Acts 9–11. Yet, "Joppa" mentions remain conspicuously absent from the rest of Luke–Acts and the entire New Testament. By repeating this unique word and memorable location, Luke indicates his desire for his readers to upload the Jonah story.

Readers can remember the prophet in Joppa, who also once received God's word, inviting him to offer God's forgiveness to Israel's enemies. However, Jonah does not want God to extend mercy to this brutal empire for all the harm they caused his community, so he flees.[16] As Phillip Cary states, "Sending an Israelite to preach to Nineveh in the eighth century BC is a little like sending a Jew to preach to Berlin in the 1930s."[17] However, with a storm, some very upset sailors, and a giant fish, God drags Jonah to Nineveh anyway. Despite Jonah doing the very minimum by delivering a message one sentence long, all of the enemy Assyrians repent—even their animals. God was working in the lives of the Ninevites before Jonah arrived. God wanted to teach Jonah something as he witnessed their response. Yet, Jonah was stubborn. He was convinced he had interpreted God's words correctly but completely missed God's character and expansive love. Jonah perceived God's lavish mercy upon the gentiles as a great evil because God was showing favor and kindness toward his enemies. God's grace invites Jonah's relationship with the Ninevites to change, but Jonah declines the invitation. In the end, his gentile hatred turns to anger at God's love and inclusion.[18]

---

16. Berger, *Jonah in the Shadows*.
17. Cary et al., *Jonah*, 40.
18. Jonah 4; Cary et al., *Jonah*, 127.

Two messengers of God, in the same city, hundreds of years apart, face a similar decision: Will God's extravagant love guide them to uproot the social division of their world and embrace the expansion of God's family? Interestingly, Peter's Aramaic name is Simon bar-Jonah. Matthew portrays Jesus referring to him with that name right before Jesus famously declares, "And I tell you that you are Peter, and on this rock, I will build my church. . . . I will give you the keys of the kingdom of heaven. Whatever you bind on earth will have been bound in heaven, and whatever you release on earth will have been released in heaven." (Matt 16:18–19). Matthew connects Peter's role in the gentile mission by referring to Peter as "Simon bar-Jonah." Luke knows this name but never refers to Peter that way. It is possible that Luke intentionally refrains from using that name to reserve the direct connection between Peter and Jonah for his Acts 10 story.[19]

Peter Fulfills Daniel's Dream

Luke then ties Peter's and Daniel's visions together in his attempt to suggest that the Son of Man has arrived in Jesus, which means that the time to enact an indiscriminate welcome of all people has now come. Luke embeds a command in Peter's vision—"rise " (ιστημι) and "eat" (εσθιω)—linking these divine dreams. Readers unfamiliar with strict dietary practices connected to religious identity mistakenly reduce the meaning of Peter's dream down to a picture of old food rules and struggle to grasp its significance. While keeping kosher is at play, there is so much more.[20]

By the first century, circumcision, Sabbath keeping, and kosher eating had become the three hallmark identifiers of faithful followers of Judaism. Parents told their children heroic tales of women and men

---

19. Luke also alludes to Jonah in his Gospel. In Luke 11:29–32, Luke uses "Jonah" four times and nowhere else in Luke–Acts. Here, Jesus raises Jonah's Ninevites and other foreigners (the Queen of the South/Sheba) to stand in judgment over his Jewish kin. Luke captures Jesus using the sign of Jonah to highlight the great faith of gentile figures against the nonexistent faith of Jesus' Jewish audience (Cary et al., *Jonah*, 79). Luke uses this narrative section to surprise his readers with who God will include as a part of God's family. Some scholars suggest that Luke deliberately crafts this story to point forward to the gentile mission. See Wall, "Peter, 'Son' of Jonah," 79.

20. The foundation of Judaism is the belief that God graciously rescued the people of Israel and entered a covenant together as his chosen people. Torah observance is a way to demonstrate their loyalty to God. This idea that grace comes first as a gift from God and his people work to show their faithfulness defined Judaism in antiquity; Sanders and Chancey, *Paul and Palestinian Judaism*, 656.

who were willing to suffer and even starve because they refused to break the food laws.[21] Similar lore emerged during Antiochus Epiphanes IV's reign.[22] Those who compromised on food regulations were seen as enemies of God and not a part of the true Jewish community.[23] The Torah identifies what kinds of animals were permitted and prohibited for eating.[24] These food laws offered ancient Israel a clear and regular way to identify those who followed Yahweh as they lived among many cultures and religious practices. Kosher rules acted as symbols pointing to the division between the unclean gentiles and the clean Israelites. Over time, the animals in the food laws began to represent different peoples.[25] Jewish literature could metaphorically speak about forbidden people through the imagery of unclean animals.[26] The Hebrew Bible depicts foreigners as forbidden animals, including the book of Daniel.[27]

Daniel 7 depicts one of Daniel's dreams, which uses animal imagery to present the history of the nations.[28] The four extraordinary monsters—or mutated beasts—that rise from the sea represent the warring nations against Israel.[29] The second creature is told to "rise and eat."[30] Luke copies the wording in Acts 10 to help readers meditate on and interpret what is happening in Peter's vision. Daniel's mutated monsters are devouring many nations in his vision, imagery that offers a scathing social critique on the vicious ways that human empires ingest people groups through deadly conquest. Empires consume people and turn people into resources to use. The monsters are like chaotic waters that oppose life; they embody

---

21. Daniel is one of those heroes. He refused to eat the food the Babylonians offered (Dan 1).

22. Dunn, *Beginning from Jerusalem*, 392–93.

23. Wright, *People of God*, 168.

24. Specifically Lev 11 and 19.

25. The Animal Apocalypse of 1 Enoch, written between 300 and 200 BCE, retells the history of the world by using animals to delineate between the different peoples of the earth; the Testament of Naphtali depicts nations as beasts who will take the tribes of Israel into captivity. (5:6–8); 4 Ezra 11.1—12.39 uses animal imagery to refer to the nations.

26. Staples, "'Rise, Kill, and Eat,'" 3–17.

27. Ezekiel 34 depicts nations as unclean "beasts of the field" who prey on Israel, the clean "sheep."; Jer 5 represents the nations as animals ready to attack a rebellious Judah.

28. Goldingay, *Daniel*, 185.

29. Bryan, *Cosmos*, 217.

30. These are the Greek words used in the Septuagint (Greek translation of the Old Testament) that was readily available during the first century.

turmoil and violence.[31] Notice Luke is not merely making a connection between two evils. More specifically, he suggests that at the core of this evil is a willingness to think of certain "kinds" of people as worthless, so much so they are worth destroying or disregarding.

Daniel 7 concludes with a vision of the Son of Man, a ruling figure who looks like a human sitting on the throne of God. Like everyone else, he gets trampled by the beasts but rises and ascends to the Ancient of Days. This divine-human ruler removes the beastly empires from the world, not the people of the empires, as the nations come to worship him (Dan 7:12–14). When the Son of Man takes his seat, it represents the vindication and victory of Israel's God over the nations who are crippled by constant war.[32]

Luke intentionally links Dan 7, presumably as a way to acknowledge the pain and suffering caused by these *mutated monsters*—these non-Jewish nations that have been wreaking havoc for too long. Yet, now that Jesus has arrived, it is time to join with the Son of Man, who is fulfilling his intent to dismantle imperialistic efforts and welcome the peoples of the earth to trust in the way of the divine-human seated on the throne of God.[33] Luke expects his audience to upload these ideas and imagine what Peter is wrestling with in his vision and its implications for rejecting formerly acceptable social division.

Luke notes that this dream repeats three times (Acts 10:16). God is testing Peter in this vision.[34] Jesus had already taught Peter that food

---

31. Daniel mentions the sea these monsters emerge from, harkening back to the lifeless and chaotic waters in the Genesis creation narrative. These empires have no regard for the well-being of the communities they conquer.

32. Wright, *People of God*, 294. Furthermore, scribal evidence demonstrates first-century Jewish people interpreted Dan 7 in light of the earlier mentioned temple desecration caused by Antiochus Epiphanes, which would also strengthen the vision's connection to Acts 10. See Bryan, *Cosmos*, 235.

33. The prophet Isaiah provides a metaphor for a future day when the wolf and the lamb will graze together, and the lion will eat straw like an ox (Isa 65:25). It seems unlikely that Isaiah uses this image merely to predict a day when wild predators and prey become friendly toward one another. The prophet assumes his audience understands these animals to represent warring peoples whom the Son of Man will bring together in peace. This imagery creates a more poignant picture of a multicultural community of "others"—now joined in genuine love.

34. Throughout the Hebrew Bible, the number three often symbolizes a testing time (Abraham [Gen 22], Egypt [Exod 10], Israel in the wilderness [Exod 15], and Israel preparing to enter the promised land [Josh 1] are a few examples of testing). Peter experienced two similar tests with the three denials (Luke 22:55–62) and the threefold restoration (John 21). Luke highlights the moment's significance by presenting this

does not make a person clean or unclean (Mark 7:1–19; Matt 15:10–20)[35] and that sentiment is emphasized through the divine voice declaring, "Do not call anything impure that God has made clean" (Acts 10:15). Peter has to decide: Will he deny the way of Christ again and uphold a narrow Jewish mindset that ostracizes non-Jews? Or will he be loyal to Jesus' ways and live in a new reality where God shatters the barriers between people and creates a new family? Luke uses Peter's test to invite the reader into their own decision point. Luke ultimately challenges his readers to imagine those they have previously assumed were opposers or enemies, recognize that God has made them "clean," and invite them to participate in his new family. Jesus, the Son of Man, has come, so it is now time to enact the inclusion of every person on earth.

Peter Witnesses the Gentile Pentecost

Luke recalls the Holy Spirit's work in Acts 2 and depicts Peter as a witness to a gentile Pentecost. He links the two Pentecost stories with the keyword "tongues." At the first Pentecost, the Holy Spirit moves, and then Peter speaks. In Acts 10, Luke inverts the order so that the Holy Spirit interrupts the end of Peter's speech. Through this new Pentecost story, Luke asserts that God welcomes all humans, not certain kinds of people, and a commitment to loving people with impartiality demonstrates loyalty to Jesus, who consistently did the same.

The Holy Spirit

The Holy Spirit is the central figure in this chapter. "Spirit" (πνευμα) appears five times in Acts 10, once as the voice speaking to Peter, once about God anointing Jesus, and three times concerning Cornelius and his gentile community. The same divine presence that empowers Jesus and guides Peter now dwells within these foreigners. This moment begins a thorough reimagining of the concept of the people of God—there is no "us" versus "them."[36] Luke designs his depiction of the Holy Spirit's

---

vision as the third time Peter experiences a threefold test.

35. Luke, who most likely used Mark's Gospel in writing his Gospel account, omits this story. It seems that Luke reserves this teaching topic for his second volume and this narrative in Acts 10. Dunn points this out in Dunn, *Beginning from Jerusalem*, 385.

36. Bond, "Acts 10:34–43," 81.

empowerment as the culminating act of Peter's speech, emphasizing that if God, through the gift of the Holy Spirit, does not separate people based on their ethnic, social, or religious identity, then neither should the church.

Peter's Speech

Peter's speech begins with his acknowledgment that "God does not show favoritism" (Acts 10:34) and a recognition that "Jesus is Lord of all" (Acts 10:36). These are a direct link to Deut 10:17–19, a speech ascribed to Moses who invites the Israelites to demonstrate loyalty to God by embodying his character and treating people fairly, including foreigners. This passage also emphasizes God's lordship over all—a deeply rooted Judaic idea. Judaism's first-century monotheism presented tension because if there is only one God over all, then he is the God of all people, the Israelites *and* the others.

Moses's speech defines why God initially set Israel apart. They were supposed to show the world God's love through how they interacted with one another in their distinctiveness, which is the heart underneath being kosher.[37] When God first calls Abraham and promises to give him a massive family, his stated purpose is so that Abraham's family would become a blessing to "every family of the Earth" (Gen 12:1–3). The point was to bless and care for, not to dominate over other nations or to create social hierarchies of who does and does not matter to God. Moses's instruction hopes to enable Israel to reveal the "otherness" of God's way, not to differentiate between whom God loves and blesses. So, in Acts 10, Luke uses Peter's speech to return to this original goal—if Jesus is Lord of all, then all people of every nation are God's beloved. Luke moves Jewish monotheism further than before, where one does not need to be Jewish to belong to God's family.[38] To make his point, Luke describes the Holy Spirit as an interrupter who "joins" Peter's speech by falling upon, or coming down upon, everyone who heard Peter speaking. Luke does not distinguish between the repentant hearers or the hearers who believed, but "*all* who heard" (Acts 10:44). Whatever theological reservations or anthropological fears Peter had that caused him to favor one kind of person over-against another, the Holy Spirit shatters them. Luke shows

---

37. Wright, *Acts for Everyone*, 160.
38. Thiede, *Simon Peter*, 146.

Peter participating with God to set the trajectory for Jesus' church that welcomes, includes, and grafts in all people without partiality.

Tongues

Luke uses the Spirit's outpouring as evidence that those who receive the divine presence join with Christ, whom God anointed by the same Spirit (Acts 10:38), and they will live as equal partners in the community. He supports this mutuality by referring to "tongues." Luke uses this word only six times in the book of Acts and always connects it to the Holy Spirit's work (Acts 2:3, 4, 11, 26; 10:46; 19:6). The first four appearances are in Acts 2 when the Holy Spirit empowers the disciples on the day of Pentecost. Here, Jewish persons throughout the diaspora hear the good news of Jesus in their native languages. In Acts 10, a new Pentecost is happening because gentiles are now speaking in tongues, too.[39] Speaking in tongues means that people could spontaneously communicate in foreign languages they did not previously know, which meant they could talk with people present from other native cultures without any language barriers. Language and culture are inseparably linked.[40] Therefore, speaking in tongues is a symbol of diversity and unity. It honors the other's cultural identity and uniqueness by including their language and not requiring them to conform, which allows them to keep elements of their culture while they join this new community. They are included in the family of God and welcomed with their differences. Previously, gentiles were allowed to enter the family of God, but doing so required a willingness to conform to Jewish cultural customs (e.g., circumcision, dietary laws, Sabbath keeping) and a renunciation of previous cultural identities.[41] In other words, you could join as long as you became fully "Jewish." Luke's narrative intentionally keeps the idea of circumcision out of the story, as if previous boundary markers like this were no longer on Peter's mind.[42] Now, the boundary marker for identifying with God's family has shifted; allegiance to Jesus and his teaching of loving one's neighbor, even enemies, fulfills observance and faithfulness to the Torah (Acts 10:34–36).

---

39. Dunn, *Beginning from Jerusalem*, 399; Helyer, *Life and Witness*, 77.

40. Barreto, "Negotiating Difference," 132.

41. Judaism did not have missionary endeavors, but they did welcome outsiders who wanted to follow their ways. See Dunn, *Beginning from Jerusalem*, 391.

42. Thiede, *Simon Peter*, 147.

Doing Right

Detractors of this interpretation may contend that God still discriminates based on Peter's words in Acts 10:35: "But [God] accepts from every nation the one who fears him and does what is right." The Hebrew Bible ties the "fear of God" and "doing right" together to describe loyalty to Israel's God. In the first century, Torah keeping was the way to demonstrate faithfulness. However, Peter defines "does what is right" by connecting it to what God did through Jesus in the next verse, "announcing the good news of peace" (Acts 10:36). It seems Peter describes the "right thing" to do is what Jesus did, to bring peace where division once ruled. Peter says God empowered Jesus with the Spirit, who "went around doing good and healing all under the power of the devil" (Acts 10:38; some translations use "oppressed"). Peter does not qualify those under the power of the devil. Jesus did not only heal the repentant oppressed or the oppressed who believed. Jesus healed "all" without qualification or preference.[43]

Luke uses the word "all" or "everyone" fifteen times throughout the entire chapter and seven times throughout Peter's six-verse speech (vv. 34–43), to emphasize God's complete impartiality.[44] Peter talks about Jesus' life, death, resurrection, and ongoing work throughout his speech, all of which point to how he brought peace and his unwillingness to diminish his enemies, fight Rome, or condemn people. Instead, he extends forgiveness to everyone. Peter says Jesus commanded them to preach that Jesus is "the one God appointed as judge of the living and the dead" (Acts 10:43). Jesus is the judge, not the church's leaders or the participants. Jesus does not empower his disciples to judge or differentiate between people, including Peter. Therefore, according to Peter, "doing what is right" is defined by Jesus' willingness to extend a message of peace, heal all, and teach others not to judge who is in or out, good or bad, including the living and the dead. Peter ties "doing what is right" to Jesus' love, welcome, and inclusion of everyone.

---

43. "All" has to be connected to impartiality; it cannot mean everyone who was oppressed. In addition, recognizing the devil's oppression ought to lead to the realization that no one is an enemy. The apostle Paul arrives at this conclusion when he declares, "Our struggle is not against flesh and blood" (Eph 6:12). People aren't the problem; the oppression of the deceiver, or the devil, is the problem (Acts 10:38), and God's love in Christ (not violence) heals that problem.

44. The number seven symbolizes completeness in the Hebrew Bible.

Mutualistic Engagement

Luke portrays Peter and Cornelius's interaction in this anti-imperial, mutualistic way. Cornelius, the wealthy Roman soldier, falls humbly before Peter, a Jewish fisherman. Social status in the kingdom of God turns upside down, and Peter's response indicates that he and Cornelius are on equal footing and status.[45] Before Peter even arrived, God was already working in Cornelius to upend his approach to social order by noting that Cornelius was a generous man, a sign that Cornelius understands the way of God revealed in Christ. God had prepared Cornelius to embrace a new mutualistic community that lays down social status. Unlike Jonah, Peter trusts and follows God's instruction and listens to the Spirit, and he and Cornelius reject the social status game to love one another as mutual friends. This bond creates the foundation for radically inclusive communities within first-century Christianity that align with God's expansive love.[46]

Conclusion

In Acts 10, Luke presents a way forward for the first-century church that rejects a purely Jewish-centric emphasis or a complete capitulation to Hellenistic customs but aligns with Jesus' way. He carefully designs Peter's encounter with Cornelius to present Peter as an inverse of the prophet Jonah, a fulfillment of Daniel's dream, and a witness to another Pentecost. Through the narrative, Luke contends that everyone is God's. God works beyond the community's imagination, as seen with the Ninevites and Cornelius's household. As the church lives out Jesus' teaching to love all others—including enemies (Luke 6:27; Matt 5:43)—they will realize no human is *actually* their enemy.

Second, Luke affirms the church is an anti-imperial mutualistic community. Luke links Peter's and Daniel's dreams together (Dan 7), suggesting that followers of Jesus must resist the temptation to think of the church as a human empire. Empires view people as objects to use to expand and secure power to lord over others. But people are not numbers or resources. They are unique persons with cherished backgrounds and experiences for whom God cares deeply—each one bearing his image,

---

45. Thiede, *Simon Peter*, 145; Jennings, *Acts*, 104.
46. Bond, "Acts 10:34–43," 81

each his own miraculous, intentional creation. As such, people's differences can be celebrated and viewed not as threats but as ways to improve the community. Only when churches yearn to honor differences will tangible unity emerge. In Jesus' community, everyone is loved and treated without favoritism and has the resources to thrive.

Lastly, Luke argues faithfulness to God, or doing what is right, is following the way of Jesus, who broke down division and fostered peace. God invites all people, regardless of ethnic, social, or religious identity, into this Jesus community. The true identifying marker is not loyalty to observing Torah (circumcision, eating kosher, Sabbath keeping) but loyalty to the way of Jesus, which Peter defines as Jesus' love, welcome, and inclusion of everyone. Luke legitimizes this theological and social expansion through the blessing and presence of the Holy Spirit.

Religious communities, past and present, often face the temptation to use their beliefs as boundary markers of who is in and out.[47] In most cases, these do not arise from malicious intent but from a desire to protect their faith or identity. Still, these misguided practices miss the trajectory of the biblical narrative and the heart of God. The Bible does not, by nature, present timeless rules but offers principled wisdom, requiring readers to examine their contexts and imagine new ways that they live out God's wise principles.[48] Acts 10 urges contemporary Christian communities to dismantle false theologies and societal barriers that categorize people as less-than or more-than and to, instead, invite them to embrace others-loving and mutualistic inclusivity anchored in Jesus's way.

Bibliography

Barreto, Eric D. "Negotiating Difference: Theology and Ethnicity in the Acts of the Apostles." *Word & World* 31 (2011) 129–37.
Berger, Yitzhak. *Jonah in the Shadows of Eden*. Bloomington: Indiana University Press, 2016.
Bird, Michael. *A Bird's-Eye View of Luke and Acts: Context, Story, and Themes*. Downers Grove, IL: IVP Academic, 2023.
———. *Jesus and the Origins of the Gentile Mission*. London: T. & T. Clark, 2007.
Bock, Darrell L. *Luke*. Downers Grove, IL: IVP Academic, 2010.
Bond, Helen K., and Larry W. Hurtado. *Peter in Early Christianity*. Grand Rapids: Eerdmans, 2015.
Bond, L. Susan. "Acts 10:34–43." *Interpretation* 56 (2002) 80–83.

---

47. Bond, "Acts 10:34–43," 81
48. McKnight, *Bible Is Not Enough*.

Boyarin, Daniel. *The Jewish Gospels: The Story of the Jewish Christ*. New York: New Press, 2013.

Brown, Raymond E., et al., eds. *Peter in the New Testament: A Collaborative Assessment by Protestant and Roman Catholic Scholars*. 1973. Reprint, Eugene, OR: Wipf & Stock, 2002.

Bryan, David. *Cosmos, Chaos and the Kosher Mentality*. Journal for the Study of the Pseudepigrapha Supplements 12. Sheffield: Sheffield Academic Press, 1995.

Cary, Phillip, et al. *Jonah*. Grand Rapids: Brazos, 2017.

Crossan, John Dominic. *God and Empire: Jesus Against Rome, Then and Now*. New York: HarperOne, 2008.

Cullmann, Oscar. *Peter: Disciple, Apostle, Martyr*. 2nd ed. Waco, TX: Baylor University Press, 2020.

Dunn, James D. G. *Beginning from Jerusalem*. Christianity in the Making 2. Grand Rapids: Eerdmans, 2020.

Fredriksen, Paula. "Philo, Herod, Paul, and the Many Gods of Ancient Jewish 'Monotheism.'" *Harvard Theological Review* 115 (2022) 23–45. https://doi.org/10.1017/S0017816022000049.

Goldingay, John E. *Daniel*. Word Biblical Commentary 30. Dallas: Nelson, 1989.

Green, Joel B. *The Gospel of Luke*. New International Commentary on the New Testament. Grand Rapids: Eerdmans, 1997.

Helyer, Larry R. *The Life and Witness of Peter*. Downers Grove, IL: IVP Academic, 2012.

Jennings, Willie James. *Acts: A Theological Commentary on the Bible*. Unabridged ed. Louisville: Westminster John Knox Press, 2017.

Karrer, Otto. *Peter and the Church: An Examination of Cullmann's Thesis*. New York: Herder & Herder, 1963.

McKnight, Scot. *The Bible Is Not Enough: Imagination and Making Peace in the Modern World*. Minneapolis: Fortress, 2023.

Moffitt, David M. "Atonement at the Right Hand: The Sacrificial Significance of Jesus' Exaltation in Acts: New Testament Studies." *New Testament Studies* 62 (2016) 549–68. https://doi.org/10.1017/S0028688516000217.

Rowe, C. Kavin. *World Upside Down: Reading Acts in the Graeco-Roman Age*. Oxford: Oxford University Press, 2010.

Sanders, E. P. *Judaism: Practice and Belief, 63 BCE–66 CE*. Minneapolis: Fortress, 2016.

Sanders, E. P., and Mark A. Chancey. *Paul and Palestinian Judaism: 40th Anniversary Edition*. Minneapolis: Fortress, 2017.

Sim, David C., and James S. McLaren, eds. *Attitudes to Gentiles in Ancient Judaism and Early Christianity*. London: T. & T. Clark, 2014.

Staples, Jason A. "'Rise, Kill, and Eat': Animals as Nations in Early Jewish Visionary Literature and Acts 10." *Journal for the Study of the New Testament* 42.1 (2019) 3–17. https://doi.org/10.1177/0142064X19855564.

Teeter, Andrew. "Biblical Symmetry and Its Modern Detractors." In *Congress Volume: Aberdeen 2019*, edited by Grant Macaskill et al., 435–73. Vetus Testamentum Supplements 192. Leiden: Brill, 2022. https://doi.org/10.1163/9789004515109_020.

Thiede, Carsten Peter. *Simon Peter: From Galilee to Rome*. Grand Rapids: Zondervan, 1988.

Wall, Robert W. "Peter, 'Son' of Jonah: The Conversion of Cornelius in the Context of Canon." *Journal for the Study of the New Testament* 9/29 (1987) 79–90. https://doi.org/10.1177/0142064X8700902904.

Oliver, Isaac Wilk. *Torah Praxis after 70 CE: Reading Matthew and Luke as Jewish Texts*. WUNT 355. Tübingen: Mohr Siebeck, 2013.

Wright, N. T. *Acts for Everyone. Part 1: Chapters 1–12*. Louisville: Westminster John Knox, 2008.

———. *The New Testament and the People of God*. Minneapolis: Fortress, 1992.

Wright, N. T., and Michael F. Bird. *The New Testament in Its World: An Introduction to the History, Literature, and Theology of the First Christians*. Illustrated edition. Grand Rapids: Zondervan Academic, 2019.

11

Peter the Intercessor (Acts 15)
Peter and the Apostolic Council

ROBERT D. ANDERSON

MARKUS BOCKMUEHL NOTES THAT Simon Peter is the second most mentioned individual in the New Testament, second only to Jesus. Among the disciples, Peter is mentioned most frequently in the Gospels and dominates the first half of the Acts of the Apostles. Even Paul affirms that Peter was the first of the twelve to witness the resurrection of Jesus (1 Cor 15:5).[1] Yet despite his importance, he fades from Luke's story after Acts 15:21 where James, not Peter, makes the final decision for what is commonly called the Jerusalem Council (hereafter referred to simply as "the Council"), circa 48 CE.[2] Indeed, this event provides Peter's final interaction in the second volume of Luke's account, after which the focus for the rest of the narrative remains on Paul. The Council, for many exegetes, becomes a turning point in the narrative with Paul's ministry taking center stage, and Peter's role, in the words of Bockmuehl, "ends on something of a whimper."[3] What is at stake with the Council is whether the identity and unity of the Jesus movement, which began in Galilee, will remain in

---

1. Bockmuehl, *Simon Peter*, 4–5.
2. Thiede, *Simon Peter*, 158.
3. Bockmuehl, *Simon Peter*, 195.

continuity with what Jerusalem represents, or whether Paul's new outreach to the gentile world would become something else.[4]

This pivotal event reflects a tension in the Jerusalem church that began between Hebrews and Hellenists, moving through the death of Stephen, the conversion of Saul (Paul), the acceptance of Cornelius, and Paul's mission in the diaspora.[5] In the narrative, all these events have led us toward the Council. The Council itself prepares us for the subsequent events in Paul's journeys and the final conflict of views in Jerusalem.

My purpose in this chapter is to examine Peter's role in this council as he takes his final narrative bow in the events of the early church. A brief review of the events leading up to the Council with the events at Antioch will be provided to set the stage. To evaluate this meeting and Peter's role, I am using a methodology called field theory, as proposed by Fligstein and McAdam. This method examines the roles of individuals in events that result in conflict and dialogue for resolution.

Field Theory Categories of Evaluation

Field Theory is a sociological framework for examining interactions between groups. This model examines "mesolevel" (midlevel) social order (the field) where various actors, individuals, or collective groups interact with each other. The theory was first introduced to me by Scot McKnight in the class at Northern Seminary, "DM 7852: The New Testament in its World 3," an exploration of the world of the New Testament and the Pharisees. The theory shows how embedded actors fashion and maintain order in a field of challenge and engagement.[6] Events within a strategic action field can be mapped across the following seven elements.

1. Strategic action fields are "fundamental units of collective action in society."[7] The stability of the field can be determined by the ability of actors to reproduce themselves. These are arenas of encounter where different views interact. In our case, the nature of the field is social, not a specific geographical location.

---

4. Dunn, *Acts of the Apostles*, 195.
5. Dunn, *Acts of the Apostles*, 195.
6. Fligstein and McAdam, *Theory of Fields*, 3. Fields can be defined at various levels and can interact with other fields, each with its own set of actors.
7. Fligstein and McAdam, *Theory of Fields*, 9.

2. There is also a broader field environment, where other fields may impact, or be impacted by, the outcome or requirements for the resolution.

3. Incumbents, challengers, and governance units—these are the actors in play within the fields. Incumbents will hold to the existing paradigm or conventions that are being challenged. Governance units make decisions that may affect both incumbents and challengers.

4. Social skill and the "existential functions of the social" define how the actors support their positions. That is, people build meaningful and normative structures that are a collaborative product shared by a group.[8]

5. Changes or disruptions from the outside of a group (exogenous shock), mobilization, and the onset of contention will generate the episode of contention that is being examined. We might ask the question, what is going on that caused the contention?

6. Episodes of contention consist of "a period of emergent, sustained contentious interaction between . . . actors utilizing new and innovative forms of action vis-à-vis one another."[9]

7. The settlement is the final resolution of the interaction. The settlement is usually determined by the governance unit.

These mappings may help us better understand how Peter plays a key role in the dynamics of the Council as various views of participants are presented in Acts. The order of the evaluation will follow the order of events in the text as we view how the interactions take place. I will incorporate the elements of the theory as we evaluate the text.

Defining the Conflict (Acts 15:1–5)

Acts 15:1–5 introduce us to the strategic action fields and the episode of contention, which are defined by the individuals from Jerusalem to Antioch (15:1). The episode of contention is also defined by the Pharisees in the church (15:5). If salvation is for the Jews, then gentiles should become Jews to receive it. Therefore, circumcision and following the

---

8. McAdam, "On the Existential," 232.
9. Fligstein and McAdam, *Theory of Fields*, 21–22.

laws of Moses are required for them to participate in the new Jewish/Christian community.

As noted by Charles Talbert, this opening unit can be arranged in a chiastic pattern to highlight the issues for the Council. The opening can be summarized as follows:

> A—Men from Judea teach that circumcision is necessary for salvation (1)
>
>> B—Paul and Barnabas are appointed to go up to Jerusalem about the question (2)
>>
>>> C—On their way, they report the conversion of the gentiles, bringing joy to the brethren (3)
>>
>> B'—When they come to Jerusalem, they are welcomed by the church and give their report (4)
>
> A'—Some of the Christ-followers who are Pharisees say that circumcision and keeping the law were necessary for gentiles (5)[10]

This paragraph defines two issues for the Council. First, there is a question of whether the gentiles can be saved and be part of the covenant community apart from circumcision. That is, did gentiles need to become Jews to participate in God's kingdom? The second is whether gentiles can fellowship with Jews without becoming proselytes.[11] Gentiles who did not observe the law would be seen, at least by some, as ritually unclean. This was the position of the individuals who came from Jerusalem to Antioch, and the initial position of the Pharisees at the Council. The second issue is whether Jews could have table fellowship with gentile believers without the gentiles being circumcised (becoming Jews), and with full adherence to the law.[12] There was no single answer to these questions from the Jews. Extreme positions, such as found in the book of Jubilees (from the first century BCE), claimed that those who were not circumcised on the eighth day were children of destruction and destined to be destroyed (Jub. 15:26–27). Others allowed for "righteous gentiles" without conversion to Judaism.[13] The question of the responsibility of righteous gentiles who affirmed the God of Israel is not unique to Christianity. It existed

---

10. Talbert, *Reading Acts*, 128.
11. Talbert, *Reading Acts*, 128.
12. Marshall, *Acts*, 257.
13. Parsons, *Acts*, 208–9.

in the Judaism of the first century. We can see this contrast in the story of King Izates, as told by Josephus, where two different Jewish teachers (Ananias and Eleazar) have two quite different views of whether gentiles who worship Israel's God should be circumcised (*Antiquities* 20.2.3-4, 34-36). The same question would arise in the early community of Christ-followers, which was predominantly Jewish in character.

These events establish the fields for the Council where the engagement of dispute and dialogue occur. In this case, two interacting fields are in view:

- The Jerusalem church.
- The church in Antioch, representative of the issues for the churches of the diaspora communities.

In the events occurring before the Council, we find a greater response of gentile proselytes to the gospel in Antioch than we would see in Judea and Jerusalem. The entry of these gentiles into the church generated an "exogenous shock," destabilizing the broader field environment that is the church. Both the individuals visiting Antioch from Jerusalem and the Pharisees represent the incumbents who seek to preserve the purity of the church by stating that the gentiles need to be circumcised, making them ritualistically covenant members. This response was probably natural for Judeans, particularly for the Pharisees in the church. For them, the purity of the fellowship would have been the main concern.[14] In addition, another possible reason for the tension over the entry of gentiles into the church was the increase in Zealot activity in the late forties. Zealot hatred was directed first toward the Roman occupation, and then toward mingling with gentiles.[15] As such, the issue of gentile involvement may have come to the forefront in the early church. As noted by one commentator, the text does not say that the individuals from Jerusalem were composed of believers.[16] The letter sent to Antioch by the apostles and elders indicates that these persons went out without their authorization (15:23-29). Therefore, it is possible that these individuals were not Christ-followers, but representatives of the broader spectrum of Judaism. However, they must have had some association with the church since the letter to the gentiles suggests that they "went

---

14. Sanders, *Judaism*, 349-50.
15. Riesner, *Paul's Early Period*, 280.
16. McKnight, *Acts*, 175.

out from us" (*ex hēmōn exelthontese*), and the Pharisees within the Jerusalem church initially agreed with them (15:5).

We also should not assume that this was the position taken by all Pharisees. Paul is a self-proclaimed Pharisee (Acts 23:6–9; Phil 3:4–6) who challenges those holding the requirement that gentiles needed to be circumcised. Later in Acts 23:9, in his encounter with the Jewish council and high priest, Paul gained support from non-Christian Pharisees.

At this point, we want to analyze the fields in play partially. The Jerusalem church and the resulting Council acted as a state field, with some authority to intervene in situations, and it had decision-making authority for the broader church environment. This extended to intervening in the current situation and making rules of conduct that would stabilize the field/environment.[17] Antioch was a "proximate field" with ties to Jerusalem, and actions at Antioch could have a ripple effect on the whole church.[18] The embassy from Antioch, which included Barnabas and Paul, acted as the challengers to the position of the incumbents. As a result of the dispute between the incumbents of the church and the Antioch delegation, the apostles and elders withdrew to consider the matter (15:6), resulting in much debate (15:7a).[19] While the issue of gentile requirements was presented to the whole of the church, a decision was required by the church leadership. That there is debate among the church leaders implies that some may have been members of the Pharisees.

While the "B" verses (vv. 2 and 4) report the decision to go to Jerusalem for a resolution and the arrival and report in Jerusalem, the central verse (3) is often overlooked. The Antioch delegation traveled through Phoenicia and Samaria, probably along the coastal trade route called the Via Maris. Along the way, they gave reports to the Christian communities about the conversion of the gentiles and garnered support from those communities.

This journey may have more importance than we would initially realize. It exhibits both the social skills of the delegation from Antioch and the existential function of social interaction among the churches. By

---

17. Fligstein and McAdam, *Theory of Fields*, 19.

18. Fligstein and McAdam, *Theory of Fields*, 15.

19. Witherington, *Acts of the Apostles*, 453. Witherington does not see this as a separate meeting but notes that others hold this view. In my opinion, there is a shift in focus to the apostles and elders that excludes the whole church. The ongoing "free for all" (Marshall) may suggest that Pharisees were included in one of these two groups. See also Marshall, *Acts*, 263–64.

gaining support from the existing churches of the region, the Antioch delegation established that the position of those demanding circumcision of the gentiles was not universal within the churches. Even more the support was coming from regions where the church had been scattered in Acts 8 and Acts 11 after the death of Stephen. The region of Phoenicia was along the Mediterranean coast next to Syria and would have been more Hellenistic than Judea. Samaritans were seen as distinct from Jews, although they also claimed to be part of Israel. The Christian communities would be sensitive to law compliance issues since Samaritans had their own version of the Torah. Given the dispersion of Acts 8 and 11, these communities also had ties to Jerusalem but would include Hellenists and possibly gentile Godfearers. Their support bolstered the position of the Antioch delegation as it approached Jerusalem.

However, upon arrival in Jerusalem, after Paul and Barnabas report their activities, Peter is the one who gives voice to the challengers' argument.

Up until the Council, Peter was the dominant figure in Acts. Peter proposes a replacement for Judas, resulting in Matthias's appointment (1:15–22), acts as the spokesman for apostles at the temple after the descent of the Spirit during Pentecost (2:14–36), participates in healings (3:1–26; 5:12–16; 9:32–35), is resisted and persecuted by the temple authority (4:1–22; 5:17–42), rebukes dishonesty in the community (5:1–11), and imprisoned by Herod Agrippa I and miraculously freed by an angel (12:1–19).[20] As noted by Markus Bockmuehl, even Paul is "a distant, almost derivative second."[21] Viewing these events and the parallels we can see in the Gospels, one might suspect that Peter is the successor to Jesus. The story of Peter's encounter with Cornelius (Acts 10:1—11:18), is an important factor in the decision of the Council, considering Peter's appeal to that event. Our last report of Peter before the Council is that he departed Judea for "another place" (12:17), possibly going to Rome.[22] In Acts 13 and 14, Barnabas and Paul take center stage. Yet at this point in the Council, Peter reappears and is central to the decision-making process.

---

20. Bockmuehl, *Simon Peter*, 27–28.

21. Bockmuehl, *Simon Peter*, 124.

22. Thiede, *Simon Peter*, 153–58. The location of Peter's imprisonment is implied as Judea since Herod leaves Judea and departs for Caesarea in 12:19.

Peter's Argument

Peter's role in the Council has been debated. Some have suggested that Peter plays a decisive role by citing his own experience in the conversion of Cornelius, where God gave the Holy Spirit to the gentiles (Acts 10:44–48). However, this does not tell us much about the dynamics of events in the Council and how Peter's speech influenced the church. Moreover, it was James who gave the final judgment of what should be done. It is the interaction between competing views that we may learn something about how Peter's influence worked.

While the embassy from Antioch only names Barnabas and Paul, Peter's appearance in the narrative gives voice to the challengers' argument. We need to review Peter's argument in detail to understand the challengers' position.

> ⁷ After there had been much debate, Peter stood up and said to them . . .[23]

In Acts 12:17b, Peter had departed "to another place," but now reappears for the Council. While some suggest that he possibly went to Rome at that point (around 42/43 CE), a more likely scenario would be that he ministered in the area of Syria or Antioch.[24]

> "My brothers, you know that in the early days God made a choice among you, that I should be the one through whom the Gentiles would hear the message of the good news and become believers."

Peter appeals to a precedent, his encounter with Cornelius, and the gentiles receiving the Holy Spirit (Acts 10 and 11).[25] While not the first to minister to gentiles, Peter received divine revelation to minister to Cornelius and raises this as a prototypical example of what God was doing in the communities that included gentiles. Peter had been chosen to present the gospel, the message of the resurrected Christ, to Cornelius.[26] Peter, therefore, was the first to receive a commission from God specifically for a gentile ministry.

---

23. Unless otherwise noted, all Scriptures quoted are from the NRSV. Greek text is from Holmes, *Greek New Testament*.
24. Hengel, *Saint Peter*, locs. 558–60 of 2652.
25. This appeal has parallels to Gamaliel's defense of the apostles in Acts 5:34–39.
26. Fitzmyer, *Acts of the Apostles*, 546–47.

This seems contrary to what Paul wrote in Gal 2:7–10, where Paul says that Peter was entrusted with the gospel for the circumcised, the Jews, while Paul was entrusted with the gospel for the uncircumcised, the gentiles. We also have Paul and Peter placed in opposition to each other in Gal 2:11–14, where Peter does not show unity with the gentiles in a meal.[27] Paul does not give us many details, but he does rebuke Peter for his withdrawal from the gentiles once "certain people came from James" (Gal 2:12). This withdrawal was scandalous because it did not conform to the gospel that Peter himself preached.[28]

Several suggestions have been made to reconcile these two texts.[29] These can be reduced to three basic views:

1. The events of Gal 2:11–14 are contemporaneous with the events leading up to the Council (Acts 15:1–5).
2. The events of Gal 2:11–14 take place *after* the Council.
3. The events of Gal 2:11–14 take place *before* the Council.

The first view can be supported by similarities we see in the text. Both speak of a Jerusalem visit and a decision. Both are prompted by Jewish legalists from Judea. They both have the same participants—Paul and Barnabas, Peter and James. In both cases, a decision is reached for a law-free gospel for the gentiles. However, the differences in these two texts outweigh the similarities. The letter to the Galatians does not mention the famine visit (Acts 11:27–30) where Paul (Saul) and Barnabas bring relief from Antioch to Jerusalem. Paul also calls the individuals from Jerusalem "false believers" (Gal 2:4) and, in his dispute with Peter, Paul suggests that James sent them (Gal 2:12). In the events leading up to the Council in Acts 15, they are associated with the church of Jerusalem (15:5, 24), but they were not sent by James (15:24).

James's decision in Acts 15 (see below) is not mentioned in Galatians. Such a major decision, the result of Paul and Barnabas's visit to Jerusalem, surely would have been mentioned by Paul in the letter if the events coincided with or were after the Council. It is also unlikely that

---

27. Bockmuehl, *Simon Peter*, 91. Bockmuehl gives F. C. Baur is an example of an exegete who sees Peter and Paul in tension.

28. Green, *Vox Petri*, 282–83.

29. Longenecker, *Galatians*, lxxvii–lxxx.

Peter and Barnabas would have submitted to the influence of these "certain people from James" (Gal 2:12).[30]

It is best then to understand the events of Gal 2:1–14 as occurring before the events of the Council, coinciding with the famine visit of Acts 11:27–30. This would place the confrontation between Paul and Peter (Gal 2) around the time of Herod's persecution. The gospel was preached initially to Jews (11:19), followed by Hellenists (11:20), with Paul joining Barnabas in Antioch teaching for an entire year. Peter's arrival may have coincided with his departure "to another place" (Acts 12:17), outside of the region under Herod Agrippa's control.

Peter's defense of the Antioch view continues:

> [8] "And God, who knows the human heart, testified to them by giving them the Holy Spirit, just as he did to us; [9] and in cleansing their hearts by faith he has made no distinction between them and us."

Peter argues that since gentiles have received the Holy Spirit (Acts 10:44–48) and have a cleansed heart, they will be saved. For Peter, the heart is purified by faith (15:9).[31] He sees this act of God in defining faith as the means of purification for both Jews and gentiles. As noted by Green, "All hear the message of Jesus the Christ, everyone must turn in faith to God and be baptized, and each receives the promise of forgiveness, renewal through the Holy Spirit (2:38), and life (11:18)."[32]

The giving of the Holy Spirit to the gentiles—the household of Cornelius—was a "final confirmation of Peter's authority in admitting gentiles into the church," an act of God that amazes Peter's Jewish companions who participated with him in this ministry.[33] Citing this historical precedent makes Peter's argument more powerful since a conclusion, even if somewhat informal, had already resulted in the receiving of the Holy Spirit by gentiles.

> "If then God gave them the same gift that he gave us when we believed in the Lord Jesus Christ, who was I that I could hinder God?" When they heard this, they were silenced. And they praised God, saying, "Then God has given even to the Gentiles the repentance that leads to life." (Acts 11:17–18)

30. Longenecker, *Galatians*, lxxix.
31. Fitzmeyer, *Acts of the Apostles*, 547.
32. Green, *Vox Petri*, 279.
33. Thiede, *Simon Peter*, 147.

The argument in Acts 15:8–9 follows the same pattern as in Acts 11:17–18. In 11:17–18, Peter argued that since God had given the Spirit to the gentiles and had given them the repentance that leads to life, to resist this was to hinder God's work among them. In Acts 15:8–9, Peter recapitulates this, stating that God both knew and cleansed their hearts, and it is God's testimony for them (not the challengers') when he gave them the Holy Spirit. Therefore, there was no distinction made between Jews and gentiles. As Dunn notes in his review of Acts 11:17–18, the point Peter made was that as far as salvation and the granting of new life, the giving of the Spirit rendered circumcision irrelevant.[34] The same applies to the argument in Acts 15.[35]

> [10] "Now therefore why are you putting God to the test by placing on the neck of the disciples a yoke that neither our ancestors nor we have been able to bear?
>
> [11] On the contrary, we believe that we will be saved through the grace of the Lord Jesus, just as they will."

As Trites and Larkin note, the "burdening" of the gentile believers, establishing the keeping of law as a criterion for salvation is not a contradiction to Peter's own piety (10:14; 11:18), but an acknowledgment of the difficulty that even Jews had with keeping the law.[36] This comment may reflect Peter's Galilean background, particularly with attempts to extend various priestly requirements to all Jews.[37] Rather Peter argues that all are saved by God's grace. Thus, this also can be viewed as an appeal to historical precedence and an appeal to let God's work stand. We can also see this "unburdening" for the gentiles as an act of grace, as leniency in judgment. This grace, which we often associate with Paul's ministry, is a key concept of Peter's theology of salvation, manifested in the giving of the Spirit and the repentance that leads to life (Acts 11:15–18). Grace becomes a dominant theme in 1 Peter as well.[38]

---

34. Dunn, *Acts of the Apostles*, 151.

35. This argument from historical precedent follows the same pattern as Gamaliel's defense of the apostles in Acts 5:34–39, where historical precedents were raised, and Gamaliel warns the Sanhedrin that they may be resisting the work of God by resisting the activity of the apostles.

36. Trites and Larkin, *Gospel of Luke and Acts*, 516.

37. Witherington, *Acts of the Apostles*, 454.

38. Green, *Vox Petri*, 287.

Acts 15:12 notes that after Peter presented his case, an argument from a historical precedent, the assembly kept silent, in much the same way as they did in Acts 11:18. This allowed Paul and Barnabas to make their case for the gentiles' faith apart from circumcision. At this point, Peter is aligned fully with Paul. For Peter, Jesus' lordship is not restricted to the house of Israel. It applies to all who acknowledge the work of God through Jesus the Messiah.[39]

Two things can be said about Peter's intercessory argument in Acts 15:7–11. As noted by Cullmann,

> Later times have often been unjust to Paul by putting him in the shadow of Peter. Theologically, however, scholars seem to me to be unjust to Peter when they put him entirely in the shadow of Paul, or regard him as Paul's antagonist, devoid of understanding for the great Pauline insights.[40]

Yet when we examine Peter's argument, it looks surprisingly like Paul's argument in Romans and elsewhere. This is seen in the following mapping of Acts 15:7–11 to comparable statements in Paul's letters.

- Acts 15:7—Rom 1:5; Gal 1:15–16
- Acts 15:8—Rom 5:5
- Acts 15:9—Rom 3:22
- Acts 15:10—Rom 3:23
- Acts 15:11—Rom 3:24; also Eph 2:8–9

Peter's view as depicted in the Council corresponds to what Paul teaches in his letters. Consequently, we might conclude Luke's summary of Peter's argument is based on the ministry of Paul. However, we might just as easily conclude that Paul's ministry is based on Peter's view of the gospel for all persons. Peter's Pentecost sermon (Acts 2:14–36) alludes to the prophecy of Joel 2:28–32, where God's Spirit would be poured out on all flesh and all who call upon the Lord would be saved (Acts 2:17, 21). The pouring out of the Spirit on the household of Cornelius (Acts 10:44–48; 11:17–18) provided evidence to Peter before the ministry of Paul to the gentiles. At the Council, it is Peter who makes the argument for gentile salvation apart from circumcision based on his prior experience. It may

---

39. Green, *Vox Petri*, 280.
40. Cullmann, *Peter*, 70.

be possible that Paul is simply executing Peter's vision of a Jewish gospel that is applicable for all humanity.

Second, we should be careful not to overextend Peter's statement by suggesting that Jews no longer needed to be circumcised, that the law had been abrogated for Jews, or that gentiles somehow have a different gospel than Jews. What we see in Peter's argument is that we cannot ignore the fact that God sometimes works in ways we do not expect, but his working among the gentiles is the same as his working among the Jews, which is through the Spirit. Jews, despite their love for the law, often struggle to remain compliant with it. This does not negate the goodness of the law but amplifies the need for God's grace. Peter is not suggesting something new for the gentiles that is different from what Jews require. There is one gospel, one grace, one faith for both Jews and gentiles.

Governance Unit—James, the Decision-Maker, and Settlement

While Peter sides with the challengers, he is not the ultimate decision-maker. James takes that role here, giving voice to the governance unit of the Council. However, he bases his decision on Peter's message, noting that Simeon (Peter) had provided evidence that God had looked favorably on the gentiles. Again, the appeal is to a historical precedent in the life of Peter. However, James takes this further, pairing Peter's argument with Jewish Scripture by citing Amos 9:11–12 (from the LXX).[41]

> [16] After this I will return, and I will rebuild the dwelling of David, which has fallen; from its ruins I will rebuild it, and I will set it up, [17] so that all other peoples may seek the Lord—even all the Gentiles over whom my name has been called. Thus says the Lord, who has been making these things [18] known from long ago. (Acts 16:16–18)

James notes that "in every city, for generations past, Moses has had those who proclaim him, for he has been read aloud every sabbath in the synagogues" (15:21). The recognition of Godfearers and proselytes in the synagogues of the diaspora seems to have been known in the Jewish community of Jerusalem and was probably seen in the journey of

---

41. Trites and Larkin, *Gospel of Luke and Acts*, 516–17. The MT reads, "Israel will possess what is left of Edom." The LXX reads, "The rest of humanity might seek." For evidence of later conflict between Peter and Paul, see Hengel, *Saint Peter*, locs. 720–24 of 2652. Hengel appears to see an ongoing conflict in the ministries of both apostles.

Barnabas and Paul (Acts 13:16, 43, 48; 14:1). By citing Amos 9:11–12, James provides additional legitimacy to Peter's argument by establishing that gentiles seeking the Lord was an expectation in the prophets for when the dwelling of David was rebuilt. The Lordship and regency of Jesus the Messiah was preached by Peter in the first sermon at Pentecost, where Peter applies Davidic texts to the events of the death, resurrection, ascension of Jesus, and the coming/giving of the Holy Spirit (Acts 2:25–36). The throne of David had already been established when Jesus sat at the right hand of the Father (2:34–36). Therefore, the salvation and giving of life to the gentiles, as testified by Peter both before and at the Council, was a natural consequence of the messianic reign of Jesus, and the fulfillment of prophecy and the teachings of Moses.

The imposition of a settlement generally comes from state actors; when "field rules are uncertain, actors tend to be more receptive to new perspectives and to engage in search processes to identify alternatives."[42] This often occurs through sustained opposition and mobilization of allies, causing the field to gravitate toward a new institutional settlement. This results in a general sense of order again, with a sense of order for both incumbents and challengers.[43] While the church and the Council may be the overall governance unit, it is James who gives voice to the group with a settlement that meets the needs of all parties.

James agrees with the challengers that gentiles do not need to be circumcised to participate in God's eschatological salvation. However, they should restrict their diet and modify their behavior to allow Jews to fellowship with them. This is a reasonable solution based on the prophetic texts (Jer 12:15; Amos 9:10–11; Isa 45:21; and Lev 17–18 for the behavioral and dietary restrictions). With the restoration of God's blessing to Israel, other peoples would seek the Lord, even the gentiles. We also know that in the cities visited by Paul and Barnabas, there were Godfearers and proselytes, and some level of fellowship would be required for them to participate in synagogues. At the same time, food laws were important for Jews, and Pharisees in particular.[44] The admonition would allow fellowship between Jews and gentiles, particularly in settings outside of Jerusalem and Judea. In terms of the broader field environment, this allowed diaspora communities that might be mixed to interact with and even provide benefits for Jerusalem. Jerusalem

---

42. Fligstein and McAdam, *Theory of Fields*, 22–23.
43. Fligstein and McAdam, *Theory of Fields*, 22–23.
44. Sanders, *Judaism*, 678–86.

maintained (for now) its authority as a state field, providing rulings and guidance to other communities or fields.

We can classify this as an act of mediation on the part of James. It seems to satisfy both sides of the argument and there is no record of Pharisees contesting this settlement. Based on the lenient perspective of Pharisees, this would settle the matter. The assembly ended with a delegation from Jerusalem carrying a letter that presented the decision of the Council, which also noted that the initial party did not represent the Jerusalem church and had no instructions from them (15:22–29).

A Theory of Fields—Mapping the Events

Throughout this study, I have described the events surrounding the Council in the language of the Theory of Fields. We can diagram these events as follows:

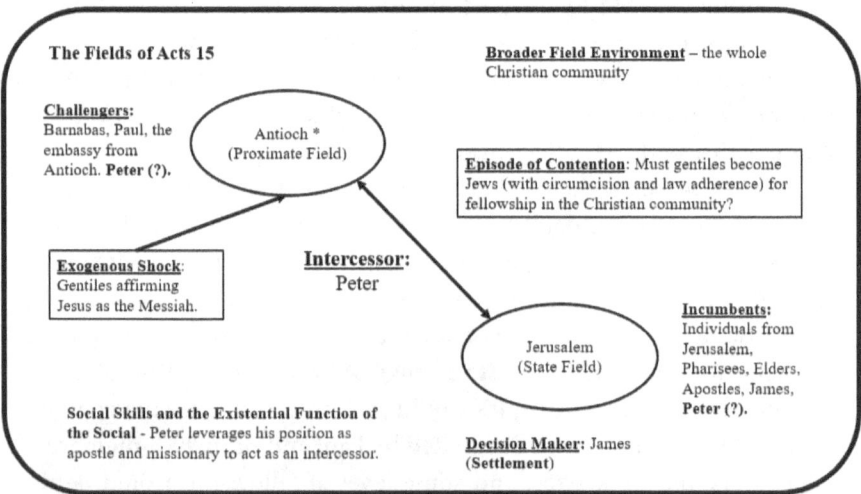

* Antioch is representative of the situation in the diaspora communities of faith.

In summary, the entry of gentiles into the church created an exogenous shock to the church that had a precedent with Peter's encounter with Cornelius but was not expected to be normative (11:17–18; 14:27). This generated an episode of contention in the Antioch church, a proximate field that fell under the authority of Jerusalem, which acted as a state field. This episode revolved around the question of the nature of the church as a Jewish community, and whether gentiles needed to become proselytes to Judaism, with circumcision and compliance to the law of Moses. The individuals from Judea represented the incumbent position of Jerusalem, that full conversion was necessary for community fellowship. The challengers' position, represented by Paul and Barnabas in Antioch, was that gentiles could be considered righteous based on faith in the Messiah (15:1–2). The decision to appeal to the church of Jerusalem and the garnering of support of communities in Phoenicia and Samaria provides us with an example of the use of social skills and the existential function of the social in applying external pressure to the Jerusalem church.

The episode of contention shifts to Jerusalem, where the Pharisees of the Jerusalem church also advocate that gentiles move toward becoming Jews. Incumbents here include the members of the Council, the elders and the apostles. In the Council, James operates in the role of the decision-maker by supporting Peter's argument by referencing the passage in Amos 9.

Peter's role is included in the incumbents since he is a member of the apostles, but he also takes the side of the challengers based on his own history with Cornelius. This puts Peter in a unique position. He can mediate between the challengers and the incumbents, occupying a position in both groups. As such, he becomes an intercessor, one who stands between the incumbents and challengers. This is not a role identified in field theory but one that is clearly biblical.

Peter on Church Leadership

In the study on Simon Peter, we might conclude that Peter's story in Acts ends with his departure to "another place" in Acts 12:17 and he is left with only a supporting role in the apostolic Council in Acts 15.[45] As we have seen, this certainly is not the case. Peter acts directly as an intercessor for the challengers and influencer on the decision voiced by James. Peter effectively bridges the gap between incumbents and challengers in this event. As part of the apostles and elders, and his historical involvement with the founding of the early church in Jerusalem, he positionally had the role of an incumbent. Yet it is precisely based on that history that he can side with the challengers concerning gentile inclusion apart from circumcision based on the evidence of the Spirit. Diversity in the church can be expected not just from divergent gifts of the Spirit, but

---

45. Bockmuehl, *Simon Peter*, 179.

through the expansion of the gospel beyond the boundaries we often set. Building on Peter's history and testimony, James mediates a position that preserves both groups while allowing fellowship among all Christ-followers. Church leaders need to recognize where God is working and seek to affirm the work of the Spirit.

Second, Peter's intercession moves the church from conflict to dialogue, leading to a "one-minded" decision (15:25). This term "one-minded" speaks to the harmony of the decisions and unity in actions of all parties going out from the Council. In a sense, this is the overriding theme of the chapter.[46] This one-mindedness does not imply there would be no problems in the church. It does suggest that ministry decisions made by the church can have a powerful effect on the world when unity in the body of Christ needs to be achieved. This intercession does not negate Israel's unique position but builds on it. Church leaders often need to step outside their paradigms of redemption to understand how God may be working through the Spirit in a new way. Interceding for the sake of the church often involves a change in thinking, like the one that occurred for Peter in his ministry with Cornelius (Acts 10–11). This allowed him to understand the position of the Antioch church and make the appeal for them.

Third, this decision is based on submission to the work of God through the Spirit and is supported by both the historical precedence recounted by Peter (15:7–10) and Scripture (15:13–18).[47] The importance of the testimony of the Spirit in the life of the church should not be neglected. It would be easy to dismiss Peter's testimony as an outlier event and retreat into traditions that may not encompass all of Scripture. The desire for gentiles to be circumcised and obey the whole law would seem good in a Jewish context since Moses prescribes these actions. However, when we repeatedly see the Spirit working in other ways, we need to creatively empower the ministry of the church without compromising Scripture. This is what James is doing by leveraging Peter's testimony (15:14) and the prophets (15:15–18).

Finally, communication of the decisions made by the church is critical. In the case of the Council, this was done by a letter and delegation sent by Jerusalem to Antioch, which was received with rejoicing by the church of Antioch. The letter also attributed in part the success of

---

46. Brown et al., *Peter in the New Testament*, 50.
47. Dunn, *Acts of the Apostles*, 202.

the ministry among the nations to the synagogues and the proclamation of Moses that took place there (15:21). Such an approach anchors the decision of the Council and the success of the gentile mission not just in the work of the Spirit, but also in Moses himself. This affirms, in part, the desire of that portion of the church who seeks to be compliant to Moses (the Pharisees), while at the same time affirming both Peter's and Paul's ministry to gentiles. This approach is not a compromise, but a correction in the understanding of how Moses is applied to the ministry to the nations. Resting on the decisions and working through them benefits the whole church.

As noted in the introduction, this is Peter's final bow in the book of Acts. If there is one other thing we can learn from him it is to listen to the voice of the Spirit and to speak the truth of what God has done, not just in our own lives but in the lives of others. Peter's willingness to intercede for Barnabas and Paul allowed their message to finally be heard by the church. Peter was not the final decision maker in this process, but his intercession moved the church from conflicts to harmony, from division to one-mindedness (ὁμοθυμαδόν). One of our key tasks as Christ-followers is to seek the unity of the church. Often that means interceding for others when our communication breaks down.

Bibliography

Bitzer, Lloyd F. "The Rhetorical Situation." *Philosophy and Rhetoric* (1968) 1–14.
Bockmuehl, Markus N. A. *Simon Peter in Scripture and Memory: The New Testament Apostle in the Early Church*. Grand Rapids: Baker Academic, 2012.
Bond, Helen K., and Larry Hurtado, eds. *Peter in Early Christianity*. Grand Rapids: Eerdmans, 2015.
Brown, Raymond E., et al., eds. *Peter in the New Testament: A Collaborative Assessment by Protestant and Roman Catholic Scholars*. 1973. Reprint, Eugene, OR: Wipf & Stock, 2002.
Bruce, F. F. *The Book of the Acts*. Grand Rapids: Eerdmans, 1988.
Cullmann, Oscar. *Peter: Disciple, Apostle, Martyr*. 2nd ed. Translated by Floyd V. Filson. London: SCM, 1962.
Dunn, James D. G. *The Acts of the Apostles*. Grand Rapids: Eerdmans, 2016.
Fitzmyer, Joseph A. *The Acts of the Apostles: A New Translation with Introduction and Commentary*. Anchor Yale Bible 31. New Haven: Yale University Press, 2008.
Fligstein, Neil, and Doug McAdam. *A Theory of Fields*. New York: Oxford University Press, 2012.
Green, Gene L. *Vox Petri: A Theology of Peter*. Eugene, OR: Cascade Books, 2020.
Hengel, Martin. *Saint Peter: The Underestimated Apostle*. Translated by Thomas H. Trapp. Grand Rapids: Eerdmans, 2010. Kindle.

Holmes, Michael W. *The Greek New Testament: SBL Edition*. Atlanta: SBL, 2011–2013.

Josephus. *The Works of Josephus: Complete and Unabridged*. Translated by William Whiston. Peabody, MA: Hendrickson, 1987.

Longenecker, Richard N. *Galatians*. Word Biblical Commentary 41. Dallas: Word, 1990.

Marshall, I. Howard. *Acts: An Introduction and Commentary*. Tyndale New Testament Commentaries 5. Downers Grove, IL: InterVarsity, 1980.

McAdam, Douglas. "On the Existential Function of the Social and the Limits of Rationalist Accounts of Human Behavior." *Seattle University Law Review* 39:225 (2016) 225–36.

McKnight, Scot. *Acts*. Grand Rapids: Harper Christian Resources, 2022.

Parsons, Mikeal C. *Acts*. Grand Rapids: Baker Academic, 2008.

Peterson, David G. *The Acts of the Apostles*. Pillar New Testament Commentary. Grand Rapids: Eerdmans, 2009.

Riesner, Rainer. *Paul's Early Period: Chronology, Mission Strategy, Theology*. Grand Rapids: Eerdmans, 1998.

Sanders, E. P. *Judaism: Practice and Belief, 63 BCE–66 CE*. 1992. Reprint, Minneapolis: Fortress, 2016.

Talbert, Charles H. *Reading Acts: A Literary and Theological Commentary on the Acts of the Apostles*. Macon, GA: Smyth & Helwys, 2005.

Thiede, Carsten P. *Simon Peter, From Galilee to Rome*. Grand Rapids: Zondervan, 1988.

Trites, Allison A., and William J. Larkin. *The Gospel of Luke and Acts*. Cornerstone Biblical Commentary 12. Carol Stream, IL: Tyndale House, 2006.

Witherington, Ben. *New Testament History: A Narrative Account*. Grand Rapids: Baker Academic, 2001.

———. *The Acts of the Apostles: A Socio-Rhetorical Commentary*. Grand Rapids: Eerdmans, 1998.

12

I Believe in Miracles?
The Miraculous Formation of Peter

James R. North

PETER HAD A VISION, and the entire trajectory of Christianity changed. In Acts 10, as Peter went up on the roof to pray, he probably did not expect to have a vision and, certainly, did not expect the magnitude of the vision he was about to experience. What could have been a simple prayer time ended up being a vision from the Lord, a vision removing any limitations on what those in covenant relationships with the Lord were allowed to eat to remain in good standing. For a community of Christ followers caught in the tension between what God had done in the past and what God was doing now, the question of how much of the law needed to be observed was a chief concern. Peter received a vision of a radical future, and while his initial response was "No Way!," the end result was puzzlement about what this meant for the future.

Little did Peter know that the day before, a day's journey away, in Caesarea, a centurion named Cornelius also had a vision. Cornelius was also praying and had a vision telling him to send for a man called Peter. Cornelius sent for Peter, and Cornelius's cohort arrived at the house where Peter was staying shortly after Peter received his vision from the Lord. Peter journeyed to Caesarea, and the meaning of the vision came into focus as he realized that the dream was about more than food but of God drawing what had previously been unclean gentiles into the community of God. Peter received confirmation the strange vision he received was from the Lord by the testimony of Cornelius and the move of the Spirit. Two strangers, two visions separated by time and space, came together to reveal God's greater plan for humanity.

About two thousand years later, a young woman called Bayley also had a vision. Bayley is a student at the Christian school where I teach the Bible, and she recently went through a significant trauma. Her father died suddenly and tragically in the night while still in his thirties. Her father was a beloved soccer coach and an important school community member. While the loss plunged the entire community into grief, it was also a beautiful picture of the community of God coming together in the midst of struggle. When Bayley returned to the sport her family loved, she nervously went onto the field for the first time shortly after her father passed. She looked up into the stands and saw her father sitting in the stands watching her. She told me that she was initially panicked but immediately felt a wave of peace pass over her. She recalled that she could see her father sitting there for several minutes, and it gave her an otherworldly sense of peace and comfort. After the game, she recounted the story to others and received one unified message. Bayley was told she missed her father so much that her mind somehow conjured him up and placed him in the stands. At no point did anyone even offer up the possibility she had a vision from the Lord. And honestly, I almost told her the exact same thing. When Bayley told me what happened, I started crying and could not immediately respond. It was in the brief time made possible by an inability to speak I felt the quiet voice of the Lord whisper, "Bayley had a vision."

The people she spoke to were all followers of Jesus, not just nominal followers. They are all people deeply committed to the difficult work of becoming a disciple of Jesus. I have been a minister in a Pentecostal denomination for my entire adult life. My initial reaction would have been the same if it had not been for truly divine intervention. How, then, does the church go from two people having a vision serving as unequivocal proof that God's fundamental mission is changing to not realizing when God shows up to comfort a young woman in deep grief? Much of Peter's discipleship happened in the context of miracles. In fact, miracles were a vital part of Peter's spiritual formation. This essential component of spiritual formation is missing from the lives of many Christians in the West. This deficiency causes good, Jesus-loving Christians to miss out when God shows up on the soccer field.

How We Got Here

How did we get from Peter having a vision that changed the trajectory of the church to visions and, by extension, miracles, being largely explained away? As the life of Peter will show, miracles did not cease when Jesus ascended into heaven. It was not just apostles and church leaders remembered for performing miracles but ordinary Christians as well.[1] Miracles continued well into the 300s, where "exorcisms and miracles are the most explicit cause of conversion to Christianity."[2] Augustine recounts a story in *City of God* 22.8 where a man with an abscess was healed before a surgeon could remove the problem. Miracles were still happening, but Origen admits that "signs of the Holy Spirit were manifested at the beginning when Jesus was teaching, and after his ascension, there were many more, though later they became less numerous. Nevertheless, even to this day there are traces."[3]

Miracles continued to occur during the medieval period, especially in the context of "groundbreaking evangelism."[4] Where the church was growing, miracles tended to follow. Many during this period sought to downplay or devalue the importance of miracles.[5] In a letter to Augustine of Canterbury, Pope Gregory praised Augustine's evangelistic work while also warning, "Beware lest the frail mind becomes proud because of these wonderful events. . . . For God's chosen do not all work miracles."[6] By the time the Reformation rolled around, miracles had come under increased scrutiny. Many healings and miracles were associated with Mary, the saints, and relics during the medieval period. Since Luther opposed the collection of relics and the veneration of the saints, he ended up opposing healings and miracles associated with relics and saints.[7] Calvin had an even more conflicted view of miracles. Calvin rejected the idea of praying to a saint for a miracle, but he also believed a prayer to St. Genevieve had saved his life.[8] In the 200 years before the Reformation, there were more than 12,500 miracle stories just from Bavaria, and the reformers credited

---

1. Kelhoffer, "Ordinary Christians," 24.
2. Keener, *Miracles*, 362.
3. Origen, *Contra Celsum* 7.8
4. Keener, *Miracles*, 367.
5. Young, "Miracles in Church History," 115.
6. Bede, *History of the English Church*, 87.
7. Keener, *Miracles*, 372.
8. Keener, *Miracles*, 373.

the devil with most of them. This rejection led to a Reformation movement that was highly skeptical about miracles bordering on anti-supernatural. Fast forward a little over a hundred years, and the Enlightenment will finish what the Reformation started, and the anti-supernatural will start to become a more widely held position.

"A miracle is a violation of the laws of nature; and as a firm and unalterable experience has established these laws, the proof against a miracle, from the very nature of the fact is as entire as any argument from experience can possibly be imagined."[9] David Hume became one of the most outspoken opponents of miracles, and because he was popular both inside and outside of philosophical circles, his influence was immense. Many others would follow in his footsteps, some with a more nuanced perspective. In the modern era, philosopher R. F. Holland was slightly more gracious concerning miracles. Holland argued that a miracle was nothing more than a beneficial coincidence understood from a religious perspective, but in no way did it signify any "divine interference."[10] While Hume used his perspective on miracles as a weapon to denigrate people who believed differently, Holland, at least, allowed people to have a positive experience based on their perspective.

This spectrum of skepticism can be seen in Christians in the West today. A community of New Testament scholars seems fully committed to Hume's line of reasoning, willing to discount not just miracles today but the miracles of Jesus as well.[11] On the far other end of the spectrum, you have Christians who believe that not only does God still do miracles, but God is required always to do miracles. Christians end up being all across the spectrum of miracles, with many not understanding where they are on the spectrum. I grew up in a religious community where miracles were normative but not expected. If someone were sick, we would pray, knowing God could heal, but we did not have an expectation that God had to heal. Even though I grew up in a community friendly to miracles, when I was healed, I did not know how to talk about it.

In 2014, I was out for a jog when an SUV hit me while I was crossing the street. I am lucky to be alive as I easily could have died but ended up breaking my spine in two places. Doctors told me that the recovery process would be long, and I could expect to be in a full back brace for four to five months. A month after I broke my back, I had the final meeting

9. Hume and Flew, *Human Understanding*, 125.
10. Holland, "Miraculous," 44.
11. Keener, *Miracles*, 103.

for my ordination as a minister. At the end of the meeting, as we were about to close in prayer, I asked if they would not mind praying for my back. I would not normally make this sort of request, as I am normally a put-your-head-down-and-struggle-through sort of guy, but my wife was weeks away from having our first child, and having a broken back would severely limit my helpfulness in caring for a new baby. They prayed for me, and I went home. The next day, I had a previously scheduled appointment with the doctor to see how I was progressing. After taking an x-ray, the doctor was surprised to find my back healed when, just two weeks prior, he thought it would be at least another four months.

I was excited to tell people that good news, but, in retrospect, I realize now that how I talked about my healing betrayed my discomfort with the subject and a lack of development in my understanding of miracles. When discussing my healing, I would say, "Either God healed me, or I secretly have the mutant powers of Wolverine, and I healed myself."[12] People knew I was joking, but now I realize it gave people an out. People uncomfortable with the idea of a miracle could default to an R. F. Holland perspective, where it was a happy coincidence viewed from a religious viewpoint. When I told the story from the pulpit, I inadvertently promoted a viewpoint inconsistent with what I claim to believe about miracles.

How should a pastor navigate a culture with widespread views on an important subject like miracles? An answer to this question can be found if we return to the story of Peter. Peter was a disciple whose spiritual formation happened in the context of many great miracles. Not only was he formed by miracles, but he also was the first disciple to perform a miracle after Jesus ascended into heaven, and several of the miracles he participated in were instrumental in steering a young community of faith in the direction God intended.[13] Peter's life can teach the modern pastor much about how to navigate the difficult terrain of miracles.

Formed by Miracles

Miracles were part of the disciples' spiritual formation because they were integral to Jesus' ministry. In Luke 4, Jesus announced the work he was anointed to do—bring good news to the poor, freedom for the oppressed

---

12. For the uninitiated, Wolverine is a character from Marvel comics who possesses the ability to heal from nearly any wound in a very short amount of time.

13. Bockmuehl, *Simon Peter*, 124.

and prisoners, sight for the blind, and favor from the Lord—and miracles were tangible expressions of those purposes. Jesus told his disciples he was going to bring sight to the blind, and multiple times he did exactly what he said he would do. When Jesus declared that he was going to set the oppressed free, Jesus was not being prophetic, merely proclaiming that freedom for the oppressed was coming. He was literally bringing an end to the oppression.[14] Looking back, we realize the fullness of what Jesus meant by that statement, and eventually the disciples would understand as well. However, the disciples also witnessed what Jesus meant in smaller, granular ways. When Jesus and his disciples met the demoniac in the country of the Gerasenes, the disciples witnessed freedom for the oppressed through the miracle of exorcism. The spiritual formation of Jesus' disciples was not just abstract concepts about the kingdom but physical moments where the power of God broke into humanity and gave a preview of the fullness of the kingdom that will be more fully established. Or, as Graham Twelftree put it, "The miracles of Jesus reveal his identity as God himself at work: indeed, God is encountered in the miracles. Thus, the miraculous activity of Jesus is the eschatological work and message of salvation."[15] Those who followed Jesus were not just formed by the miracles they witnessed but by the physical reality of the kingdom of God making things right in the world.

Peter experienced what the other disciples experienced as far as spiritual formation is concerned. However, Peter had more personal interactions with Jesus, recorded in the Gospels, than anybody else. Interestingly, half of Peter's interactions with Jesus had a miraculous component attached. Several of these encounters will be explored in greater detail to better understand Peter's personal formation. For the full list, see the chart below.

---

14. Bock, *Luke*, 408.
15. Twelftree, *Jesus the Miracle*, 343.

Jesus' Direct Interactions with Peter

Interaction	References	Miracle included?
Jesus calls Peter to follow him	Matt 4:19, Mark 1:17, Luke 5:4	Miraculous catch of fish
Peter requests to walk on the water and Jesus calls him out	Matt 14:28–33	Walking on water and calming the storm
Jesus asks Peter, "Who do you say I am?"	Matt 16:17–19, Mark 8:29, Luke 9:20	No
Jesus rebukes Peter	Matt 16:23, Mark 8:33	No
Transfiguration—"Shall I build some shelters?"	Matt 17:4, Mark 9:5, Luke 9:33	Jesus transfigured, Moses and Elijah show up
Jesus instructs Peter to pay their tax with a fish coin	Matt 17:25–27	A miracle coin in a fish's mouth
Peter asks Jesus how many times he must forgive	Matt 18:22	No
Jesus washes Peter's feet; Peter objects	John 12:6–11	No
Jesus predicts Peter's betrayal	Matt 26:34, Mark 14:30, Luke 22:34, John 13:36–38	No
Jesus tells Peter to watch and pray after falling asleep in Gethsemane	Matt 26:40, Mark 14:37	No
Peter cuts of Malchus's ear; Jesus chastises Peter	Matt 26:52, Mark 14:47, Luke 22:50, John 18:11	Jesus heals the severed ear
Jesus reaffirms Peter's call	John 21:1–19	Miraculous catch of fish

Peter's relationship with Jesus was bookended by two remarkably similar miraculous events.[16] Before Peter decided to follow, Jesus provided a miraculous catch of fish for fishermen who had worked all night and had not caught a thing. As is often the case in the Gospel of Luke, faith in Jesus follows the miraculous.[17] Faith, in this instance, looks like Peter responding to the call Jesus gave him. He left his nets and became a disciple of Jesus. About three years later, we met a different Peter. Peter was by the sea again, similar to when Jesus first called him, but this time the

16. Bockmuehl, *Simon Peter*, 106.
17. Green, *Gospel of Luke*, 233.

man on the shore was someone Peter knew. Someone Peter knew and recently betrayed. I wonder when Peter knew Jesus had forgiven him. Was it when he responded obediently to Jesus' instructions and was blessed with a miracle catch? Or was it when they sat down and talked after breakfast? The text does not betray the answer, but the timing of the miracle and when Jesus and Peter talked is significant from a formation perspective. Jesus allowed Peter to participate in the miracle before they worked things out. Peter's failure as a disciple did not preclude him from experiencing the miraculous bounty of fish. This is not the only time Peter's failure has been framed in conjunction with a miracle.

Perhaps the best-known story about Peter is when he asks Jesus to let him walk on the water, and Jesus calls him out. Jesus walking on the water is found in Matthew and John, but only the Gospel of Matthew includes Peter in the miracle. Matthew alone portrays Peter as having both faith and doubt.[18] Much has been made of Peter losing faith and beginning to sink, and it is an important point in the story. The nature and significance of this miracle need further investigation. Matthew describes the scene in a matter-of-fact way, as he does in other miracles of nature. Walking on the water was merely a "practical response to a difficult situation."[19] The other disciples' reaction when they reach the boat shows what an important miracle this was to the disciples. The miracle evoked a "suitably awed and theologically loaded response from the disciples."[20] Jesus revealed power that could subdue even the chaos of the unruly sea. However, before Jesus subdued the sea, Peter believed that Jesus could extend that power to Peter. Not only could Jesus walk on the sea, but he could also enable Peter to do so. Participating in a miracle has a much different value from a formation standpoint than just observing a miracle occurring.

Peter's discipleship was not simply watching Jesus do miracles but participating with Jesus. Though Peter doubted and started to sink, he experienced what it was like to walk on the water. There is a world of difference between watching someone and doing it. An embodied experience will always produce greater and more lasting results than just watching someone else. Further, Peter learned from this experience that trying and failing is not the end. Jesus chastises Peter for doubting, but

---

18. Bockmuehl, *Simon Peter*, 25.
19. France, *Gospel of Matthew*, 566.
20. France, *Gospel of Matthew*, 567.

Jesus does not let him sink. Jesus does not hold Peter's failure against him, which should be very encouraging news for the rest of us.

When Peter followed Jesus, he certainly learned much from his teachings. However, he must have learned much from participating in miracles with Jesus. Peter knew what it was like to be hungry and be satisfied by a miraculous bounty of food. Peter knew what it was like to feel the power of God as he walked on the chaos of the sea. He knew what it was like to fail and still be allowed to participate in a miraculous catch just before experiencing the miracle of being reconciled with a betrayed friend. It is this formation that will prepare him for taking a leadership role on the day of Pentecost.

Peter's Practice of Miracles

After Jesus ascended into heaven, Peter took up the mantle of carrying Jesus' message forward. Peter followed in Jesus' footsteps, not just in proclaiming the good news of the kingdom of God with words but tangibly through miracles. With the exception of nature miracles, Peter replicated most of the miracles that he saw Jesus perform.[21] Jesus healed a paralytic, and Peter healed a paralytic. Jesus miraculously evaded a crowd that wanted to kill him; Peter miraculously escaped prison before he could be killed. Jesus raised people from the dead; Peter raised someone from the dead. Peter illustrates what a disciple ought to do. Peter's apprenticeship to Jesus included preaching, teaching, and miracles. As Peter began his own ministry, he would copy how he was formed by following Jesus.

From Pentecost to his second escape from prison, there are many examples of Peter being involved in the miraculous.[22] We will now turn our attention to look more closely at several examples. Peter was the first disciple to perform a miracle after Jesus ascended. Acts 3 recounts Peter and John going to the temple courts and healing a man who had been paralyzed from birth. Interestingly, Acts makes clear that Peter and John frequently went to the temple courts, and the crippled man was brought daily to the temple courts. The crippled man had been in proximity to Peter and John but did not seem to know they could heal him because he

---

21. Nature miracles are a category of miracles in which the manipulation of natural elements occurs. Examples include walking on water, multiplying food, and calming the storm.

22. See Acts 2:14; 3:1; 5:3, 12, 19; 8:17; 9:32, 36; 10:9; 12:6.

only asked for money.[23] Peter only responds to the paralytic after the man initiates conversation. Peter was not searching for someone to heal but was willing to respond with healing when initiated. Healing was common for Peter, but it was not all that he did. Peter could not be diminished to just being a healer, which is an important distinction. Several chapters later, Peter chastised Simon the Sorcerer for only wanting power because Peter knew there was more to the Christian life than power.

Peter reinforces this concept later in the passage when he tells an amazed crowd that his power did not heal the man. Peter knows he was not the one who had the power and did not deserve the credit. Peter takes the opportunity to correct the crowd so there is no misunderstanding about what is happening.[24] Further, Peter goes on to make sure people know that his personal piety did not fuel the miracle. Peter knew deeply that miracles often come through broken vessels because he had experienced this reality when participating in Jesus's miracles. In this brief interaction, Peter reveals that disciples ought not to get glory for what the Lord is doing in and through us.

Another important insight into Peter and miracles can be found in Acts 5:12–16. This passage summarizes the work of the apostles and the results of this work. Peter and the apostles had been healing many, resulting in more people becoming Christians.[25] What is instructive about this passage is not the miracles themselves but what happens after the miracles. Promptly after many were healed, the apostles were taken and put in prison. The sequence of signs and wonders leading people to follow Jesus, resulting in persecution, is common in Acts. Miracles and persecution often went hand in hand.[26] Peter and the apostles are lucky in this particular instance, and God miraculously helps them escape prison. There will be another occasion where Peter miraculously escapes from prison in Acts 12, but this is not always the case.

In Acts 4, a similar sequence is present. Peter had healed the paralytic, preached to the crowd, and was immediately imprisoned. After talking to the Sanhedrin, Peter was eventually allowed to go, but there was no miraculous escape this time. Miracles did not lead to an easier life for Peter and the early Christians. Miracles greatly benefited the

---

23. Keener, *Acts*, 1047.

24. Peter has had to use a speech to correct the crowd before: see Acts 2:15. See Bock, *Acts*, 167.

25. Witherington, *Acts of the Apostles*, 227.

26. Young, "Miracles in Church History," 105.

recipient but never led to any political power to help increase the collective standing of Christians in society.[27] Miracles did not create a path to an easy life. Even after the miraculous release from prison in chapter 5, the apostles still received a flogging for the trouble they had stirred up. Despite the problems that miracles often caused, Peter and other disciples did not stop allowing themselves to be used by God to bring about miraculous ends.

Inevitably, there were other problems miracles were likely to generate. In Acts 9, Peter travels around Lydda and hears of a faithful disciple called Dorcas who had recently died.[28] Peter goes to Joppa to see the woman, and, after a short time, he tells her to get up. Dorcas, by the power of God, rises from the dead. On the surface, it does not seem like rising from the dead could lead to difficulties. However, once it became clear that resurrection was possible, the inevitable question would be, why is Stephen still dead? Stephen was specifically picked to serve widows, and Dorcas served the poor.[29] Why would God raise Dorcas from the dead while Stephen stayed dead?

The text does not give us insight into why the Lord was willing to raise one from the dead but not the other. It does give us some insight into Peter. It shows that Peter was willing to step into the mess that miracles can make. When Peter receives word that a faithful disciple is dead, he has a choice. He could go and see what God would do, or he could let the dead stay dead. Peter had been one of the few present when Jesus responded to Jairus's request to heal his daughter and ended up raising her from the dead. Peter was present when Lazarus came out of his tomb. Peter knew what God could do. He also knew that his coworker in the gospel, Stephen, stayed dead. Ultimately, Peter chose to have compassion for Dorcas and the widows present by asking God to do something amazing despite the questions it might raise. Peter was willing to enter into the mess that could develop when God makes the unexpected occur. It illustrates Peter's trust in the Lord that though miracles could create more problems, ultimately, the kingdom would benefit.

27. Witherington, *Acts of the Apostles*, 221.

28. The use of disciple to describe Dorcas is significant because it is the only time in the New Testament that *mathetria* is used to describe a female. I am unsure what that means for our endeavors, but it is worth noting. Bock, *Acts*, 377.

29. Widows are only mentioned three times in Acts: twice in this passage and in the passage describing the work Stephen was called to do. It is beyond the scope of this writing to connect the two, but it seems plausible that Luke was doing just that. Bock, *Acts*, 378.

Peter's life illustrates what happens when someone is formed into the likeness of Jesus and is willing to accept the responsibility of carrying Jesus' mission in the world forward. Peter understood that Jesus did not come to bring a theory that would change the world but acted in tangible ways to make the in-breaking of the kingdom known. It was not an easy task. Acting like Jesus meant that life would be messy and hard, but that did not stop Peter. If I am being honest, I think that difficulty makes me uncomfortable with miracles.

Challenged by Miracles

I have been miraculously healed, yet I am uncomfortable talking about it. When my student Bayley came to me with her vision, my initial response was similar to everyone else's, rejecting it as just in her head. I am grateful she came to me that day, though, because it made me start to take seriously an area I needed to grow in. I realized that I inadvertently was like R. F. Holland, looking for a coincidence that could get credit instead.

When I heard about a miracle, my default setting was skepticism, not praise. Instead of being filled with the joy of the Spirit, I was filled with the spirit of Scooby-Doo. If I asked the right question and stayed skeptical long enough, I could unmask the carnival owner with a hidden agenda masquerading as a ghost. Now, that is not to say discernment is not important. Peter had to show discernment to recognize Simon the Sorcerer was up to no good and had selfish motives. Discernment and skepticism are two different dispositions, and only one is a gift of the Spirit. However, at the end of the day, skepticism is easier, and it gets me off the hook for why miracles are not happening around me. It is understandable why Pope Gregory warned Augustine of Canterbury about miracles because a lack of miracles was an indictment of Pope Gregory's ability to reflect Jesus properly.

How do we reform our thinking? How do we work against two thousand years of steady decline away from miracles? The key can be found in Peter's life. First, formation in miracles is essential. Since getting in a time machine and following Jesus around is not an option, pastors formed in the anti-supernatural West would benefit from a greater understanding of what God is doing in the majority world. Skepticism is not the default setting for global Christianity, and it would behoove pastors in the West to start listening to stories from the majority world where miracles are occurring in greater numbers.[30] Further, pastors need to get better at seeing the miracle at work around them, owning the reality that the miracle is present, and talking about it as a real miracle.

Second, like Peter, pastors would do well to realize that our righteousness will not compel the Lord to allow us to participate in the miraculous. God uses broken vessels and a contrite heart to make his glory known in the world. Pastors cannot wait until they have reached a certain level of personal piety before they allow themselves to explore the possibility of the miraculous. On the flip side, those pastors who have been blessed by seeing miracles in their ministries need to embrace a level of humility about what they have experienced and embrace that their supreme righteousness is not the source of the healing.[31]

Third, ask God to move. I often wonder how many miracles I would have seen if I had the boldness to ask. Fear that a miracle will not occur has often kept me from asking. Peter's life illustrates that sometimes an angel leads you out of prison, but sometimes you are just stuck. Being willing to ask ultimately puts your trust in God's knowledge so that even when God does not heal or provide a way out, God will find a way to work it for good.

Fourth, give up your illusion of control and embrace the mess of miracles. Peter could have controlled the situation and not had to deal with the question, "Why is Stephen still dead?," if he did not try to raise Dorcas from the dead. The illusion of control would have meant two dead saints instead of just one. Dead people staying dead is far easier for me than death of my control.

Peter illustrated the potential of what a life reflecting Christ could do for a community. Miracles formed Peter, and miracles, in turn, formed the nature of his ministry and the world around him. As pastors, we have the responsibility to point people toward Jesus. People come to us hoping to get the perspective that Jesus would give them. There is a good chance that if we are not properly formed in miracles, we might give them David Hume instead of Jesus. While it is not our intent, people might walk away thinking that the miracle God gave them to encourage or strengthen them was just something they made up.

---

30. Craig Keener wrote a wonderful book to assist in this project. I highly recommend it. See Keener, *Miracles Today*.

31. I once met a minister who had a healing ministry. I went to shake his hand, and he refused because he did not know me. He said he would not touch those who he did not know because he did not want his power "tainted."

Bibliography

Augustine. *The City of God Against the Pagans*. Vol. 7: *Books XXI–XXII*. Translated by William M. Green. Loeb Classical Library 417. Cambridge: Harvard University Press, 2007.

Bede. *A History of the English Church and People*. Translated by Leo Sherley-Price. Revised by R. E. Latham. New York: Barnes & Noble, 1993.

Bock, Darrell L. *Acts*. Baker Exegetical Commentary on the New Testament. Grand Rapids: Baker Academic, 2007.

———. *Luke*. Baker Exegetical Commentary on the New Testament 3. Grand Rapids: Baker, 1994.

Bockmuehl, Markus N. A. *Simon Peter in Scripture and Memory: The New Testament Apostle in the Early Church*. Grand Rapids: Baker Academic, 2012.

Cotter, Wendy. *Miracles in Greco-Roman Antiquity: A Sourcebook*. London: Routledge, 1999.

France, R. T. *The Gospel of Matthew*. The New International Commentary on the New Testament. Grand Rapids: Eerdmans, 2007.

Green, Joel B. *The Gospel of Luke*. The New International Commentary on the New Testament. Grand Rapids: Eerdmans, 1997.

Holland, R. F. "The Miraculous." *American Philosophical Quarterly* 2 (1965) 43–51.

Hume, David, and Antony Flew. *An Enquiry Concerning Human Understanding*. Paul Carus Student Editions. La Salle, IL: Open Court, 1988.

Keener, Craig S. *Acts: An Exegetical Commentary*. Grand Rapids: Baker Academic, 2012.

———. *Miracles: The Credibility of the New Testament Accounts*. Grand Rapids: Baker Academic, 2011.

———. *Miracles Today: The Supernatural Work of God in the Modern World*. Grand Rapids: Baker Academic, 2021.

Kelhoffer, James Anthony. "Ordinary Christians as Miracle-Workers in the New Testament and the Second- and Third-Century Christian Apologists." *Biblical Research* 44 (1999) 23–34.

Lewis, C. S. *Miracles: A Preliminary Study*. San Francisco: HarperSanFrancisco, 2001.

"N. T. Wright on Paul, Hell, Satan, Creation, Adam and Eve & More." *Unbelievable?* (Podcast). June 23, 2014. https://www.premierunbelievable.com/unbelievable/unbelievable-nt-wright-on-paul-hell-satan-creation-adam-eve-and-more/11783.article.

Origen. *Origen: Contra Celsum*. Translated by Henry Chadwick. Cambridge: Cambridge University Press, 1980.

Richardson, Alan. *Christian Apologetics*. San Francisco: Harper, 1947.

Twelftree, Graham H. *Jesus the Miracle Worker: A Historical and Theological Study*. Downers Grove, IL: InterVarsity, 1999.

Witherington, Ben. *The Acts of the Apostles: A Socio-Rhetorical Commentary*. Grand Rapids: Eerdmans, 2009.

Young, William. "Miracles in Church History." *Churchman* 102.2 (1988) 102–21.

13

Tracing the Steps of the Suffering Servant
Peter's Theology for Christians in Pain

MATTHEW MCBIRTH

DEFENSE OF THE CHRISTIAN faith dates back to the first generation of Jesus' followers. Peter, in his epistle to Christians in Asia Minor, urges them to be prepared to make a defense (*apologia*) for their hope in Jesus (1 Pet 3:15). This tradition continues today with individuals dedicated to defending the faith against external detractors and internal false teachings. For as long as defenses for the Christian faith have been around, there has always been alongside it the question of suffering.

The apostle Peter indeed addressed this question as he wrote to believers that were suffering simply for being Christian (4:16). Although nearly two thousand years have passed since the time of 1 Peter's letter, contemporary Christians still struggle with the issue of unjustifiable suffering. When this type of suffering takes place, a natural reaction is to have an anthropocentric approach. One asks, "What have I done wrong to deserve this?" Many Christians default to the idea of divine punishment for their (or others') suffering. Statements like "I have not read my Bible enough," "I have not prayed in a while," "I have not been serving lately," are offered as causes of suffering, neglecting the fact that many disciples of Jesus who do these practices still suffer.

So, how should Christians approach suffering? Peter posits an eschatological perspective of suffering that allows believers to acknowledge the grief of suffering but also the power of God's redemption in the face of it. In essence, Peter urges the believers to understand suffering as a cue to contemplate the grace of God situated in the undeserved suffering of Jesus, which ended in his glorification and his followers' liberation from sin. Peter asserts three implications from contemplating Jesus' suffering, and he lays these out in 1 Peter by redefining suffering, anticipating glory to follow suffering, and extrapolating how Jesus' sacrifice enables the followers to pursue holiness amid suffering. Peter addresses suffering all throughout his first epistle. Yet, it is within 1 Peter 2:18—3:20 that Peter applies his eschatological perspective to real life situations of Christian slaves and wives, encouraging them to follow in the steps of Christ Jesus.

Understanding Suffering

Suffering as a Christian

Suffering is an "experience of bearing physical, psychological, economic, or social pain, distress, or loss."[1] This definition recognizes the complexity of suffering. Since it is an experience of immense loss, suffering does not only occur physically. Let this counter the flippancy from some pulpits saying that suffering only occurs with physical persecution. As will be demonstrated later, the Jesus-followers that Peter addressed were primarily dealing with nonphysical persecution, and Peter labeled this suffering (1 Pet 1:6). Before analyzing Peter's urge to approach suffering as a cue to contemplate Jesus' suffering, one must first understand the suffering addressed in 1 Peter and why Peter links everyday suffering to Jesus' crucifixion.

First Peter portrays first-century Christian suffering in Asia Minor as similar to that of Christians across the empire (5:9), linked to the label "Christian" (*Christianos*, 4:16), and related to believers "doing what is right" (3:14).[2] The church's obedience to God created conflict within their gentile communities. Social-conflict theory defines this as intergroup conflict, which arises when individuals or specific groups fail to meet social expectations, prompting the community to address the breach in the social contract in order to restore the status quo.[3]

---

1. Tabb, *Suffering in Ancient Worldview*, 25.
2. All verbatim Bible quotations are taken from the NET.
3. Williams, *Persecution in 1 Peter*, 38–39.

From Peter's perspective, suffering was occurring because they were living holy lives. From a non-Christian perspective, the Christians were disrupting social and familial mores tied to the fabric of Greco-Roman culture. Biblical and historical analyses illuminate three major causes of the suffering referenced in 1 Peter.

First, the suffering arose from neighbors because Christians' strange beliefs led to their nonparticipation in communal functions. A regular complaint about Christians was that they were atheists (Tertullian, *Apology* 40.2). The Roman historian Tacitus (56–120 CE) commented that Christians believed in superstition, practiced vice, and hated humankind (Tacitus, *Annals* 15.44). These three statements likely refer to Christians' exclusive worship of the crucified-yet-resurrected Jesus, and their declaration that he is Lord of all (Acts 10:36). Since Christians no longer worshiped the traditional pagan gods, they did not participate in some community celebrations (e.g., theaters and festivals) because they were entwined with pagan worship.[4]

This abstention was likely not only noticeable visually and financially. Acts 19 illustrates the connection between idol worship and the economy (Acts 19:25). This is also noticeable in early second-century Bithynia, where Christians (and Jewish people) had grown so numerous that the local temples and sacrificial animal businesses were disappearing (Pliny the Younger, *Epistula* 10.96.9–10). Christian abstention from pagan rituals and the financial ramifications led to accusations of them being evildoers (*kakopoios*, 1 Pet 2:12), creating the disorienting experience of being foreigners and outcasts within their own communities (2:11).[5]

Second, the communal bombardment of slander and accusations of disruption likely rose to a place where local police investigated the claims. In most cities throughout Asia Minor there was at least one elected official who was responsible for policing the community. Much of the *eirenarch*'s

4. Gonzalez, *Story of Christianity*, 1:45; Williams, *Persecution in 1 Peter*, 250.

5. Scholars have debated if *paroikos* and *parepidēmos* (1 Pet 2:11) should be interpreted literally or figuratively. There are three approaches. One is the metaphorical reading. The believers are not literal foreigners or exiles but are experiencing conflict akin to these demographics. For a strong argument for this reading see Horrell, "Aliens and Strangers," 100–132. A second approach is that some in the audience are foreigners, but the terms are utilized figuratively to connect the believers to the experience of Abraham. For a strong argument for this reading see Green, *Vox Petri*, 311. A third approach is that the terms are literal, that the believers are in fact resident aliens, and some are exiles. John Elliott is the scholar who made this approach compelling. However, for a good summary of this approach read McKnight, *1 Peter*, 48–51. This paper respects all three approaches but lands on the first reading.

role was to investigate the accusations made of community members and quickly end the disruption.[6] Investigations often led to interrogations. If the accusations were validated, official trials would follow. Christians throughout Asia Minor experienced, therefore, not just social ostracism but also legal ramifications that could easily result in imprisonment or capital punishment.[7] This historical reality adds weight to Peter's instruction to "be subject to every human institution" (1 Pet 2:13) and to be prepared to peacefully answer questions pertaining to their faith (3:15–16). Contemporary Western Christians would do well to heed this instruction as the West becomes increasingly skeptical of our faith.

Lastly, Christians experienced suffering at the hands of fellow household members. Many have noted the peculiarity of Peter's household codes (2:18—3:7). Most household codes address three common pairs present within urban households: husbands and wives, parents and children, and masters and slaves. However, Peter only primarily addresses slaves and wives, spending a very small amount of time on husbands.[8] Peter likely highlighted these two groups within the church due to their unique roles within pagan households.

Slaves in the Greco-Roman world were, legally speaking, property and had no right to make their own decisions.[9] The slaves addressed in 1 Peter 2:18 are specified as *oiketēs* which refers more specifically to household slaves rather than agricultural estate slaves. Due to their proximity to the head of the household and family cult, a Christian *oiketēs* would have experienced daily vulnerability regarding their faith.[10] How should a slave respond when commanded to participate in pagan religious rites? Or, how should a slave respond if commanded to participate in sexual immorality? These very well may be the sort of scenarios the enslaved Christians found themselves in, and maintaining obedience to Christ may have been the good acts that they were being beaten for (1 Pet 2:20).

---

6. Williams, *Persecution in 1 Peter*, 143–46.

7. Horrell, "Label Χριστιανός," 210.

8. Peter also addresses elders and "youngers" later in the epistle, but not as part of a household code. He does this to reinforce his dominant metaphor of "Church is Family."

9. For more on the realities of slaves in the Greco-Roman world see Hunt, *Ancient Greek and Roman Slavery*.

10. Davids, "Exalted Lord," 260.

Christians married to pagan husbands also found themselves in precarious situations. Since a man's honor was closely tied to his wife's lifestyle, how a wife conducted herself not only impacted her but the entire household.[11] This not only dealt with dress (1 Pet 3:3–4), but also with worship of the *paterfamilias*'s gods. The ancient philosopher Plutarch instructed wives to worship and hold in reverence exclusively the gods of their husbands.[12] This pagan worship looked like making the daily ritual offerings to the household's gods and cooking for the large-scale familial celebrations.[13] Christian women thus found themselves not only in tension with society but with their husbands who expected strict obedience; and any evidence of participating in a foreign religion would be perceived as rebellion.[14]

Thus, Christians experienced intergroup persecution for no longer adhering to community expectations. Their nonparticipation in the local celebrations, household religions, and their new belief caused the communities to shame them through accusations of doing deplorable acts (1 Pet 2:12). Intergroup conflict was likely made even worse by the occurrence of intragroup conflict (1 Pet 2:11; 4:3)[15] and by the low social status of many of the believers. The fact that these believers made up the lower levels of the economy means that they were often marginalized, consistently overlooked by the very authorities they were told to honor and respect (1 Pet 2:13, 17).[16] Therefore, their suffering is not just because they are Christian but also a suffering that comes from being disenfranchised. Peter's message to these suffering Christians, therefore, also applies to Christians today who either suffer as they reside in a hostile province or experience scarcity of resources, relationships, or well-being.

Christian Perspective on Suffering in Context

With all this pain, how did these early Christians think of their suffering in relation to God and the world? In the Mediterranean world during

11. Lu, "Woman's Role," 10.
12. Smith, *Strangers to Family*, 75.
13. Davids, "Exalted Lord," 260.
14. Jobes, *1 Peter*, 203.
15. The occurrence of apostasy would have caused issues of mistrust—maybe even division—especially if those who apostatized may have gone on to act as informants. For a historical case for this reading see Williams, *Cultural Christians*, 61–82.
16. McKnight, *1 Peter*, 51.

antiquity, there were two dominant options of making sense of suffering that would have been readily available to Peter's audience. Lucius Annaeus Seneca the Younger (4 BCE–65 CE)—a Roman Stoic philosopher—argued that suffering categorically was natural, as opposed to coming from a place of malice. He understood that hardships such as poverty, losing reputation, public hatred, and even loss of children were "for the good of the persons" suffering.[17] Seneca understood these pains as ultimately building virtue in a person and community. In fact, this is one of the characteristics that humans held above the gods, that humans could suffer and thus build character.[18]

Jewish thought in antiquity took a different approach to suffering, often correlating it to divine punishment. For example, 4 Maccabees depicts a theology of suffering coming from the hand of God. The martyrdom of a family is portrayed as divine retribution for Israel's years of sin, with the suffering of the righteous martyrs serving vicariously as the required sacrifice.[19] A prayer of the martyred family head showcases an understanding that their suffering satisfied divine punishment (4 Macc 6:27–29).[20] The Mishnah, as another example, also posits suffering as consequence for sin and brought on by God.[21]

As the Jesus followers in Asia Minor faced suffering, some likely wondered if God intended it. Others may have sought to find a purpose in their suffering but found no respite. Peter offers a pastoral call to see suffering through a third option: an eschatological worldview. While there are similarities between Peter's understanding of suffering and that of Seneca and 4 Maccabees, there are also strong contrasts. Seneca deems suffering as natural and neutral. Peter on the other hand understands suffering as evil. He describes suffering as part of the war that sin has waged upon humanity (1 Pet 2:11). It is not something natural. It should not be. This is portrayed in three main ways in Peter's letter.

First, Peter demonstrates this eschatological battle by reminding the believers to not respond to conflict like the pagans do. Notice that Peter acknowledges the wrongdoing of the persecutors (3:12; 4:5) but he nevertheless tells the Christians to continue to honor the leaders and conduct themselves peacefully (2:12; 3:1, 16). The social shame that they

17. Tabb, *Suffering in Ancient Worldview*, 84.
18. Tabb, *Suffering in Ancient Worldview*, 29.
19. Tabb, *Suffering in Ancient Worldview*, 75.
20. Tabb, *Suffering in Ancient Worldview*, 84.
21. Kraemer, *Responses to Suffering*, 56–57.

are experiencing should not lead to an isolationist mentality, where the Christians avoid their pagan neighbors. To be honest, only those with a great amount of privilege—such as those in the modern West—can do such a thing and survive. Peter instead wants the followers of Jesus to hold onto hope that their good conduct will lead to the conversion of unbelievers (3:1). As we read Peter's instruction within a different time, may we not simply map his instruction to ancient Christian slaves and wives onto our current time. Peter is addressing people with little to no rights and privileges. For example, it is not as if Peter is advocating for slavery. Similarly, Peter is not advocating for women to remain in abusive situations, as his letter is sometimes utilized today. Abusing a spouse (or anyone) is a crime today, and based on Peter's words every person is to accept the authority of human institutions such as the government (2:13–14). The apostle does not find anything good in suffering itself, nor sees suffering as the only way to evangelize. Peter is simply locating the origin of suffering in another agent.

The second and third ways Peter portrays his eschatological view of suffering is by directing the church to see who the true enemies are. He first highlights the evil spirits in prison that Jesus announced his victory to when he ascended (3:19–20). He later mentions that the devil is part of the real enemy, seeking to devour the believers all over the world (5:8–9). Peter wants Christians to have the eschaton in mind as they follow the way of Jesus (1:20), nearing the end and final judgment (4:7, 17). As they perceive the world in this way, they see that the true enemy is not their neighbors; but instead, is sin that terrorizes creation.

This eschatological perspective of suffering coming from evil encourages the believers that they are not being punished by God. Additionally, Peter does not want anyone acting as if suffering is a small thing. That, in fact, what they are experiencing is unnatural. Peter was raised on the tradition of the Psalms and the book of Lamentations. He knows the devastation of suffering, and the need to lament. May pastors do the same today, letting grief have its time. Unjustified suffering is wrong. The good news, however, is that God will make it right. Peter assures them that suffering does not get the final say by bringing the suffering of Jesus to the forefront of their minds, demonstrating that suffering leads to glory.

Contemplating Jesus' Suffering and Glory

Part of a pastor's role is to help his or her siblings in Christ see things for what they are. A Christian worldview lovingly pushes against harmful perspectives, inviting the Spirit to transform our minds to become more like Christ's mind. This is what Peter sets out to do. As he asserts the eschatological worldview, pastor Peter submits a reconfiguration of suffering. It is a perspective that not only pushed against ancient ideas of suffering, but modern ones as well. Peter's eschatological worldview runs contrary to the Prosperity Gospel. As Peter will illustrate, people who obey God do not always receive long, comfortable lives. Additionally, Peter's perspective on suffering pushes against the idea of God waiting for us to mess up. That as soon as we do, punishment comes. Certainly, there are consequences for sin; but how often have Christians labeled unjustified suffering as a punishment from God? Peter, on the contrary, urges believers to rethink suffering within the eschatological matrix, seeing that unjustified suffering actually leads to glory. Peter supports this new sequencing (suffering to glory) by having believers contemplate God's grand narrative climaxed in the suffering servant Jesus (2:20–25). He then provides exemplars of godly people who suffered yet were blessed afterwards (2:18—3:12), allowing the believers to anticipate God's justification.

The Suffering Messiah

The suffering servant hymn found in Isa 52:13—53:12 is frequently referenced in the New Testament. Of all the engagements with this hymn, Peter quotes and paraphrases it the most extensively. He integrates the suffering servant hymn with Jesus' passion to remind believers that suffering for obedience to God leads to God's favor (2:21–25). By connecting the suffering servant to marginalized Christians, he gives two affirmations to believers: in their suffering, they are near to God and they are becoming more like God.

In Isa 52–53, the nameless sufferer is referred to as God's *ebed*. This Hebrew term can be translated *slave, servant, official,* or *follower*. When modified by the word "my," this suffering servant joins the likes of people near to God such as Moses (Exod 4:10; Josh 1:2), Joshua (Josh 5:14); and David (1 Sam 23:10). It conveys an intimacy with and dependence on God.[22] Peter explicitly identifies this close-to-God servant as the Messiah (*christos*). Peter, having referenced Jesus as Messiah (1 Pet 1:1), integrates this Christian view of the Messiah as the suffering servant by linking the hymn to Jesus' trial (2:22–23) and crucifixion (2:24). Peter asserts, therefore, that though Jesus suffered unjustly, he was (and is) near to God. In doing so, Peter beautifully conveys that disenfranchised Christians are likewise near to God.

Peter creates a connection between the Christian slaves and the suffering servant Jesus. Though there is no terminological similarity between *oiketais* (2:18), *doulos* (2:16), and *pais* (Isa 52:13, 53:2 LXX), the words nevertheless connect conceptually. All words pertain to submission under authority, and the action of the *ebed* is commonly referred to as that of a slave (*doulos*).[23] The suffering servant may in fact be referred to as *pais* (LXX) to convey the warmness between the servant and his master, and thus that same warmness converges onto the suffering Christians. They are not merely God's servants, nor are they simply marginalized members of society. Though times are bleak, they are God's cherished possessions.

Peter's linking of Christians to the suffering servant acknowledges a second affirmation: that they are indeed becoming more like Jesus as they reflect his crucifixion. Contrary to Seneca, Peter believes that God did indeed suffer in the incarnation. Peter wants the Christians to see their suffering as a prompt to contemplate Jesus' suffering. They are abused (*loidoria*, 1 Pet 3:9) and he was abused (*loidoreo*, 2:23). They suffer (2:19–20) and so did he (2:21, 23). For Christians, suffering unjustly points us to our suffering savior. In contemplating his suffering, we are assured that we have not chosen wrongly as his suffering resulted in blessings for the world. This eschatological perspective leads to joy as Christians become more like Jesus, sharing in his suffering (4:13). As Peter says, "But if you do good and suffer and so endure, this finds favor with God. For to this you were called, since Christ also suffered for you" (1 Pet 2:20b–21). Peter in this "call" statement is not saying that God desires for them to suffer. Instead, it is God's will for them to be blessed, maintaining Christ-likeness in the midst of suffering.

Peter talks about Jesus' suffering throughout his epistle. It is like a large bucket of water that continues to spill out with every step. If

---

22. Brettler and Levine, "Isaiah's Suffering Servant," 160.
23. Isaiah 42:19, 48:20, 49:3, 56:6, 63:17, 65:9.

one had to give a climatic point where Peter's eschatological perspective shines most through it would likely be 1 Pet 3:18–22. In this passage, one sees that suffering for obedience to God leads to glory. Peter attests that Jesus suffered for sins, put to death in the flesh (3:18); but the story ends not in the tomb but in a heavenly room. Peter comments later in the passage that Jesus did indeed resurrect (3:21), and that in his resurrection, ascension, and sitting at the right hand of God, Jesus proclaimed victory over the evil dominion (3:19–22). Suffering for Christ's sake, therefore, does not end in shame. It ends in glory. It ends in receiving honor from God, what Peter calls God's grace and credit (2:20).[24] In contemplating the grace found in Jesus' suffering, they are reminded of their hope. He suffered, they suffer. He was abused, they are abused. He was glorified, they will be exalted by God (5:6).

The Invitation to Suffer Well

Telling people to continue to do the same acts that are resulting in their suffering is not an easy task, however. It is certainly not an easy message to receive. A common practice in the ancient world was to provide exemplars of people who suffered well. Seneca did this in his conversation on suffering, referring to them as heroes. For Roman men, the way to earn glory and honor was by fighting for their country. Seneca took this concept and mapped it upon every person's life as they faced suffering, asserting that those who are remembered by the culture are the ones who embraced harm inflicted upon them.[25] Fourth Maccabees does this as well, portraying the martyred Eleazar, the brothers, and their mother as ideal Abrahamites and examples to be emulated.[26]

Peter similarly gives Christians exemplars to emulate in their suffering. Jesus is, of course, *the* exemplar; but Peter highlights three other examples in the pericope. All of these examples model a person of God who faced suffering and afterwards received a blessing.

One exemplar is highlighted indirectly through the quotation of Ps 34 in 1 Pet 3:10–12. Psalm 34, as the superscription says, pertains to the time David was displaced, a foreigner in the land of the Gath (1 Sam 21:10–15). In this episode, David had to behave like he had lost his mind

---

24. Edwards, *1 Peter*, 117.
25. Tabb, *Suffering in Ancient Worldview*, 30.
26. Tabb, *Suffering in Ancient Worldview*, 87.

to avoid being attacked by Philistines. In the psalm, David sings that, despite being treated poorly by the surrounding community, he will remain obedient to God's will and not speak evil (Ps 34:13). Within this psalm—as well as the narrative in 1 Samuel—David's experience offers encouragement that those who cry to God will be redeemed by the Lord (22). Peter utilizes the psalm to draw a parallel between his audience and the ancient hero David, encouraging believers to remain steadfast, as they too will be blessed just as David was after his exile.[27]

A second exemplar that Peter provides to Christians is the Jewish matriarch Sarah. Whereas Peter referenced David indirectly, Sarah is referenced explicitly in 1 Pet 3:5–6 as an example of a godly woman who obeyed God amid adversity. Modern Christians often highlight Sarah's harmful treatment of Hagar and Ishmael, which Genesis clearly notes, but Scripture remembers Sarah as the faithful mother of Israel (Isa 51:2; Heb 11:11) who received God's blessing after suffering barrenness. Peter's main point is that Sarah was holy because she put her hope in God (1 Pet 3:5). He follows by saying that Christian wives are Sarah's children when they continue to do good and do not succumb to fear (3:7). Sarah exemplifies one who is blessed after remaining obedient to God in the face of tragedy.

Lastly, Peter highlights the Christian slaves and the wives as exemplars for the Christian community. As noted above, Peter does not follow the traditional household code format. This was because Peter wanted to focus on those most vulnerable in society, but also because he wanted to showcase the most vulnerable as people who demonstrate the character of Jesus. It is in Peter's instruction to slaves that he tells them they resemble Jesus. It is in Peter's instruction to wives that the call to holiness is mentioned. Thus, those who are at risk of receiving the most shame are held up by Peter as those who will receive honor from God, and thus exemplars of the way of Christ.[28]

Contemporary Christians should also have exemplars of siblings in Christ Jesus who suffer(ed) well. These may be people popular or particular; deceased or alive. May we look to someone like Oscar Romero—former archbishop of San Salvador—who chose to live on the grounds of a hospital in order to be in proximity with the poor of his community. The nearness to the "least of these" was reflected in

---

27. Christensen, "Solidarity in Suffering," 351.
28. Edwards, "Jesus and the Disinherited," 256.

Romero's preaching, calling for God's kingdom to reign in the here and now. Romero lived under threat of death, in an atmosphere where disenfranchisement was the reality. Nevertheless, Romero kept preaching the way of Jesus, to love and reflect Jesus to all around him, and he did so until his assassination in 1980. Likewise, may we hold up the mothers and fathers of our local churches who have endured much suffering yet have remained in the faith. It is the testament of the widow who lost her husband after a long fight with disease, but continues to hold onto Jesus even as loneliness or past pains resurface, that churches need to give platforms and microphones to.

By prompting believers to contemplate Jesus' suffering and presenting exemplars, Peter encourages Christians to follow Jesus' steps through suffering to glory. Jesus' obedience in the midst of suffering is not just an encouragement, it is an invitation. He has left an example for them to follow. *Hypogrammos* (1 Pet 2:21), used once in the New Testament, pertains to someone tracing over another's work. Similar to how kindergartners receive sheets of paper with dotted letters to be traced over, Jesus' obedience in the midst of suffering is also to be traced over by Christians. In following his steps, Christians will not only face suffering, but they will also receive glory. In positing an eschatological perspective, one where the future judgment is lived presently, Peter assures the believers that their suffering will too fade away, for they have already experienced the grace of God. Their suffering does not go unnoticed, and they will indeed be justified just like the rejected cornerstone.

Enduring Suffering

In contemplating the suffering of Jesus, Peter asserts that not only should they be encouraged for they know glory is to come, but they also are reminded that Jesus' suffering liberated them from the evil of sin. Now that Peter has assured the believers that they are still on the right path, he has to tell them how it is possible to remain on the path. Is the suffering they are met with too strong? How can one face insult and shame not just from community members but from family members and maintain the same way of life? The trial on this trail of following Jesus truly does intensify the temptation to go back to the former life. Yet, Peter is confident that the Christians can endure in following the steps of Christ because his suffering liberated the cosmos. By his bruises, Jesus detached people from the power of sin. Affectively, Jesus has not only paved the way for his followers, he has given his servants the strength to persevere. Peter urges the believers to live in the power of God's redemption by preaching about separation from sin and Jesus' healing atonement.

First Peter 2:24–25 contains some of the most theologically rich content in the entire Bible. Within these verses Peter directly talks about the ramifications of Jesus' crucifixion. Firstly, Peter states that Jesus bore our sins on the cross so that (*hina*) we would be *apoginomai* from sins (1 Pet 2:24). *Apoginomai* can be translated in a variety of ways. The word, etymologically, means "to become away from." It connotes a separation of objects. However, the word can be understood figuratively and thus intensified to mean "to die to" something. Peter asserts that Christ's crucifixion effectively frees us from the power of sin, a radical separation where the liberated have been separated from its influence.[29] Now liberated from the power of sin, Christians are able to follow God's call on their lives to be holy. This freedom from sin is not some theoretical assertion that is posited as a future reality. Peter believes this reality is now, and it is actualized as Christians abstain from concrete sins such as malice, deceit, insincerity, envy and slander (1 Pet 2:1), all sins that one may resort to in the midst of persecution. To fight fire with fire. However, now that they are liberated from sin, they do not need to fear their persecutors or fear the things their persecutors fear (3:14). Their holiness has been made possible by Christ liberating them from fearing evil.

Peter then concludes this section on the suffering servant in saying that Jesus' sacrifice not only liberated but also healed the believers (2:24b). Peter quotes from the LXX, stating that Jesus' bruises (*mōlōps*) causes healing for the believers. Drawing upon a medical term (bruise), Peter metaphorically explains the believers' current condition. Prior to Jesus, they were attached to sin. A parasite, foreign to God's will for creation. In being tethered to sin, it consistently sickened them. Yet, Jesus—the great physician—healed them. Greek and Roman physicians believed that bruises functioned as the body's mechanism of drawing harmful diseases to one place in order to facilitate health to the rest of the body.[30] A bruise indicated the two parts of recovery. First, bruises indicated that the individual had suffered some sort of trauma. Second,

---

29. Edwards, *1 Peter*, 119.
30. Reese, *1 Peter*, 164–65.

as a bruise changed color and began to lighten and eventually fade away, this indicated healing.

How does this conceptual metaphor help us understand Peter's thoughts on atonement in regards to Christian suffering? Peter eloquently argues that the devastating trauma of sin and its consequence, death, wreaked havoc upon Jesus, and his sacrifice enables believers to flee from sin and the devil.[31] Therefore, Jesus' death is not simply a substitution. Jesus' suffering liberates the world from sin and maintains believers as they face the enemy's tactics. So, how are they to remain steadfast in the midst of suffering? They are to put their faith in God, believing the truth that the Spirit of Christ is more powerful than the spirit of evil.

Conclusion

Peter emphasizes holy living in the midst of suffering. Following in the steps of Jesus sometimes means being pushed into mud. We should not be surprised when ridicule comes toward the kingdom. As the proverb states, "if they did it to Jesus, only time will tell." Or as Jesus himself said, "If they persecuted me, they will also persecute you" (John 15:20). Christians may think unjustified suffering indicates a misstep or that they are walking the wrong way. Peter assures us that this is how evil behaves. In a sermon I heard him preach six or seven years ago (unfortunately no longer available online), Dr. Robert Smith Jr. once said, "If you haven't met the devil, it's probably because you are on the same way."[32]

The way of Jesus is being pushed into the mud, and it is in the mud that we are to continue to walk like Jesus. Slog through the mud by praying to God, knowing that God is near. Slog through the mud like Jesus by not returning abuse for abuse, or slander for slander. Slog through the mud by fearing God alone. All of this, however, is only possible because of God's powerful grace. Glory follows suffering. This reality is only made possible by Jesus' conquering of death and his liberation, taking us from slaves to freed people. Simply put, Peter wants suffering Christians to believe the words of his Savior and friend, Jesus.

> Blessed are you who are poor, for the kingdom of God belongs to you. Blessed are you who hunger now, for you will be satisfied.

---

31. Elliott, *1 Peter*, 536–37.

32. Robert Smith Jr. is the Charles T. Carter Baptist Chair of Divinity Christian Preaching Professor at Beeson Divinity School.

Blessed are you who weep now, for you will laugh. Blessed are you when people hate you, and when they exclude you and insult you and reject you as evil on account of the Son of Man! Rejoice in that day, and jump for joy, because your reward is great in heaven. For their ancestors did the same things to the prophets. (Luke 6:20b–23)

Bibliography

Achtemeier, Paul J., and Eldon Jay Epp. *1 Peter: A Commentary on First Peter*. Hermeneia. Minneapolis: Fortress, 1996.
Brettler, Marc Zvi, and Amy-Jill Levine. "Isaiah's Suffering Servant: Before and After Christianity." *Interpretation* 73 (2019) 158–73.
Christensen, Sean M. "Solidarity in Suffering and Glory: The Unifying Role of Psalm 34 in 1 Peter 3:10–12." *Journal of the Evangelical Theological Society* 58 (2015) 335–52.
Coxe, A. Cleveland. *The Ante-Nicene Fathers*. Edited by Alexander Roberts et al. 10 vols. Rev. ed. Carol Stream, IL: Hendrickson, 1996.
Davids, Peter H. "Exalted Lord and Suffering Servant: The Response to Jesus in James and 1 Peter." In *The Earliest Perceptions of Jesus in Context: Essays in Honor of John Nolland*, edited by Aaron White et al., 253–67. New York: T. & T. Clark, 2018.
Edwards, Dennis R. *1 Peter*. Edited by Tremper Longman III and Scot McKnight. Grand Rapids: Zondervan Academic, 2017.
———. "Jesus and the Disinherited and 1 Peter." *Journal for the Study of the Historical Jesus* 17 (2019) 256–70.
Elliott, John H. *1 Peter*. Anchor Yale Bible. New Haven: Yale University Press, 2001.
Gonzalez, Justo L. *The Story of Christianity*. Vol. 1: *The Early Church to the Dawn of the Reformation*. 2nd ed. New York: HarperOne, 2010.
Green, Gene L. *Vox Petri: A Theology of Peter*. Eugene, OR: Cascade Books, 2019.
Hagewood, Lee. "Psalm 34:12–16 in 1 Peter and the Apostolic Fathers." *Restoration Quarterly* 64 (2022) 147–56.
Horrell, David G. *1 Peter: A Critical and Exegetical Commentary*. Vol. 1: *Chapters 1–2*. New York: T. & T. Clark, 2023.
———. "Aliens and Strangers? Socio-Economic Location of the Addressees of 1 Peter." In *Becoming Christian: Essays on 1 Peter and the Making of Christian Identity*, 100–132. New York: T. & T. Clark, 2013.
———. "The Label Χριστιανός (1 Pet. 4.16): Suffering, Conflict, and the Making of Christian Identity." In *Becoming Christian: Essays on 1 Peter and the Making of Christian Identity*, 164–210. London: T. & T. Clark, 2013.
Hunt, Peter. *Ancient Greek and Roman Slavery*. Hoboken, NJ: Wiley-Blackwell, 2018.
Jobes, Karen H. *1 Peter*. Illustrated ed. Grand Rapids: Baker Academic, 2005.
Kraemer, David. *Responses to Suffering in Classical Rabbinic Literature*. New York: Oxford University Press, 1994.
Lu, Shi-Min. "Woman's Role in New Testament Household Codes: Transforming First-Century Roman Culture." *Priscilla Papers* 30 (2016) 9–15.
McDonald, Brett M. "Exile, Suffering, and Holiness: The Use of Psalm 34 in 1 Peter." *Presbyterion* 48:2 (2022) 67–84.

McKnight, Scot. *1 Peter*. The NIV Application Commentary. Grand Rapids: Zondervan Academic, 1996.

Pliny the Younger. *Letters, Volume II: Books 8–10. Panegyricus*. Translated by Betty Radice. Cambridge: Harvard University Press, 1969.

Reese, Ruth Anne. *1 Peter*. New ed. Cambridge: Cambridge University Press, 2022.

Schnabel, Eckhard J. "Jewish Opposition to Christians in Asia Minor in the First Century." *Bulletin for Biblical Research* 18 (2008) 233–70.

Smith, Shively T. J. *Strangers to Family: Diaspora and 1 Peter's Invention of God's Household*. Waco, TX: Baylor University Press, 2016.

Tabb, Brian J. *Suffering in Ancient Worldview: Luke, Seneca and 4 Maccabees in Dialogue*. Library of New Testament Studies 569. London: T. & T. Clark, 2017.

Tacitus. *Tacitus: Annals, Books 13–16*. Translated by John Jackson. Loeb Classical Library. Cambridge: Harvard University Press, 1937.

Williams, Nadya. *Cultural Christians in the Early Church: A Historical and Practical Introduction to Christians in the Greco-Roman World*. Grand Rapids: Zondervan Academic, 2023.

Williams, Travis B. *Persecution in 1 Peter: Differentiating and Contextualizing Early Christian Suffering*. Novum Testamentum Supplements 145. Leiden: Brill Academic, 2012.

Winsbury, Rex. *Pliny the Younger: A Life in Roman Letters*. London: Bloomsbury Academic, 2013.

14

Reimagining Politics
First Peter's Vision for Public Witness

Taylor Terzek

Many of us have been told not to engage in conversation about religion or politics. These are taboo topics—things you don't bring up on a first date or subjects you intentionally avoid at Thanksgiving dinners. One could say that we ignore religion and politics because they are heavy, complicated topics. But more likely, we don't speak to these things because of the intensity and vitriol that can accompany them, especially as it pertains to politics.

Politics can be a dirty word in American society today. It conjures up images of division, corruption, and disillusionment. Just recently I posed a question on my social media account: *When you hear the word "politics," what comes to mind?* I asked people to simply note their associations with the term, and they responded with words like corruption, conflict, power, money, division, debate, and manipulation. There was a lot of pessimism connected to this term "politics," but I was not surprised. In many ways, this is a warranted association. As Michael Wear puts it in the opening line of his book *The Spirit of Our Politics*, "Our politics is sick."[1] Our current political culture in America consists in contests for public domination and a political psychology that is

---

1. Wear, *Spirit of Our Politics*, xii.

centered on "fear, anger, negation, and revenge over perceived wrongs."[2] However, the problem with this is that we (Christians) typically turn this into a pointed finger at *them*.[3] We assume the sickness is due to a toxin that grows in culture with its increasing secularism, or we consider the sickness to be the result of some agenda or misplaced values across the partisan aisle. But this sickness is not simply an out-there problem. Christians in America, specifically "evangelicals" (if that reference isn't too slippery), are experiencing their own political sickness.[4]

I'm breaking the taboo. We need to talk about politics. There have been numerous books recently published that help modern Western Christians better engage with politics. The various books help provide a biblical theology on politics,[5] scrutinize the sociological and historical impact of Christians in politics,[6] give hermeneutical guidelines for how to use the Bible in politics,[7] as well as provide practical suggestions for how to vote, engage in dialog, seek the public good, etc.[8] In this essay, I want to take my cues from 1 Peter and explore how Peter provides us with a vision for public witness that can help reimagine our politics.

I have three primary questions. First, what is the political context for 1 Peter? I provide a brief sketch of the early Roman Empire under Augustus and the emperors that followed, attempting to trace how the empire made its presence known in Asia Minor, and what this meant for Christians in that region. Second, how does Peter instruct Christians living in their political context? I will highlight a key passage from 1 Peter (2:11–25) and explore it within its first-century context.[9] Third, considering Peter's instruction to first-century Christians in Asia Minor, how should the American church interact with politics today? Surfacing some of Peter's implicit posture toward politics and a possible narrative theology in 1 Peter, I suggest that American Christians should (1) acknowledge the distance between modern American Christians and first-century Anatolian Christians when it comes to access to political power, (2) disentangle

---

2. Hunter, *To Change the World*, 104.
3. Hunter, *To Change the World*, 105.
4. See Alberta, *Kingdom*.
5. Sprinkle, *Exiles*.
6. Alberta, *Kingdom*.
7. Schiess, *Ballot and the Bible*.
8. Wear, *Spirit of Our Politics*; Giboney et al., *Compassion*; Butler, *Party Crasher*; Wright and Bird, *Jesus and the Powers*.
9. I will assume throughout this paper that Peter was the author of 1 Peter.

and distinguish between the "public" and the "political," and (3) scrutinize the social imaginaries of our culture and replace it with a gospelized imagination, utilizing the three main movements of the story of Jesus to construct a more faithful way forward.

The Political Context of 1 Peter

Before we explore Peter's political prescriptions in 1 Peter, we need to situate the letter in its political context. Peter writes this letter to a group of congregations, largely gentile, that were spread throughout Asia Minor.[10] This makes the precise audience difficult.[11] Nonetheless, we know that the letter was likely taken to cities in the provinces that were "thriving and growing according to the pulses of the Roman Empire."[12]

From Republic to Empire

The Greco-Roman world of the first century was politically structured under the Roman Empire. The Roman Republic moved into the realm of nostalgia, the remnants of which were loosely held as an homage to the past, but real political power had shifted from the Senate to the emperor.[13] The first emperor of the empire was Octavian, but the Senate conferred upon him a new name, Augustus, which meant "revered one."[14] Augustus led Rome into what could be considered a golden age, ruling through *auctoritas* (*Res gestae* 34.3).[15] This is a difficult term to translate into English, but one scholar notes how this was a kind of moral and transformative leadership that did not seek to forcefully impose authority through pure military force.[16] And too often we do not

---

10. Michaels, "1 Peter," 915. The gentile audience is evident from 1 Pet 1:14, 18; 4:3–5. But it is also probable that these gentiles had "become attached to Judaism through local synagogues and other forms of Judaism" (McKnight, *1 Peter*, 22).

11. Michaels, *1 Peter*, xlv.

12. McKnight, *1 Peter*, 22.

13. Karl Galinksy argues that the essential characteristic of Augustus's rule concerned the "conscious return to and rearticulation" of the *res publica*, which was a "central attitude" or "traditional value system that placed the common good . . . ahead of private interest." See Galinsky, *Augustan Culture*, 6–7.

14. Goodman, *Rome and Jerusalem*, 35.

15. See Galinsky, *Augustine Culture*, 10–11.

16. *Auctoritas* is "a quintessentially Roman and therefore untranslatable term," but

factor this into our view of Rome. Yes, we must acknowledge Rome's oppressive empire on the one hand, but we cannot negate the grassroots devotion extended to Augustus as well. This is best seen in how Rome extended its influence into Asia Minor, not through military domination, but through the appeal of a new, collective story.[17]

The Gospel of the Roman Empire

Rome exercised its imperial power "through the symbolic arrangement of public space, the presence of images, and the performance of rituals."[18] It put forward a "new mythology"[19] that boasted of providing the residents of Asia Minor with the fortunate opportunity to live in such a time as this—a moment in history marked by peace and prosperity.[20] A prime example of this symbolic arrangement of public space is the Calendar Inscription of Priene.

The Calendar Inscription of Priene (9 BC) documents a decree from the League of Asia. In this inscription, we read Paulus Fabius Maximus's proposal to the Provincial Assembly, where he strongly suggests that the calendar should shift to begin on Emperor Augustus's birthday. We know that the Assembly approved the proposal and then honored Maximus for such a suggestion, but then multiple copies of the letter and the decree were inscribed on stone and sent out to the surrounding cities. Here is the portion of the inscription that notes the Provincial Assembly's reply to Paulus Fabius Maximus:

> In her display of concern and generosity on our behalf, Providence (πρόνοια), who orders all our lives, has adorned our lives

---

Galinksy notes that it expresses "material, intellectual, and moral superiority" and is "the ultimate power of the emperor on a moral level." Augustus is seeking more than just power or prestige. He wants to provide a "higher kind of moral leadership." See Galinsky, *Augustan Culture*, 12.

17. In fact, "no Roman legion was stationed in the province of Asia during the first centuries." See Price, *Rituals and Power*, 54. Some have claimed that this was a "propaganda campaign" by Rome. See Liebengood, "Roman Imperial Claims," 259. Galinksy challenges whether the label "propaganda" is the best fit for Augustus's actions, and his insights push me away from using that word. It seems that much of the coinage, for example, was not by imperial fiat, but more a "subtle system of mutualities" (*Augustan Culture*, 39).

18. Horsley, *Scribes*, 6.
19. Zanker, *Power of Images*, 4.
20. Liebengood, "Roman Imperial Claims," 260.

with the highest good, namely Augustus. Providence has filled Augustus with divine power for the benefit of humanity, and in her beneficence has granted us and those who will come after us [a Savior] who has made war to cease and who shall put everything [in peaceful order].... And Caesar, [when he was manifest], transcended the expectations of [all who had anticipated the good news], not only by surpassing the benefits conferred by his predecessors but by leaving no expectation of surpassing him to those who would come after him, with the result that the birthday of our god signaled the beginning of good news [*euaggelion*] for the world because of him. (ll. 34–41)[21]

One scholar observes how this inscription was "for the Romans, a new narrative, being told in its fullest and perhaps first form about Augustus"—one that could be packaged as a "gospel."[22] This was the Roman gospel: "Thanks to one man, a man sent by god, a new age had dawned."[23] It was good news of a *realized eschatology*, and it permeated the empire in the form of literature, inscriptions, coinage, and through the imperial cult.[24]

The Imperial Cult

Devotion to this Roman gospel was exercised through participation in the imperial cult, and this includes provinces in Asia Minor. Seventy-seven imperial temples have survived in Asia Minor alone, a majority of which were likely constructed by the close of the first century.[25] The cult framed much of public space, but also public *time*. For example, in Asia Minor, the provinces instituted a calendar that restarted on Augustus's birthday, declaring the dawn of a new age.[26]

---

21. Noted in Stanton, *Jesus and Gospel*, 32, quoted with minor modifications from Danker, *Benefactor*, 216–17.

22. Porter, "Paul Confronts Caesar," 168.

23. Liebengood, "Roman Imperial Claims," 260.

24. Such a marketing campaign was upheld by the Julio-Claudian and Flavian emperors that followed Augustus, but these emperors devolved into more cruelty; see Liebengood, "Roman Imperial Claims," 261.

25. Perrin, "Imperial Cult," 131.

26. Price (cited by Liebengood, "Roman Imperial Claims," 260) observes, "All of Asia Minor instituted a calendar that began the New Year on Augustus's birthday with similar inscriptions that declared that a new epoch, a golden age, was initiated with Augustus."

But again, scholars make the point that this was more of a grassroots phenomenon. The council of Asia's representative elders desired to showcase their loyalty to the new emperor, and so *they* requested to establish a cult in his name.²⁷ Augustus was even sensitive to accepting their overture, but he eventually recognized their request. Nonetheless, even if the imperial cult was not an authoritarian imposition, it still reflects a public norm or social expectation that was tied to cultic honors and political allegiances.²⁸ For residents of Asia Minor, there was a new political reality that was informed by a gospel, which was then embodied and acknowledged in the public-saturated worship of the emperor.²⁹ This was a kind of socialization into the Roman story, and those who opted out would be considered strange and suspicious.

A Strange, Suspicious Religion

In the words of Nijay Gupta, early Christians were perceived as a "strange religion."³⁰ However, there was no official policy that persecuted Christians during the time of Nero's reign, especially in Asia Minor. Across the empire, cultic groups were persecuted by the state inasmuch as they became publicly disruptive, disturbing the peace. For the most part, the early Roman Empire was (what we would call) "multicultural" and "tolerant."³¹ But if a cultic group slipped into civic disruption or warranted a "suspicion of political subversion," the hammer would drop.³² Najeeb Haddad notes that Rome expressed tolerance "*only* if these cults and practices did

---

27. Dio Cassius, *History* 51.20 and cf. Tacitus, *Annals* 4.37, both cited in Perrin, "Imperial Cult," 125.

28. One could also argue that the imperial cult became more imposing and cruel as the Julio-Claudian and Flavian emperors came to power, which has influence for 1 Peter if it was written under Nero's reign (see McKnight, *1 Peter*, 29). Liebengood notes that the Julio-Claudian and Flavian emperors appealed to this Roman gospel of Augustus to legitimize their own rule and "compel loyalty," in Liebengood, "Roman Imperial Claims," 261.

29. Obviously, this is oversimplified, which calls for caution. For a more nuanced presentation of the imperial cult and how it relates to the writings of the New Testament, see the recent Burnett, *Paul and Imperial Divine Honors*.

30. Gupta, *Strange Religion*.

31. Goodman, *Rome and Jerusalem*, 147.

32. Relations between Rome and the Greek cult to Dionysus or the Egyptian goddess Isis are evidence of Rome's possible intolerance; Haddad, *Paul and Empire Criticism*, 10–14.

not pose a threat to the civic order."[33] These parameters for social engagement and political navigation are revealing for Peter's instructions in the letter. It also implies that the persecutions referenced in 1 Peter "are not official imperial persecutions," but "discrimination and abuse on a local level, which occurred with or without imperial sanction."[34]

All this forms the backdrop for understanding Peter's instructions to the Christian communities in Asia Minor, to which we now turn.

Peter's Instructions in 1 Peter 2:11–15

Peter first addresses them "as foreigners and exiles" (2:11).[35] While some people are quick to read this as a metaphor of a spiritual situation, J. H. Elliott has argued that the primary reference is to their real social situation.[36] Socially, they were marginalized and disenfranchised. Further, this self-realization is a Christ-realization, rooted in Jesus himself being "the true outsider."[37] This redeems their social location, but also redefines it within a new frame—i.e., the gospel, the story of Jesus.[38] For he also declares that they are "chosen" by God (1:1–2; 2:9), included in the holy, royal priesthood (2:5, 9), and a holy nation (2:9)—having been mercifully brought into God's people (2:9, 10). They are the homeless who have found their home in God (2:10), the disinherited that have been given an imperishable inheritance in Christ (1:4), "free people" who are "God's slaves" (2:16). But this identity—paradoxical, brimming with tension—is a vital part of thinking about their social engagement, for their very identity struggles with a tension, and so will their relation to society.

Good People for the Public Good

Next, Peter writes that they are to "abstain from sinful desires" (2:11), which is connected to living "good lives among pagans" (2:12). They are

33. Haddad, *Paul and Empire Criticism*, 10.

34. Davids, *First Epistle of Peter*, 10; Michaels, *1 Peter*, 126; see also Kruse, "Persecution."

35. All citations from the Bible are from the NIV unless otherwise stated.

36. Elliott, *Home for the Homeless*.

37. Jobes, *1 Peter*, 3. She also cites Volf, "Soft Difference," 17.

38. Jobes observes how Peter also "encourages a transformed understanding of Christian self-identity as to redefine how they can live out the gospel in a hostile world," in Jobes, *1 Peter*, 3.

to do this to combat accusations of wrongdoing ("though they accuse of doing wrong," 2:12) and so that pagans "may see your good deeds and glorify God on the day he visits us" (2:12). It is an ethic of personal holiness *and* public witness.

While some take the exhortation to "do good" as a call to perform general moral acts,[39] Bruce Winter demonstrates how benefaction inscriptions often use this language of "doing good" to refer specifically to the Greco-Roman system of benefaction.[40] In Greco-Roman society, there were not government assistance or social programs like we have today. Instead, they relied on the wealthy of society, the benevolent, to "do good" for the sake of the city.[41] As such, we can see Peter's call to do good "as a means of establishing Christian credibility" in the public sphere by participating in the system of benefaction.[42] When they do this, it combats accusations of wrongdoing, and it showcases the Christian concern for the public good.

Now, Peter gives no hint that public recognition will be successful *until* "the day"—a future time of God's culminating justice. The good deeds they do today might lead to present suffering. Peter knows this well (cf. Acts 4:1–21).[43] But there is a time when accusations of wrongdoing will be scrutinized under the weight of God's glorifying radiance of light. In the meantime, Christians are to continue doing good even in the face of suffering (1:6–7; 2:19–21; 3:13–14, 17–18; 4:1, 12–19; 5:9–10). One could argue that Peter is contrasting the realized eschatological claims of Rome's gospel with the future realization of the gospel of Jesus Christ.[44] True peace and vindication are not yet realized (despite Rome's claim), and the Christians of Asia Minor still wait for that day. For now, they seek to do good.

---

39. One teacher commented, "The idea is to live a radiant and compelling life, not hidden away in a Christian utopia, but 'among'—*right in the thick of*—'the pagans,'" in Comer, *Practicing the Way*, 141.

40. Winter, *Seek the Welfare*, 35–36.

41. Walker, "Benefactor."

42. Winter, *Seek the Welfare*, 39.

43. Peter labels his healing of the lame man as a "good deed" in Acts 4:9, which could also be a "technical word associated with the benefaction system" in the Greco-Roman world; see Parsons, *Acts*, 63. Peter challenges the authorities for why they are condemning rather than honoring them for their act of benefaction. As Keener notes, for the authorities "to reward benefaction with contempt or accusations was considered reprehensible," in Keener, *Acts*, 194.

44. See Liebengood, "Roman Imperial Claims," 262–63. He claims that hope appears to be of primary concern for Peter in the letter.

From this prefatory instruction, we discern a basis for public engagement of public witness for the common good that can then inform more specific political engagements. In other words, there is an orientation to the public that shapes a particular orientation to politics, and that particular orientation to politics should not negate (or completely overwhelm) the basic public orientation to seek the public good. What does this look like in practice, specifically as it pertains to the church's relation to politics? Peter continues.

Political Relations

From this general instruction, Peter gets more specific. He instructs them to "submit yourselves . . . to every human authority" (2:13). This includes "the emperor, as the supreme authority, or to governors" (2:13b–14a). The governors would be extensions of imperial authority that were sent "to punish those who do wrong and to commend those who do right" (2:14). As Christians who are committed to "do right," Peter's recipients should have no issue submitting to these authorities. However, their submission to these authorities is also connected to (1) their obedience to God's will, (2) the implicit demotion of the emperor, and (3) their willingness to suffer for doing good.

1. Obedience to God's Will

Regarding the first point, there are some translation details that help us clarify Peter's instruction. One commentator argues that the imperative *hypotagēte* ("submit" in NIV) is better translated as "respect" or "defer to," referencing "a secondary and more limited" commitment.[45] Peter reserves the more forceful term *hypakoē* (obedience) "for a person's relationship to Christ," which is to be their "primary and radical commitment."[46] Considering these nuances of translation, Peter is instructing them to "respect the emperor and his status."[47] In other words, it is not a blanket endorsement for unswerving submission to the state. And this is reinforced by Peter's affirmation that this is "God's will" for them (2:15) and they are to defer to earthly authorities "for the Lord's sake" (2:13). They are to respect human

---

45. Michaels, *1 Peter*, 124.
46. Michaels, *1 Peter*, 124.
47. See also McKnight, *Second Testament*, 1 Pet 2:13.

authority not simply because of the legitimate authority of the state, but also because of the ultimate authority of Christ.

2. Demotion of Rome

Caesar was typically given the title of "Lord" in the Roman world; and Peter conspicuously refers to Jesus as Lord right before his command to submit to other authorities.[48] In other words, Peter relativizes Rome in relation to Christ. This is best seen in Peter's four commands in 2:17, where he expands on his command in 2:13. He instructs them to "Show proper respect to everyone, love the family of believers, fear God, honor the emperor" (2:17). These commands encapsulate the behaviors that Christians should prioritize, but there is an equalizing effect that defines the emperor in "human terms," which might have carried a sharpness in light of the imperial cult.[49] It provides a rhetorical effect similar to if someone asked me if I loved my wife, and I responded with "I love everyone." Such a response calls my love for my wife into question. I suspect Peter's readers might interpret the call "to respect everyone" in a similar way.

3. Willingness to Suffer

Peter then turns to give more specific instructions based on their social locations—slaves (2:18), wives (3:1), husbands (3:7)—before returning to instruction for them all (3:8—4:19). For the sake of space, I simply want to note how Peter acknowledges that the act of doing good might incite suffering. Yes, they are called to defer to their social authorities and to do good, but Peter is under no illusion that all human authorities are good actors. Instead, he prepares them that they will "suffer *for doing good*" and they must "endure" such suffering (2:20). Why? Because "this is commendable before God" (2:20), and they were "called" to such a way of life as followers of Christ (2:21). As an example, a pattern, a model (*hypogrammon*), Jesus suffered *for* them, but also *before* them so "that [they] should follow in his steps" (2:21). Peter points them to an image of Jesus' suffering as to strengthen their willingness to suffer for doing good. Before I expand on this last point, let's summarize Peter's political instructions so far.

---

48. Green, *1 Peter*, 73.

49. Green, *1 Peter*, 75. See also Liebengood, "Roman Imperial Claims," 255.

Simplistic Summary

Returning to the second primary question: how does Peter instruct the recipients of his letter to interact with politics? In one sense, it is fairly simple: "Live holy, be good citizens, participate in society in your own way, endure suffering, and don't make waves."[50] However, as McKnight states, "this simplistic procedure will not do."[51] It is not as much that this is insufficient instruction on Peter's part, but more than that, such a blunt regurgitation of these instructions ignores several things. It ignores the nuances of Peter's priority of Christ's supreme lordship and his implicit demotion of the emperor; and more, it ignores Peter's larger scheme—one that I prefer to label as the gospelization of their imagination. Another way to say it: Peter instructs them by grounding and substantializing his instructions through the image of Jesus' story, which is the gospel. Peter meets story (a Roman gospel) with story (the gospel of Christ).

Gospeling the Imagination

Jeff Dryden speaks to this, noting how Peter is providing not just moral instructions, but a moral vision.

> He [gives] not simply a theological worldview; but a *narrative* theological worldview. He is not giving simply ontological statements about how the world is, but weaving together a *story* of how the world is; and this becomes the context for their own stories as individuals and as a community.[52]

Returning to 2:18–25, Peter exhorts them to suffer well for doing good, but he strengthens this exhortation by telling them the story of Jesus centered on his suffering, death.[53] Later in 3:18–22, he does it again, but he adds Jesus' resurrection and ascension (3:21–22). In other words, he reminds them of the V-shaped story of the gospel.[54] From his exalted state as the preexistent Son of God, Jesus moved downward, took on

---

50. McKnight, *1 Peter*, 22.
51. McKnight, *1 Peter*, 22.
52. Dryden, *Theology and Ethics*, 64.
53. Liebengood adds that Peter's presented narrative is "implicitly Davidic at its core," highlighting the connections between elements of 1 Peter and Zech 9–14 ("Roman Imperial Claims," 265; for a list of parallels between 1 Peter and Zech 9–14, see pp. 268–69.)
54. Bates, *Salvation by Allegiance Alone*, 35.

human flesh, bore the sins of humanity, suffered and died for sins in accordance with Scriptures, was buried, raised on the third day, appearing to many witnesses, and he ascended to be the ruling Christ, sending the Spirit to effect his rule in and through the church until he returns one day to consummate his rule. This is the gospel. This is the "master story" of the church.[55] And it is this story that Peter encourages the Anatolian Christians to find themselves in.

Through their baptism, they have already been brought into the story (3:21). Baptism is an event of extensive "resocialization" that initiates people into the community and into their shared story.[56] As such, baptism is a ritual that reenacts the V-shaped story of the gospel, performing "two nearly symmetrical movements," where the first is a "descending action," and the second is "a rising action."[57] The baptismal candidate is identifying with the story of Jesus, reinforcing the "mythic pattern" of Jesus' descent and ascent.[58] To use language from Michael Gorman, they are participating *in* Christ, embodying his story, and "becoming the Gospel."[59] In the face of the Roman gospel that boasted a realized eschatology in the providential arrival of Augustus, Peter provides a storied image that recharacterizes the Anatolian Christians into a new identity that *not only* provides explanatory power for their current suffering, but also stirs them to practice a new way of life in their community and world. It is this embodied practice in community that substantializes faithful witness.[60]

Peter's Instructions for the American Church

Taking my cues from 1 Peter, I encourage us to do three things: (1) acknowledge the distance; (2) distinguish between the public and the political; and (3) improvise with a gospel imagination.

---

55. Gorman, *Becoming the Gospel*, 133.
56. Meeks, *First Urban Christians*, 78.
57. Meeks, *First Urban Christians*, 156.
58. Meeks, *First Urban Christians*, 181.
59. Gorman, *Becoming the Gospel*.
60. This re-storying also accounts for the recharacterization of Rome, especially seen in Peter's use of "Babylon" in 5:13. Just as Peter connected the Anatolian Christians to the story of God as found in the scriptures of the Hebrew Bible, he does the same with Rome, casting them as the oppressive, archetypal empire of Babylon.

Acknowledge the Distance

The recipients of 1 Peter were a socially marginalized community that had little to no influence on the politics of their day. In other words, they had no reasonable claim or access to political power. Today in America, Christians are presented with an opportunity that was largely unthinkable to the Anatolian Christians of the first century. One scholar wrote, "Today we can entertain conversations about the exertion of moral authority by the church on the political scene, whether from the religious right or religious left," but this "could scarcely have entered the thoughts of exilic aliens and strangers."[61]

It raises the hypothetical but important question: What instruction would Peter give if he were writing to people in our social location, in our political context? We cannot, must not assume that the instructions would be identical. Different social contexts call for different social instructions.[62] Space does not afford a comprehensive answer to the question, but the question itself is a critical reorientation for many American Christians—to the Bible and to politics. Nonetheless, while the Bible was not written directly *to* us, it was written *for* us.[63] There are some aspects of Peter's instruction that we need to acknowledge as we approach the question, and one of those aspects is how Peter prioritizes the public over the political and does not conflate the two.

Distinguish the Public and the Political

Peter's reframing (and implicit demotion) of state power is critical for us to take seriously. In our contemporary American culture, the public has become conflated with the political.[64] And this is not simply a Conservative Christian problem, but it is an American Christian problem that plagues the right, the left, and even neo-Anabaptists.[65] Many of us need to recognize that "there are no political solutions to the problems most people care about."[66] We have too high of expectations for politics. Hunter writes,

61. Green, *1 Peter*, 283.
62. McKnight, *1 Peter*, 22.
63. See Walton, *Lost World*.
64. Hunter, *To Change the World*, 168.
65. Hunter, *To Change the World*, 97–175.
66. Hunter, *To Change the World*, 171.

> There are no comprehensive political solutions to the deterioration of "family values," the desire for equity, or the challenge of achieving consensus or solidarity in a cultural context of fragmentation and polarization. There are no real political solutions to the absence of decency and the spread of vulgarity . . . the state's role addressing human problems is partial and limited. It is not nearly as influential as the expectations most people have of it.[67]

We assume that if we are to influence the public with our moral values, we will need to do so through the political. But we need to scrutinize that assumption, and 1 Peter can help us. Peter puts forward a strategy for public witness that includes the political, but the political does not dominate the conversation. Like Paul, Rome is relatively "insignificant" to Peter on the cosmic scale of things.[68] Politics is not the frame by which Peter organizes his instructions for seeking the public good. Instead, politics is a secondary concern—one that is tied to one's ability to seek the public good. They only need to be concerned with politics inasmuch as the community's political position (i.e., the empire's suspicion of their civic disloyalty) could disrupt their public witness.

To carry this into our day, we need to ensure that our political engagement is not disruptive to our public witness. As Wear puts it, "Christians will think of politics best when we do not think of politics first."[69] And I fear that in our contemporary conflation of the public and the political, our political engagement (which is typically satisfied by simply voting) ironically delegates our responsibility for seeking solutions to public issues. We are satisfied with seeking the public good through voting for the candidate that best aligns with our ideological values, which for Christians are typically communicated as biblical values (which is an issue for another time). In a dangerous irony, our political actions provide us with an appearance of seeking the public good, soothing the impulses of our perceived responsibility; but this is an illusion that is upheld in the conflation of the public and the political.[70] Said another way, politics has become the "social imagery" that "defines the horizon of

---

67. Hunter, *To Change the World*, 171.

68. Barclay, "Why the Roman Empire," 363–87.

69. Michael Wear (@MichaelRWear), "Christians will think of politics best when we do not think of politics first," X, June 6, 2024, 11:48 a.m., https://x.com/michaelrwear/status/1798743747188150590.

70. Hunter, *To Change the World*, 173.

understanding and the parameters for action."[71] Our imaginations need renovation—*semper reformanda*.

Improvise with a Gospel Imagination

American history is riddled with people appealing to the Bible to support their political positions. And, interestingly, the same Bible would be used in support of opposing political positions.[72] How does this happen? It often assumes the Bible is a moral handbook that is universally, immediately applicable. But the solution to this problem is not less scriptural engagement, but rather a kind of engagement—a Spirit-led improvisation—that gets at our imaginations.[73]

We are embodied, affective beings, not purely cognitive, rational, or intellectual beings. Therefore, if we want to live for God, we will need to be governed by a love for God and what he loves. Our hearts will need to be renovated. But how does this happen? As James K. A. Smith has forcefully argued, it chiefly concerns our loves and desires. Our loves are shaped by liturgies—embodied, love-shaping practices and rituals.[74] When we participate in certain practices, we are yielding to the guiding love that is embedded in that practice, drawing and driving us to some vision—to some image—of the good life. Therefore, our pursuit of the public good must be tied to our imaginations, to us *seeing* that good life.[75]

Smith demonstrates how our "imaginations get stuck in a rut, and it becomes difficult to get out of them to imagine things differently."[76] When this occurs, Charles Taylor warns that the modern social imaginary "has become so self-evident to us that we have trouble seeing it as one possible conception among others."[77] Therefore, in order to be shaken loose of our dominating social imaginary, "we need more affective pictures."[78] I suggest that the picture of the gospel story can be one such affective picture.

---

71. Hunter, *To Change the World*, 168.

72. Schiess, *Ballot and the Bible*. See also Noll, *In the Beginning Was the Word* and *America's Book*.

73. McKnight, *Bible Is Not Enough*.

74. Smith, *You Are What You Love*.

75. For more on the imagination, see Smith, *Imagining the Kingdom*; and Prior, *Evangelical Imagination*.

76. Smith, *Desiring the Kingdom*, 28.

77. Taylor, *Modern Social Imaginaries*, 2.

78. Smith, *Desiring the Kingdom*, 29.

As the church looks to the Bible, I suggest that the Word of the words of Scripture be the frame and the reflection point for wise application. Put differently, the gospel—the V-shaped image of the story of Jesus—should always be at the center. A different master story, a different gospel (often a distortion of the true one) will produce different discipleship, distorted discipleship, and therefore a distorted public witness. But story must be combated with story, gospel with gospel. And, again, Peter can be interpreted as putting forward such a scheme.

How then do we practically improvise our political engagements with the image of the gospel? Matthew Bates argues that the gospel can be a composite of ten plot points of Jesus' story, but this can be further summarized as three major movements: Jesus became human, died for sins, and was raised and ascended to be the ruling Christ.[79] As we meditate on each of these three major movements in the story, we can live in and live out this great story.[80] So practically, we can ask three dense questions to spark our political engagements: (1) How should the incarnation shape our public lives? (2) How does the cross shape our public lives? And (3) how does Jesus' resurrection and ascension shape our public lives?

Rather than simply offer you my musings to these questions, I would strongly encourage you to struggle through these questions for yourself. However, struggling *for* ourselves must not slip into struggling *by* ourselves. We need to be in the wrestling ring together—and none of this WWE evangelicalism kind of wrestling ring (one dominated by personas and hollowed out for performance in service to market consumers). No, we need the wrestling of the Greek philosophers—a serious, sophisticated, honorable struggle. We need to wrestle like Jacob; and it may dislocate our hips, but it will relocate our loves, resulting in us bearing the name that God wants us to bear as his people (Gen 32:22–32).

Conclusion

The letter of 1 Peter offers rich insights into the political posture that Christians are to adopt within a challenging sociopolitical context. By examining the Roman Empire's political landscape, Peter's instructions to seek the public good, and the call to a respectful yet discerning engagement with governing authorities, we can discern a blueprint for

---

79. Bates, *Why the Gospel?*, 74.
80. Wright, *Great Story*, 13.

faithful witness in our own time. For the American church today, this means a strategy of faithful presence (not withdrawal), creative subversion (not complicity), and invitational witness (not coercion). As Christian pastors and leaders, let us continually point people to this gospel-centered vision. The question is: will we live into our dangerous calling to be the salt of the earth (Matt 5:13), or will we continue to be "salt in the wound" of America's political carnage?[81]

Bibliography

Alberta, Tim. *The Kingdom, the Power, and the Glory: American Evangelicals in an Age of Extremism*. New York: Harper, 2023.
Barclay, John M. G. "Why the Roman Empire Was Insignificant to Paul." In *Pauline Churches and Diaspora Judaism*, edited by John M. G. Barclay, 363–87. Grand Rapids: Eerdmans, 2016.
Bates, Matthew W. *Salvation by Allegiance Alone: Rethinking Faith, Works, and the Gospel of Jesus the King*. Grand Rapids: Baker Academic, 2017.
———. *Why the Gospel? Living the Good News of King Jesus with Purpose*. Grand Rapids: Eerdmans, 2023.
Burnett, D. Clint. *Paul and Imperial Divine Honors: Christ, Caesar, and the Gospel*. Grand Rapids: Eerdmans, 2024.
Butler, Joshua Ryan. *The Party Crasher: How Jesus Disrupts Politics as Usual and Redeems Our Partisan Divide*. Colorado Springs, CO: Multnomah, 2024.
Comer, John Mark. *Practicing the Way: Be with Jesus; Become Like Him; Do as He Did*. Colorado Springs, CO: WaterBrook, 2024.
Danker, F. W. *Benefactor: Epigraphic Study of a Graeco-Roman and New Testament Field*. St. Louis: Clayton, 1982.
Davids, Peter H. *The First Epistle of Peter*. 2nd ed. New International Commentary on the New Testament. Grand Rapids: Eerdmans, 1990.
Dryden, Jeffrey de Waal. *Theology and Ethics in 1 Peter: Paraenetic Strategies for Christian Character Formation*. WUNT 209. Tübingen: Mohr Siebeck, 2006.
Elliott, John H. *A Home for the Homeless: A Social-Scientific Criticism of 1 Peter, Its Situation and Strategy*. 2nd ed. 1990. Reprint, Eugene, OR: Wipf & Stock, 2005.
Galinsky, Karl. *Augustan Culture*. Princeton: Princeton University Press, 1998.
Giboney, Justin, et al. *Compassion (&) Conviction: The AND Campaign's Guide to Faithful Civic Engagement*. Downers Grove, IL: InterVarsity, 2020.
Goodman, Martin. *Rome and Jerusalem: The Clash of Ancient Civilizations*. Illustrated ed. New York: Vintage, 2008.
Gorman, Michael J. *Becoming the Gospel: Paul, Participation, and Mission*. Grand Rapids: Eerdmans, 2015.
Green, Joel B. *1 Peter*. Two Horizons New Testament Commentary. Grand Rapids: Eerdmans, 2007.
Gupta, Nijay K. *Strange Religion: How the First Christians Were Weird, Dangerous, and Compelling*. Grand Rapids: Brazos, 2024.

81. Switchfoot, "The Beautiful Letdown," from *Beautiful Letdown*.

Haddad, Najeeb T. *Paul and Empire Criticism*. Eugene, OR: Cascade Books, 2023.
Horsley, Richard A. *Scribes, Visionaries, and the Politics of Second Temple Judea*. Louisville: Westminster John Knox, 2007.
Hunter, James Davison. *To Change the World: The Irony, Tragedy, and Possibility of Christianity in the Late Modern World*. New York: Oxford University Press, 2010.
Jobes, Karen H. *1 Peter*. Baker Exegetical Commentary on the New Testament. Grand Rapids: Baker Academic, 2005.
Keener, Craig S. *Acts*. Abridged ed. New Cambridge Bible Commentary. Cambridge: Cambridge University Press, 2020.
Kruse, Colin G. "Persecution." In *DNTB*, 775–78.
Liebengood, Kelly D. "Confronting Roman Imperial Claims: Following the Footsteps (and the Narrative) of 1 Peter's Eschatological Davidic Shepherd." In *An Introduction to Empire in the New Testament*, edited by Adam Winn, 255–72. Resources for Biblical Study 84. Atlanta: SBL, 2016.
McKnight, Scot. *1 Peter*. NIV Application Commentary. Grand Rapids: Zondervan Academic, 1996.
———. *The Bible Is not Enough: Imagination and Making Peace in the Modern World*. Minneapolis: Fortress, 2023.
———, ed. *The Second Testament: A New Translation*. Downers Grove, IL: IVP Academic, 2023.
Meeks, Wayne A. *The First Urban Christians: The Social World of the Apostle Paul*. 2nd ed. New Haven: Yale University Press, 2003.
Michaels, J. Ramsey. *1 Peter*. Word Biblical Commentary. Dallas: Word, 1988.
———. "1 Peter." In *Dictionary of the Later New Testament and Its Developments*, edited by Ralph P. Martin and Peter H. Davids, 914–23. IVP Bible Dictionary Series. Downers Grove, IL: InterVarsity, 1997.
Noll, Mark A. *America's Book: The Rise and Decline of a Bible Civilization, 1794–1911*. New York: Oxford University Press, 2022.
———. *In the Beginning Was the Word: The Bible in American Public Life, 1492–1783*. New York: Oxford University Press, 2015.
Parsons, Mikeal C. *Acts*. Paideia. Illustrated ed. Grand Rapids: Baker Academic, 2008.
Perrin, Nicholas. "The Imperial Cult." In *The World of the New Testament: Cultural, Social, and Historical Contexts*, edited by Joel B. Green and Lee Martin McDonald, 124–34. Grand Rapids: Baker Academic, 2017.
Porter, Stanley E. "Paul Confronts Caesar with the Good News." In *Empire in the New Testament*, edited by Stanley E. Porter and Cynthia Long Westfall, 164–96. Eugene, OR: Pickwick Publications, 2011.
Price, S. R. F. *Rituals and Power: The Roman Imperial Cult in Asia Minor*. New York: Cambridge University Press, 1984.
Prior, Karen Swallow. *The Evangelical Imagination: How Stories, Images, and Metaphors Created a Culture in Crisis*. Grand Rapids: Brazos, 2023.
Schiess, Kaitlyn. *Ballot and the Bible: How Scripture Has Been Used and Abused in American Politics and Where We Go from Here*. Grand Rapids: Brazos, 2023.
Smith, James K. A. *Desiring the Kingdom: Worship, Worldview, and Cultural Formation*. Grand Rapids: Baker Academic, 2009.
———. *Imagining the Kingdom: How Worship Works*. Grand Rapids: Baker Academic, 2013.

———. *You Are What You Love: The Spiritual Power of Habit*. Grand Rapids: Brazos, 2016.

Sprinkle, Preston M. *Exiles: The Church in the Shadow of Empire*. Colorado Springs, CO: David C. Cook, 2024.

Stanton, Graham N. *Jesus and Gospel*. New York: Cambridge University Press, 2004.

Switchfoot. *The Beautiful Letdown*. Columbia/Sony BMG, 2003. Spotify.

Taylor, Charles. *Modern Social Imaginaries*. Durham: Duke University Press, 2004.

Volf, Miroslav. "Soft Difference: Theological Reflections on the Relation Between Church and Culture in 1 Peter." *Ex Auditu* 10 (1994) 15–30.

Walker, Donald D. "Benefactor." In *DNTB*, 157–59.

Walton, John H. *The Lost World of Genesis One: Ancient Cosmology and the Origins Debate*. Downers Grove, IL: IVP Academic, 2009.

Wear, Michael R. *The Spirit of Our Politics: Spiritual Formation and the Renovation of Public Life*. Grand Rapids: Zondervan, 2024.

Winter, Bruce W. *Seek the Welfare of the City: Christians as Benefactors and Citizens*. Grand Rapids: Eerdmans, 1994.

Wright, Christopher J. H. *The Great Story and the Great Commission: Participating in the Biblical Drama of Mission*. Grand Rapids: Baker Academic, 2023.

Wright, N. T., and Michael F. Bird. *Jesus and the Powers: Christian Political Witness in an Age of Totalitarian Terror and Dysfunctional Democracies*. Grand Rapids: Zondervan, 2024.

Zanker, Paul. *The Power of Images in the Age of Augustus*. Translated by Alan Shapiro. Ann Arbor: University of Michigan Press, 1988.

15

Peter's Shift in Christology
It's Not A Mission, It's A Way of Life

J. Leland Stephens

Introduction to Story

Our brains are hardwired to create stories. In fact, right now your brain is creating your story by processing all the new data you are receiving and adding it to all the data stored in your long-term memory[1] to build for you a coherent picture of your present reality. Put another way, your current story is being shaped by your past story (i.e., your family of origin, your culture, your painful or traumatic experiences, your education, etc.) because your brain filters all your present conclusions through the assumptions created by your memories.[2]

Our brains combine our memories and our current reality to build a different kind of story that is sometimes called vision. Our vision is a projection of a wanted or expected outcome informed by all the past data

---

1. Neuroscientific research has proven that memory is multifaceted in function and brain location. I am generically talking about the function of "long-term" memory as it relates to our self-awareness and decision making. I assume throughout this chapter that these memories can be received through both individual experiences and through social/cultural conditioning.

2. There are a lot of resources that talk about our brains and the power of story but for a quick theological introduction, see Green, "Practicing the Gospel," 387–97. See also Johnson, *Human Rites*, for his discussion on how embodied practices shape our story.

and assumptions stored in our memory, that tells us how to act to either accomplish or avoid the expected outcome. Combine these two types of story created by our brains and we can begin to grasp how our past story informs both our present perspective and our future decision making.

In this chapter, I want to take this fundamental idea of story and use it to explain Peter's inability to grasp that Jesus was the Messiah who would usher in God's kingdom by dying. Then I'll turn and show how Jesus transformed Peter's common Judaism memory into the cruciform[3] Jesus vision. And finally, we'll look at how Peter used his shift in Christology to disciple the next generation of followers through communal memory.

Peter's Story

What information about Peter's story before Jesus do we actually know?[4] Based on the four Gospel accounts, we can say that Peter's[5] name before Jesus was Simon Bar Yona (son of John/Jonah), he was married, he had a brother named Andrew (who was a disciple of John the Baptist), they were both fisherman, and Peter was originally from Bethsaida and either he moved to, or his mother-in-law had a house in, Capernaum. One other detail, not found in the four Gospel accounts, that is pertinent to Peter's backstory is that Acts 4:13 tells us that the Jewish leaders viewed Peter as an "uneducated man." This is not enough information to build a nuanced picture of Peter's story before Jesus, but knowing Peter's occupation, the location of his home, and that he is referred to as uneducated[6] does give us enough information to conclude that Peter

---

3. Cruciform simply means to be conformed to the way of the cross. A good article that unpacks this is Hays, "Crucified One."

4. Many theological historians have taken up the task of using what data is available to piece together a more detailed backstory than I will present here. For a robust list of these sources see Green, *Vox Petri*, 35–51.

5. Cephas (*Kephas*) is the Aramaic version of the Greek name Peter (*Petros*); both mean rock/stone.

6. Many authors, especially at the popular/non-scholar level, have tried to paint a picture of first-century Judaism's education path as robust and solidified for all male Jews which makes it seem like all would have been "educated," but this is almost assuredly a projection of a post-AD 70 developed Rabbinic Judaism onto a diverse, temple-centric Judaism of the early first century. One popular example is Comer, *Practicing the Way*, 24–26. My point is not to speak specifically against Comer's conclusions, as I agree with most of them; it is instead to point out that not only is this an unhelpful picture of who Jesus was claiming to be, it is almost always an unnecessary foundation

was most likely not affiliated with any major sects within first-century Judaism (i.e., Pharisees, Sadducees, Essenes, etc.) and allows us to identify him as a member of "common Judaism."[7]

Common Judaism's Expectations

Common Judaism is simply one of the terms that have been used to describe the majority population within first-century Judaism. This group was not as focused on an exact interpretation of Torah but would still have been dedicated to the central particularities within the Jewish faith. Therefore, we can argue that Peter was circumcised, most likely prayed multiple times a day, recited the Shema daily, fasted regularly, attended the local synagogue on the Sabbath, sacrificed at the temple during the festivals, ate kosher, overall desired to follow the law, and longed for the fulfillment of the prophets' promise concerning the return of YHWH, Israel's God, and the restoration of Israel.[8] All of this builds a picture of Peter prior to Jesus but it's this last piece that will help us better understand Peter's story as it relates to who he thought he was meeting when Jesus beckoned him to come and follow.

All first-century Jews agreed that something wasn't right about their current circumstances. This was driven by the reality that the Jews were captive in their own God-promised land, Israel was still disunified and scattered throughout the known world, and the land was infiltrated with gentiles which only increased concerns over ritual purity and cleanliness. There was also a chasm between the status of the Jewish leaders and the common Jews, taxation was high which led to increased debt, and famine and disease were a reality to many. Each of these factors were not equally felt by all first-century Jewish groups but in different ways they contributed to the longing for the restoration of Israel among all the groups. The major disagreement between the groups was *how* this restoration was going to come.

---

for the theological point trying to be made.

7. For more detailed info on the perspective of common Judaism than will be presented here, see Sanders, *Judaism*; Dunn, *Jesus Remembered*, 255–324; and Wright, *New Testament*, 213–14.

8. While this is beyond the scope of this chapter, I want to point out that the terms Israelite/Israel and Jew/Judaism are not synonymous in the New Testament. For the position I hold, and will be using in this chapter, see Staples, *Idea of Israel*.

Common Jews were waiting on an intervention from YHWH to step in and solve all of these problems by sending the Davidic king/ messiah (arguably interchangeable titles) to come in the power of the Spirit, judge the disobedient, cleanse and gather Israel, and inaugurate a time of great blessing and prosperity for God's people.[9] All of these expectations had been neatly packaged into a single metaphor called the kingdom of God. Given that Peter's brother Andrew was a disciple of John the Baptist, it seems reasonable to conclude that the Baptist's proclamations had also influenced Peter to expect this intervention immediately, not just sometime in the future.[10] All of this anticipation and expected outcome shaped Peter's vision of Jesus which postures us to understand why he struggled with Jesus' cruciform agenda.

Peter's Journey with Jesus

To change our interpretation of our present story, we must go through a process that enables our brains to correct our past story. Peter's journey with Jesus clearly illustrates this as his expectations of the Messiah blocked his ability to comprehend Jesus' teachings (Mark 4:13; 7:17–18)[11] and authority (Mark 4:35–41; 6:45–52; 8:14–21).[12] This is because Peter filtered everything Jesus said and did through his memories which produced an interpretation that was misaligned with Jesus' agenda. Jesus was aware of this and was intentionally working to shift Peter's vision.

Jesus' intention to shift Peter's stubborn vision is first foreshadowed by Mark's placement of Jesus healing the blind man in 8:22–26. In this scene, Jesus spits on and touches the blind man's eyes, but this only results in the man having blurry and hazy sight. Then Jesus touches his eyes again and he is able to see completely. The man regaining his sight requires a two-phase process which is meant to be startling to the reader as the expectation is that Jesus' healing would be instantaneous. This story serves as an illustration for how Jesus is overcoming

---

9. These expectations are rooted in a conglomeration of Old Testament texts and summarized in Second Temple Jewish texts like Psalms of Solomon. McKnight, *Kingdom*, 47; and Staples, *Idea of Israel*, 325.

10. This all seems to be supported by John 1:40–41, esp. where Andrew says, "We have found the Messiah!" and Peter seemingly leaves with him without further discussion or explanation.

11. I will explain why I am only using Mark's Gospel account later in the chapter.

12. Hooker, *Saint Mark*, 20–21.

the blindness in Peter's story through a journey filled with many small shifts instead of all at once.[13]

Peter's Proclamation Reveals Continued Blindness

In the following scene (Mark 8:27–33), Jesus asks the disciples who they think he is, and Peter boldly answers, "You are the Messiah." Behind these words can be heard both Peter's assuredness that Jesus was YHWH's king and anticipation that the time for the inauguration of God's kingdom was upon them. Through the lens of Peter's story, the only way this could come to fruition was an eventual clash with Rome, and given Jesus' special status with the Father and his miraculous power, they were guaranteed to win. This aspect of Peter's expectations was most likely rooted in the communal memory of the Maccabean revolution in the face of oppression by Antiochus Epiphanes IV (168–160 BC). Peter would have celebrated this victory every year during the festival of Hanukkah, so some final version of this victory is most likely the outcome Peter expected.

Like the man who didn't clearly see the first time Jesus touched his eyes, Peter is correct in identifying Jesus as YHWH's king, but he still can't see Jesus' agenda clearly. Jesus is aware of this and, according to Mark 8:31–40, turns immediately to address how the kingdom of God would be inaugurated and how Jesus' followers are expected to participate in its arrival. Peter pulls Jesus to the side and rebukes him, convinced there is no way the kingdom can come through the Messiah's death. Jesus in turn rebukes Peter by calling him Satan due to his inability to discern and participate with God's plan. The shame Peter felt in this moment would have been deep, as Jesus ensures Peter's rebuke is heard by the other disciples, but this is still not the watershed moment for Peter's shift,[14] so the journey forward continues.

---

13. For agreement with my position on the blind man as a pattern see Garland, *Mark*, 312.

14. To Peter's credit, despite the deep shame he felt by Jesus' rebuke, he demonstrates that he truly does believe Jesus is the Messiah by continuing to follow even though the vision forward is obscured. In Mark's Gospel account, this is the mark of true faith: unwavering allegiance even when the path forward is not clear.

Peter's Denial—Jesus' Faithfulness

In Mark 14:66–72, after Jesus is arrested and led away, Peter is portrayed as bravely following Jesus and his captors while all the others had abandoned him. His willingness to follow Jesus takes him all the way into the courtyard of the building Jesus is taken in to be interrogated. And then things take a turn. A person in the courtyard accuses Peter of being a follower of Jesus. Peter denies and moves to a new location so he can be ready if Jesus chooses to act. Jesus doesn't; by the end of the night Peter will have denied he is a follower of Jesus three times. The dichotomy of this episode is clear: Jesus remains committed to the Father's agenda, even in the face of death, and Peter again fails to recognize the path of faithfulness, resulting in shame.

A quick excursion into the mind of Peter reveals that he couldn't have come to a different conclusion in that moment. Why? The part of Peter's story that still envisioned the accomplishment of all the expectations concerning Jesus and the inauguration of God's kingdom had not been fully corrected, so when Peter is in the courtyard deciding whether to become a martyr or not, his brain could not produce a positive vision that aligned with martyrdom. Thus, he lied and fled.[15] To be clear, this is not a fear of death problem, this is a story problem. We see in the garden scene that Peter was willing to fight, and therefore die, within the bounds of Jesus ushering in the kingdom of God. Peter almost assuredly saw death as a reasonable outcome as long as it could be understood as a faithful death. The beauty and hope that flows from all of this is that while Peter's story blinded him from rightly interpreting the moment, his failure highlights Jesus' power to heal even the most stubborn stories.[16]

This complete failure is what was necessary to posture Peter for Jesus' cruciform vision. This is portrayed clearly when, after the resurrection, Jesus finds a much more pliable and humbler Peter. In John 21:15–19, Jesus comes to Peter offering forgiveness, restoration, and recommissioning and Peter humbly accepts. This is the moment we've been waiting for; Peter's story was finally re-storied into Jesus' story, resulting

---

15. Second Maccabees 7 presents a theology of resurrection as a logical reason for martyrdom, but this does not apply to Peter's scenario because the Maccabean accounts are tied directly with the scenario of holy war and apostatizing. Peter probably expected a holy war, but Jesus' silence ruled that out in Peter's mind and he also did not see his unwillingness to become a martyr as somehow rejecting his Jewish faith.

16. Garland, *Mark*, 312.

in the Christological shift of the cross from an impossibility to a central component of Jesus' enthronement as king of God's kingdom.

The Cross as a Way of Life

Peter's shift in Christology did not stop with Jesus' sacrificial death and resurrection as so many reduce it to today. In Peter's mind, the cross was now to be understood as the way of life, or the vision, for all who desire to faithfully follow Jesus. Peter seems to be convinced that Jesus beckoning his followers to take up their own cross (Mark 8:34–38) meant that the cross was to be seen as more than just a redemptive act; it was also to be seen as a representative act. In other words, Jesus' death did not exempt his followers from suffering, but instead invited his followers to understand their suffering as divinely empowered participation with God's redemptive movements in the world.[17]

We see this most clearly in Peter's life through his martyrdom, as actions always speak louder than words. The church historian Eusebius succinctly addresses this event, stating,[18] "It is recorded that Paul was beheaded in Rome itself and that Peter also was crucified in Nero's time, and the title of 'Peter and Paul' over the cemeteries there, which has prevailed to the present day."[19] He later provides a more detailed account: "Peter seems to have preached in Pontus and Galatia and Bithynia and Cappadocia and Asia to the Jews of the Dispersion, and at last, having come to Rome, was crucified head-downwards,[20] for he himself had asked to suffer so."[21] This depiction of Peter's martyrdom represents his faithful influence, even in death, that shaped much of the early church's understanding of Jesus' death as more than just a substitutionary sacrifice, but also as a way of life.

---

17. Hays, "Crucified One," 33–35.

18. It must be said up front that while Eusebius is generally regarded as a reliable witness for church history, his distance and bias does not always produce confidence among historical scholars. For the reader who is looking for a resource that robustly addresses the arguments for and against Peter's stay and martyrdom in Rome, I recommend Cullmann, *Peter*, 71–157. For a quick summary see Bruce, *Peter, Stephen, James*, 43–45.

19. Eusebius of Caesarea, *Ecclesiastical History*, 132.

20. This is highly contested because it is not mentioned by the earliest writers that mention Peter's crucifixion.

21. Eusebius of Caesarea, *Ecclesiastical History*, 138.

Peter's Story Re-storied

Returning to Peter's story one last time, during the scene of his denials, we saw a Peter who couldn't imagine martyrdom as a path to victory, as his story was shaped by common Judaism's expectations of redemption. Fast forward to the end of his life, Peter is again faced with a similar choice: save himself and flee Rome, or stay and strengthen the church in Rome, even at the cost of his life? The difference this time is that Peter's story has been re-storied. When Peter's brain sees death as a cost of following Jesus, it's no longer processed through the memory of his former expectations and assumptions; it's now processed through his experiences with Jesus. This motivates him to face death because this is now a reasonable and joyful outcome since it can be understood as a faithful sacrifice to God with the promise of vindication in light of Jesus' example.

Discipleship for the Next Generation

Peter's shift in Christology also became the vision for how the gospel[22] would be used to make disciples of the next generation. This vision is best illustrated in the Gospel according to Mark, primarily due to the close relationship between Mark and Peter. The most credible source that provides a detailed account of Peter's relationship with Mark is Papias, who was the bishop of Hierapolis around AD 130.[23] While Papias's original writings are lost, Eusebius introduces him and captures his words as follows:

> Papias, an ancient man, who was a hearer of John and a companion of Polycarp, attests in writing in the fourth of his books, for five books were composed by him. . . . Papias himself, however, according to the preface of his treatises, makes it clear that he was never a hearer or eye-witness of the holy Apostles, but he shows that he received the doctrines of the faith from those who knew them. . . . We shall now of necessity add to his words already quoted a tradition about Mark who wrote the Gospel, which he gives in these words: "This also the Presbyter used to say, 'When Mark became Peter's interpreter, he wrote

---

22. When I use the word gospel, I am referring to the oral and written proclamations concerning Jesus' birth, life, teachings, miracles, death, resurrection, and ascension and the way of life/story these proclamations beckon others into.

23. For a more in-depth argument in favor of Papias's position see Hooker, *Saint Mark*, 5–6.

down accurately, although not in order, all that he remembered of what was said or done by the Lord. For he had not heard the Lord nor followed Him, but later, as I have said, he did Peter, who made his teaching fit his needs without, as it were, making any arrangement of the Lord's oracles, so that Mark made no mistake in thus writing some things down as he remembered them. For to one thing he gave careful attention, to omit nothing of what he heard and to falsify nothing in this."[24]

The text of Mark also supports Peter's influence. A few quick examples include Mark consistently sharing information from the standpoint of Jesus' twelve disciples, which contrasts with Luke (e.g. Mark 1:36 vs. Luke 4:42). Several times Mark shares details from the inner circle's perspective (Peter, James, and John), which contrasts with Matthew and Luke (Mark 5:37 vs. Matt 9:23 and Luke 8:51). Moreover, Mark even shares the very thoughts and emotions of Peter in certain situations (Mark 9:6, 11:21), revealing a more personal knowledge of Peter's experiences.[25] Given this evidence, we can confidently argue that the best way to understand how Peter shared the story of Jesus is by examining the Gospel according to Mark.

One last side street to explore before turning to the Gospel itself is the circumstance that led to the writing of Mark's account. Mark was likely Peter's interpreter[26] in Rome because Peter did not speak Latin and probably only spoke Greek at a business level, necessitating assistance in explaining complex aspects of Judaism and Jesus to the churches in Rome. After Peter's martyrdom, a significant shift occurred.[27] Mark decided to go to Egypt to proclaim the gospel in Alexandria, creating a need within the Roman churches to transition from an orally based gospel of Peter, translated by Mark, to a written Gospel based on Mark's memory of Peter's teachings.[28] In response, before Mark left for Egypt, the churches

24. Eusebius, *Ecclesiastical History*, 202–6.

25. Farmer, "Mark."

26. Admittedly, there are different versions of Mark's relationship to Peter found in second-century Christian writings and not all of them would support this theory that Mark was Peter's interpreter. However, all of them acknowledge Mark's close relationship to Peter. For a detailed introduction to Mark, see Witherington, *Mark*, 20–25.

27. Church history is somewhat in agreement that Peter was martyred by Nero so the latest possible date for Peter's death is AD 68. Cullmann, *Peter*, 71–157.

28. Helen K. Bond, summarizing Jan Assman, says, "If [for our purposes, Peter's] memories are to survive, these oral memories must be transformed into cultural memory . . . which extends beyond the present generation and becomes embedded in the authoritative cultural repertoire of the group. Writing the memories down into

commissioned him to create and copy multiple copies of Peter's Gospel for distribution among the churches.[29]

Peter's Gospel Through Markan Eyes

Mark's Gospel account is divided into two sections: chapters 1–8 and chapters 9–16. Chapters 1–8 focus on Jesus' ministry, teachings, and miracles to reveal Jesus' unique identity. But even amid this narrative-supported high Christology,[30] Jesus is presented as aware that his path must lead to the cross (e.g., 2:19–20). Then, in chapters 9–16, the pace of the Gospel slows down, providing a detailed account of Jesus' final days before the cross. Yet even though his death is moved to the forefront in this section, Jesus is still teaching and performing miracles until his arrest (e.g., 11:20–25 and 13:28–31). The Gospel is structured in this way to ensure the themes of Jesus' divine identity, suffering, and death for the sake of many cannot be separated to fit any other story than Jesus'.[31]

In between these two sections is Mark 8:31—9:1, which acts as a hinge point in this Gospel account. Jesus, aware that his time on earth is almost up, predicts his death and beckons the disciples to follow him, even if it leads to their death. Through this lens, Mark proclaims that "Jesus died (as an inclusive substitute) for the many who will participate in his death in their own lives and hearts through faith and perhaps even

---

some kind of a literary text provides an effective way of transforming them into cultural memories, of stabilizing group identity, and of providing an expanded context . . . in which the writer of the text can speak to new generations of hearers without actually being present." Bond, "Was Peter," 53.

29. I take this perspective based on Eusebius, "Church History," 115–16 combined with pp. 261 to say that the church in Rome asked Mark to write down Peter's teachings because Mark was leaving Rome to go to Egypt which would have left them without their oral source of the gospel teaching.

30. "Recent investigation of Mark has stressed the importance of the fact that he presents his Gospel in narrative form. A great deal of Mark's Christology is implicit, conveyed by the way in which he presents the material." Hooker, *Saint Mark*, 20.

31. "Jesus was an enigmatic and forceful figure, and Mark, probably more than any other Gospel writer, has given us the flavor of what it might have been like to encounter him in a world with a wide variety of hopes and dreams about redeemer figures. He did not wish to be defined by others, but rather to redefine the Christological categories. Mark would also have us know that spiritual things are spiritually discerned—only by revelation can the Christ be truly comprehended, but once comprehended, he could be confessed with a variety of royal titles—Christ, Son of God, Son of Man, King, Son of David." Witherington, *Mark*, 54.

through their own martyrdom."[32] When this is still not understood in 10:45, Jesus goes one step further to explain that his death will have a redemptive purpose—that victory for many will come through the cross. Therefore, "the courage to look death in the face derives from the hope of vindication" (8:34—9:1; 10:29–31; 12:9–11; 14:62; 16:1–8) and the path to vindication is the way of Jesus and the cross, for the sake of others.[33]

Through this high-level lens, we can see that Peter has not only learned from his past failures but has also learned how to leverage his past failures to beckon and disciple the next generation of believers, in hopes they don't make the same mistake as him. They may hear his teachings about Jesus and reject them, but they won't misunderstand who Jesus is claiming to be nor what it means to follow him. For those who choose to follow the way of Jesus, Peter's cruciform gospel will form communal memories so that even though they did not walk with Jesus, hear all of his teachings, and see his miracles, Peter's memories will become the memories of the community. And out of these communal memories will flow servanthood, sacrifice, and suffering as the most normal elements of their story, shaping their expectations of life and success.

Future Generations

Peter's communal memories, as shared through Mark's Gospel account, shaped communities to live the cruciform way of Jesus. Two situations in church history clearly portray this reality. The first is the persecution of the church in Rome during the reign of Emperor Nero, when Peter proclaimed the gospel in Rome, showing immediate impact. The second is the plague that struck Alexandria around AD 260, demonstrating Peter's legacy across multiple generations.

In AD 64, Emperor Nero set fire to a section of Rome and blamed Christians which led to an intense period of persecution. Tacitus recounts the story like this:

> To scotch the rumour [that the fire had taken place to order], Nero substituted as culprits, and punished with the utmost refinements of cruelty a class of men, loathed for their vices . . . whom the crowd styled Christians. . . . (4) First, then, those who confessed . . . were arrested; next, on their disclosures vast

---

32. McKnight, *Jesus and His Death*, 357–58.
33. McKnight, *Jesus and His Death*, 357–58.

> numbers ... were convicted, not so much on the count of arson as for hatred of the human race.... And derision accompanied their end: they were covered with wild beasts' skins and torn to death by dogs; or they were fastened on crosses, and, when daylight failed, were burned to serve as lamps by night. (5) Nero had offered his gardens for the spectacle, and gave an exhibition in his Circus, mixing with the crowd in the habit of a charioteer, or mounted on his car. Hence, in spite of a guilt, which had earned the most exemplary punishment, there arose a sentiment of pity, due to the impression that they were being sacrificed not for the welfare of the state but to the ferocity of a single man.[34]

As mentioned above, Peter's death is portrayed as occurring during Nero's reign. While we cannot assert with certainty that Peter was martyred in this specific scenario, it is evident that Peter's oral gospel was already circulating throughout the churches in Rome by this time. Consequently, it can be argued that the steadfastness of many believers in the face of tremendous suffering can be traced back to the hope they found in Jesus through Peter's faithful proclamation. The immediate impact of Peter's gospel provided early Christians with the strength and encouragement needed to endure persecution, demonstrating how his ministry fortified their faith and resilience.

Let's now fast forward around 200 years into the future and see how Peter's legacy was shaping the second generation through Mark's Gospel account. In Alexandria[35] (circa AD 260), a plague begins to sweep through the area with a seemingly high mortality rate.[36] Eusebius records the writings of Dionysius, the bishop of Alexandria during this time, as such:

> [After] a very brief season of rest this pestilence assailed us; to them [the pagans] more dreadful than any dread, and more intolerable than any other calamity; and, as one of their own writers has said, the only thing which prevails over all hope. But to us this was not so, but no less than the other things was it an

---

34. Tacitus, *Annals* 15.44-2-5, cited in Dunn, *Beginning in Jerusalem*, 56–57.

35. We have already mentioned that Mark went to Egypt after leaving Rome, but I include Alexandria in my locations of Peter's influence because Eusebius notes that Mark was the first to establish churches in Alexandria with the Gospel account he had composed in Rome. Eusebius, "Ecclesiastical History," 116.

36. "Dionysius emphasized the heavy mortality of the epidemic by asserting how much happier survivors would be had they merely, like the Egyptians in the time of Moses, lost the firstborn from each house. For 'there is not a house in which there is not one dead—how I wish it had been only one.'" Stark, *Rise of Christianity*, 82.

exercise and probation. For it did not keep aloof even from us, but the heathen it assailed more severely.[37]

Later he adds,

> The most of our brethren were unsparing in their exceeding love and brotherly kindness. They held fast to each other and visited the sick fearlessly, and ministered to them continually, serving them in Christ. And they died with them most joyfully, taking the affliction of others, and drawing the sickness from their neighbors to themselves, and willingly receiving their pains. And many who cared for the sick and gave strength to others died themselves having transferred to themselves their death. And the popular saying which always seems a mere expression of courtesy, they then made real in action, taking their departure as the others' "offscouring." Truly the best of our brethren departed from life in this manner, including some presbyters and deacons and those of the people who had the highest reputation; so that this form of death, through the great piety and strong faith it exhibited, seemed to lack nothing of martyrdom.[38]

The communal memory of Peter's Christology was powerfully alive, still guiding believers in Alexandria into its third generation. Despite the immense suffering and loss, these Christians demonstrated unwavering commitment to their faith by selflessly caring for the sick and dying. Their actions reflected the sacrificial love of their crucified king, embodying the hope and assurance that vindication through Christ was worth any cost. This enduring legacy of faith and sacrificial love highlights the profound and lasting impact of Peter's ministry, inspiring generations to live out the gospel even in the face of death.

Final Reflection: It's Not a Mission, It's a Way of Life

There is a foundational lesson at the heart of all this that I want to ensure we don't miss: when we focus solely on the mission, the outcome becomes our vision. This means our minds will lead us to make decisions aimed at manipulating this outcome. We see this clearly in Peter's story before Jesus' crucifixion and resurrection. Peter was focused on the messianic

---

37. Eusebius, "Church History," 306–7.
38. Eusebius, "Church History," 306–7.

mission according to common Judaism, which led him to completely miss Jesus' cruciform agenda.

Let me illustrate this point. Many churches would say that the mission they are pursuing is some form of evangelism and discipleship. This often results in the desired outcome of getting more people to come to their Sunday morning worship service. The argument for this is often: if they can get them attending, they can beckon them to make a decision for Jesus and assimilate them into the community by serving or attending a small group. In this scenario, success is measured by numbers. To achieve the outcome of more people gathering and serving, they look at the latest trends within churches and culture and realize that they need an engaging speaker, good music, a good children's ministry, an influential social media presence, a professional looking flow of service that looks and sounds good on their streaming platform, etc. And if the numbers dip, they just need to update to some new "special sauce" to bring the people back.

I use this example because the data of this outcome-based model is in, and we can easily see what outcome we actually create: pastors and worship leaders who care about influence and performance, burned-out volunteers who end up struggling through church hurt, and preference-driven churchgoers who are moved by the show but leave unchanged. This is not the only model that has failed over the years. The American church has been chasing outcomes, and failing to produce the outcomes we've chased, for so long that you'd think we would've learned our lesson by now. Yet our minds keep convincing us that this time it will work. News flash: it won't! Why? We haven't been given the power to control outcomes! God controls the outcomes, we control the faithfulness.[39]

The difference between the outcome-based model and Peter's shift in Christology is profound. Peter's shift was not merely a cognitive belief that Jesus was God in the flesh; it was a transformation into a new vision of faithfulness that re-storied Peter's entire story. This new vision was the cruciform way of Jesus as the only way to the kingdom of God. Through

---

39. To be clear, when I say faithfulness, I mean that we must love the Lord our God the way Jesus modeled love for the Father which, in the power of the Spirit, propelled him into the life of loving people sacrificially but never in a way that violated his obedience to the Father nor the Father's definition of good. Most of the failures I see in the church stem from the mission focusing on loving God, but the way it is lived out hurts persons or the mission focusing on loving people, but it is lived out in such a way that violates our obedience to God and his definition of good. If we don't feel this tension, we probably aren't living faithfully.

this shift in vision, Peter no longer projects a mission to be accomplished; instead, he sees people to be loved and beckoned to a new way of life. And by making this the cultural memory all who enter the community are formed into, in just over three hundred years, Christianity grew from a small Jewish sect into the dominant religion of the Roman Empire. God accomplished his mission through their way of life, the community did not accomplish God's mission through their strategies.

For an American church who is so focused on accomplishing the mission with the least amount of uncomfortableness and inconvenience as possible, the takeaway is clear: *our call is not to a mission, it is to the vision of a new way of life.* This way of life is the way of Jesus, and the way of Jesus is the way of the cross. Jesus' cruciform vision is the only vision powerful enough to change our story into a life that is unfazed by the circumstances surrounding it:

> Again and again, the forward march of Roman power and world organization was interrupted by the only force against which political genius and military valor were utterly helpless—epidemic disease. . . . And when it came, as though carried by storm clouds, all other things gave way, and men crouched in terror, abandoning all their quarrels, undertakings, and ambitions, until the tempest had blown over. [But for the Christians] we have begun gladly to seek martyrdom while we are learning not to fear death. These are trying exercises for us, not deaths; they give to the mind the glory of fortitude; by contempt of death they prepare for the crown.[40]

Bibliography

Aland, Kurt. *Synopsis of the Four Gospels*. Bellingham, WA: Logos Bible Software, 2009.
Bird, Michael F. *Jesus the Eternal Son: Answering Adoptionist Christology*. Grand Rapids: Eerdmans, 2017.
Blomberg, Craig L. *Jesus and the Gospels: An Introduction and Survey*. 3rd ed. Nashville: B&H Academic, 2022.
Bockmuehl, Markus N. A. *Simon Peter in Scripture and Memory: The New Testament Apostle in the Early Church*. Grand Rapids: Baker Academic, 2012.
Bond, Helen K. "Was Peter Behind Mark's Gospel?" In *Peter in Early Christianity*, edited by Helen K. Bond and Larry Hurtado, 46–61. Grand Rapids: Eerdmans, 2015.
Bond, Helen K., and Larry W. Hurtado. *Peter in Early Christianity*. Grand Rapids: Eerdmans, 2015.

---

40. Stark, *Rise of Christianity*, 74–81.

Brown, Raymond E., et al., eds. *Peter in the New Testament: A Collaborative Assessment by Protestant and Roman Catholic Scholars*. 1973. Reprint, Eugene, OR: Wipf & Stock, 2002.

Bruce, F. F. *Peter, Stephen, James, and John: Studies in Non-Pauline Diversity in the Early Church*. Nashville: Kingsley, 2017.

Comer, John Mark. *Practicing the Way: Be with Jesus; Become Like Him; Do as He Did*. Colorado Springs: WaterBrook, 2024.

Cullmann, Oscar. *Peter: Disciple, Apostle, Martyr*. 2nd ed. Translated by Filson V. Filson. Waco, TX: Baylor University Press, 2020.

Dunn, James D. G. *Beginning from Jerusalem*. Christianity in the Making 2. Grand Rapids: Eerdmans, 2009.

———. *Jesus Remembered*. Christianity in the Making 1. Grand Rapids: Eerdmans, 2003.

Eusebius of Caesarea. "Church History." In *Eusebius: Church History, Life of Constantine the Great, and Oration in Praise of Constantine*. Edited by Philip Schaff and Henry Wace. Nicene and Post-Nicene Fathers, series 2, vol. 1. New York: Christian Literature Company, 1890.

———. *Ecclesiastical History, Books 1–5*. Edited and translated by Roy Joseph Deferrari. The Fathers of the Church 19. Washington, DC: Catholic University of America Press, 1953.

Farmer, J. H. "Mark, the Gospel According to." In *The International Standard Bible Encyclopaedia*, edited by James Orr et al., 1990–91. Chicago: Howard-Severance, 1915.

Garland, David E. *Mark*. NIV Application Commentary. Grand Rapids: Zondervan, 1996.

Green, Gene L. *Vox Petri: A Theology of Peter*. Eugene, OR: Cascade Books, 2020.

Green, Joel B. "Practicing the Gospel in a Post-Critical World: The Promise of Theological Exegesis." *Journal of the Evangelical Theological Society* 47 (2004) 387–97.

Hays, Richard. "The Crucified One: Jesus's Death and Discipleship in the Gospel of Mark." In *Cruciform Scripture: Cross, Participation, and Mission*. Edited by Christopher W. Skinner et al., 22–36. Grand Rapids: Eerdmans, 2021.

Helyer, Larry R. *The Life and Witness of Peter*. Grand Rapids: IVP Academic, 2012.

Hengel, Martin. *The Cross of the Son of God*. Translated by John Bowden. London: SCM, 1986.

———. *Saint Peter: The Underestimated Apostle*. Grand Rapids: Eerdmans, 2010.

Hooker, Morna D. *The Gospel According to Saint Mark*. Black's New Testament Commentary. London: Continuum, 1991.

Hurtado, Larry W. *Mark*. Understanding the Bible Commentary Series. Grand Rapids: Baker, 2011.

Johnson, Dru. *Human Rites: The Power of Rituals, Habits, and Sacraments*. Grand Rapids: Eerdmans, 2019.

McKnight, Scot. *Jesus and His Death: Historiography, the Historical Jesus, and Atonement Theory*. Waco, TX: Baylor University Press, 2006.

———. *The King Jesus Gospel: The Original Good News Revisited*. Grand Rapids: Zondervan, 2011.

———. *Kingdom Conspiracy: Returning to the Radical Mission of the Local Church*. Grand Rapids: Brazos, 2016.

Orr, James, et al., eds. *The International Standard Bible Encyclopedia*. Chicago: Howard-Severance, 1915.

Rutledge, Fleming. *The Crucifixion: Understanding the Death of Jesus Christ*. Grand Rapids: Eerdmans, 2017.

Sanders, E. P. *Jesus and Judaism*. Philadelphia: Fortress, 1985.

Skinner, Christopher W., et al., eds. *Cruciform Scripture: Cross, Participation, and Mission*. Grand Rapids: Eerdmans, 2021.

Staples, Jason A. *The Idea of Israel in Second Temple Judaism: A New Theory of People, Exile, and Israelite Identity*. New York: Cambridge University Press, 2021.

Stark, Rodney. *The Rise of Christianity: A Sociologist Reconsiders History*. Princeton: Princeton University Press, 2020.

Witherington, Ben, III. *The Gospel of Mark: A Socio-Rhetorical Commentary*. Grand Rapids: Eerdmans, 2001.

Wright, N. T. *Christian Origins and the Question of God*. Vol. 1: *The New Testament and the People of God*. London: SPCK, 1996.

———. *Christian Origins and the Question of God*. Vol. 2: *Jesus and the Victory of God*. London: SPCK, 1992.

———. *Mark for Everyone*. London: SPCK, 2004.

16

Feed My Sheep
Failing Forward in Ministry—A Pastoral Reflection

MATTHEW TREXLER

THE YEAR IS 1984. Jeff Wilson is a freshman and a star running back on his high school football team. One morning, Jeff is driving to school in his beat-up Plymouth Duster, and on this particular morning, the sun is glaring through the windshield. He is busy adjusting his visor when the unthinkable happens: he feels a thud, stops, and then immediately pulls over. As he gets out of the car, his stomach drops: lying on the asphalt unconscious is one of his classmates, Tammy Baird.

A horrible thought goes through his mind: did I just accidentally kill someone? He quickly checks her pulse and realizes she's still breathing. Running to the nearest pay phone he calls an ambulance. Tammy is immediately rushed to the ER and paramedics are miraculously able to save her life. But Jeff is never the same again.

In the days following the event, Jeff is so overwhelmed by guilt, he doesn't even want to live. Horrible thoughts race through his mind: *"What kind of person would ever hurt someone like that? What kind of person am I? How could anyone ever live with themselves again?"*

After some time of recovery, Tammy makes her way back to school, but Jeff is so overwhelmed with the guilt of what he has done that he can't make eye contact with her. Every time he sees her walking down the hallway, he turns around and walks the other way. Eventually, they graduate and go to different colleges, and Jeff hopes to never see her again. But twenty years later, Jeff wakes up one morning to see an email in his inbox from Tammy.

His heart immediately drops. The guilt comes rushing back. "Surely, she's out to get me. She's going to let me have it." But instead of ignoring or deleting the email, he summons the courage to finally open it. "*Dear Jeff, you may have been the first person to hit me with your car but you certainly weren't the last.*" Tammy then goes on to explain that she has become a fairly successful stuntwoman in Hollywood, working on a variety of movies and TV shows like *Mr. and Mrs. Smith*, *Sons of Anarchy*, *NCIS Los Angeles*, and *Fear the Walking Dead* just to name a few. "*When people ask me how I got so good at car hits, I explain how a guy hit me my freshman year walking to school. I credit you for helping me determine my calling in life.*"

That email healed something deep in Jeff. For so long he carried this guilt that he had ruined Tammy's life. He never thought himself worthy of forgiveness, but now, unexpectedly, something good and beautiful emerged from it all.

When we think about God at work in our lives, the one place we are pretty confident he can't be at work is in our failures. Many of us in ministry are weighed down by our past sins or frustrated by our constant and continuing failures to love Jesus and to love those he has entrusted to us. Some of us have said things that we can never take back; we have relationships that are riddled with regret and many times we wonder if we should even be in vocational ministry.

Simon Peter is no stranger to failure. I find him to be a man with whom I can easily sympathize. Even after beautiful displays of loyalty and faith: "You are the Christ!" coupled with ringing endorsements from our Lord: "On this rock, I will build my church," Peter seems to follow it up with some stinging failures: "But you can't go to the Cross!" followed by scorching rebukes from Jesus: "Get behind me, Satan!"

So, which is he? Rocky or Satan? Follower or failure? The question I'm afraid is all too familiar. And the most famous failure of all, the three-fold denial, almost shipwrecks his entire faith. But this beautiful passage at the end of John's Gospel teaches that Jesus can take even the most painful of failures and turn them into vehicles of blessing.

A Failed Fishing Expedition

After his disastrous Easter weekend, Peter decides to go fishing. Has Peter given up and returned to his former life? Is Peter comparable to a pastor who, worn out by ministry, skips Sunday service to play golf instead? I think it's safe to assume that whatever is motivating this fishing trip, Peter is ashamed and discouraged.

There are countless times in my own ministry experience that I am ready to throw in the towel. I give a sermon and the blank, bored faces of my students make me wonder if anything is really happening or if I'm even cut out for ministry. It is usually after those especially discouraging days that I am looking up other job possibilities or throwing myself into some kind of activity or hobby that gives me immediate results. For Peter, this was usually fishing. Not today.

The fishing trip turns out to be another discouragement. Peter and his friends catch nothing that night. Already we are getting echoes of Jesus's initial meeting of Peter in Luke 5, but there are also echoes of Jesus's farewell speech to his disciples in the Upper Room. "Apart from me," Jesus said, "you can do nothing" (John 15:5). The word for nothing (*ouden*) is the exact same word used by John in this passage: "That night they caught *nothing*."[1] But it is in the midst of Peter's embarrassment and failure that Jesus will appear.

I find the resurrection appearances of Jesus in the Gospels quite fascinating. He rarely if at all appears before giant crowds in his resurrected form—he does not reveal himself to Pilate, or the Roman soldiers, or the Jewish leaders, or those who crucified him—instead he reveals himself to beleaguered, battered, and doubting disciples in quiet obscure episodes like this one with Peter and the disciples. Just like in his ministry, he reveals himself to the poor in spirit. They are the ones who are able to see him. Even today, Jesus is ready to reveal himself in fresh ways to disciples who are deeply disappointed in their work.

Jesus, at this point a mere stranger on the shore, asks a question that seems to only highlight their failure: "Did you guys catch anything?" The answer of course is a resounding "No!" But Jesus offers some unsolicited advice: "Try the other side."

What is Jesus doing here? He's saying to Peter: "Peter, if you are going to be my disciple you have to follow me in the areas where you think

---

[1]. Bruner, *Gospel of John*, 1208

you know better." Are we ready for Jesus to confront not only our failure, but our entire way of doing ministry?

But the disciples are ready to listen to Jesus. It would have been laborious to move a heavily lead-weighted net from one side of a boat to the other but the disciples nevertheless obey.[2] Immediately, the long failure of their entire night is reversed by this small act of obedience as the disciples haul in an enormous catch of 153 fish.

Failure Confronted

Jesus seems to conduct most of his ministry over meals. Pastors take note: Jesus wants not only to talk to us but also to eat with us. Jesus isn't giving a lecture; he's giving a meal. Some of the most important ministry moments will happen not behind the pulpit but behind the table. The act of eating with someone can be a profound experience.

Upon arrival at the shore, the disciples see that a meal has been prepared: a charcoal fire with fish lying on it along with some bread. Jesus has made breakfast. And now the Savior invites his wayward and ashamed disciple to a meal that will enact forgiveness and reconciliation. Is this not a hint of how Jesus will primarily commune with his erring people every Sunday when we are invited to partake of the Lord's Supper?

The charcoal fire of course is also meant to remind Peter of his awful evening by a similar fire just a few days before. Jesus's threefold questions of "Peter do you love me?" will directly mirror Peter's threefold denial. Jesus's question is penetrating and necessary: "Do you love me?" I cannot think of a more important question. Jesus does not say, "What do you think of me?" nor does he even say, "Do you believe in me?" which of course is important. Instead, he goes straight for the jugular: "Peter, do you love me?"

Before Christ commits his sheep to Peter's care, he wants to know that Peter does truly love him. How can we love the people of God if we do not love Jesus? Every ordination, installation, or commissioning exam should primarily be focused on this one, true penetrating question: "Do you love Jesus?" Doctrine, knowledge, gift set, Bible memory will all be worthless if we do not have love for Jesus. We could preach

---

2. Bruner, *Gospel of John*, 1209.

with the tongue of angels but if our love for him is not true or sincere then we are a noisy gong or clanging cymbal.[3]

But there is another angle to Jesus's question as well. Perhaps you are discouraged with your ministry—it feels as though your staff, congregation, elders are all constantly disappointed and critical. It is easy to feel like a failure in those moments. But Jesus's gentle question is clarifying: "Do you love me?" If we can feebly respond, "Yes, Lord you know that I love you," then Jesus is deeply satisfied. It is enough.

Jesus's encounter with Peter in this passage is deeply pastoral. Upon first reading, the setting of a charcoal fire and Jesus's repeated questions about Peter's love for him could seem a bit shaming, or to put it in modern parlance, triggering. Is Jesus seeking to cast doubt on the sincerity of Peter's answers? Is our Savior throwing in a bit of shame with his forgiveness?

I believe Jesus is taking a more pastoral approach: Jesus wanted Peter's last memory of their encounter to be Peter's threefold, "I do love you Lord." All of us, if we are honest, are familiar with regret. Anyone who has experienced feelings of deep guilt knows that even forgiven sins have a way of haunting our memory and experience. We will see very soon that the work of the church can only go forward when we are unburdened of our destructive memories and truly encounter the forgiving love of God.[4] Jesus wants to provide Peter with a new and deeper experience: "Peter I know that despite your failure and denial, you really do love me."

Pastors and ministry leaders, take note. Many times, sermons and talks want to cast doubt on the sincerity of our love for Jesus: "But do you *really* love him? Have you *really* surrendered fully to Jesus? Have you *truly* counted the cost?" Sometimes these questions are necessary but it's just as important, if not sometimes more important, to affirm that those under our care, especially those struggling, doubting and failing, are in fact sincere and trying Christians who do love the Lord.

Of course we must exercise wisdom—especially when counseling others in matters of repentance. Growing up, we called insincere and pretended shows of sorrow "crocodile tears." The fruit of repentance is always necessary—whether it be our own personal failure or the failure of those we shepherd.

---

3. 1 Cor 13:1 (NIV).
4. Burge, *John*, 595–96.

But notice that Jesus is not the Great Criticizer in this passage. He does not follow up Peter's threefold assertion of love with probing and doubting questions: "But Peter how much have you actually wept? How much have you fasted and afflicted your soul?" Instead, our Lord accepts Peter's weak but sincere love. If Jesus does this for us, let us also do this for those under our care.

Peter's response is the response of all true believers: "Yes Lord, you know that I love you" (John 21:17). It's interesting to note that Peter has changed his tone from previous occasions. Just a few nights before, Peter declared his loyalty to Jesus by *comparing* his love to the love of the other disciples: "Even if they desert you, I won't!" This may be what Jesus means by his initial and perplexing question: "Simon, son of John, do you love Me more than these?"[5] Peter has wrongly elevated himself above his fellow disciples, but now Jesus seems to be gently asking Peter if he is still so sure of himself.[6]

But Peter's failure has led to a transformation. Peter no longer directs his gaze horizontally, but vertically. In other words, what matters now to Peter is not human comparison but true divine knowledge. "Lord, you know that I love you!" Peter no longer appeals to his perceived loyalty but to Jesus's knowledge of him.

This is important to remember when our own hearts accuse and condemn us. Even if our hearts rightly condemn our lack of love for God and neighbor, God who is gracious is able to see the love and faith that we truly have, even if it has disappeared from our own sight. Like Peter, we too can come boldly before the throne of grace and assert our love for the Lord. Even in our failure, he knows that we love him.

Peter's declaration of love is then followed by an accompanying charge from Jesus: "Feed my sheep." Translation: "Okay, Peter, I believe you. Please continue to demonstrate this love by taking care of the people I have entrusted to you." Of all the tasks that Jesus could have assigned to a failed disciple, this seems the most unexpected. I would have expected a probation not a promotion. But when the Good Shepherd gives Peter the high calling of shepherding his flock, Jesus is teaching Peter and all future shepherds that failure is sometimes the best prerequisite for shepherding his people.[7]

---

5. John 21:15 (NIV).
6. Bruner, *Gospel of John*, 1227.
7. Bruner, *Gospel of John*, 1226.

Why is this the case? It's sometimes helpful to imagine the type of shepherd Peter might have become if he had not experienced this threefold failure. Before his denial, Peter seemed quite confident in his loyalty and allegiance to Jesus—again measuring his faithfulness by comparison to others. If we were to imagine that Peter never failed, and continued to live with his own sense of spiritual superiority, we can probably guess the type of shepherd he would become.

If he were around today, maybe he would become a motivational speaker or social media influencer with endless podcasts, TED talks, and TikToks calling others to live a higher life of deeper discipleship (like himself). When it came to dealing with doubting, erring, and struggling disciples, I doubt his posture would have been one of empathy or patience. I'm certain he would talk about Jesus, but he would most likely give people himself. The best ministry however, is when we have come to the end of ourselves and give people the only person who truly matters: Jesus. As one of my mentors once told me, "You'll never know that Jesus is all you need until Jesus is all you've got."

But failure has now prepared Peter to look downwards, not in introspective shame, but in compassion toward the lambs now under his care. Jesus instructs him to feed, that is nourish, those whom Jesus wins into his fellowship. Leading the church and caring for those who need spiritual nourishment will now be his primary calling as a shepherd.[8] And we are to notice whose lambs they really are: "My lambs!" If we truly love Jesus, then we will take care of the sheep Jesus lovingly entrusts to us.

Peter seems to have taken this command to heart as he writes in his first letter: "Be shepherds of God's flock that is under your care, watching over them—not because you must, but because you are willing, as God wants you to be; not pursuing dishonest gain, but eager to serve; not lording it over those entrusted to you, but being examples to the flock. And when the Chief Shepherd appears, you will receive the crown of glory that will never fade away."[9]

It is interesting to note that Jesus repeats this command three times. Why does Jesus not say for example, "Peter if you love me: feed my sheep; also, be diligent in praying and fasting, and make sure to help the poor"? Why does Jesus seem content to keep it at: "feed my sheep"? Certainly, the Christian calling includes prayer, Bible study, social justice, visiting

---

8. Cullman, *Peter*, 65.
9. 1 Pet 5:2–4 (NIV).

the sick, showing hospitality. Why is feeding the sheep, "the one thing needed"?[10] Maybe because it is the one thing needed.

I find Jesus's command to Peter deeply focusing and refreshing: "please feed my sheep." New Testament scholar Dale Bruner humorously points out that Jesus does not tell Peter to "go win the Mediterranean world"[11] but instead "feed the sheep I have brought into your care." Perhaps this one thing will be enough. Bruner goes on to say, "If we will make our single passion the good care of the little flock entrusted to us, all the other responsibilities of discipleship will fall into place—such as prayer, Scripture, Church, love, and justice. But lose this flock-centered focus and everything will be skewed."[12]

Nadia Bolz-Weber is a Lutheran minister and public theologian who is known for her unconventional approach to reaching others through her church. Whether it's through sporting tattoos that mark the liturgical year and tell the story of the Gospels, or her sermons and blogs directed at the abuse of purity culture, Bolz-Weber has cultivated a ministry that many burned-out Christians and honest seekers have found deeply healing and refreshing. I find her writings fascinating and thought provoking and when she published a blog post a few years ago entitled "If you can't take it anymore, there's a reason" it immediately caught my attention.

She begins the article by telling a story of her old apartment building where sketchy electrical wiring made it hard to accomplish even the most ordinary of tasks. She wasn't able to dry her hair and listen to the stereo at the same time because the circuit breakers would blow a fuse when modernity asked too much of it. She makes the connection with the old circuit breaker and our own finite minds and bodies:

> I just do not think our psyches were developed to hold, feel and respond to everything coming at them right now; every tragedy, injustice, sorrow and natural disaster happening to every human across the entire planet, in real time every minute of every day."[13]

The COVID-19 pandemic revealed some of the worst sins of our society and brought an onslaught of bad news to our screens: income inequality, homelessness, racial injustice, white privilege, corrupt

---

10. Bruner, *Gospel of John*, 1229.
11. Bruner, *Gospel of John*, 1228.
12. Bruner, *Gospel of John*, 1230.
13. Bolz-Weber, "If You Can't Take It," para. 2.

governments and institutions, the lack of affordable healthcare, not to mention the collapse of toxic churches and their religious leaders. It's enough to make one want to crawl into a cave and never come out. The human heart and spirit were not made to hold, feel and respond to all of these global injustices all at once.

I was personally perplexed about what to do: As a disciple of Jesus, how can I be obedient without totally burning out? As followers and disciples of Jesus Christ we cannot turn a blind eye nor can we retreat from the sorrows and evils that surround us. Jesus entered into the suffering and sadness of his neighbors and commanded his disciples to love the poor, the needy, and the outcast. To retreat into our comfortable lives and homes, focused only on our own concerns, is disobedience to the call of Christ and an abandonment of the mission of the kingdom. However, to attempt to solve all the problems around us as individuals is a betrayal of our human finitude and a recipe for burnout and frustration. As my friend and professor Kelly Kapic so eloquently put it: are the only two options before us to *do everything* or *do nothing*?[14]

It was here that I believe the Lord directs us to his command in John 21: "Feed my sheep." How we care for those under our charge is of upmost importance in the Savior's eyes. To put it in the language of Jesus from a Lukan parable: will we be faithful with the "few things that are entrusted to us"?[15] How we care for and nourish those entrusted to us: congregants, students, clients, patients, children or aging parents will be worth a stadium full of converts in the Savior's eyes on the last day.

Failure Reimagined

Peter must show his love for Jesus by caring for the sheep entrusted to him—although Peter does not know it yet, this will cost him no less than everything. Jesus tells him:

> "Very truly I tell you, when you were younger you dressed yourself and went where you wanted; but when you are old you will stretch out your hands, and someone else will dress you and lead you where you do not want to go." Jesus said this to indicate the

---

14. Kapic, *You're Only Human*, 174.
15. Luke 19:17 (NIV).

kind of death by which Peter would glorify God. Then he said to him, "Follow me!"[16]

A wealth of ancient pagan as well as Christian texts associated "stretching out the hands" with crucifixion.[17] Jesus tells Peter that this vocational call of caring for his sheep will lead to martyrdom. Who said ministry was going to be easy?

Jesus says here what he has always said: following him will include a cross. Ministry is cruciform. It is this cross that Peter famously did not want for his Lord, and now he himself will be led "where he does not want to go." Committing himself to the way of the Good Shepherd will mean laying down his own life for the sheep.

This needs to be said again and again in modern American evangelicalism. As a minister, I am tempted many times by my pride and selfish ambition to feed off of the sheep instead of feeding the sheep. There of course is no real comfort or joy or love in this, only crushing performance.

David Letterman was a famous host of the *Late Night Show*. Near the end of his career he did this interview about what it was like to go out in front of a crowd every night. Here is what he said:

> Every night you're trying to prove your self-worth. It's like meeting your girlfriend's family for the first time. You want to be the absolute best, wittiest, smartest, most charming, best-smelling version of yourself. If I can make people enjoy the experience and have a higher regard for me when I'm finished, it makes me feel like an entire person. If I've come short of that, I'm not happy. How things go for me every night is how I feel about myself for the next 24 hours.[18]

For many pastors, including myself, this can be what every Sunday feels like. How will I feel about myself this week? How did people receive my sermon? Which is really a way of asking: how did people receive me? But Jesus wants to set us free to truly love him and by so doing, truly love the sheep he has entrusted to us.

In the desert Jesus is tempted by the evil one.[19] If one pays attention to the landscape of each successive temptation, you will notice that Satan takes Jesus from the desert floor, to the top of the temple, and then onto the highest hill overlooking the kingdoms of the world.

16. John 21:18–19.
17. Bockmuehl, *Simon Peter*, 66.
18. Cited by DeGroat, "Am I Doing Enough?" para. 13.
19. Luke 4:1–13; Matt 4:1–11.

Satan's temptation is upward mobility: higher, higher, higher. But Jesus chooses the will of his Father and he goes down toward Jerusalem. The divine way of glory is always downward.[20]

The way of success in the kingdom will look like failure in the world's eyes. Crucified to the world and its worldly ambition, it may look like small ministries, churches in perpetual conflict, biting criticism not only from the world but many times from Christians, discouragements from within and without, and a string of loose ends only the resurrection can tie up. Jesus ended his public ministry nailed to a cross; are we above our Master?

Jesus's call to Peter means an "undeviating discipleship all the rest of his days."[21] Why is Jesus giving Peter, and through Peter all future ministry leaders, such a depressing outlook? Of course, we know there is much joy in ministry and it can be filled with parties and celebrations that mirror the angels of heaven. But perhaps Jesus wants us to know that good and faithful ministry will not feel triumphant. It entails suffering, persecution, hate, and a giving up of one's life. Even when Paul wrote about joy, he did so from a prison.

It may have in fact been kinder and wiser of Jesus to tell Peter this depressing news. Peter could have easily mistaken his own future suffering in ministry not as a badge of honor worthy of belonging to the Messiah, but as a punishment and payback for his previous failure.[22] Jesus wants Peter to know that suffering and hardship in ministry is not a sign of failure but a standard companion of mission. And just as Jesus came out the other side into resurrection glory, so Peter will too if he continues to follow Jesus. What looks like failure to the world (and to our own discouraged soul) may in fact lead to a crown of glory in the resurrection. What matters is that we follow behind the crucified and risen Jesus.

Conclusion

Peter has experienced quite the transformation. This change is only because of the grace of the merciful Master who has not only called, but re-called the failing and errant disciple to his mission and kingdom work. This second-chance discipleship, called *grace* in the New Testament, is

---

20. Bruner, *Gospel of John*, 1231.
21. Moloney, *Love in the Gospel*, 186.
22. Bruner, *Gospel of John*, 1232.

at the heart of the Jesus Movement and "it is the continuing heritage of Peter's memory among all the Christian churches."[23]

It is good news that Jesus entrusts his global mission with exactly such humans as Peter—problematic disciples. But these are repentant people, disciples who confess their sins and their love for Jesus. They are in short, sincere and trying Christians. Jesus can work with such people—in fact he delights to take failing and struggling disciples and use them to feed other needy lost human beings.[24]

Love, according to the Johannine Jesus, is the mark of true discipleship. Loving Jesus will never be a private affair, nor is it measured by emotional states of ecstasy—rather it is worked out on the ground in earthy and faithful ways—feeding the lambs that Jesus has entrusted to our care. And sometimes those precious little lambs are critical, angry, cynical, disgruntled and look more like "our enemies" rather than our friends.

We are to care for the people that Jesus brings into our churches and into our lives. This is Jesus's great ordination charge. He is only willing to entrust it to disciples who are most qualified for this high calling—the poor in spirit who fail and feel their failure but have also felt the forgiving embrace of God. May he give us his grace and his power in this incredible and awesome undertaking.

Bibliography

Bockmuehl, Markus N. A. *Simon Peter in Scripture and Memory: The New Testament Apostle in the Early Church*. Grand Rapids: Baker Academic, 2012.

Bolz-Weber, Nadia. "If You Can't Take It Anymore, There's a Reason: An Essay on Circuit Breakers, Empty Buckets, and the Shame-Show of Social Media." *The Corners*, Aug. 17, 2021. https://thecorners.substack.com/p/if-you-cant-take-in-anymore-theres.

Bruner, Frederick Dale. *The Gospel of John: A Commentary*. Grand Rapids: Eerdmans, 2012.

Burge, Gary M. *John*. The NIV Application Commentary. Grand Rapids: Zondervan, 2000.

Cullman, Oscar. *Peter: Disciple, Apostle, Martyr*. Translated by Floyd V. Filson. 2nd rev. ed. Reprint, Waco, TX: Baylor University Press, 2011.

DeGroat, Chuck. "Am I Doing Enough?" *In All Things*, May 9, 2016. https://inallthings.org/am-i-doing-enough/.

Kapic, Kelly. *You're Only Human: How Your Limits Reflect God's Design and Why That's Good News*. Grand Rapids: Brazos, 2021.

Moloney, Francis J. *Love in the Gospel of John: An Exegetical, Theological, and Literary Study*. Grand Rapids: Baker Academic, 2013.

---

23. Bockmuehl, *Simon Peter*, 183.
24. Bruner, *Gospel of John*, 1233.

17

Pastor Peter's Paradigm

Bethany Covenant
Laura Tarro Celebration
August 4, 2024

Scot McKnight

It is one of my career's great honors to be invited to speak to you this AM on the day celebrating Laura Tarro's ordination.

Laura was in a New Testament cohort at the seminary. She was alert. She asked good questions and interacted with her peers and professors—from Day One. As you may know she had a previous career as an editor. Some women who believe they are called turn their gifts toward the publishing industry rather than fighting church folks over their becoming pastors. As a student, Laura's papers revealed an excellent mind and a wonderful grasp of the techniques of writing. Her grasp of the significance of the New Testament for the church, and the ministry to which she was (more than obviously) called and her availability, led me to ask her to be my graduate assistant and cohost of the *Kingdom Roots* podcast.

What I'm saying about Laura is that she was "first among equals," which is a line used of the apostle Peter. *Primus inter pares*. Laura was never "above her peers" but always treated her peers as equals. So she knows what I mean when I say she was not alone in being "first among equals."

Peter was not alone either. I want to take some lessons from Peter in our time together this AM. By the way, Peter would not have been irritated that we are in a brewery today. Galilean Jews of Peter's sort did not have bottled water. The most common drinks, and you may not know this, were wine, red of course, but also beer (e.g., Isa 5:22; 24:9; 28:7; 29:9; 56:12; Mic 2:11). Wheaton professors know about this, but some don't tell their students.

But this morning I want to talk to you about your pastor. The pastoral calling is *hard work*. The major reason it is hard work for the lead or senior pastor is because it is *loadbearing*. In our basement, which doubles as my library, we have loadbearing metal poles that brace up the floor big boards (I'm not sure about the terms), which hold up the floors and braces and joints and studs for a two-floor home. Pastors bear the load of responsibility as a full-time mission. More than they should but who else will bear that load?

The pastoral calling is *never over*. No nine-to-five job. No "take the weekend off." The apostle Paul, who at times had words for the apostle Peter, after flouting a list of his sufferings and persecutions, said, "Besides everything else, I face daily the pressure of my concern for all the churches" (2 Cor 11:28). Loadbearing. He daily ruminated over whether or not the church folks liked him, or whether or not they were angry over his decisions, or whether or not they would welcome him when they were face-to-face again. Pastoring is never-ending relational engagements. And if it weren't for people, pastoring would be fine. Which is why Pastor John Ames, in one of Marilynne Robinson's novels, made known he liked to go to the church early in the morning because no one was there.

And the pastoral calling is *constantly shifting*. Gone are the days when pastoring meant studying the Bible and praying every morning, lunch at home, and afternoon meetings with staff, and community leaders, and pastor friends. When it meant Thursday morning golf with one's pastor friends. Pastoring means a constantly shifting set of loadbearing concerns. I've learned enough about Bethany Covenant to know this year has presented a number of loadbearing shifts.

Well, I'm not here to talk about the challenges Laura faces so much as exhort you to help her. In serving her you will free her up to serve you in the pastoral calling. In helping her you will help her wonderful husband, Geoff, and her young adult children, Hayley and Owen.

Peter, unlike Paul, never griped about his churches nor did he talk about how hard of work it was to pastor such persons throughout Asia Minor. So, Peter's life and words will aid us in the time remaining.

Peter as a Pastor

A few features of Peter's life that made him the pastor-presbyter (elder) that he was. He was a *convert*, and that story is told very well by Luke in Luke 5:1–11. We know it as the fisherman becoming a fisher of men, but the essence of that story is that Peter learned *who he was* when he finally learned *who Jesus was*. It led him to confess his sins, drop the nets, and give himself to Jesus and follow him all over Galilee and down to Judea— and in the process his conversion was not always on display.

And Peter was a *fellow elder* (5:1). When I mentioned that Peter was "first among equals" being a co-elder reveals Peter's own heart. He did not see himself as the first pope but as one who pastored people with others who were pastoring people. Let this sink in: the original "first among equals" knew that pastoring was a shared ministry rather than a hierarchical one. Even if Peter will yank out in 2 Peter that old argument that "I was there so I know," the tone of his life and letters was not authoritarian.

Then Peter tells us in the passage read this morning that he was a *witness*. Peter's emphasis in 1 Pet 5:1 was that he was a witness of the sufferings of Christ, which—truth be told—yes, he did witness but he didn't exactly do so from a place of courage or faith. He stood at a distance, he denied Jesus three times, and he disappeared from the cross. But he saw it and later confessed sin and became a witness for the importance of cruciformity, or conformity to the cross of Christ. First Peter 2:21–25 is one of the New Testament's great passages about cross-shaped discipleship. But Peter was a witness in a much larger sense: his life was about transferring all he witnessed about Jesus—life and death, crucifixion and resurrection and ascension, transfiguration and trial, teachings and miracles—transferring all of that into language for the moment he found himself in. One has to think that Galilean fishermen from a mostly gentile village never dreamed he'd become a church planter in Asia Minor, and he surely never anticipated Saint Peter's in the Vatican! But witnesses to Jesus at times end up in places they never expected, with histories that far surpass their realities.

Peter then was a convert, an egalitarian when it came to pastoring people, and he was a witness to Jesus.

Permit me now to make a simple point and then explain its two dimensions. You will permit Laura to do what she is called to do if you do what you are called to do. I'll say that again with one new word: You will permit her to do what she is called to do *only* if you do what you are called to do.

Laura's Calling

Her calling is outlined by Peter, and the major words speak volumes of truth to anyone who has ever been called to loadbearing.

I begin with a recent translation of 1 Pet 5:2: "Pastor God's flock among you, mentoring." The NIV has "Be shepherds of God's flock that is under your care, watching over them." I'm no fan of the NIV's use of "*under* your care" when the Greek term, *en*, does not mean over or under but among. The idea is more a shepherd being surrounded by sheep than a shepherd standing alone on a rock or hill looking down on them.

> Pastor, or "be shepherds": the role of a church leader naturally flowed in the Jewish world into metaphor of shepherd because (1) David was one and (2) God was one and (3) upper-level leadership in that world often gravitated toward that expression. Shepherds feed and protect and worry and rescue and shear and wander around with wandering sheep. Laura is called to shepherd/pastor.
>
> Then he says pastors "mentor." The NIV has "watching over them" because the NIV is afraid to admit the Greek term could be translated with "bishop" or "bishoping." The idea is oversight in the sense of holistic care for each person in the fellowship, and an element of that holistic care is mentoring and spiritual direction. Laura is called to mentor.
>
> Peter next gives a list. He knew this list because he had planted churches with mentors who brought these items to his attention:

1. Mentoring willingly, not "from necessity"

    Pastoring people is not a job or a duty. It is a relationship. In fact, it is a sacred relationship.

Recently Kris and I attended a funeral. What struck me, as a seminary professor, was the role the pastor played in this family: meeting with them, listening to their sorrows, their concerns, their plans, their desires. She—the pastor was a "she"—was relatively new to the church. There is no more sacred moment between a pastor and a congregant than the funeral. She did all this *willingly*.

This is what Laura wants to do with you. And in doing this, Laura mentors the family and the congregation.

2. Mentoring in a way consistent with God's ways

The NIV's "as God wants you to be" is a good translation. The recent translation I mentioned has "consistent with God's ways." All the Greek has is, literally, "according to God." Pastoring-as-mentoring is *an act of mediating God to people*. As God is the Greatest Shepherd, God's mentoring of God's people becomes the paradigm into which Laura is called—to mediate God to you.

3. Mentoring *emotionally* and not for money

One of the pastor's great challenges is finances. They are always present, and they are important. But income is not the intent of mentoring others. Peter knows some try to pastor out of greed.

So, the alternative to greed is *eager to serve*. The Greek term is wonderful: it means something like "full of passion and commitment." That recent translation has "emotionally," which I quite like (since that translation is mine).

4. Mentoring as a *model* instead of a heavy-handed authority

Authoritarian people are attracted to positions of authority. Not so, according to Peter, for pastoral mentors. Notice how he opened chapter 5: as a "fellow elder." Not as an "apostle," which could pull rank.

Instead, they are to model what it means to be a follower of Jesus. Not perfectly of course. Peter surely wasn't, and he's the one saying this. Rather, pastor-mentors follow Jesus and invite others to join them so they can *together* follow Jesus. As Paul said, "Become copies of me just as I am of Christ" (1 Cor 11:1).

5. Mentoring *toward* the First Shepherd's approval

    The aim of the pastor-mentor is not a large church or a big platform or a mega-reputation. The aim is the "First Shepherd's" approval when he returns, when we meet up with God.

Remember our theme: You will permit Laura to do what she is called to do *only* if you, Bethany Covenant, do what you are called to do.

Bethany's Calling

If that is a sketch of dimensions of Laura's calling, here is a sketch of how you can help her by doing what you are called to do.

1. Avoidance of status climbing (5:5–7).

    Status was the way of life in the Roman Empire, and Asia Minor's churches planted by Peter were never going to escape that cultural mindset. Nor do we. Some people want the platform; some people want to preach (who should not be preaching); some people want to sing (who can't sing). Some people want power (and wanting power is a big problem). So, Peter urges "all of you" to avoid status climbing.

    Instead, want it for others and clap for them when they get it. And go for a walk and yell a bit and cry a bit and wait until God grants you that spot.

    In this way you will permit Laura to do her work.

2. Alertness (5:8ab)

    "Be alert and of sober mind!" Whatever your intoxicant is, discipline yourself away from it. It might be movies, it might be politics, it might be the Chicago Cubs or Bears or Bulls or the Sky. It's OK to be inebriated with Caitlin Clark. Whatever clouds your mind and heart, and so blocks your capacity to give priority to following Jesus . . . go on a fast.

    In this way you will permit Laura to do her work.

3. Awareness (5:8c–9)

   Satan is the enemy of Bethany Covenant. Satan's intent has always been death, and Satan accomplishes death by swallowing up humans—distracting and diminishing and destroying. If you are aware, and don't get kooky about it, of Satan's ways, which are simple and sometimes subtle, you will be on the right path. And don't blame everything on Satan. C. S. Lewis once wrote in the preface to *The Screwtape Letters,*

   > There are two equal and opposite errors into which our race can fall about the devils. One is to disbelieve in their existence. The other is to believe, and to feel an excessive and unhealthy interest in them. They themselves (the devils) are equally pleased by both errors and hail a materialist or a magician with the same delight.

   Avoid the extremes, and in this way you will permit Laura to do her work.

4. Empowerment, and you can spell Empowerment with an A if you'd like to keep the points alliterated. No one but an editor will mind (5:10–11).

   God is at work in you. God's work is to glorify his Son through you, through Laura, through living the gospel in your community and neighborhood, and through the preaching of the gospel about Jesus. But this is God's work, not yours and not Laura's.

   God equips each of us to participate in this great gospel work in the world, and so much as we surrender to God's equipping and not to our powers, we will achieve what God calls us to achieve.

   In this way you will permit Laura to do her work. As you surrender to God's empowerment of you, you will permit Laura to God's empowerment.

   This is how it works: You will permit Laura to do what she is called to do *only* if you do what you are called to do. In this way, she will not do what you are called to do, and you will not try to do what she is called to do.

The pastoral calling may well be loadbearing and never-ending and constantly shifting, but it is also exhilarating, glorious, fulfilling and, an expression I most like for pastors who are in their sweet spot, "gift-exploiting." Laura has a loadbearing responsibility at Bethany Covenant but you have the responsibility of embracing your calling (and hers) so she can do what God has called her to do.

www.ingramcontent.com/pod-product-compliance
Lightning Source LLC
Chambersburg PA
CBHW030821230426
43667CB00008B/1315